A Daily Devotional

Quiet Moments for Women

A Daily Devotional

Quiet Moments for Women

JUNE·MASTERS·BACHER

HARVEST HOUSE PUBLISHERS
Eugene, Oregon 97402

QUIET MOMENTS

Copyright ©1979 Harvest House Publishers
Eugene, Oregon 97402

Library of Congress Catalog Card Number 79-84722
ISBN 0-89081-187-3

Printed in the United States of America.

CONTENTS

Dedicated
to
My loving husband
George

My New Year's Prayer

DEAR LORD, it is difficult to conceive of you in my mind, but you are present in my heart this New Year's Day. I turn to you now, assured that you will hear because of your mercy—not because of my goodness.

"Peace on earth" seemed possible during the wintry holidays as I saw seriously divided families, neighbors and nations brought together. As the Christmas tree goes out and the bills come in, strengthen me. I don't want the January frost to take over in my heart. May my heart be warm and my temper cool as I store ornaments and freeze leftover turkey. May I meet this year's challenge with a light heart, casting last year's shadows behind, lest I make the same mistakes. Be patient with me, Lord, as I make a fresh start, for I am fallible.

The bells which rang so sweetly and clearly in last midnight's air are "as sounding brass or tinkling cymbal" without the love I need to be a better Christian, wife, mother, daughter, teacher, friend—all the things that are *me*. Make me worthy of my role: *that of being a woman!*

Remind me often, Lord, that it's the little things that count. Help me to understand that "good will to men" includes my family. Understanding is more important than an overdone pot roast when my husband is late for dinner. High-decibel squeals of the children are their joyful noise. The dog underfoot needs affection. Let me remember, Lord.

Help me, Lord, to meet each day with the same hope, courage and determination I feel today. I am persuaded that I need to review the three R's: *Restoration* of spirit; *Renewal* of compassion; *Refreshment* of love—for You, my family, my friends and the people who pass my way. Grant me grace to bridle my tongue and hear them all before offering my opinions. I am guilty of being attentive to my wants, unmindful of their needs. Forgive me when I become too busy to be kind.

May this born-again spirit remain alive within me that I may touch the lives of others. Bless us with Your peace which passes all understanding. Amen.

Peace Be To This House

JANUARY is the month of the "full underground moon." Far in the north the beaver, the woodchuck and the black bear slumber. Their hearts beat slowly as they live on comfortable layers of fat underneath their winter coats. We mortals should have such rest!

This January in initiating my family into another new year, I feel God has given me a gift of opportunity—opportunity to make "peace on earth" more than wistful thinking. Maybe what each family member needs most of all is a chance to be still; to rest in a near-forgotten quiet; and to reacquaint himself with God, friends and with me. I love my job as mother: to tease my family's palates and tickle their toes back to normal appetites for meals and humor. *I love it!* But do they really need to be overfed? Maybe I should consider a different hunger they may have. Do they need constant entertaining? Or am I overlooking the obvious: giving them my time.

I'm sure we gave our loved ones everything but our time during the pre-Christmas rush. Now can we spare a moment to love them, and then leave them alone to be restful in themselves? Is overprotecting—maybe hovering—a common fault we women share? Secretly, I take pride in coaxing, don't you? I am so proud of being "Adam's rib" and a mother that I often put myself in an overbearing position. But sometimes my family needs to rest from me, too.

Actually, aren't we all like the January snow? There is stillness and purity; and underneath the drifts lie a thousand colors of spring. Maybe animals *need* to hibernate and flowers *need* to go dormant to think and pray.

TO THINK AND PRAY ABOUT: How and when do we get together in a quiet way as a family? Do we manage a moment of loving-quiet for each family member every day?

January 3
Luke 21:1-4

A S A CHILD I used to enjoy the conversation my father carried on with his mules. "Enjoy your oats tonight, fellows. Tomorrow it's 'back in the harness' for you." Daddy meant that literally. It has been a figure of speech in our family ever since.

Today it's back to work for millions of Americans. "Back in the harness" for me is back to the classroom to wipe away the overlooked glitter, remove the red and green ornaments and listen to endless autobiographies—each beginning with "I got." I'm trying to remember one child who ever said, "I gave."

As a teacher I am exposed to a wider spectrum of child-thinking than the full-time homemaker; but the "getting attitude" is not restricted to children. It surrounds all of us. Come to think of it, what we now call "gift exchange" really isn't *giving of ourselves* at all. I look at my crumpled-up Christmas list and feel a little ashamed. What does it really mean to give? Daddy's team worked six days a week pulling a plow in return for a bag of grain. Reread the Bible story of the widow's mite; recall the legend of "Why the Chimes Rang"; and hum the old hymn "I gave my life for thee, what has thou given to me?"

As Christians we are commissioned by God to seek blessings for the poor, the oppressed, the aged, the sick, the lonely and the handicapped. Go beyond contributing to some collection or dropping loose change into a cup—offer help to "the least of these." Wouldn't it be nice to take a more it's-up-to-me attitude? A letter, a visit, a smile: any such small but personal gesture might warm over the Christmas spirit. Then I could really say, "I gave."

TO THINK AND PRAY ABOUT: Reflect on an experience in which you truly *gave* .

Gentle Dew From Heaven

YES, I should be mopping the kitchen floor or hiding the fudge before we all get sick. Instead, I stand drinking in God's creation both from nature and from the poetry of His word.

Do you see God where you look? Today I see Him reflected in a single drop of dew. In the creation-fresh morning it trembles uncertainly upon a blade of grass, giving back the light of the world like an uncut diamond. "Where did it come from, Lord? Where will it go?"

A dewdrop is a marvelous thing—so fragile and yet so powerful. In liquid form water sustains life. Solidified, it's the silver ice of winter, the reservoir of spring. Then, at the sun's bidding, it rises heavenward, forming cumulus clouds, carrying rain to Oregon evergreens, Illinois cornfields and Appalachian slopes.

In the beginning God parted the earth from the water. The Psalmist sang of the voice of the Lord above the waters, His glory thundering. I think of the great rock formations fractured by the rush of many waters, and the breast of the earth heaving into mountains through which gushing water flowed. "How cooling and refreshing to the molten masses of land the tumbling waterfalls and laughing rivers must have been, Lord, filling the valleys and watering plains as they hurried to the seas."

"What greater manifestation of Your care could I ask, Lord?" I long to cup this pearly beauty in my hand, but the droplet moves into the cycle of God's plan to drop somewhere like Shakespeare's "gentle dew from heaven."

Now, back to the mundane but necessary tasks that sustain the family. No, not yet. One must write such thoughts, else they, too, will go:

> It isn't the distance of heaven's arched blue
> The whole sky reflects in one drop of dew.
> It isn't the size of the deed that we do,
> But light of the eye as love sparkles through. J.M.B.

TO THINK AND PRAY ABOUT: Do you see God in all things which are of Him? How can your small deeds reflect your concern and His love?

January 5
Hebrews 13:1-2

We entertain them all the while—
Those angels unaware—
Though they add substance to our lives,
We hardly know they're there—J.M.B.

THE SYMBOLISM of this month's snow or last month's
heavenly chorus sets us thinking about angels. Maybe one
crossed your path the preceding year. Maybe you had an experience that witnessed to you as Kathy's act of kindness
witnessed to me.

The doctor had put up a "No Visiting" sign. I had made it
through surgery, but a long recovery lay ahead. I was dissected
in four directions and wired for sound. I needed rest. My husband needed rest, too, so the doctor had sent him home. I was
alone in great pain, wanting no company, yet wanting to cry
from loneliness. White figures had tiptoed in and out for awhile,
but then I was left in the vast darkness, undisturbed by sound.

Suddenly, she was there: a very young nurse with a beautiful
face. I recognized her as a former student. "Stay!" my heart
cried out. "I will," her eyes replied. There were no words.

Each time I drifted out of a fitful sleep, I was aware of Kathy's
presence. There was nothing clinical in her manner, not even a
look of over-concern—just reassurance. She was a special
visitor. I remember thinking, "Nurses are busy people. How
does she have time? Tomorrow I will thank her. Tomorrow . . ."

When I was fully awake, the shifts had changed. Kathy was
gone.

"The night nurse—where is she?" I asked the attendant.

"She's not a regular here," the woman said. "She was visiting
her parents."

"But how . . . ?"

"She recognized your name on the list, sat with you all night,
then flew East."

Was Kathy what is meant by an Angel of the Lord in the
flesh? Her bond of love brought reassurance to my frightening
silence.

TO THINK AND PRAY ABOUT: How can you be an
angel in human form? Ask God.

Anacani

> . . . Full many a flower is born to blush unseen
> And waste its sweetness on the desert air . . .

LITERARY scholars say that Thomas Gray took seven years to polish his immortal poem, "Eulogy Written in a Country Churchyard," before he gave it to the world. If so, they were years well spent. Hundreds of phrases from the rich verses have passed into the treasury of our language. The flower quotation is one of my favorites, because its sad-sweet message reminds me of students I have had—some discovered, others not. The story of "Anacani" is especially dear to me.

Each Saturday evening I listen to Anacani's beautiful voice on the Lawrence Welk Show and remember . . . The noted band leader calls the petite young singer "our purty little *senorita.*" Her friends call her "Connie," but to me she's the little lost girl Central School's principal brought to my classroom one Monday morning. He introduced her as "Consuelo Gil," and said, "She speaks no English. I'm sure you'll manage well." Then he was gone.

"Dear God, how?" I whispered. I wonder who was more scared, the child or the teacher. We looked at each other and somehow understanding broke through the language barrier. The principal trusted me, but more importantly, Consuelo trusted me. Then, as if in answer to my prayer, Maria, a bilingual student, came and said: "I can help." *(Bless the Marias of this world, Lord!)* Maria became our translator, and I resolved to learn as much Spanish as possible while Consuelo learned English.

Anacani loved to sing then, as she does now. After her initial shyness wore off, she sang in Spanish, translating for her classmates, as she does now for the T.V. audience. Anacani pursued her career with the same perseverance she tackled a second language. Like Thomas Gray, she polished her art. How our lives are transformed by trust!

TO THINK AND PRAY ABOUT: How can you trust God more completely in order to trust yourself and others more?

The Silver Pear

"**I** HAVE to be Jonathan, or I won't be in it!" yelled our son, Bryce. Casting was in progress for "The Silver Pear," the annual school operetta. My husband and I looked at each other in despair. How could we gently explain that there can only be *one* "lead," and it's unlikely to be assigned to a nine-year-old boy who can't carry a tune?

The main character, Jonathan, owned a pear orchard where the legendary silver fruit grew, which gave life to all the trees. It was no surprise that Bryce did not get the coveted role, but he was crushed.

"There are other parts," I told him. "What about Smudgie? It was Smudgie who came to the rescue that fateful evening Jonathan forgot to light the smudge pots and the Frost Folk came." Bryce seemed encouraged. But . . . he failed to get that part, too. Again I looked over the cast of characters: Moon Maidens, Kathy, Princess Gray Dove—hardly suitable! The Frost Folk wouldn't work; they were too shy to speak and hurried to join the chorus. Wait! "Who is Archibald?" I asked. "Moth-er! A *dog!*" Bryce replied disgustedly.

That afternoon Bryce ran in from school. Too breathless to make sense, he handed me a note from his teacher, Mrs. Davis. I was to make a dog suit "with a nose" and spectacles. Bryce found his voice: "Archibald's a *hero*, too. A rockhound! He looks for a mastodon bone and sniffs up Mt. McLoughlin and finds the bone under the Frost King's chair and that leads 'em all to the magic fruit . . . "

I have to admire Mrs. Davis for taking the time to point out the value in a smaller role, and giving Bryce a sense of direction, even when it meant leading with his nose. It led to the high rock and the silver pear! Years later, when our son was considering the ministry, he was confronted by his limitations. Then he remembered *"Archibald."* Our minister worded it a little differently when he said: "It doesn't take a pulpit to serve: *all* work can be a ministry."

TO THINK AND PRAY ABOUT: Do you have a sense of direction? Where is it taking you?

The Inside Lane

OUR CHEVY gave us trouble throughout the day's little trip. George's mechanical touch had seen us safely to the last stretch. Suddenly the car stopped without making a signal! A stalled automobile on a freeway seems to bring out the worst in people—and this was no exception. Horns tooted wildly. Insulting words (people feel safe in making when their vehicles are moving and yours isn't) came from four lanes.

What *do* we do? Supposedly my husband can fix anything. But on a freeway? We had to get from the inside lane to the right shoulder—but not by being rear-ended! As for pushing the car to the shoulder manually or walking to a telephone, I knew the statistics concerning pedestrians on Highway 15. How could we get a tow truck? The answer to our dilemma came in an odd way.

There was a sudden screech of brakes. I closed my eyes and grabbed the back of my neck. But no crash! We were being approached on either side by two bearded men with hair hanging down the backs of their leather jackets. I fumbled for my billfold and began taking off my rings. The men were talking with my husband, but I was unable to hear above the pounding of my heart.

George got back in the car. "The kids are giving us a push," he said. Soon we were crawling at a snail's pace. "Isn't that risky for them?" I asked. "Very," he replied as we gained speed. Gradually we moved into the proper lane and subsequently into a service station. As they were driving away, one of the young men yelled: "Thanks for letting us help." Helping was a privilege!

What if we had refused their kindness because of their outward appearances?

TO THINK AND PRAY ABOUT: Do you receive the love from others as God chooses to send it? Do you undiscriminately help others to the safe shoulder of God?

Wednesday's Child

January 9
James 5:11

THERE'S a hint of rain when Bertha enters the room. To her, red sails at night portend a storm. When she phoned this morning she couldn't speak above a whimper. "Laryngitis . . . this time from the cold front . . . another one's approaching . . . doctor's offices filled . . . and look what the hospital costs are." But the burdens she bore weren't all hers—all the obituaries, news of men who left their wives for younger women, cost of living and flying saucers.

"I wish you'd hang up on her," my mate has suggested countless times. "You're not doing her a favor letting her run on like that, you know." I knew something else, too—some of her was beginning to rub off on me. I found myself depressed and wondering if I did to others what she did to me. Then I felt ashamed of such thoughts, because wasn't it my Christian duty to bear her burdens?

"Wednesday's child is full of woe," Bertha was fond of quoting—as though the accident of her birthday left her with no control over her life. She even knew the number of times "woe" was listed in her reference Bible.

The next morning during our telephone conversation an idea popped into my head. "When *is* your birthday?" I asked. It was like her to tell me that nobody remembered before she told me the date. As she talked on-and-on, I looked at my desk calendar and some quick calculations showed me that June 27, 1915, did *not* fall on Wednesday! Bertha wasn't going to like the news, but something had to break through her gloom. I had endured all I could, even after reading James 5:11. "Guess what?" I sang out cheerfully, "You were born on Sunday—not Wednesday. Do you know what that means? 'But a child that's born on the Sabbath day is fair and wise and good always'.' Feeling a little deceptive, I congratulated her.

Bertha called this evening to tell me about her new cold wave, but her laryngitis seemed to have disappeared. Maybe that's a start.

TO THINK AND PRAY ABOUT: How can you approach woeful people positively? "Berthas" need to know that you and God love them and are listening.

We need wisdom when our hearts ache;
We need vision and a will
We need power when our hands shake
As we climb each other's hill . . .

                                    J.M.B.

I CONFESS a lack of patience for food addicts. Make that past tense. I see the problem differently now.

I know a beautiful person who became obese. She tried pills, all-liquid diets and starvation, only to go on a binge of banana splits. Believing in moderation in all things (and being a twig), I shrugged when she asked for advice on WEIGHT WATCHERS. "All you need is exercise. Walk," I suggested. "With this flab?" she replied. "You don't know how it feels; and besides, habits are hard to change."

She was right. What I found out was a riot; but I learned there's only one way to empathy—to be "where it's at." Can you imagine two enormous pillows around my middle, draped with a tent-dress to hide the simulated bulge? My reflection was enough to make me reach for a chocolate cream. I pulled my son's dumbbell set from beneath the bed, and just rolling it was a workout, but I planned the impossible—to lift and carry it each step all day. You want a confession? My experiment lasted about as long as my friend's diet. I was ready to hit the mat with the first try. Walk? I couldn't even breathe. Is this how my friend feels—**ALL** THE TIME? I called her: "Bring over the WEIGHT WATCHERS' rules, I'll *help*."

Small (sometimes ridiculous) incidents can teach us humility. Why do we impose more upon others than God? He has promised us help in times of need. Let's try to remember God's love and withold judgment. Habits are hard to break; but like my friend, we can ask for help.

TO THINK AND PRAY ABOUT:
Lord, help us to withhold judgment—
Weighing every word we choose—
Give us greater understanding;
Let us walk in others' shoes. Amen.

$\mathcal{A}$ Prayer List

I T IS GOOD to have friends to comfortably talk over concerns without having to weigh every word. I shared a weakness with a friend yesterday, and she gave me strength. What's more, I freed her of the illusion that I'm organized. It had always made her feel self-conscious.

Organized! My desk, my house, my marriage, my *head* would be in shambles without my lists (which I often cannot find). A scribbled list on my desk indicates to which editor I owe an article or which friend I owe a letter. There's a scrawled list of calls to make by the hall phone and an undecipherable list of emergency numbers by the den phone. There's a list where our valuables are (safe because nobody can read it). . . appointments . . . menus . . . and iron-bound budgets that hang on the wall. I would resolve to organize my lists if I made a New Year's resolution, but I don't . . . I make lists.

After my friend and I laughed together about my lists, we started talking about prayer. I brought it up because I'd been thinking about how to pray: "I have so many people to pray for and so many things to pray about, I need to be asking for strength to pray."

"Of course, you do," she replied. "You have to look to God's strength for daily strength—even strength to pray. And if you discover weaknesses in your life, ask God to shoo them away." Then she shared with me one of *her* lists: "It's a PRAYER LIST!"

Now I have another list in my life. Daily, as I find new things to pray about, my list grows. I am grateful to my friend.

TO THINK AND PRAY ABOUT:

1. List all things you feel you need to discuss with God.
2. Identify your strengths and weaknesses.
3. List ways you can develop your strengths and eliminate your weaknesses.
4. List long-term plans for improvement. Be realistic—but daring.

Remember that God and you are working on these lists together. It was Christ who taught the disciples to pray. He will help you.

The Offering Tree

THE OFFERING TREE looks ragged. It had a lot of use during the holidays. For as long as I can remember, our family has had the custom of providing a Christmas tree for the birds. It is such fun preparing the tree as a group. Conifers look more traditional, I suppose, but even an avocado tree looks festive looped with tinsel, a star on the top and sweetmeats hidden among the leaves. We hear the happy twitters like thanksgiving prayers among the branches. I know it would please God if we were half so grateful.

It was our son who decided we should call it an offering tree. "What's an offering?" I asked Bryce one day. He was four years old at the time. Without hesitating he replied, "Something you give and nobody can take it back." How true! Once a migrating bird has visited the offering tree and dined from the colored paper cups filled with dried fruits and grain, the gift is gone. There is no way he can return the gift, reward us or repay us. Maybe that is our most unselfish offering of the giving season.

There should be the same spirit with gifts between friends; there *is* the same spirit in God's gift of love to us. He offers it so freely, and He never takes it back. All He requires of us is to accept His gift unquestioningly—like the birds accept from the offering tree.

Even now as I refill the containers, a lone bird is settled on a low branch gathering strength to fly higher. I share hope.

The little bird flew down to perch upon a fragile limb;
It swayed beneath the tiny weight; 'twas much too small for him.
And yet, as it bent towards the earth, the bird had notes to sing:
A message for the world to hear; it, too, must trust its wing.
I found the place inside of me where wings of faith must start;
The hope came up to sing a song and perched upon my heart.

J.M.B.

TO THINK AND PRAY ABOUT: What is your definition of offering? Do you share without hoping for return?

The Heart Of The Home

"FOLLOW the sun!" travel folders exclaim. End-of-the-month sales emphasize the importance of finding exactly the right clothes for the trip at reduced costs. The sun spends the winter here, and "right clothes" aren't my hangup; but I have given some thought of visiting Monaco some day. When I saw the photo of the little principality bordering the Mediterranean Sea, I read the article with interest. As it turned out, the newspaper item devoted most of its time to the Prince and his Princess Grace.

What makes us think these royal families are so different from us? I laughed when I read Her Highness' account: "You should see how the children behave, turning my room into something like Grand Central Station," the article quoted her. "Albert rushes in to grab the shower, followed by the girls. Caroline wants to borrow my curlers when she's not taking my clothes or makeup. Stephanie prances in to talk about her problems. Meanwhile, I'm sitting at my dressing table, propping up a telephone holder with my chin, carrying on a conversation . . . It all ends with me doing Stephanie's hair, then going into the kitchen to fix breakfast. That's my so-called relaxed morning before I rush off . . . ."

It sounded so familiar I could have written it myself. The former actress even said, "Like any other mother, I've often been tempted to strangle my daughter but have overcome the desire." That reminded me of an occasion when my frustration was so great I gave my son a swat, then hugged him, and we cried together! But through it all, as Princess Grace said, "Children are my proudest achievement."

I guess frustration, discipline and reconciliation are a part of the price we pay for the ultimate pride we feel in our children. She added "sacrifice" to her list. "It's the woman who keeps the family together. She has to sacrifice; but she is the heart of the home . . . ."

The article made me feel proud and humbled—proud of my accomplishments as the "heart" of the family; humbled by the knowledge of how often I have leaned on God in my "reign." He has made me a joyful mother!

TO THINK AND PRAY ABOUT: Take time to praise God for your estate.

Coping With Inflation

"CLOSED FOR INVENTORY" signs hang on the door of first one store then another. It puzzles me that merchants should have to pay taxes on their merchandise-in-stock, then pay again on their profits. It's hard enough to cope with inflation without (by my definition) being taxed twice. The subjects of inventory and high cost of living came up when some of my neighbors came over to sew on buttons and mend sox. Hilda opened up the topic by saying, "Who has to keep up with the Joneses? Keeping *down* with them would be more like it!"

Here it is the middle of January and what little money there is left from Christmas seems to melt faster than the snow in the Midwest. Alta, a recent bride, called it *"catastrophic."* Her word depicts young couples' dilemma. They want to buy a new house but lack the down payment. As she put it, "You can't borrow money from the bank unless you're able to prove you don't need it!"

Hilda and her husband own their home, but do I remember how expensive children's shoes are, she wonders? I shudder, remembering the cost of having one child—she has six! One thing we shared in common: increase in food prices. Food cost is literally gobbling up our budgets. "I'm thankful our son can buy his own shoes, food and incidentals," I said. And somehow the word "thankful" turned our talk 180°. We talked a lot about the tribulations of the times, but what about the *blessings*.

"I'm glad for one thing," Alta said. "We've shredded our credit cards! We sleep better not having to worry about due-day!"

"Actually," Hilda admitted, "I sort of enjoy working part-time. It's good for the kids to have to pitch in and help around the house. Getting up early for the paper route doesn't hurt John a bit!"

Thoughts flew as we bit off the last threads: "We *do* spend more time together at home . . . Del's mother feels she's an asset now that I need help . . . The garden trimmed me down along with the budget." We'd taken a *positive* view.

TO THINK AND PRAY ABOUT: Ask God to help you find ways to cope in a positive way. Then believe.

January 15
I John 4:17-18

THE CHILDREN were as busy as proverbial beavers cleaning clutter from their desks. Next week parents were to visit, and the boys and girls were sure they would give their desks the white-glove test. They were happy in their work, for they wanted to please Mom and Dad.

Fortunately the knock on the door was loud; otherwise I wouldn't have heard it above the noise. I was surprised to see two women, neither of whom was a mother of a fourth-grader The older appeared about seventy-five; the younger, a teenager, wore a tight, frightened smile and a telltale billowing smock. I fumbled for words as I gestured toward the children, "We 're expecting visitors." "So are we!" the older woman readily replied. "Please go on—may we watch for awhile?"

For a few minutes the pair just stood. Then they moved quietly around the room, bothering none of the activity. Now and then a phrase would reach me. "Like 'em?" the older woman asked the girl, who nodded mutely. "Lots of 'em, huh?" Again, the nod. "See how happy?" Gradually the girl's pale face took on color. I looked carefully at her, and, yes, her eyes were even sparkling. "They come to please us!" encouraged the older.

The bell rang and the children lined up at the door waiting for me to dismiss them for recess. The expectant mother looked ready to romp with the chattering children. Mrs. Andrews (I learned) brushed aside a wisp of gray. "Well," she said patting the mother's stomach, "that's how we all got here!" And then it occurred to me what the kindly neighbor was doing—something the girl's mother, her doctor and her husband had been unable to do—alleviating the youngster's fears by letting her associate with children—see the happiness and love in them.

I remembered the comforting words of the angel to Mary when she learned that she was to bear the Son of God. I marveled at the way this woman had comforted a young girl in such a simple way. As Sophocles said, "Much wisdom often goes with fewest words."

TO THINK AND PRAY ABOUT: Take today's fear to God. His love will handle it.

One Definition Of Prayer

LITTLE LEAGUE was in full swing. "It's obvious we don't have a Babe Ruth," my husband commented of our son's progress—or lack of it. He'd missed first team and barely made it on second (judging by the amount of time he sat on the bench).

"Did you get up to bat today, Bryce?" one of us asked each evening at dinner, until we saw how painful the question was. Always his answer was the same, "But I will tomorrow. I've asked God."

"That bothers me a little," I confided to George, whose rational "Why?" threw me.

"Supposing he doesn't make it at all?" I was becoming more anxious.

Calmly George replied, "Who has the greater faith? (That bothered me a little, too!) My grandmother used to say prayer was like our two water buckets. When one's let down into the well, the other comes up." George's grandmother did not know about Little League, but I thought she knew a lot about prayer.

No more questions, I promised myself. Maybe one day the bucket will come up full.

I longed to comfort Bryce. No mother likes to envision her son suiting up enthusiastically day after day and getting nothing from it but a sunburn. I thought a lot about Paul's question, "Lord, what wilt thou have me to do?"

I waited. Then one day it happened. Bryce burst into the house like Hurricane Camille. "I made . . . I made it . . . one kid was sick . . . I got up to bat, and I smashed it clear over Fuller's fence. YIPPEEE!"

After that our boy was a regular hero. "First up every day," he said.

At last there was a game, and Bryce's team won! (Oh, yes, he was Captain then.) "Did you pray?" I asked him after the game.

"Yes, real hard, but not for me. The others need it worse now."

TO THINK AND PRAY ABOUT: "A prayer in its simplest definition is merely a wish turned Godward," wrote Phillips Brooks. Pray for others.

Sky-Watching

"Clouds are God's lace stretched across the sky."

Anonymous

EARLY in life I learned to be a sky-watcher. I loved clouds. My grandmother taught me to see "animal shapes" in clouds, and I spent hours picking out my favorite animals. The soft cumulus clouds were "good"; the harsh nimbus ones "bad." I scanned the skies for my grandparents' signs: "Red sails at night, sailor's delight; red sails at morning, sailor's warning." My grandparents planted and harvested by the shape and colors of clouds.

My mother, too, steeped in age-old weather signs, dressed me accordingly. She needed neither push-button news nor barometer to know a proper wash day. She used to paraphrase a hymn: "He taught me how to wash and pray."

Looking up is still a vital part of my life. The delicate fibers of cirrus clouds that thread themselves in and out of cumulus-animal patterns are all a part of God's communication. Matthew tells us so. There is peace in the puffs of white; power in the smokestacks of black. The earth needs the rain God wrings out of the clouds and the sun He sends to follow.

Our lives, too, can be purified by storms. Science has developed warning systems for tornadoes, hurricanes and typhoons. Maybe some day they'll be able to harness all that power. God desires that we harness the power He sends us through storms in order that we may grow in faith. We need not fear the terror of the tumult, for joy cometh in the morning—blessings will *follow*. God is up there keeping our world (our lives) in motion.

TO THINK AND PRAY ABOUT: Find ways to let storms draw you closer to God.

Welcome, Miracle Child

January 18
Matthew 19:13-14

"A baby is God's opinion that life should go on."

Carl Sandburg

NO JOY can compare to that of being new parents. A baby is a miracle—there is nothing like it! However, another miracle that takes place after the birth process is the fulfillment the couple shares in their gift of love to each other.

"She was to be my Christmas present to you," Chris said to Will.

"I'd rather have a New Year's gift anyway," Will answered. Both seemed oblivious to our presence. They were busy counting little Carla's fingers and toes, tracing the button-nose and smoothing the silky-fine hair. "Oh, thank you, thank you," they kept murmuring over and over. It was hard to tell whether they were speaking to each other or to God—both, I think. My husband and I slipped out of the hospital room. It was a reverent scene . . . the moment belonged to them.

I thought of the song of the Psalmist as we left: "I will praise Thee, for I am fearfully and wonderfully made; marvelous are Thy works, and that my soul knows right well."

No invention of mankind can compare with that of creating human life. All the fine jewels that keep a watch ticking; all the thrust that keeps supercargo planes airborne; all the cogs and wheels . . . chemical solutions . . . *all* are replaceable. But each baby is unique—the breathing image of God. The young parents were remembering what I in the hustle-bustle of each day sometimes forget. Their baby is a miracle! Life is a miracle!

TO THINK AND PRAY ABOUT: Do you thank God—and each other—for the wonderful gift of life? Do you remind your child/children of His continued welcome in your home?

A Soft Answer

WE ALL KNOW the effectiveness of a soft answer, but I wonder if we practice it often enough for the right reasons. At work . . . at home . . . ?

My friend, Jackie, has been planning a weekend trip to Mexico City since January first. Three times she has called the travel agency to change the date. "I can't believe how understanding the girl is," Jackie told me. "You'd think I was doing her a favor, when actually she probably thinks I'm a pain!"

"Probably," I replied, "but how long would she remain with her job if she said so?"

I had a similar experience recently with a telephone repairman. My line blew down when the dreaded East Winds (Santa Anas) struck full force. I *wasn't* glad: I had a dozen calls to make multiplied by five because nobody's ever at home. I think I was more aggravated by the assignment than by the dead phone. The repairman treated the small inconvenience as a real emergency and had my phone repaired and me subdued (I used him as my sounding board) in five minutes. I invited him for coffee. Now, how did I find time for *that*?

Well-trained personnel are essential to good business. Firms which train employees to respond to discourtesy with courtesy are the most successful. And some individuals who work on commission or depend on tips are masters at it. Even listening to a complaint, problem or customer's advice may bring him back. How often, I wonder, do these nice people really long to lash out at the human pests of the day?

Jackie's and my experiences remind me of two important things: 1) If I expect pleasantries, am I pleasant? 2) Do I deal with others pleasantly for the right reasons? It is "good business," yes, but is it motivated by love? Do others see Jesus in me?

TO THINK AND PRAY ABOUT: How do you handle anger? Define Christian love.

The Gift Of The Butterfly

January 20
James 1:17

A BEAUTIFUL, unusually large butterfly just flew past the window. It was easily recognizable as a Monarch because of its bright orange-brown color and white markings. Monarchs, like the sun and tourists, spend winters in Florida and California. Protected by law, they feed on milkweed and oleander, happy and unafraid. Occasionally, one of the butterflies gets its calendar confused and leaves a moon-green cocoon attached to a Monterey pine twig.

A little boy ran into our home one day holding one of the cocoons: satiny and brittle, tenderly cupped in his hands. "Look!" he cried excitedly. "Mother Butterfly left us a gift!" It seemed the perfect definition: a *gift*.

"What will we do with it?" I asked the eight-year-old. His answer was so obvious it made my question sound foolish.

"You have to accept gifts," he told me. "It's just a worm now, but one day it will be a big, BIG butterfly—unless we crush it. And it will fly—unless we bend its wings."

It was not the first and will not be the last caterpillar to spin a cocoon. The world of butterflies goes on. But that butterfly was special and unique to the child and to the other children and adults in the neighborhood who watched the miracle take place in the garage. "Nothing may come of it," I warned, but the children were unconvinced. "It will be a beautiful Monarch," the finder insisted. *But we musn't crush it—or bend its wings.*

God has so many gifts in store for us: gifts of nature, friends, family—which, after all, need the same tender, loving care. The lowly worm hiding in the cocoon can emerge and soar to the sky. The butterfly did!

TO THINK AND PRAY ABOUT: Count the blessings of nature. What lessons can you learn? Seek people cocooned in fear and shame and help them "emerge."

I Think I'm Going To Cry, Lord

I THINK *I'm going to cry, Lord! And I have no shoulder to cry on, but yours. The rest of the world is busy; and, besides, I don't want them to see me crying . . . .*

At moments like these, my tears are my prayers. Today is one of those days that I'm too choked up for words—God understands. This morning I forgot to put water in the coffee pot, the bacon burned, and I went into a fit of sneezing (sure sign of a cold) just when I was planning to shampoo my hair.

The sky is dark and it has begun to rain, but why tell others? Or is that my problem? I never want to burden anyone. I gave up crying a long time ago—in public, that is. When I became "too big" to cry over a scratched knee, I decided my parents meant that included other hurts, too.

I never wanted my husband to think I was a self-pitying wife, or my son to misunderstand: it took me hours to comfort Bryce one day when he saw my tears while peeling onions for the meat loaf. I'd heard in "methods" courses that "A *good* teacher shows no emotion." And who wants to be a *poor* teacher? Plus, I was raised with the concept of not burdening friends with one's "family problems."

Life without tears can be difficult, because things build up inside. Sometimes one ache piles on another. A lot of little things brought me to my knees right by the kitchen sink with my rubber gloves still on and water dripping all over the floor. Maybe it's good I can't handle my problems alone. Today's reading tells me there is a time to weep—*And this is it, Lord!* It also tells me that God knows the end from the beginning. *Thank you Lord, for letting me cry and understanding.*

TO THINK AND PRAY ABOUT: Tell God your problems. Leave the solutions with Him.

I'm A Free Woman

January 22
Galatians 5:30-6:1

DUSTING seems so pointless—moving dust from one place to another. It takes very little diversion to get me to stop. I was sneezing away from the dust flying from the feather duster when Sadie, my next-door neighbor, called: Would I come over and see "something," she wondered.

I felt like declining because: 1) Leaving my dreaded job would make me feel guilty. Remembering what my grandmother always said didn't help: "If a task is once begun, never leave it till it's done—especially if it's something you don't want to do!" 2) And Sadie's housekeeping depresses me. Never have I seen a ball of lint, a cobweb or a molecule of dust. She must have discovered a way to blow it over the hedge between our two houses.

Feeling a second pang of guilt, I went. Sure enough, there was the odor of lemon wax mixed with the scent of fresh flowers and something else I couldn't identify. "Glue," Sadie explained, bringing out her newest scrapbook: CHRISTMAS THIS YEAR. It was complete with family photos, annotated gift tags, notes, ribbons . . . truly a thing of beauty. And I hadn't even brought my mailing list up to date!

"Been to Sadie's house?" George asked when he saw me furiously dusting half an hour later. "Why do you feel our house has to look like hers? Are you bound to her?" That brought to-day's Scripture to mind.

"No, I'm not!" I realized and put the duster down gratefully. It was time to check George's chocolate cake in the oven. He never complains about dust; and he doesn't complain when the cake splits in the middle and I have to put it together with toothpicks. As a matter of fact, I seriously doubt that Sadie finds fault with they way I keep house, either. Yet, I was in such a "bondwoman" frame of mind that I had closed my eyes to see-ing the important "something" at Sadie's house.

What would God have had me do? Be free, of course, to offer *my* best, which doesn't have to be like my friend's best. I should appreciate *me* as I appreciate *her!*

TO THINK AND PRAY ABOUT: God says you are a "freewoman." Are you free to be yourself?

I Wish I Had A Mouse In My Pocket!

January 23
I John 4:8

A MOTHER learns so much reading to her children. I remember a very special book that neither Bryce nor I could get away from: BEN AND ME. Amos was the little mouse who told Ben Franklin all of his secrets and helped him in diplomatic conferences. When Ben wanted to test for electricity, it was Amos who went up in the kite. Ben kept the little mouse up, even when he tried wildly to get down. Then, after undergoing the stiffening shock of lightning during the electrical storm, Amos returned to earth—enlightened, but frightened. He refused to rest or share his knowledge until he reached the shelter of Ben's vest pocket. "Oh, mommie," my little boy used to say, "I wish I had a mouse like Amos to help me! He could solve my problems and be my friend."

After enjoying the little fantasy with my son, I shared a conversation I had with my grandmother many years before. She used to spend hours telling me folk tales and reading me Bible stories. It was probably after this conversation that I realized there's a difference between make believe magic in stories and God's real-live miracles. "Grandma, how big is God?" I asked.

"So big He can cover the whole world with His love, and so small He can curl up inside your heart," she explained.

"How can that be?" my son wondered.

He, too, was satisfied with the answer, "God *is* love."

"That's better than having a mouse in my pocket, I guess," Bryce concluded.

Yes, there is magic in the story of Amos, but there is a miracle in the story of God's love. It is a wonderful, wonderful thought that His love reaches out and embraces the entire world. It is a source of comfort to know that it lies within me: He helps me through and solves my problems. He is my constant friend in this world and in the world to come. GOD AND ME.

TO THINK AND PRAY ABOUT: What books do you share with your family? Do you find ways of relating incidents to your relationship with God?

Good Medicine

"LAUGHTER is the best medicine," says the old adage. Today's Proverb calls it the "merry heart." I praise God for the sense of humor passed down to me by my Irish ancestors. It is the marvelous ingredient I use to oil the sticky places in everyday life: a drop can reduce friction and release tension. Oh what a blessing to be able to see the "laughing side" of myself and others. Humor can prevent symptoms from becoming an illness. Without it situations become problems, and cures take much longer.

Maybe I'm somewhat of a "Polyanna," but so many trials just seem to dissipate with a smile or a light word. I remember when our son reached the stage where he challenged "Father knows best" and claimed "Mother doesn't understand!" Bryce and I were at a stalemate over a rule I had laid down. I was determined to enforce it. Infuriated, he yelled, "Mother, you remind me of the words that great man said—I can't remember his name!" . . . Then seeing me calm (although I was seething on the inside) he yelled louder, "And I'm so mad now, I can't even remember what it was he said!" We burst into laughter. "My king's in check," Bryce grinned.

I praise God also for people He has sent into my life with their "medicine droppers" of good cheer. My doctor has relieved my mind so many times with light words; my parents raised me with an easygoing philosophy; and my husband laughs *with* me—not *at* me when I have "one of those days."

God has me convinced He wants us happy. I am also convinced that happiness is the *way* we travel instead of a destination to seek. Jesus told the world that He came so that we might have LIFE and have it more abundantly. Let's share joy with those who lack it.

TO THINK AND PRAY ABOUT: Are you able to laugh at yourself and others? In what way does Christ contribute to your happiness? Pray for those who are broken in spirit.

God As Our Source Of Power

January 25
John 8:12

W E USUALLY take our electrically-operated homes for granted, because it's seldom necessary in this land of mild winters to worry. But lately both Lady and Gentlemen Hurricanes have forgotten their manners and blown into unfamiliar territory. They have uprooted trees and tossed them playfully across power poles—as those living in hurricane territory well know. The problem in California is that most people are not prepared with the necessities: fuel oil, candles, lanterns, flatirons, etc. . . . and they panic.

In last night's blackout (result from a storm on the Pacific Coast) our neighborhood was without power. Neighbors called us so frequently to ask if our power was restored yet, we began to wish the tree had fallen on a telephone line instead of a power line. Feeling around in the dark for the ringing telephone over-and-over was frustrating, especially when so much needed to be done. "I don't have time for all these unnecessary calls!" I wanted to shout. *No time?* Isn't it strange how illogical our minds become in crisis? Just what was there that could be done in the dark? Or could I do something constructive to help the situation?

In the first place, our livingroom need not be dark. We could build a fire in the fireplace. Why not turn the dark evening into an *adventure!* We could pop popcorn . . . or better yet, heat chile in an old pot over an open fire! The evening was a huge success. "Wow!" Bryce exclaimed, "You ought to send this 'new' idea in to some magazine, Mom. I betcha other women don't know about it."

Feeling the warm glow of the fire, I knew I should do something else: call the friends I had insulted by tone of voice if not by choice of words and share about our adventure. Maybe they would like to enjoy a similar evening with their families. Sharing would be a way of saying, "I'm sorry."

TO THINK AND PRAY ABOUT: God's power shines more brightly in the dark. Sometimes we need to be reminded, "Many waters cannot quench love." God would have us share love.

This Day Belongs To God

SUNDAY is the Lord's Day, but each day should be set aside for Him as we walk in the Spirit. Supposing we go about our business as usual today but with a song in our hearts—a hymn of praise. Set aside today in a special way as you pray the following prayer with me:

"Thank you, Lord, for this new day. It is Yours. Help me to keep it lovely for You by thinking no unworthy thoughts, doing no unkind acts and speaking no unpleasant words.

"Thank You for the precious hours which appear to belong to me, but in reality belong to You. Let me know they come through Your grace. Let me know we all live on "borrowed time" for a unique purpose. Let there be no moments of this day spent in coveting worldly things; rather, let my purpose be to better myself and others for Your Kingdom.

"Thank You for Your love and the sacrifice of Your Son. Let me follow the Blessed Example by sacrificing for my family, friends and all others who need me with no expectation of a reward. You have rewarded me already, and You will reward me further; not because I am deserving, but because of Your goodness and mercy.

"Thank You for the mind You gave me. Lead me to use it wisely. Erase the temptation of ill thoughts. Replace them with humility. Then and only then can I be loving, understanding, and forgiving, as You would have me be.

"Thank You for the responsibility of my 'free will.' It is awesome, but I desire to make the right choices. Help me choose to look for the good and holy things You place in others instead of fault-finding to make myself look better.

"Thank You, Lord, for yesterday for I learned from it; but let me put it behind. Let me go forth to make this day 'sufficient unto itself.' Then I can say in truth: 'This day belongs to You.'"

TO THINK AND PRAY ABOUT: Today is a precious gift. Praise God for it, then give voice to the new song He puts in your heart for today.

Resuscitation

January 27
Genesis 2:7

A HEART ATTACK victim, someone choking to death or unconscious from swallowing too much water—what does the bystander do to help? A trained member of our local police will be demonstrationg CPR (cardiopulmonary resuscitation) tonight for our Emergency Training Program.

Results of CPR have been dramatic. Parents reportedly have saved lives of their children, and now children themselves are receiving instruction on life-saving skills. Some schools are adding a fourth "R" (resuscitation training) as a requirement for graduation.

Recently one teenager trainee's hands set a man to breathing again. The girl kept a cool head, felt for a pulse and, finding none, used gentle pressure to help air flow into the stranger's lungs. "You saved a life!" someone proclaimed after the medics arrived and took over. Until then the high school student had been too busy to think about it. Suddenly she marveled, "Hey, yeah, maybe I really did." Of course it was God who restored the man, but He used the hands of a young girl as instruments to free the air passageway.

We are all God's instruments to "massage a heart" or "dislodge obstructions," but sometimes it's in the spiritual rather than the physical sense. The importance of mouth-to-mouth breathing needs no further proving. It works! Are we overlooking some other important things, however: the heart-to-heart talk or the hand-in-hand walk? If we distribute these small helps in time of need, God will take over with a spiritual heart. Kindly deeds are life-giving. Can you lead someone just a little closer to LIFE? "Hey, yeah, maybe I really can!"

TO THINK AND PRAY ABOUT: God needs our hands, our hearts, our minds and our practical skills for Himself. All of us are "trainees" for His Kingdom.

Wider Dimension

I HAD HOPED to discard some old books in this year's January inventory. My little library just won't hold them all. Periodically, I restack them. Last night I got as far as the first book I picked up: WINNIE-THE-POOH. No cover, pages dog-eared, and the center section smeared with chocolate kisses. I deliberated . . . then made the mistake of opening it.

There sat Pooh Bear where my son and I had left him, unable to get out of Rabbit's burrow because he had eaten so much. I began to read. When Rabbit heard that Pooh must remain until spring, he asked, "Do you mind if I use your back legs as a towel-horse? Because, I mean, there they are—doing nothing—and it would be very convenient to hang towels on them." Bryce's crayon squiggles in the margins were like recorded laughter, reminders of our discussions: "His legs *should* be used, huh, Mommie? And hands, too, huh?"

I turned a page. Christopher Robin tried to comfort the bear: "We will read to you." Pooh replied: "Then would you read a Sustaining Book, such as would help and comfort a Wedged Bear in Great Tightness?" Bryce saw the dialogue as more than make-believe and asked if he could give his teacher a "Sustaining Book" for Christmas. He gave her the Bible.

I have no idea how "wedged in" Bryce's teacher was, but I know the comfort of God's Word when our world becomes one of "great tightness." It is one means He reaches out with to draw our hearts closer to Him. I appreciate the inspired author of WINNIE-THE-POOH, but far beyond that is my appreciation of God's Word. I closed the book—and replaced it on the shelf.

TO THINK AND PRAY ABOUT: Cicero said, "A room without books is like a man without a soul." *Dear Lord, make room in our hearts for Your Great Book.*

LIFE IS God's most precious gift. Handle it with prayer.
Memories can be beautiful; this one is tragic, but it carries
a reminder of the value of preparedness. It happened in
January—here in Southern California.

Weather reports said, "Clear skies . . . heavy snow-pack . . .
all roads open to mountain resorts." Happily a cub-scout troop
(many of whom had never seen snow before) packed their gear
and headed into the peaks. In the white, fairy-like forest they
tumbled like a litter of puppies, built snowmen, engaged in
snowball battles and rolled backwards downhill.

Suddenly a lovely white mountain-wall became an avalanche-
wall descending upon the boys. Before even realizing what was
happening, four frolicking boys were buried in graves of snow.
Mercifully, three were able to dig out; but rescuers were too late
to save the fourth: a nine-year-old lad who fell face-down in the
innocent looking white.

"Why?" asked a shocked public when they heard the sad
news.

"Why?" There could be any number of explanations. The sun
came out quickly and the snow slid without warning. Maybe
the children had become too daring and had ignored the warning signs; or possibly some overexuberant children had removed
the signs entirely. Then, there is always a chance of a slide in a
previously safe area. Looking back and trying to answer "why"
is sad. What we can do is help our children prepare as much as
possible—to know the rules and abide by them. They must be
familiar with their HANDBOOKS FOR SAFETY which caution: "Stay away from unmarked areas."

God offers His HANDBOOK, the Bible, to us. In it He shows
us where to walk, warns us of the dangerous places, instructs us
when we're off course and comforts us when we don't make it.
Answers are in God's HANDBOOK.

TO THINK AND PRAY ABOUT: In life's adventures
there are risks, but the love of God surrounds us. How should
you prepare for life, both physically and spiritually?

A Happy Ending

A RECENT newspaper story was so uplifting I felt a surge of joy (they're often so depressing). The story ended happily with a New Year's resolution from a teenage alcoholic.

The child started drinking alcohol at nine. Her source was the family refrigerator. Her unaware suppliers were her parents. Her audience was friends who thought it extremely funny to watch her antics and even somewhat envied her. One year later, even though she did not realize it, she was addicted.

By the time the child was in her teens, she could no longer learn in school. Her body was weak and her mind fuzzy. She had a session with a psychiatrist who said she was "depressed," and a physical examination by a medical doctor who said she was "hyperactive." Both prescribed drugs, but as she expressed in the article, "I was on a drug already."

At long last her mother, who had hung the millstone around her daughter's neck in the first place, recognized her as an alcoholic. Understandably disturbed, the mother gave up drinking. "Ironically," the girl stated, "that only solved *her* problem. It created two more for me. She and my father divorced, which added to my stress. Also, since there was no longer any liquor in the house, I took up shoplifitng to get money to buy it." After she was arrested, the 18-year-old decided to take her life.

"Maybe it's just as well," she told the reporter. "It brought my mom and me together. 'My darling, you're an alcoholic—like me—like your father—we have to get help.' We cried in each other's arms and she went with me to the hospital."

By New Year's Day the child-alcoholic had progressed to a halfway house. Her resolution: "I will pray every night, 'Dear God, please let me be sober for twenty-four more hours. I praise you for today'."

TO THINK AND PRAY ABOUT: Pray for this girl and all alcoholics. Praise God for His strength and His mercy.

Lord, thank you for this bright New Year,
Please teach me to unfold it
So I can share unmeasured joy—
So great my heart can't hold it.
Lord, lend me strength and give me peace;
And I need aspiration;
Lord, lend me dreams and give me Hope
With great anticipation.
Then to the strength You lend me
I'll add an ounce each day;
And to the peace I'll add a pound—
And give the rest away . . .

J.M.B.

THERE IS a special kind of anticipatory joy that comes with turning our calendars. Tomorrow a new month begins. February is a month of surprises. Every now and then, quite out of season, a branch blossoms. Occasionally, there is a cheerful rose. Flowers, like children, are spontaneous. When they feel warmth after a gentle rain, they come popping out to take a look at the sun.

Tomorrow is full of unexpected things. It belongs to God. We only need the courage to face what He has in store; accept it willingly; enjoy it to the fullest; function within it the best we are able; and finally, share it freely with others. There is so much we can do to bring an early spring into the lives of those around us.

There is another joy in the challenge of facing the unknown: the "resting joy" of leaving the future in God's hands. It is enough to know that I am in His keeping.

TO THINK AND PRAY ABOUT:

I'll sing along with practiced song;
Help others learn to pray;
Lord, turn my Hope to you each hour
That lies beyond today.

My Prayer For February

DEAR LORD, on this first day of February I need more love. I know you have a boundless supply—the kind that never fails—and I need an armful so that I can scatter it among family and friends, because I have been unable to show love as I ought.

Remind me, Lord, that You are the Potter and I am the clay. Do a bit of work on me each day that others may see I am Your vessel. Allow me to be a bridge that leads to Your, storehouse of love; not a barricade built with ignorance and prejudice.

Make my life an inviting gateway to the excitement and adventure of walking with You. Let me read Your Word with greater understanding that I may share it as a source of wonder and delight. Let me unhesitantly step on the ladder that leads upward; then let me unhesitantly move over that others may ascend to greater heights of joy and vision. Your horizons are limitless, Lord! Give me—give us all—of Your infinite wisdom that we may deal with little everyday things in knowledgeable ways.

Let me remember that prophecies shall pass away, so destroy the preachiness inside me. Lord, You say that tongues shall cease. Let mine slow down now. Stop me from giving my husband unnecessary nudges. Stop me from being so all-knowing with my children, so eager to enter into their decisions, or so ready with "I-told-you-so" looks. Teach me your "silent language" so that we understand each other without uttering a word. Blindfold me to their errors now and then.

One day all knowledge shall vanish away, but for now, equip me with enough to deal with those around me as tenderly as if I were painting, sculpting, composing music, tending a garden or writing a letter to a dear friend. Make me worthy in Your sight and fit to be loved and imitated by those around me. This is a big order, Lord, but You can fill it. Just give me an armful of love this February day. Amen.

Fear Of Shadows

All is locked in winter's ice; the heavy clouds hang low;
The roads are glazed in silver; each roof is heaped with snow.
And yet I feel within me a winter-gone-away;
The groundhog saw no shadow this February day!

                                                    J.M.B.

THIS IS Groundhog Day! According to legend, the wood-chuck emerges from hibernation. Should the sun be shining, the furry little animal sees its shadow and, being a coward, scurries back to sleep out the six more weeks of wintry weather. Some of our ancestors, steeped in Old World lore, refused to light early-morning lamps lest they disturb the little rodents. But others scoffed, "You're as scared of the critter's shadow as he is!"

Whether due to childhood experiences, environment or other influences, I possess a whopping amount of fear. One such fear is of electrical storms. They *can* be dangerous, but I cry, "Good-by, Cruel World" each time I plug the iron in. I grew up where lightning storms were common and spent a lot of time with my head beneath the covers. Have you done that? I used to pray a lot about my fears when I was a little girl, but in my innocence I asked God to make the storm go away instead of asking Him to take care of my fear. And, yes, I wondered why He didn't answer. I kept my terror knotted inside, embarrassed because I felt I was the only coward around.

It was when I began teaching a roomful of children, all eyes towards Teacher during a storm, that I maintained serenity by praying, "Keep me calm, Lord—for them." Something happened when I thought of others first.

Now, we know some fear is a healthy thing. It is the aching tooth of wisdom, but it must be extracted when it renders one helpless. Have I conquered all my fears? No, but they grow dimmer with each prayer: "Keep me calm, Lord."

TO THINK AND PRAY ABOUT: What are your fears? Pray and fear loses power.

Grandma, Definition Of . . .

February 3
Hebrews 12:11

GRANDMOTHERS all over the world, we love you! You are:

The nurse who took over when Mommie worried about my fever, and bragged about my first tooth.

The peppermint-scented lady that held me while she told Grandpa how to fix my broken toy.

The capable hand holding mine during my first haircut; then, after calling tears "foolishness," stooped down to save a curl.

The picture of courage walking me to nursery school, blowing my nose and powdering hers—never telling a soul we both cried like babies.

The banker who insisted I give of my small allowance to Sunday school, then slipped dimes in my piggy bank so I could have the softball after all.

The firm believer in "spare the rod and spoil the child," (with a switch "just in case").

The historian of horse-and-buggy days when I wanted to drive a car.

The "late reader" when I came back home from my first date.

The only family member who recalled choosing her mate without help.

The schemer who helped me plan my wedding by taking over completely—all the while talking of the estimated seventy-percent giving—on both sides.

The not-too-subtle spokeswoman, telling me what a beautiful grandchild I was and that my parents deserved the same thrill.

The memory whose teachings lead me to deal tenderly with my children, understandingly with my parents, lovingly with my husband, kindly with my friends and obediently with God.

J.M.B.

TO THINK AND PRAY ABOUT: Do you practice the art of loving—grandparent, parents and *all* older people?

Here's My Problem, Lord

A LITTLE STORY my father used to tell me came to my rescue last night.

"There was this man who owed his next-door neighbor a hundred dollars. Now, the bill was due the next day and he had less than thirty dollars. The night before he tossed and turned till his wife wormed the truth out of him. The good woman then got out of bed, threw open the window and yelled: 'Hey, Ruben! About that hundred bucks—he ain't got it!' 'Now,' she said to her husband, 'let *him* worry'. And they went to sleep."

At 1:30 A.M. I was lying awake worrying about the cake I could not bake for Fellowship Sunday. Of course! All I had to do was call Sylvia—not tonight, of course, but the first thing in the morning. She would understand that I could not bake a cake and be out of town at the same time. That settled that, but I had some questions to ask myself before I fell asleep. Why had I worn myself out over a trifle? Why hadn't I shared the problem with Sylvia? As a matter of fact, if it was worth losing sleep over, why hadn't I raised the window and called out to God?

The cake was no big deal, but it made me realize what I had been doing—behaving like Homer's Titan who was forced to support the heavens on his head and hands. In a sense I had been robbing God of His right to help. This self-imposed martyrdom is contrary to God's wishes. I slept after I had said a prayer: *Here are my problems, Lord—the big and the small. Forgive me when I forget that they are Yours.* Amen.

TO THINK AND PRAY ABOUT: Do you practice casting your burden upon the Lord as the Psalmist advises in today's Scripture? In what ways does God then sustain you? Remember that putting Him in charge takes practice, but it works!

■ December • January • February 2000-2001

OUR DAILY BREAD

By the breath of God ice is given, and the broad waters are frozen.

Job 37:10

Love Begets Love

DO I *keep* the Golden Rule? No, I prefer to *share* it! That way it becomes an exciting game. Small considerations bounce back and forth, keeping the ball of kindness in play. There's no score-keeping and no trying to win. It's simply an interaction with points rising on both sides. Rules of the game? Examples may be more helpful.

Two customers are waiting in the Friday afternoon line of a bank-teller's booth. A young man notices he's directly ahead of a tired-looking business man. "Would you like to go ahead?" he asks. "No," the older man responds, "You're very kind, but you have only a check to cash. I'll save my business transaction for the Merchants' Window."

Two ladies are waiting to check out at a grocery store. As the first pays her bill she sees the customer behind her trying to place purchases on the counter with her left hand, holding a baby with her right. "I'll hold the little one," the first customer offers. The mother gratefully hands over her child. "I can't thank you enough," she sighs.

You've seen it happen. Two drivers pull out from a four-way stop simultaneously. One yields, the other waves. . . fellowship at an intersection.

Will there always be a courteous response? No. Kindness may be new to the other party, but those who share the Golden Rule introduce the only rule needed. It helps to remember that as servants of God we are not out to win over people; we are out to win people over. There's no losing, either. Once we introduce people to Christian ways, God takes over and enriches their lives. Washington Irving said, "Love is never lost. If not reciprocated it will flow back and soften and purify the heart."

TO THINK AND PRAY ABOUT: Can you find ways to apply today's Scripture verse to your daily life? This single sentence prayer helps me: *Lord Jesus, let my light so shine that others may be guided by it. Amen.*

For Women Only

AN ARTICLE entitled "For Women Only" caught my eye. Why men were excluded puzzled me. I wonder who collects this life-and-death information, and for what purpose. I wonder even more why I read it! Still they do; and I do.

"Your life expectancy is seventy years," the cheerful newsbreak began. "And here's how you're going to spend it: five years, eating; twelve, toiling; five, dressing and undressing; six, walking; three, talking; three, educating yourself; eight, amusing yourself; three and one-half, reading; twenty-four, sleeping; and half a year, worshipping God." How depressing!

As for my longevity, who says it's seventy years? Look at Methuselah. My spirits began to lift. Eating five years? Perhaps, since I eat slowly. Toiling twelve? I love my work! Five dressing and undressing? One logically follows the other—unless I choose to retire fully clothed. Three and a half reading? Fine. I'm a fast reader. Six-walking- three-talking I'll lump together and double it, since my husband and I walk six miles daily—and he says I talk all the way. Three in education? Lop that off altogether, for education is a lifetime proposition. Twenty-four *sleeping*. Does anybody really sleep that much? *I* don't. Maybe others don't wake the roosters up to crow like I do, but I doubt that there are that many Lady Rip Van Winkles around. And as for worshiping, the data gatherers must have years spent in formal services.

I wonder if they know about those of us who talk to God morning, noon and night: Thank you, Lord . . . Help me, God . . . Oh, what a beautiful morning!

TO THINK AND PRAY ABOUT: Look for a new definition to "Life Expectancy!" And live your life in the expectancy of the Lord—every moment of every day.

The Greater The Claim

PROMISSORY breezes tease the sleeping trees and rearrange the cloudpuffs in the February sky. Now and then they are able to push aside the purgatorial darkness of mankind's smog and give Earthlings a glimpse of Eternal Blue. When this happens, I feel a new spring in my steps: A miracle is about to come to pass! Oh, scientists can explain it. No miracle really, just the order of things. It is my private miracle that I can look up and find beauty. It is time to open the shutters—shutters which closed out the storms and the light as well. So it is time to open the shutters of my heart and humble myself to meet the needs of others without reserve—as children do. It is time to share the beauty I see.

Sharing myself, the beauties of nature, the Good News of Christianity—all these involve risks. Investors say "The greater the claim (for profit) the greater the risk." Or, on another level, I remember the lesson of the poke-sallet, which in early spring pushed through winter leaves in tender shoots. Those who were "brought up on poke-sallet" knew it made fine table greens in its youth—a rare delicacy since no other greens were ready so early. Ultimately, in its maturity, the plant turned blood-red and its leaves and its berries were poisonous. Even in its safest stage, parboiling was recommended. Risky, yes; and the timing had to be just right. The same is true of my task.

There is a man who lives a short distance from me that I am trying hard to like. The fact that others have given up must not deter me: *My job is to love the unlovable.* Maybe he never looks to the sky; but if he did, who knows but what a little green sprout would reach towards the light?

TO THINK AND PRAY ABOUT: If you have an "impossible situation," pray with me: Lord, when we take risks and fail, let us not feel ashamed. Let us make new plans, try different ways, knowing the miracle is there through Your Son, who taught us to love.

Bridle Your Thoughts

THIS IS the season for the common cold—something everybody wants to share with me. As I waited for my doctor's appointment, I saw this sign:

"Any man can spoil himself for himself. He can allow himself to grow so sensitive that he lives in constant pain. He can nurse his grudges until they are intolerable burdens. He can think himself insulted until he is apt to be. He can believe the world's against him until it is. He can insult his friends until they are no longer friends. He can think himself so important that no one else enjoys his friendship. He can become so wrapped up in himself that he becomes very small."

It was interesting as I sat in the waiting room to watch the reaction of newcomers. Invariably they paused and read the sign. Some smiled. Some frowned. A few sneered. And I saw a few prospective patients flee while they still had the chance! Unknowingly, the readers were revealing themselves as they evaluated the doctor's philosophical sign. As a matter of fact, I did a little self-analysis myself—between sneezes.

How easy it is to coddle myself and suffer self-inflicted pain; to cling to all the little hurts the day brings; to imagine a friend has betrayed a confidence; to become so small I could slip down ALICE'S "rabbit hole" and hide—not wanting to be found or comforted. Self-pity is a dreadful malady, but it isn't incurable! The treatment, I suppose, varies with the patient; but I profit from reading I Corinthians, Chapter 13. I simply can't lick my wounds after that! I strongly recommend it to everyone. It costs nothing. There are no side-effects. And it has the healing power of making the reader long to be out of the doctor's office helping others! Helping others, incidentally, is step number two of my self-help program. I left the clinic with a grateful heart that my doctor is a medical missionary.

TO THINK AND PRAY ABOUT: How important is to-day's Proverb in your life? Do you praise God for unfailing love? How can we keep our thoughts pure?

The Wonder Of Wonderful Neighbors

OUR LIVES would be lonely without our neighbors. We appreciated our good neighbors and desired to be good neighbors in return.

The avocado-shaded backyard of our home provides privacy and a place to bathe the boxer. In front the window above the sink provides a view of our neighbor's property. How nice to have people who take pride in their property! As I did dishes this morning I looked to the right where lemons sparkle on the trees like chandeliers against a well-manicured lawn. The yard on the left looked ready for a garden wedding with its giant bouquets of hibiscus and carpet of strawberries. Just below are the lush vegetable gardens tucked away by a shapely hedge. The owner is always grooming the grounds—or trotting across the street with overflowing baskets of fresh produce. Yes, we need our neighbors . . . .

There's so much to the "good neighbor policy." And it all begins with love.

TO THINK AND PRAY ABOUT: God tells us to love our neighbors; today's verse tells us how much. Maybe the Golden Rule is all we need; but I made out a little checklist for myself. See where you fit on a scale of one-to-eight:

1. Do I keep my premises as clean as theirs, thereby sharing beauty?

2. Do I share from my grove and my garden that which I have?

3. Do I refrain from borrowing except in emergencies? Then, do I pay back immediately—always taking a little something extra in return?

4. Am I friendly and helpful, withholding advice unless it is invited?

5. Do I keep my pets off their property but understand if theirs visit?

6. Do I keep radio, TV, and my voice at a reasonable volume?

7. Do I teach my children to have fun without being obnoxious?

8. Do I pray for my neighbors? Do I find some way to share Christ?

Empty Nests

THE DECIDUOUS TREES have finished dropping their leaves. After raking and burning, I can enjoy the nests that only the birds knew about last summer. It is amazing how many nests I see. Some swing like tiny hammocks suspended with fragile cobwebs; and yet they weathered the strong east winds. Some have mud foundations and look as if the feathered architects had soldered them to the forks of a tree for future generations. I wonder where they found the mud and how long it took the little beaks to haul it to the building sites? One nest I am unable to identify is woven of eucalyptus bark; the pale blue feather barely visible between the twisted white bark tells me that the nest is warmly lined. The tiny nest suspended from the tip of a slender twig could house nothing bigger than a hummingbird.

The marvel of it all is that although I can count a dozen nests, all made from a different blueprint, I know that up in the mountains, down in the valley and out in the desert there are countless more made of thorns, roots, moss, sticks and strings—each different, constructed by God's little creatures with only their beaks and feet. Last spring each happy couple selected its piece of real estate, shopped for building materials and set up housekeeping for a family. Mama Bird and Papa Bird fed their fledglings a nourishing diet, gave them the proper flying lessons and sent them out into the world to raise families of their own. And now the nests are empty . . . .

I read a lot about the "empty nest syndrome" these days. Psychiatrists should refer mothers afflicted with this depression to articles on ornithology. One can learn a lot from birds. How happily the parents tend their young and what a quick adjustment they make when their children grow up! They resume their singing as if they are secure in the knowledge they've done a fine job. Having done their best, they are able to give their young up to live their own lives, confident they in turn will do their best.

TO THINK AND PRAY ABOUT: Are you able to put your children's futures in the hands of the Lord?

Why Are You So Happy?

ONCE UPON A TIME there lived a family of happy owls. The barnyard animals, who were forever squabbling, demanded, "Why are you so happy?"

"When spring comes we are happy to see everything come to life after the long winter sleep. The trees put forth their buds and leaves; the meadows are covered with thousands of tiny flowers; and birds everywhere are singing merrily. Later, around every flower, bees and bumblebees are buzzing, and all kinds of little flies are humming. Butterflies flit to and fro gathering honey from the golden sunflowers. Then we know that summer is here . . . . Then autumn comes, and the spider, who has waited through the glorious summer under a leaf, comes out and spins her web to hold up the tired leaves a little longer. We rejoice to see her, and finally when the leaves are fallen and the earth is covered with snow, we come back and are cozy in our old home—for winter is here again."

Celestino Piatti's delightful story reveals a pattern of sensitivity to the beauty of life. Baudelaire, the French poet, said it another way: "Most blessed, most fortunate is he whose sensitive soul soars up to the earliest larks, and lets him listen to the language of the flowers and all the voiceless things." There's a tucked-in moral here. I pause and ask myself just what kind of an image I present to others. Am I a soaring lark, a happy owl—or do I appear to be one of those fighting, pecking-at-each-other fowls, seeing no loveliness, sharing no love? If so, who would want my brand of Christianity?

When the Lord appeared to Paul, telling him to go to Rome to testify as he had done in Jerusalem, He said, "Be of good cheer." Obviously God had no need for a long-faced missionary to sadly bear the Good News of his apostleship and the redemptive power of Christ. The birth of Christ brought joy to the world. It should shine in my face so brightly that others ask of me, "Why are you so happy?"

TO THINK AND PRAY ABOUT: Are you a happy Christian? Pray that you may become more sensitive to God, your environment and others around you.

Divided Houses

THE USUAL "Lincoln's Birthday Sale" flyers fill today's newspaper, and rickety-looking log cabins decorate the children's windows. No "Marked Down" tags or sketches of the Sixteenth President's birthplace can capture the spirit of the man: principle above privilege; patriotism above politics; and love of country above all personal gain. The best way to honor the memory of one of our greatest Americans is by following his examples of compassion and tolerance.

"A house divided against itself cannot stand," Abraham Lincoln said in his acceptance speech to the United States Senatorial nomination. "Either the opponents of slavery will arrest the further spread of it and place it where the public mind shall rest in the belief that it is in the course of ultimate extinction; or its advocates will push it forward, till it shall become alike lawful in all the States, old as well as new—North as well as South." Ironically, it was his pursuits of equality of peoples that brought his defeat. Lincoln took his downfall philosophically: ". . . and though I now sink out of view and shall be forgotten, I believe I have made some marks which will tell for the cause of civil liberty long after I am gone." He was only partially correct. He did *not* sink from view; he went on to become President. He *did* leave marks. His untimely death is a dark page in our history, but what gift could be greater than that he offered? His gift was a way of tolerance and peace.

Is there a more lovable and livable quality to life than tolerance? Tolerance is vision, generosity of spirit and breadth of mind. It enables us to see things from another's point of view; concedes to others the right of personal opinion; and softens the hard core within us that seeks to have its own way. It leaves no room for divided houses.

TO THINK AND PRAY ABOUT: Is yours a divided home? God can chink together the broken heart, the broken dream, the broken relationship if you will but ask for help. Nothing can separate you from His love. Pray for tolerance at home and peace for the world. Let it begin with you!

Lamps Of Love

THE WORLD can be a dark, chilly place or it can be warmed by lamps of love. Our young Associate Pastor and his lovely wife expressed the following gratituity after a surprise housewarming.

"An evening to remember, as this was the night our house was warmed by people we love! Cathy and I will have many happy memories as we reflect on the housewarming. We have decided to purchase lamps for our home with your financial gift. We trust that these lamps will be used to brighten our home and enable us to see our way more clearly. In a parallel manner, Christ came into the world that lives could be brighter and we might see life more clearly. '. . . God is light . . .'

"As the lamps will help us see our home better, so life in Christ enables people to see life better. Being in Christ helps people see others as God sees them. Then, because there is no darkness in God, having the light of Christ enables us to see the hurts which are so prominent in the lives of men and women today. There are many times when people avoid the pain and suffering surrounding them because a life in Christ brings light to life and we are able to see those hurts, accept them and do something constructive in His name. Last, the light that Christ gives enables us to see the joy and happiness that can be such a great part of life. A warm smile, a healthy laugh or an infectious grin can be lost so easily in the dark. Yet, when there is light, they can spread so quickly and give vitality, warmth and enthusiasm to life. Jesus Christ helps us to see more joy in life as well as to be a source of joy in the lives of others.

"As people are entertained in our home, there will be physical light so that we can see one another better and feel the freedom that comes from being in the light. Thank you, Friends, for helping us to provide that light. On a spiritual level, we also want people to see the light of Christ shining through as they look at our home. It is our prayer that God will use it in a way to make it a light in our community."

TO THINK AND PRAY ABOUT: Praise God for lamplighters! Let your light shine.

Old-Fashioned Sentiment

This lacy heart has words to say:
"I love you in the same sweet way
As when our love was new and bright
With laughter, stars, and candlelight—
Of which the poets love to sing—
In lilac-twilight of our spring . . .
For there's a rapture, there's a thrill
Knowing we are sweethearts still!"

J.M.B.

MAYBE it's kind of corny putting a little ditty alongside my husband's breakfast tray each Valentine's Day. He always knows a poem will be there—just as I know there will be a ceramic mouse perched on my plate to add to my collection together with the first violet of spring.

Once, many years ago, we were away from home and he spent his last dime for a little bunch of the fragrant flowers he knows I love. Nobody told me to invert the blooms so the violets could drink at night, so the next morning they were hopelessly wilted. I cried and cried and awkwardly he tried to comfort me, but both of us knew it wasn't their death I mourned. I am simply a sentimental simpleton, a woman born to love and be loved—and I thank God for that . . . The violets died of thirst, but our love is alive.

St. Valentine's Day does have a place in ancient history—as do violets. Valentinus of Third-Century Rome is considered "patron saint of lovers." Valentinus, a Christian priest, refused to worship the Roman gods, so Emperor Claudius II sentenced him to death. While in prison Valentinus saw a clump of wood violets growing just within reach of his cell window. He picked a bloom and a heart-shaped leaf on which he inscribed with a pin: REMEMBER YOUR VALENTINE for the jailer's blind daughter. The practice has grown and become somewhat commercialized, but the base still is LOVE.

TO THINK AND PRAY ABOUT: Valentines used to be unsigned. Think of some lonely person to surprise. And remember anytime is "I love you" time!

Where's My Sense Of Humor, Lord?

February 15
James 5:11-13

THE CITY bus was late, and my feet were complaining about the new shoes I'd worn shopping. The waiting bench was filled so that the only two standing were a giggling little girl and me. Between giggles, the girl asked, "Do you know what 'mim' people are?" I admitted that I did not. "They are most proper. They sit with their lips pursed up tight and disapprove of everything you do and they hold their hands tight together." I laughed, because although I was doing none of those things, it summed up the way I felt. Pleased by my appreciation, the bouncy child consulted her book and went on. "Mim people always have 'worgs' in their gardens. You know what worgs are? They're plants that just practically never grow—" A grind of gears told me the bus had come. The happy voice was lost in a din of adult voices—too bad, for she was trying to explain about "gnurr" on the plants' leaves.

The small stranger had brightened my day. Isn't it wonderful the way children laugh so readily and so wholeheartedly? God sends them to us equipped with a delightful sense of humor. They are able to reduce friction and tension with a laugh. When Bryce was growing up we set aside a small corner in our library for our "humor shelf." When the going got rough we would pull down a fun-book and share a laugh. Many times when things were not as great as I thought they should be I asked, *Where's my sense of humor, Lord?*" He helped me to laugh. Then, I was no longer a "mim" person!

TO THINK AND PRAY ABOUT: All of us have unpleasantries in life. A laugh puts us halfway through a cure. "Life by the yard is very hard, but by the inch, it's really a cinch." Today's reading encourages us to be happy as we "endure" and to sing when we are merry. Can you see Our Lord with a smiling face? Would He want "worgs" in His garden?

Let Us Imagine . . .

February 16
I Chronicles 28:9

"Imagination rules the world."

Napolean Bonaparte

RIGHTLY EMPLOYED, imagination is a wonderful thing. There's a great imaginative story that kept Bryce from eating too many sweets as a little boy: after over-indulging, the suffering child in the story has a "spaghetti dream" in which he is being overcome by spaghetti. Then he enters the land of ice cream where he eats and eats until he and the ice cream turn purple, green and blue. Invariably after this story, Bryce had no desire to over-indulge.

Children live in a world of imaginary characters doing whimsical things. As they grow older they must sort reality from fantasy; yet hopefully each child keeps a scrap of imagination from his childhood. For it is imagination that allows one to see a golden daffodil within the brown bulb, the seed that will sprout from a clod of earth or the goodness within each person he meets.

Imagination also allows us to see the things of God. We can picture our Father in heaven with His Son, who is preparing a place for us. There is a quotation that suggests, "If man does not imagine his future, then, indeed, he will not have one." This can be applied spiritually. Of course, the Bible makes frequent mention of the wrong kinds of imagination: vain things, evil things, mischief among friends. But the right kind of imagination allows others to see "Jesus in me." It implies responsibility on one part; a spark of spiritual imagination on the other.

TO THINK AND PRAY ABOUT: "Imagination is the quality that raises men most above animals." Play a "Let Us Imagine" game—imagine a world without sin.

Push Button In Case Of Emergency!

February 17
Proverbs 20:22

"**D**ID YOU TELL your teacher what happened in the elevator, Jody?" the delighted mother asked her seven-year-old boy. He looked from his mother to me, brown eyes shining.

"I was all by myself and I got stuck. I had to unlock the words!" he said triumphantly. I shared Jody's excitement, for his learning to read had been a struggle for both of us. I had tried every teaching method I knew and wondered how he unlocked the words in a crisis.

"I sounded out *push*," Jody went on to explain. I knew *p* had a puffing sound and the *u* was short and says 'uh' between two consonants and *sh* is the shushing sound and I already knew *button* and *in* and the *a's* long in *case* because there's an *e* on the end—" Jody finally paused for breath. "But the other word was so BIG." He looked thoughtful. "Till I broke it up like you told me, a piece at a time." The child referred to dividing the word "emergency" into syllables. This made me wonder if I practiced what I preached in terms of everyday problems: *a piece at a time*.

Jody resumed his story. "So I pushed the button. I knew somebody would save me. I just sat down." Lesson Two: *Wait*.

I complimented Jody on how well he had handled the emergency and told him that's why we need to be good readers. But, too, I was thinking of what my student had shown *me*. From the mouth of a child had come two practical reminders: (1) Handle life bit by bit; and (2) Push the button and wait! So often I see giant-size problems as insurmountable instead of realizing they're conquerable a piece at a time. When I exercise my "reading skills" and turn to God's Word, I expect an immediate cure. And do I tackle today knowing that tomorrow will take care of itself? Am I able to push the button and wait?

TO THINK AND PRAY ABOUT: How can you apply Jody's faith? Of such is the Kingdom of Heaven.

An Inside-Out Rainbow

February 18
Genesis 9:11-16

"Oh, rainbow, that gracious thing, made up of tears and light."
Coleridge

RAINBOWS are a favorite subject of writers. Nature-poets sing of "rainbow bridges"; Christian writers find God's promise "faithful to its sacred page"; and mythologists speak of "the smiling daughter of the storm."

During World War II when young men needed dreams, a popular song was "I Saw a Rainbow at Midnight." The tune was catchy. The lyrics were sentimental. Scientists paid no attention to inaccuracy: no sun, no bow.

Then, last night, those of us still up after midnight caught sight of the phenomenon! The moon, like a half-disk, lay flat on top with swirly "stars" around the bottom. Surrounding it was a rainbow-colored ring. But this rainbow was unique in that it started out light blue—lighter than the surrounding sky—and melted into the red end of the spectrum closer to the moon. In other words, it was an inverted rainbow.

In response to calls, a spokesman at Palomar College, California, told us the illusion was "common in the East . . . result of off-ocean air approaching warm land . . . producing an in-side-out rainbow (it's usually red on the outside, moving to blue of the spectrum on the inside) . . ." I bogged down in the technical explanation. I only knew that it was indescribably beautiful in earthly terms.

While God placed the bow in the sky as a sign of His covenant with Noah, writers tend to use it as an analogy: the smile following tears.

TO THINK AND PRAY ABOUT: We should be rainbows that coax colors after "storms of life."

A Healing Power

MY GRANDMOTHER had a sampler hanging on the parlor wall. The hand-stitched title was: SURE-CURE. As a child I found the words fun to read, but as I grew older I realized they held a deeper meaning. Each time I repeat them now I realize Granny's prescription truly has a healing power to "restore my senses."

"One pound of resolution, two grains of common sense, two ounces of experience, twelve ounces of dislike, one large sprig of time, three quarts of cooling water, and a great quantity of consideration. DIRECTIONS: Set these over the gentle fire of love, sweeten with the sugar of forgetfulness, skim with the spoon of melancholy. Put the best part inside, cork it with the conscience, let it remain, and you will find quick ease to restore the senses. These articles can be had at the apothecary's, at the Home of Understanding, next door to Reason, on Prudent Street, in the Village of Contentment, built on Prayer. This is a sure-cure for the disease, 'We-Never-Speak-As-We-Pass-By'."

How easy it is to let little dislikes and petty irritations build until I am alienated from a friend. How easy to allow small hurts to close me off from my family. And how quickly I find myself, because of these things, out of communion with God. God gave me the precious gift of loving through His Son. He adds to this gift of loving when I come to Him in prayer and as I practice the art of loving others. I need to talk to God about each little irritation that creeps into my life; prayer is the vital ingredient of Christian health. How is it that I neglect to use prayer for all my emotional aches and pains? Prayer brings us closer to God and to others.

TO THINK AND PRAY ABOUT: What petty differences do you have to bring to the Lord in prayer? *Lord Jesus, restore us with the sure-cure of prayer. Amen.*

What God Hath Joined

ALL AROUND US I see marriages crumbling, but I never expected to see it happen to two of our dearest friends. How could they have lived in a state of confusion and conflict, so overwhelming it affected their happiness to the point of a divorce without our being aware? But, even had we known of their struggle, could we have helped? One comfort I have is knowing that in everything there is access to God. I shall mail them a copy of "Prayer at the Time of Divorce." (Permission given by the publisher of THE LUTHERAN PRAYER BOOK.)

TO THINK AND PRAY ABOUT: Dear Lord, a sad tragedy has come to our family. When we were married we heard Your admonition "What therefore God hath joined together let not man put asunder." But something happened, Lord. I remember from my confirmation instructions that unfaithfulness or desertion are biblical reasons for divorce.

Lord, in whatever way I have been directly or indirectly responsible for this divorce, I pray for Your forgiveness. If it be possible for us to get together again and continue our married life, I would thank You. If this is not possible, then help me in the future to dedicate my life more fully to You, Lord, and to accept with grace whatever joys or sorrows You may have in store for me.

Dear God, You have something to say in Your Word about remarriage. Help me to understand Your direction before I consider any remarriages, lest I put my will above Your will. Lord, I want and need Your blessings in my life.

Grant this according to Your divine will for Jesus' sake. Amen.

Arbor Day Meditation

THE ARBOR DAY movement began in the 19th century when a number of public-minded persons, alarmed by the rapid deforestation in the United States, urged that trees be planted systematically. Dates vary with climatic conditions, but at least three states have "plant a tree" day in February.

If a tree could speak it might tell us: "I am the oldest factory working for mankind. I take carbon dioxide and convert it into oxygen for breathing. I can supply enough oxygen—me, one tree—to keep eighteen people alive. And, in a sort of gift exchange, I can use up the air man does not need, carbon dioxide. I am sort of an air conditioner, using the sun's energy to evaporate moisture in my leaves and releasing it to cool the atmosphere. Would you believe that an acre of trees like myself can give off as much moisture as an acre of water?

"I help control floods by holding raindrops and letting them down gently. I add to underground water so there will be springs. My leaves on the ground make soil rich and fertile for food and flowers. I soak up noise. A row of us can absorb deafening sounds from skyways and highways. I serve as a shield from wind when farmers plant my friends and me in fence-rows. We hold the wind in our branches or it would carry away the soil.

"There is much I do to protect our nation's resources; and if you'll forgive my pride, may I add that I lend beauty with my restful green leaves—a sort of outdoor patio where anyone can rest and meditate? If you look closely at my leaves, you'll see something else. They have a fuzzy surface that traps and filters out ashes, dust and pollen from the air. I look paper-doll flat, but I am sort of three-dimensional. Have you really looked me over?"

The "Talking Tree" is right. It can do all these things—and more. Joyce Kilmer said, "Only God can make a tree." But we can conserve it.

TO THINK AND PRAY ABOUT: Examine a leaf. Meditate. A miracle is there. Thank God for trees He planted in the Garden of Eden and the Tree of Life which awaits us in Eternity.

Preserving Tradition

February 22
Matthew 22:37
John 5:23-24

AS I PIT the fruit for the traditional cherry pie, I find myself wondering how many Americans only remember our First President's powdered wig, velvet pants or his minuet with Martha Dandridge Custis. Do they think of George Washington on his birthday as "Father of our country?" Or, on the other hand, do some people take his memory too seriously, confusing the phrase with Our Heavenly Father? As adults, we are symbols of authority to children. Whether we would choose the role has nothing to do with it. It comes to us packaged. They watch, listen and interpret our every move. And, sobering as the thought may be, we Christians are scrutinized by a watching audience of non- Christians. How do we measure up?

I pop the pie in the oven and close the door—hard, as if to drown out my thoughts. They persist, taking me back to Christmas. Did I emphasize fruitcake, evergreens and gifts more than the significance of the Holy Birth? On the other hand, did I keep the Baby Jesus too little too long—never getting to the significance of His walk among men?

It is so easy for things to be overdone, which reminds me to check the cherry pie. It is doing fine, brown crust with thick red juice oozing a wee bit the way my family likes it. In a sense, I wish it had run over in the oven. Sometimes such a crisis is less disturbing than my thoughts. Ahead lies Easter—hot-cross buns, lilies and nests of colored eggs. My family would be crushed if I dropped the little traditions. Looking back on my childhood, I recall ministers who denounced such "paganisms," then preached a Good Friday sermon on Easter Sunday—leaving Christ on the cross. I agonized over that, for the Hope, the Joy of Rebirth, the Eternal Promise never came . . . .
My pie is done!

TO THINK AND PRAY ABOUT: *Lord, let us share Your Truth, as we preserve the small traditions. Amen*

February 23
Isaiah 47:13

"We have seen his star . . .
and are come to worship him."

Matthew 2:2 (KJV)

THOUGH IT is not the case this year, now and then
February gives us an extra day. There is (so they say) some
sort of cosmic mystique to this day. For instance, past practices
allow for fair ladies to invite young men to dinner, or, were they
bold enough, to propose marriage.

Couples married on Leap Year, no matter who pops the question, will have an exhilarating life together, maybe because they
have less anniversaries together. They will have to work hard,
according to the "sayers," but they will reap bountiful rewards
careerwise, becoming "names" in show busines or politics.
Supposedly, people have their consciousness raised on Leap
Year and elect good leaders; so we can look forward to a year
extraordinary! This is, no doubt, why election year falls at this
time.

Astrologers would have us believe that any Leap Year is a
thrust toward more auspicious times ahead. It's a time to expand business, buy property or make investments. Children
born during Leap Year will, supposedly, be "extroverted and
precocious."

Making predictions by the stars is not new, as we see by the
Bible. The one Star followed by the Wise Men led them to
God's Son. Putting our faith in the stars is a common (but risky)
practice now; however, letting the right Star lead us can bring
us bright tomorrows.

TO THINK AND PRAY ABOUT: What Star are you
following? Where is it taking you?

The Last Day

The greatest gifts God gave to me:
Love and its power of memory. J.M.B.

REMEMBER the hard-to-please English teachers? We thought they were harsh then, but in retrospect, do you find that their teachings were wise, their advice to "press toward the mark" sound? I remember one assignment that meant so much—even then. Now it means more.

I interviewed an older woman. My question was: "If this were your last day on earth how would you spend it?" My subject talked with closed eyes; her words came out in colorful phrases instead of sentences; and I had to take notes quickly. She said:

"I should wear a morning-face, so I could watch earth's full rotation from dawn to wherever day and night meet in twilight. I should rest, reliving other days filled with God's blessings: friends . . . old hymns . . . porches . . . children's laughter. . . . I should watch narrow sunbeams turn windows gold, blind the eyes of sleepy pigeons and filter through the cobwebs. I should listen for the mockingbirds that know all earth-songs and a few of heaven's, too. I should watch the earth drowse at noon when even the sun seems to pause . . . but I should not sleep lest I miss the building of white cloud-cathedrals and their fall when the thunder-organ sounds. And in the hush that follows a storm, I should look at the washed sky, filled with a million invisible stars, waiting for the night. I should look upon rain-washed hills, mute like the stars, with strength lying their silence. . . . Then happily, I should watch the golden disk sink in the west, leaving me the molton silver of a day well spent, while, like the energy of the stars, never spent at all. . . . And I should hope to take my memories with me. In nothing else am I rich . . . in nothing else could I be poor. . . ."

TO THINK AND PRAY ABOUT: "This is the day which God hath made; let us rejoice and be glad in it." Is every day a gift from God?

Rose Of Sharon

ROSES ARE nothing out of the ordinary in Texas, but I hope the cutting I brought back from there takes root. I was "back home" at a reunion when I saw the rose so out of season.

There was a dream-like quality in the soft-vowel speech flowing around *potpourri* that day. It is easy to forget how thick East Texans slice ham, how refreshing buttermilk pie is after seconds on everything else—and how drowsy and contented one feels afterwards. It was nice being among old friends. One asked the blessing: he had become a minister. One shared a seascape in oils: she had become a painter. Another showed slides of exotic places service to his country had taken him. One wrote a book; one patented a safety device . . . blessed ties. Going home (whether to friends or family) can restore fidelity to old dreams. It reminded me of "When We All Get to Heaven" and "When the Roll Is Called up Yonder."

The rose was in the centerpiece on the dining room table. "Isn't that the Rose of Sharon?" I inquired of the hostess when there was a lull. She nodded, and soon we were remembering the garden from our childhood. That's the advantage of keeping in touch with friends and extended families.

Winters can be cruel to roses there, but my friend's mother had one that bloomed constantly in a little secluded corner. "I named it the Rose of Sharon," she told us, "because it ignores the blizzards and droughts." On raw days we used to watch the determined buds swell with promise—half-concealing, half-revealing the handiwork of God.

"It's like life here and hereafter," she said one day, "what it is and what it will be." (*Thank You, Lord, for such teachings.*)

The "Rose of Sharon" was symbolic of friends here and hereafter. The lovely lesson lingered, sharing memory and tradition.

TO THINK AND PRAY ABOUT: Lord, let our lives be a rose-out-of-season for someone.

The Good Samaritan

IT IS SO EASY to look out for "my kind." The problem of showing compassion for "a different sort" is an old one. The people of Samaria were looked upon by the Jews as "foreigners of a Gentile tongue," and yet in the parable of the Good Samaritan (Luke 10), it was the lowly man from Samaria who bound up the wounded man when the priest and a Levite had ignored him. I had reason to think of the story I had known since childhood just last week—not in some faraway place, but in the Safeway parking lot. I also saw my husband in a new light.

George and I saw a man lying face-down beneath the street light. Cars were passing dangerously close to the helpless person and pedestrians were either gaping in curiosity or hurrying past to avoid getting involved. Getting involved can be dangerous. The whole thing can be a hoax, a trick to set up a victim who offers assistance; or for real the person can be injured, but one is made liable in certain cases. Offering aid (like offering any other service that Christ would have us offer) involves risk.

My husband leaned down to see if the man was injured. "Are you hurt?" When he answered his speech was slurred and there was a heavy odor of alcohol. George had a choice to make. He could walk away and be safe, or he could render help and endanger himself. It was dark and I was frightened. I'd never been in such a position. "Let's go—"

But George had made a different kind of decision. "Are you able to stand?" The man shook his head. "Try!" my husband said briskly.

It was then that we saw the gash on the stranger's forehead. He needed medical attention, but he was babbling, "Don't turn me in . . . no money . . . 'fraid of hospitals . . . done nothing . . . no police." We persuaded him he needed a doctor and took him to a hospital. My husband's risk helped to meet the stranger's needs.

TO THINK AND PRAY ABOUT: Do you think God requires us to show mercy—at a risk?

The First Commandment With Promise

RECENTLY as a beloved neighbor sorted through the souvenirs of a now grown-up family, she said, "June, I want you to see this." And, oh, I am glad she shared it! It's the kind of letter every father should receive from his daughter.

When Bess read it to me (I never seem to have my reading glasses) her voice was halting and there was a lump in my throat, too. We parents remember all the little baby-things; but I, for one, forget that children remember with tenderness, also. When a grateful offspring takes time to mention all the things that make a "Pop" so special, then doubles twice her greeting with "We thank God for you," the first commandment fulfills a promise for the parent as well as the child.

"Dear Pop: Somehow I just couldn't find a birthday card that said the right things. They don't mention the show of concern, the understanding and the expressions of love. They don't seem to know about a guy that seems at times to be so hard and stern on the outside, yet is always there when anyone needs a helping hand. They don't say a thing about the Grandpa that spends hours playing with his grandkids even if it hurts—and never lets on. There was nothing there that noticed the talents in almost every area. Some day maybe someone else will have the privilege of having a Pop like you; and then, maybe they will make just the right card. Until then, all we can say is that we thank God for you.

Happy Birthday, Pop! From those who love you."

TO THINK AND PRAY ABOUT: God knows we love our families, but do we thank Him for them often enough? Do we express our love to them? *Lord, teach us not to expect too much of our children but rather to tell them of their special qualities. It is such a privilege—being a parent. We thank You now.*

"I have been driven many times to my knees by the overwhelming conviction that I had nowhere else to go. My own wisdom, and that all about me, seemed insufficient for the day."

Abraham Lincoln.

THE COUPLE was contemplating divorce. There was no villain—just a chain of circumstances in which one break led to another and another, and neither party seemed willing to make an effort to weld the links together.

We friends urged until we finally persuaded them to see their minister. We had such high hopes that the sessions would go well. Instead, each ended in a shouting match.

"We're getting nowhere—nowhere at all. I'm ready to call a halt," Sue told a group of us. "Come with me. Just once. You'll see!"

And we did see. Both Sue and Reggie sat stiffly in their chairs. Their faces were closed and it was easy to imagine that their hearts were, too. The minister began tactfully where the couple had left off at the preceding session. "Now, let's try just once more—"

"I don't want to try!"

"See! What did I tell you?"

And suddenly both were talking at once, their voices rising, their language abusive.

The minister stood up. "There really is nothing more I can do," he said quietly. "But before you go, I would like to have you quiet down. Just bow your heads and be still." They complied. "Lord, I commend this couple who once knew love to Your loving care. There is nothing more I can do. You must take over in their lives. Amen."

The couple stood. There were tears in Sue's eyes—probably the first she had shed. Reggie reached out awkwardly and put his arm around her. "Don't cry, honey—please. I—you—we, *we'll* work it out!"

"Thank You, Lord," said the minister softly.

TO THINK AND PRAY ABOUT: *Thank You, Lord, that we're sometimes driven to our knees—with nowhere else to go.*

The Borrowed Hand

WINTRY FEBRUARY is gone. The month, like its days, was short. Yet much can happen in twenty-nine days. I look back upon the month leaving its pain and remembering its beauty, for it held a touch of magic. Let's call it the magic of love—the emotion that brings wonder and delight from every situation. Love is that precious thing which gives wings to otherwise meaningless valentines; replaces sorrow with comfort; replaces fear with space; brings a hint of smile to come even when there remains a tear in the eye. February's cold weather allowed me to forget the gardening and catch up on my reading. Since it's the birthday month of two great Presidents, I read their biographies. I learned that the remains of the Washington family rest in the family vault at the foot of the vineyard of his beloved Mount Vernon—by his last will and testament. I had not known the Capitol Tomb was unoccupied when I visited it. I learned about Lincoln's Gettysburg prayer in the pre-dawn of the battle: "I told God that I had done all I could and that now the result was in His hands; and that if this country was to be saved, it was because He willed it. The burden fell off my shoulder, my intense anxiety was relieved, and in its place came a great truthfulness!" . . . And then came the loss of one of my dearest friends, a hurt too deep to talk about . . . .

TO THINK AND PRAY ABOUT:

I borrowed God's hand in my sorrow
and held it till tears went away;
I said, "I'll return it tomorrow;
Just let me hold on for today."
Somehow the time slipped thro' my fingers
(I feel that's the way He planned);
Feel of His Presence still lingers—
I can't let go of God's hand. J.M.B.

My March Prayer

TEACH ME TO *pray, Lord.* Sometimes I feel I really do not know how. Let me stop hesitating to confess. Help me humble myself to ask for help. And, Lord, let me not fall asleep when I am trying to thank You for the countless blessings of the day. I know You would have me watch and pray, that I enter not into temptation. Keep me ever watchful.

Teach me to pray, Lord. Reveal Yourself to me so that I can reveal You in everything I do and say and write. May it all reflect Your touch so that others can see "good works" and be blessed. Then bless all the secret little cogs and wheels that miraculously capture thoughts and translate them into print. Bless these hands, Lord; make them willing vehicles to carry out Your wishes. Bless my heart, Lord, and purify it as it pumps in silent rhythm to keep my body functioning, rushing vital blood to my fingertips. May my heart have no will of its own except that which is Yours. And, above all, bless my thoughts, Lord, as they shape themselves into words that others may hear or read. Take my thoughts from the dusty closet of my mind and air them often. Shake out the wrinkled phrases; replace the tarnished words with Your Words. Lead me to speak to others in simple, humble language that expresses Your profound truth. Let mine be words of hope.

Teach me to pray, Lord. I need to pray wherever I am, whatever I am doing. Let me greet each dawn ready to examine new ideas; explore them; then sort them out according to Your Will. Give me the strength to develop each idea into a blessing. Lord, I have faith in You; please give me faith in myself so that each effort in Your Name will be a message of love. You have put love in my heart—love in the hearts of us all—and You have given us the capacity to love You and love each other. Now, I would ask that You stay close beside me, guiding me when I lack the ability to express it. Then, "may the words in my mouth and the meditations in my heart be acceptable in Your sight . . . Oh, Lord, my Strength and my Redeemer."

God's In Command Of My Senses

OH, SIGHTS and sounds and smells of spring! Yes, it will be some three weeks before the sun crosses the plane of the earth's equator to officially make the announcement. But March brings a gentle awakening of nature that defies the calendar of the weather. The awakening is from within. Maybe we are "conditioned" to hear, see and smell creatively. I remember an inspired teacher who suggested that our hearts have ears! "The secret," she said, "is to listen *for* something, then *to* it." This morning I threw open the window and said, "Good morning, Spring!" and listened for a response. The gentle coo of a mourning dove and the wind-rumors spread by the swaying ferns brought season's greetings. Listening to the soft sounds of our hearts brings us to a place of comfort—away from the wails of a severe winter.

The same teacher taught that our hearts have eyes. "You can look *at* an object and never *see* it at all," she said. She encouraged us to look up for the puppet-show of the clouds and to climb low-hanging boughs and look down at earth's patterns below. "Is this the way we look to You, God?" Standing by the window this morning, looking at the street below, I whispered, "Let me be pleasing in Your sight, Dear Lord. I hope those living on the lower street will look up for something of God—and find it in me."

"Scents carry you on journeys," she said, so our hearts have noses, too! I remember so well the game we played, with our eyes closed identifying an apple, a violet or a sift of spice by its aroma. *Lord, we want to hear, see and smell your beauty from within and without.*

TO THINK AND PRAY ABOUT: Today's reading speaks of discerning with the senses. Pray that you may feel new glory in this spring's miracle. Share it with others!

In The Beginning Was The Word

IT WAS HARD sitting through Brother Brown's sermon that Sunday so long ago. We were going to have homemade ice cream after dinner! Daddy had borrowed a neighbor's hand-crank freezer and Mama and I had helped chip ice, measure rock salt and blend sugar, eggs and milk for the rare dessert. I hopped impatiently from one foot to the other as my father puzzled over the direction on top of the lid: "Stop turning handle when cream begins to freeze."

"Strange," he kept repeating as he turned, but obediently he stopped cranking when the wooden paddle became sluggish, telling him that the contents had thickened slightly. Quickly he drained the brine from the cedar bucket, covered it with a gunny sack and left it to complete its magic freezing.

After church services, I gulped my meal, saving space for the creamy vanilla goodness to come. Will there ever be another disappointment to match that day's? When Daddy opened the bucket there were a few crystals on the sides and the rest was lukewarm froth. Above my childish sobs, I heard my father re-read the directions—this time including the one little word which was hidden beneath the handle when he hurriedly read the first time: "*NEVER* stop turning . . ."

How important one word can be! Even a negative word—*no, not, never*—makes such a difference!

TO THINK AND PRAY ABOUT:

Words are the makers of music;
Words are the weavers of dreams—
Earth-things faintly remembered—
Divine in dimensions unseen.
Words can make wars or can win them,
Sway motion of wind, tree, or bird;
Words can beguile with their magic;
Please, God, let me guard every word.

A Dime's Worth Of Love

March 4
Matthew 10:7

TUESDAY I rode the city bus for the first time. California weather lets me walk generally, so I'd planned to walk to the clinic because George had the car. Of course, we didn't anticipate rain. What could have been an inconvenient bus ride turned out to be a blessing, however.

The bus was crowded (we're not conditioned to spring storms), and nerves were frayed—including the driver's. His frustration surfaced when a would-be rider did not have her fare ready. "See the sign?" he said irritably. I looked up to see an elderly lady with a ragged scarf knotted around her head standing uncertainly in the door. A draft of cold air came in; and in spite of myself I, too, felt a twinge of impatience.

"A dime, lady! I'm late already."

She's half drowned, I thought. *Or is it palsy—or fear?*

The pour soul made no effort to find a coin. As a matter of fact, I saw she had no purse—just an old plastic shopping bag filled with what appeared to be buttons, used hair curlers, safety pins and scraps.

"O.K., O.K.! Just step out!" I got a closer look at the creased face. she was older than I'd first thought—old enough to ride free, a courtesy of the city. Maybe she couldn't read the sign, maybe she was unable to understand English. Quickly, I ran up the aisle and dropped in a coin for her. The driver muttered, "Thanks," and I saw a look of understanding cross the faces of those around us. One man rose to offer her his seat. She shook her head and followed me. With a cold, wet hand, she placed a bar of partially used soap in my lap. Fighting tears, I smiled; and her answering smile took the rain out of my day. I was proud of the commuters, too. They waited until the proud lady, who had shown us she was no "beggar," was safely off the bus.

TO THINK AND PRAY ABOUT: The woman had given freely. Do you see a special kind of beauty in such a gift? Was it the object or self she shared?

Gold Lining

I watched the golden poppies spill
Like liquid gold across the hill
As petals wilted one by one
And faded with the summer sun.
The plants did not reseed themselves
To golden-glow the hillside shelves;
The rains that washed the mountain's face
Transplanted them some other place.
But when I walk their trail I find
My feet are light; my heart gold-lined—
Knowing, though they left no chart,
They gladden someone else's heart. J.M.B.
(From ALONG THE WAY, compiled by Monta
Henrichs Crane and Betty Wallace Scott)

THE CALIFORNIA POPPY has strange, elusive ways. Some years the "Golden State" is truly golden. Other years, when there is drought, not a single bright petal appears.

One year the poppies seemed determined to take over the fields. My husband's 35 mm camera captured the scene in color to bless us like Wordsworth's daffodils—in recollection only—for the poppies where long in returning. It was dry and we wondered if the state flower was extinct.

Then one March day, following a torrential rain, we saw them in the valley below—achingly beautiful. "But where were the seeds?" I asked George.

"Dormant—waiting. The rain made them germinate."

I like to think God looked after those flowers. He knew how long the seeds needed rest. He transplanted and resurrected the seeds when and where they were needed. I think kind deeds are like the poppies. They may lie sleeping, forgotten we think. But not so! They, like the flowers, eventually pop up to take a look at the sun and to bless the life of somebody somewhere—perhaps far away.

TO THINK AND PRAY ABOUT: "For lo, the winter is past . . . The flowers appear on the earth . . . ."

Half A Loaf

SATURDAY evening we were having dinner guests—two couples, close friends we scarcely call "company." The six of us take turns with our "food and fellowship" meetings; and, I guess, I'd have to confess that I concentrate more on the fellowship than the food. My husband refers to me as a "Mary" because I'd rather talk than eat. I was buzzing around like a computer concentrating on the wrong things, as usual. But as our guests' arrival drew closer, I realized that a bit of "Martha" would be necessary if anyone was to eat.

As I rolled the typewriter into the closet, I realized I'd been so busy I had forgotten to buy bread. No stores were open; and any minute Ann and Bob, Terry and Joe would ring the doorbell. Even close friends have a right to expect bread with a meal.

Quickly I dialed my emergency number. "Barbara," I said frantically. "Do you have a loaf of bread in your freezer? Friends are coming—"

"Coming up!" she answered. Five minutes later there she was with a bread basket heaped with oven-hot rolls!

"Fortunately I was baking," she said as she hurried back across the street.

It was such a pleasant evening. I felt a special glow from the loving-kindness of my friend. Barbara's yeast rolls were a conversation piece. "I can't take credit," I admitted. "My wonderful neighbor brought them." (I was embarrassed to tell the whole story!) But when we said our round-the-table prayer, I made special mention of her.

The next day I learned that Barbara and Jack, too, were entertaining! At the risk of running short, she had come to my rescue. The warmth of the previous night's glow doubled. It was a modern version of the loaves and the fishes.

TO THINK AND PRAY ABOUT: *Lord, remind me to share half a loaf in everything and let me do so with sincerity and truth. Make Your love my motivation.*

Obedience School

LAST NIGHT was "Bronchov," our boxer's first night in Obedience School. George and I took along the proper paraphernalia (we thought): the dog's record of required shots, our receipt for his tuition, and the required choke chain and leather leash. Nobody told us to ask our doctor for a prescription of tranquilizers (for us); a whip and a chair (for him); and a first-aid kit (for the other dogs)!

People who know about boxers will understand why both of us needed ice bags for our head after the evening. Just arriving and seeing twenty-five dogs of assorted sizes set him off. He began to pant uncontrollably; his tongue turned blue; and I am sure his body temperature shot to 108°. With a mighty bound he was in the middle of a circle of already frightened canines. The lady instructor maintained her cool and said soothingly: "He'll calm down." It didn't happen, of course.

"Now," she announced, "we will begin by speaking softly, 'Heel!' and moving forward." Bronchov, on command, turned around to make friends with Charlie, the dog behind him, and made the first round walking backwards.

"When I say 'Halt!' the instructor went on, 'all dog owners will count aloud 'one, two' and give the command, 'Sit'!" Wonderful! He obeyed, then leaned forward to nip the heels of the dainty white Spitz ahead of him.

I gave up my little silent prayer that our dog would conform and cease to be a distraction, an embarrassment and the clown of the group. I sent up a little prayer instead for my husband's survival.

Secretly I was seething. The dog's behavior was inexcusable. He is a highly intelligent creature, head and shoulders above some of the dull-witted creatures that were behaving like veterans. And, then, it occurred to me that my anger was directed toward some sort of image I wanted *our* dog to communicate. How could Bronchov know all these things? He would have no need of Obedience School if he knew . . . .

TO THINK AND PRAY ABOUT: *Dear God, have patience with me.*

Do I Bury My Talent?

"**I** HAVE NO talent." How often I hear the statement. How different the lives of performers would be if they had said it.

Tourists visiting Southern California comment on the marine climate, glossy-leafed orange trees that can't decide whether to bloom or fruit, so do both simultaneously, and avocado groves that hike up rocky hills and mysteriously flourish in the unlikely terrain.

We're often asked about the stars. And many times it's: "Which way to Lawrence Welk's?"

"I want to meet the *maestro* . . . Guy and Rolna . . . Tom . . ." Each has a favorite. One day a Michigan-licensed car pulled to the curb alongside my husband and me to ask for directions. "I just must meet Norma!" the lady said.

I was glad she told me, for Norma Zimmer was at the Village Mall that day autographing her book, NORMA. When later I saw the couple in the crowd surrounding the singing star, the woman came to me to say, "I've lost my courage."

"Read her book," I suggested, showing her my copy.

Norma's autobiography is clear and uncluttered. Was she always rich, successful, famous? No! She was poor and (in *her* mind) unattractive. Hers is no Cinderella story. No fairy godmother helped. It was God who performed her private miracle. He sent contacts into her life—among them "my wonderful boss," she says. Her life is a hymn of constant praise.

Oh, yes, the Michigan tourist purchased NORMA. "I'll share it with *everybody*," she said of the autographed copy. Norma Zimmer had talent before she met the persons who gave her an opportunity to share it. But don't we all? One needn't be an artist. There are other talents—like opening doors. Am I the "agent" who helps others as I ought? What greater talent is there?

TO THINK AND PRAY ABOUT: Do you bury your talent or double its measure?

The Wind-Song Of March

"**M**ARCH SINGS A wind-song of varied theme: the high soprano of approaching spring mingled with the bass echo of winter's threatened return. The elements hum with expectancy. The hawthorn buds in the hollow. Jonquils dance along the fence rows. Gardens wake up with the crocus-eyes of spring. Anemones, known as 'wind flowers' because of their mythological connection, lift their faces to the gentle breezes and raw winds—loving them equally."

Yesterday's beginning on "The Wind-Song of March" never was completed. Today I rose early to finish the article. As it happened, again I was interrupted. I'm ready to disconnect the phone and hang a "No Visiting" sign on my door. The calls came from members of my nominating committee hit by the flu bug; my neighbor lost a blind cat; my husband's shirt needed a button; and I forgot, then remembered, to thaw the roast. It's the little wordly things that wear us away . . . the candle dripped . . . somebody spilled sugar on the floor . . . one bad apple *did* spoil the box . . . was there ever a more disagreeable wind? The wind's shredding new leaves, tangling kites in the power lines, and blowing the neighbor's bills from their trash can into our front yard!

I turned to the sixth chapter of Matthew as I often do when I'm unable to cope with the day. I am less anxious when I read how God provides for the fowls of the air and clothes the lilies of the field. And it is a comfort to know where my treasures are! Life's little problems can bring the enemies of confusion and unrest to our minds, but God can chase them away just as He "maketh the storm a calm" (Psalm 107:29). I closed the Bible, said a prayer and completed my essay: "Suddenly the season sets itself on course. Winds come in sweet and pure—laden with bloom. March, like yesterday, is never perfect. But remember the lessons." The storm has passed.

TO THINK AND PRAY ABOUT: Do you feel God has power over an "emotional storm?" Pray that you may seek first His Kingdom; then seasons will right themselves.

The Total Picture

A LOT OF EXCITING printed pages help comprise my day as I review books for three publishing companies. There is no way for me to know how reading affects the lives of others; but I know what it does for me. If the over-used phrase "turned on" can be applied to my life in any one field, it would be in the area of reading. From reading I get the power I need to meet the demands placed upon my life: spiritual power, intellectual power, emotional power . . . I could go on and on.

Reading has helped me to see the entire picture: to realize the importance of the parts, but to bear in mind that the whole is more important than just the mere aggregate of the parts. How often we misjudge books just by picking them up and thumbing through, often quoting out of context. How often we misjudge people by a single act, on a certain day, under a given set of circumstances. The thought occurred to me as I was examining a new version of an old story, THE BLIND MEN AND THE ELEPHANT.

I guess everybody knows the story, but I had shelved it away until the box of bright, new books came in this morning's mail. In the fable three blind men felt of an elephant and wondered what the animal was like. The problem, of course, was that each felt of only one part. The elephant was like a tree trunk to one because he felt of the legs. It was like a big fan to the second man because he felt of the ear. No! It was like a rope, insisted the third, because he had felt of the elephant's tail. "This is what I do sometimes," I said aloud to myself, "I take little bits and pieces of people apart—and just never see the whole picture which is the sum of all these fragments."

TO THINK AND PRAY ABOUT: God and He alone knows the whole picture of me and each person that I meet. He knows the true character of our hearts—while I, like the proverbial blind men, summarize after knowing only a part.

What Love Can Do!

It comes when you're not looking—
An unexpected thing—
A something you've no name for
Which makes you want to sing.
One moment you feel wintry
And then you take a look
And suddenly a crocus
Leaps from a picture book.
A branch of pussy-willow
Will reach to touch your cheek . . .
A glimpse of cream-brown thrasher . . .
Your thoughts have reached their peak.
The season, like the catkins,
Is clinging to each bough;
You long to burst out singing—
And spring will show you how! J.M.B.

I RELISH THOUGHTS of love! I think it's rather great that my marriage has weathered many winters and renewed itself each spring . . . .

Love, like springtime, comes without a word and bursts into sudden song—that leads straight to the altar. And then, like the other beautiful things of spring, it just grows and grows and grows. Sadness fades like winter and the heart says, "Thank You, Lord, I'm not alone anymore." Does there really exist a "happily forever after?" Yes, for those who believe in spring.

The Bible is a love-packed book! Those who read it in search of love need never be lonely again. God is listening with concern to every thought brought to Him. He is the Master Teacher who loves His learners too much to let them fail! Then, when we have accepted His offering, He commands us to share its joy. Love demands that I listen to every person, caring enough to help. Love is God's way of binding us all together.

TO THINK AND PRAY ABOUT: Lord, bless us with selfless affection—unending! Let us lead others to Your altar.

The Path Of Least Resistance

March 12
I Peter 5:8-11

A FRIEND OF mine, a born skeptic, has this philosophy: "We, all of us, follow the path of least resistance." Her own life is her prime example. On some days she ignores the saucy words of her children because "showdowns" give her a headache, and she agrees to absolutely everything her husband suggests rather than risk an argument. Now, on other days, one crooked step from an offspring earns him a swat on his posterior (especially if her mother-in-law, the disciplinarian, is visiting). Or her once-catered-to husband may receive the silent treatment for two weeks for being too noisy when Mother (the unquestionable matriarch) is trying to rest. It's questionable if her philosophy is working: her family is as scattered as the Tribe of Israel.

Other areas in my friend's life are equally as unpredictable. She has been forced to cook over a campfire because she neglected to pay the utility bill and the service was discontinued. And because she feels it too time-consuming to balance her bankbook before making out another check, she's become a champion check-bouncer!

There are other brands of philosophy that I prefer. The path of least resistance is too negative—or do I tread the same trail and just call it by another name? If not, why haven't I challenged my friend when she says, we *all* look for the easy way out? Yesterday she shed a light for me on "resistance." There are things we should resist: wrong doctrine, the devil (and he will flee), or temptation (and it will not overtake us). But there are things we should not resist: an opportunity to repent, a chance to give up "my" rights in order to do God's will, or the experience of bathing in Jesus' love. Following the path of least resistance can work if properly applied.

TO THINK AND PRAY ABOUT: Check your standing; ask God to help you resist in the right places.

My Head Aches, Lord

March 13
Psalm 27:14
Psalm 55:22

MY HEAD ACHES, Lord. *My temples throb with pain—pain so deep I hear it pounding in my ears, echoing in my forehead, blurring my vision. My nerves are tied in knots; my temper is short; and I feel like lashing out at those I love. My family tries to soothe me with loving words; they tiptoe in respect for my throbbing head; but they do not understand my need to be alone. They feel rejected, Lord and I feel guilty. We all feel we have failed—because of my headache, Lord.*

Do you have such days and find yourself feeling ashamed? It was Thoreau who said he was going to the woods to live in quietude and solitude, so that he could find *why* he lived. It must be a dreadful thing to live all of one's life and never really know why one lives. I am unable to tolerate it for one day. We know God has a purpose for us, and usually we are able to bring meaning into our lives and the lives of those around us. But sometimes we have a need to get away, meditate and look for answers to what we are unable to understand. We need to walk with God; to reconstruct our day; replenish our lives with beauty, love and comfort—paving the way for a better tomorrow. We need to rest our tired minds and rid ourselves of the pressures that brought so much pain.

TO THINK AND PRAY ABOUT: Look up wherever you are. Look into God's Infinite blue. *Thank You, Lord for your sky houses us all together. How immense it is; how small our problems. I close my eyes and walk the blue skyway, the universal symbol of freedom. I have been a prisoner, Lord, but I have found comfort in my simulated walk.* God clears our pain when we look to Him. His Word often says, "It came to pass . . . " but not once, "It came to stay." Thank You, Lord.

A Letter To My Husband

DEAR GEORGE: Thank you for keeping a little corner in your heart that is mine—all mine.

Thank you for the home we planned together, for letting me fill it with furniture you could have complained about: the too-straight chairs, the curved sectional davenport which forced you to curl up when you needed to stretch out and the frilly curtains. Thank you for what you contributed: fresh coats of paint, freshly-waxed floors—and oodles of security, warmth and love.

Thank you for balancing my bankbook, reading complicated directions on household appliances, and figuring out the differences in price vs. weight of grocery items on my list. Thank you for doing the family shopping when I am too busy (which is most of the time) and saying, "No problem. I enjoy it, really."

Thank you for giving me a generous slice of your time every day—shutting the whole world out as if we were Adam and Eve. You give me your undivided attention as if I were the most beautiful woman in the world—and the most desirable. You listen to my account of the little events of my day as if they color world history.

Thank you for sharing your day with me—as if I understand it all—and for being cautious in burdening me with your insecurities and fears.

Thank you for helping me raise our son and for giving him unconditional love, for teaching him gently about the world, and for training him in the way that he should go.

Thank you for being you.

TO THINK AND PRAY ABOUT: Write your husband, your children or your parents to thank them. Ask God to increase familial love all over the world.

Mid-March Doldrums

March 15
II Peter 1:7-8

HERE THEY COME—those mid-March doldrums. It's that time of year when spring makes several false starts, then a "norther" blows in, catching peach trees at a popcorn stage, so the chances of a good fruit crop lessen. Lima beans refuse to sprout and our deacons refuse to buy another cord of firewood, so we all complain of cold feet at prayer meeting. Then March brings a burst of unscheduled heat and we fan ourselves and say there has never been such a fickle spring. There hasn't been, of course—since last spring.

Here I am, suffering from the March malady. My grandmother would have given me a dose of sulphur or suspended a bag of asafetida around my neck like a necklace.

This is a good opportunity to ask myself: "Am I a part of the season's problems, or—like my maternal grandmother—am I a part of the solution?"

My grandmother never went out and purchased a new hat to combat the blahs. Money didn't grow on sassafras bushes; and, besides, she preferred a sunbonnet. But, oh yes, she had a cure. "Let's do something impulsive!" she used to say. "Let's go for a tramp in the woods in search of the March Hare; we can be the Mad Hatters." We'd make leaf hats, which in my mind were things of splendor.

When we'd come home we'd do an impulsive deed for a neighbor. Today, I looked back and tried to recall some of the things we did—because they're exactly what I plan to do! 1) Write a letter when it's not your turn! 2) Call somebody you haven't heard from in years; 3) Make a batch of cookies and take them to a shut-in; and 4) Go out and look for a stranger to smile at! None of these things cost a cent; but how long has it been since I did them! So here goes. Will I feel silly smiling at a stranger? If so, that means I need practice. It may open a door to friendship, adventure and joy to another. It will re-open one for me.

TO THINK AND PRAY ABOUT: Who says we have to play by rules of convention?

Outreach

THE CARD CAME yesterday. The givers could have had no way of knowing its timeliness. A wreath of orchid and cream pansies surrounds a purple-backed Bible, centered with a golden cross. The message says, "A subscription to GUIDEPOSTS is coming to you with Easter Greetings." There is no signature, but the typed "Congregational Care and Outreach Committees" at the bottom tells it all—they *care* enough to *reach out*. That must be the greatest reason in the world!

Even the design of the card signifies thoughtfulness. Did the artist know that the flowers, too, say "We care?" *Pansy* comes from a French noun, *pensee*, meaning "thought." How nice to be a part of a body whose members care enough to reach out and say so. The committee, like the symbol of the flower, is well-chosen. I shall write a letter today.

Those on the Congregational Care and Outreach Committee deserve to know how I value this subscription at this particular time. As I work with words which I hope will be applicable to the daily lives of GUIDEPOSTS readers, those "quiet people" gently place a tool in my hands. I feel an inner glow; for, unaware, they have become a part of the service I am undertaking. I find myself thinking: "This is as it should be. Each of us is a part of God's family."

What a beautiful Easter Greeting—offered freely, asking nothing in return.

> The world seems every Easter
> Somehow to start anew;
> I wish its shine might linger
> To bless us all year through. J.M.B.

TO THINK AND PRAY ABOUT: Is it easier for you to do little unexpected things for others when you know the joy of receiving back from them? Examine the meaning of the "perfect gift" in today's Scripture and apply it to your life. Thank God for earthly givers—their outreach and their care.

An Old Irish Prayer

March 17
I Corinthians 2:9

S T. PATRICK is probably about as elusive as a leprechaun. "A patron saint of Ireland" is a scanty account of so mighty a man as my maternal grandmother would have had me believe—and believe it I did! She attributed more wit and wisdom to the saintly man than any one person is entitled to. He drove the snakes out of the Emerald Isle, for one thing. Snakes and I were never on friendly terms, so I used to beg her to share his method with me. There was magic in every Irish potato, with which she credited St. Patrick. She knew all the old Irish songs and legends and folk dances—the kinds of things children thrive on.

Now, my grandmother knew and she saw to it that I knew we were playing games with our imaginations. She called it "vision," and quoting her worn-out Bible said over and over, "Without vision the people perish." I think back on her quotations now and realize that without the vision she left me some meanings would be less clear. She used to read the Psalms of David, "The heavens shall declare the glory of God," and the picture I conjured in my mind was far more glorious than any commentaries I have heard on the passage. When her youngest son (my age) and I had a spat, she always reminded us that "If two make peace with each other in this one house, they shall say to the mountain: 'Be moved,' and it shall be moved." Peace and its power became so real to the two of us that we wished we lived among the hills instead of the flat farmlands. We *believed*.

That belief stuck with us as a philosophy when we entered the field of education. "Vision is discipline," she told us. "Never let people use your wings. Give them vision to grow a pair for themselves!" Could any teacher do more than that?

TO THINK AND PRAY ABOUT: "May the road rise up to meet you. May the wind be always at your back. May the sun shine warm upon your face, the rain fall short upon your fields, and until we meet again may God keep you in the palm of His hand."

Too Old To Grow? Humbug!

March 18
Romans 8:18

"**I**'M TOO OLD to learn," said the self-imposed "little old lady" as she leaned back wearily and rocked away in a manner that made me motion-sick. The comment was a response to my suggestion that she enroll in a provocative course our church was offering, "How to Be Better Than I Am." My suggestion was a response to the lady's call saying that she was lonely and that there was nothing left in life.

I studied the childless widow from where I was sitting in her tidy livingroom. She needed to shed twenty pounds, but I love life too much to have dared suggesting that she consider one of the several physical fitness programs at the Y. Her pink cheeks had no wrinkles—not even a laugh-line, which was no wonder. It occurred to me that a lot of women spend a fortune with plastic surgeons to look like that. She had held a teaching credential at one time. What a brilliant thought!

"Say!" I said with all the brightness I could muster. "Adult Ed needs a group leader for a home-care beauty course. With a complexion like yours—"

She was incensed. "I couldn't get the job and I couldn't handle it. Nobody likes me!" I was beginning to see why . . . .

I had accomplished nothing. Unknowningly, I am sure, the prematurely "old" lady had reached a stage of apathy brought about by her own indifference. Had zest for life ceased when she lost her husband? Did she feel unfulfilled because there had been no children? Or, perish the thought, had she never known that our Creator placed within us a remarkable phenomenon for growth? Age is no factor. Oh, she wasn't going to grow any taller physically; but, spiritually, the sky was the limit. She could grow some intellectual stems by taking the course at church; she could "grow" smaller by taking the course at the Y; she could grow spiritually—right up to where God is—by taking on some volunteer work. She must choose.

TO THINK AND PRAY ABOUT: Do you see people around you who have given up? Think of ways to help them move beyond the "easy armchair." God may work with them after you and I have left them in their solitude.

Faithful Flight

March 19
Isaiah 25:4

THE SWALLOWS came back to Capistrano today. The legend of their faithful return to the California mission is well-known; and there is a song about the small, long-winged passerine birds. Swallows are noted for their swift, graceful flight and for the extent and regularity of their migrations, but their selection of the mission for a homesite goes unexplained. Some call it instinct; others call it faith.

It is no legend that Father Junipero Serra dedicated the mission in 1776 and named it for the Crusader, St. John of Capistrano. Shaped like a giant cross of 180 x 90 feet, the church was one of the highest triumphs of mission architecture, with seven domes and a tall campanario visible for ten miles. Beautiful though it was, the mission delighted the eye for only six years before an earthquake wrecked the roof, cloisters, nave, five domes and campanario—killing twenty-nine persons. Heavy rains thwarted early attempts to rebuild. There was fear among the Indians, mingled with strange superstitions that the mission would never be restored. But the little swallows never gave up hope. Year after year they returned to the ruins, a tradition dating back to Spanish colonial times. The faithful little creatures returned every St. Joseph's Day, nesting in the eaves to raise their new families, then left each St. John's Day, October 23. They were late only once, delayed four hours by a storm at sea. Against impossible odds, the battered and weary birds came.

Maybe seeing the courage of the swallows gave the people faith to begin rebuilding in 1865. Undoubtedly there were numerous doubting Thomases in the parish—those who needed the "sign" the birds provided. But the swallows asked no questions. We need ask for no signs. Faith brings the miracle.

TO THINK AND PRAY ABOUT: Ask God to help you build unquestioning faith. Pray for its miracle to take place in your life—and expect an answer!

Come To Our Wedding, Lord

March 20
Jeremiah 33:11

"To love someone is to be the only one
to see a miracle invisible to others."
Francois Mauriac

LOVE IS NOT BLIND; it sees, but overlooks, accepts—and goes on with the business of living with stars in its eyes. Perhaps that is a miracle, after all.

Looking back on my wedding I think it *was* a miracle—my whirlwind courtship and marriage. George and I saw a miracle our families failed to see. Maybe my parents weren't quite ready to hand over their only daughter to someone else; and maybe most daughters are not as determined (or fortunate) as I. Are marriages made in heaven? I don't know about that either. I only knew that's where I took my prayers.

I wish I had known "Prayer On Our Wedding Day" on that day so long ago; but I'm thankful my thoughtful friend, John Leykom, sent it to me recently.

My loving Lord, the day for which we have planned and dreamed is finally here—our wedding day. Lord, the excitement of it all makes us feel as if we were walking on clouds. It is almost too good to be true. We are so thankful that You have brought us together and that today we are to be joined as husband and wife. We are so thankful that we can ask Your blessings on our marriage and to know that what we are doing is according to Your will. Therefore we pray, Lord, that You will be a part of our family. As you were invited to come to the wedding in Cana of Galilee, so we pray that You would also come to our wedding and come to live with us in our home. We need You, Lord, because we know together with the happiness of the future there will also be days of trial and stress. Help us to be forgiving toward each other so that we may also pray for Your divine forgiveness . . . .

TO THINK AND PRAY ABOUT: Our Lord will always help as He did at the wedding at Cana.

Tidings Of Spring

March 21
John 12:24

The sunshine brought good tidings today
As it rushed through meadows and trees;
It whispered first to the catkins
And I think that they told the bees.
Into my yard the gold message came
To ruffle a young daffodil:
"Don your best bonnet," sunbeams all sang,
"For spring is just over the hill!" J.M.B.

THE VERNAL equinox has come—that period in the cycle of the seasons in which days and nights are equal in length. Children, who would pipe with Pan in the spirit of eternal spring, will argue that the nights are longer (but winter-weary parents have rebuttal for that!). Surely everybody throughout the world must love the season when, as Browning put it, "God's in His heaven—all's right with the world."

Rusty pine needles are dropping and the trees thrust up new green sprays to cover the few that refused to leave the parent tree. I notice there are fat, pink buds on the Thundercloud plum—a sight that never fails to bring a sad-sweet ache of memory. I always loved hearing my father sing the old hymn, "The Uncloudy Day." It is one of those deceptively warm days today, without a cloud to mar the blue; and it takes little imagination to see the flowering plum as "the Tree of Life in Eternal Bloom," shedding its fragrance over a land where life has begun anew. Even the vulture, which wheeled over the scene looking for signs of death, has given up and sailed away.

And yet, paradoxically, it was death which brought about this unbelievably brilliant beauty. Each tender shoot of grass beneath my feet sprang from last year's seed. Each daffodil was a dull, brown bulb giving no hint of the ruffled trumpet inside. Now each bloom looks as if it carries the image of the sun itself, caught and cupped in the shining throat. Memory allows me to hear my father's voice a little louder: "Oh, they tell me of a land where no storm clouds rise."

TO THINK AND PRAY ABOUT: There is such a place; there will be such a day. And we, in His image, shall rise up to meet Him—much as the daffodils pattern the sun. Spring is a life-giving time . . . .

God's Word

March 22
Mark 10:27
Luke 17:11-19

God bless them every one, we pray;
and let them know we care—
Please make our every little verse a Universal Prayer.

"WHERE DO THE ideas of poetry come from?" people ask. We all learn from each other. Doesn't it follow we should thank each other—and praise God?

My first poem appeared in a little pulp magazine when I was very young. For it I received seventy-five cents—in stamps! But I was a "published" writer, so there was no stopping my pen. I wish I had written the editor to let her know how the small triumph changed my life. I owe so much to her. Most of us do wait too long to say, "Thank you."

But, then, we all owe so much to so many, don't we? My own daily miracle is that of words—those God hands to me to write down. He hands down something for each of us. He knows what we are to do even when we do not, but we find the outlets with God's help for our talents. In my case, I depend upon God to help me find the editor who recognizes Him as "author" and me as "ghost writer."

Just as other people bring joy into our lives, we can send joy back into theirs—in some way. It works! How do I know? Each day my mailbox bulges with blessings, appreciative letters from people in hospitals, mental institutions, convalescent homes and prisons. "Do you answer these?" my postman marvels. Yes. God is using me and with Him all things are possible.

All around us hearts cry out in loneliness. God opens a service door—a way for us to enrich their lives. And it is such a beautifully reciprocal process. As we enrich their lives, they enrich ours—pushing us on to greater heights. If we use the needs of others as our inspiration, God will direct if and when we are to "specialize." If our goal is a "book," let us take it page by page first. Too much? Try it line by line—even word by word. The world is in need of the many "small deeds" that go to make "great people."

TO THINK AND PRAY ABOUT: Wouldn't it be nice if we set aside a day for writing to say, "Thank you for encouraging me?" Christ healed ten lepers but only one thanked Him.

Moods . . .

There's a harsh and brassy wind
Playing in the timber,
Bending willows to the ground
As though their legs were limber.
There's a worn and ragged wind—
Its notes reduced to sighing—
For it has seen too much of life
and holds its breath, near dying.
But wind is noted for its change,
And, rested now, leaps sprightly
Back to where the willows lie;
"Get up!" it tells them lightly. J.M.B.

"**B**AD NEWS can be therapeutic," I read in the newspaper today. That's what it said; I read it twice to be sure, and with each reading the taco I had for lunch became a little heavier. I remembered a sociologist in college whose philosophy was as hard to digest as the taco. "Now, life is nothing but problems. The only way to be successful is to enjoy them!" I made it through his course without mastering the art. Then I read a much-admired religious writer's suggestion: "Pray for adversity." Is the newspaper article implying something similar?   I laid the paper aside, then picked it up again. "Now, it doesn't make sense to slash your wrists, beat a spouse, or take an overdose of sleeping pills because somebody burned a building you never saw—" I relaxed. True! "Or, for that matter: vomit, develop a high pulse rate or suffer heartburn." I tensed up again. The article was hitting close to home. "The first step in curing evil is to perceive it. One cannot have a tranquil soul without a degree of tough-mindedness . . . Get your alarm threshold up high enough so that it takes a real wave to go over it. Sagacious people don't lose their ability to listen to the quiet. . . ." Now that's something to think about.

TO THINK AND PRAY ABOUT: There is a quiet that can come when we stand in the midst of a storm. Pray for God to give you resiliency and added strength.

Lord, Send Me A North Wind!

March 24
Proverbs 25:23
Matthew 21:22

THIS IS THE kind of day when children "reap the wild wind." My mother does not take such delight in the "devil winds." She remembers a different time and a different place, when the wind blew in illness and fear. "Lord, send me a north wind," she prayed. The fresh north wind would drive away the east wind which was sucking the breath from my father, her youngest brother (six) and me (the same age). We were abed with pneumonia. There were no miracle drugs in those days and pneumonia was all too often fatal. All rural telephone lines had snapped from the force of the driving wind. Few people would have ventured into the contaminated house, even had they known, for the illness was considered contagious then. And the same harsh wind that threatened to bring death to our home had taken the lives of too many already.

My mother was out of touch with the world. But she was in touch with God. "I can't come down with this, Lord. Send the north wind!" "The crisis will come for each of them tonight," the doctor told my mother "I'll stay; you pray!"

All night the two of them heated bricks, wrapped them in newspaper and placed them around our chill-racked bodies when we had "sinking spells," and they laid cold compresses to our burning foreheads when we went into soaking sweats. They ran from one bed to the other forcing medicine down our choking throats, then held our heads as one by one we vomited it up. I drifted in and out of consciousness long enough to feel a heavy weight on my chest and a cool hand caressing my cheek . . . and suddenly I was wide awake. The "weight" was a hot water bottle, which I grabbed and hurled through the window. Immediately the room was filled with the soothing breeze which promised *Life*. I saw the others awake, heard the gentle patter of rain and said belligerently, "I'm hungry." My mother burst into grateful tears. "Hallelujah!"

TO THINK AND PRAY ABOUT: Keep in touch with God! The course of winds will change.

Petunia's Prayers

WE FOUND HER in the flower bed. It was an early spring morning and the blanket of gray fog almost obscured the wee, fog-gray kitten. With little eyes unopened yet, she arched her fluffy back and tried to bluff us with a hiss. Then and there Bryce (who was nine) and I knew she was special. George sounded more convincing. "We are not keeping this cat!" he announced, gingerly taking her from the budding petunias. The hissing stopped; she tried a little note that caught in her throat; and George knew she was special, too. It was my son who christened her "Petunia;" it was his father who took over feeding her with a medicine dropper; and it was the three of us who were recipients of the same amount of love we gave our kitty—for twenty-one years.

One of the special things about "Petunia" was her gift of speech. Now, all cats can "Meow," but it takes a gifted animal to *talk*. There was never a question as to what this very special cat wanted. She let out a yowl like a roving Tom if we accidentally shut her in a closet. She called coaxingly at the door when she wanted to come inside and let out a distress signal when she wanted to go out. She flirted openly in talky-tones that said, "I'll love you forever if you'll warm my milk." She sang us to sleep with contented lullabies and she woke us each day with a three-syllable greeting that sounded exactly like "Good morning!" But the real genius surfaced when we took the kitty with us on summer vacations—as we did even the last year of her life. "Petunia" sensed when it was getting too warm in the car and asked for the air conditioner in a tone which differed from any other request. Turn it on and she stretched out happily; off, and she complained bitterly.

It was George who said recently, "Petunia had everything life had to offer because she asked, then thanked me. Her voice was like a prayer."

TO THINK AND PRAY ABOUT: There's a lesson to be learned about asking, then thanking. There's power in prayer!

Music Is So Many Things

MARCH 26, 1827, Beethoven died. The ordinary man catches cold and takes a day's sick leave. But geniuses seem to be different. At least one of them composed some of the world's greatest music while suffering from chronic stomach trouble and headaches, liver disorders and nausea—not to mention deafness. The man, of course, was Ludwig van Beethoven. To mark the 142nd anniversary of his death, MEDICAL NEWS published a new study in 1969 concerning the afflictions of the immortal composer. Dr. W. Schweisheimer wrote the medical history. The writer did a skillful job disproving one of the seamy legends concerning Beethoven—the whispered rumor of his being a victim of a social disease.

According to Dr. Schweisheimer, the cause of Beethoven's tragic deafness was a disease of the inner ear known at that time as "neuritis acoustica," probably resulting from an earlier attack of typhoid fever. After that, illness followed illness—and all the while he was giving the world some of its most glorious and enduring music. It was Browning who said, "There is no truer truth obtainable by man than comes of music." And the miracle of it all was that God gave the deaf composer the gift of feeling—feeling that came from a music-filled heart and transferred through sensitive fingers to delight the ears and the hearts of generations to come with music he would never hear. What more selfless gift could there be than the universal language his music gave the world? I hope Beethoven hears applause in heaven . . . .

How much this world needs music; and music is so many things. Some compose soul-stirring numbers for symphony orchestras; play an instrument! But all can enjoy the great works of others; hear music in the winds; imagine the language of birdsong—and share with others a particular brand of "music appreciation." Come to think of it, God has gifted us with the ability to hear music in laughter . . . let's not be deaf to these blessings.

TO THINK AND PRAY ABOUT: Praise God that you can hum if you don't know the words!

I'll Be A Sunbeam For Him

BACK IN MY preschool days I belonged to the Sunbeam Band. Our responsibility was to spread sunshine, the well-meaning adult leader told us. I wasn't exactly sure how I was to go about the job. I put in my apprenticeship outshouting my five-year-old peers, "A sunbeam, a sunbeam; Jesus wants me for a sunbeam. A sunbeam, a sunbeam; I'll be a sunbeam for Him!" I look back on the Sunday afternoon calls our little band made on older members of the church who were unable to attend the morning services. I rather imagine we spread more sunshine than our little untrained minds knew. I remember entering dark rooms inhabited by cold countenances that sent chills down my spine. Eyes seemed to pierce right through me, so I made a joyful noise with more volume than tone quality—to hide my fear. How relieved I was when smiles creased those faces. My knees stopped shaking and the rooms were no longer dark; countenances no longer cold. That, I supposed, was spreading sunshine. Today I suppose the same!

I wonder if we realize how much our personalities reach out to brighten or darken the day for those we meet? This world depends upon the sun for its warmth; but I think human hearts depend upon each other.

When my husband, my mother and I visited the old home of Abraham Lincoln in Springfield, Illinois, I remembered a story I had heard about a little girl who saw a light burning in one of the windows. I looked for that light; and yes, it was still there—the one which caused the small daughter of a tourist to comment, "The President left his light on when he left, Mommie." How right she was, for it is true that Mr. Lincoln left a light in the window of every American heart. That's his sunbeam.

Our world needs light; and Jesus still needs me for a sunbeam. I can smile and share—and sing loudly. "I'll be a sunbeam for Him!"

TO THINK AND PRAY ABOUT: Sunny deeds can be unrehearsed, ordinary little everyday things. Every sympathetic hand, understanding smile, or kind word spreads a glow.

A Touch Of Love

"THERE IS SOMETHING in our society that discourages touching. Even the friendly handshake is rare. 'Sensitivity Courses' are no substitute. You can't legislate, motivate or imitate warmth. If it's real, the recipient knows." Our minister set me thinking about "Pal," the most dull-witted pet we ever owned. He was afraid of doorbells and cats but made friends with strangers and led them straight to our watermelon patch! Some watchdog.

Still, I learned a valuable lesson from him. He was a firm believer in "the laying on of hands." Never have I seen another dog so loving, eager to please and ready to seek forgiveness. A harsh word sent "Pal" creeping and crawling for a reward, the touch of a hand. Only then was his heart healed.

It was the very next day that I read that a Korean man had collapsed in a local market and, unable to communicate, died for lack of medical attention. His widow was left without family, friends or knowledge of our ways.

Our son's wife is Korean and has given our family insight into the stoicism and the loneliness of Oriental grief. "We must go to her," I told my husband. He checked the paper for the address.

What could we say? Nothing. She understood no English. What could we do? "Pal" knew!

We located the house and saw the slight figure kneeling before a lighted candle. With hands clasped and eyes closed, she was rocking back and forth in her sorrow. When the elderly lady answered our knock, I simply reached out and she walked into the circle of my arms. George took over making the necessary arrangements and helping her find a temporary job—weeding a neighbor's yard. Yesterday we saw her again. "Friend!" she cried happily. Healing has begun.

TO THINK AND PRAY ABOUT: Can you think of times when loving hands helped you through a crisis? Pray that God will lead you in helping to heal others daily.

Resurrection In A Terrarium

WE WERE GOING on a picnic, the four of us. As I bulged the lunch boxes with chicken, stuffed eggs and chocolate cake, George loaded his camera. Bryce and his wife, Sun, who are usually so eager to help, were giggling over in a corner of the livingroom. Obviously, some sort of conspiracy was in progress. Curiosity grew when Bryce called, "Mother, put in a lot of extra plastic bags!" Why? "And a big box!" Sun called next. *Why?* When Bryce went looking for a shovel and Sun asked for a clipboard and pencil, I had to inquire. The answer Sun gave was, "It's a surprise!"

Up in the hill country we all went our separate ways until lunch time. Bryce and Sun took their equipment with them and when they returned to join us, George observed mildly that he should have brought the trailer. The box was half-filled with peaty soil and clumps of green-velvet moss. It was planted like a garden with plastic bags—each housing a dainty fern, a purple thistle or a twig I didn't recognize; but Sun explained it was similar to a twig in her Korean homeland. The clipboard was filled with rough sketches of the cliffs and hillsides from where they came. I gave up. The labels were in Korean writing!

I forgot the incident until Good Friday. They had planned it as an Easter surprise, but the surprise just couldn't wait. There on our dining table stood the most beautiful terrarium I have ever seen! "We went to the mountain and the mountain came home with us," Sun said, employing her usual figurative language. In a three-feet-tall bulk mayonnaise jar she had duplicated the charm of our outing. In this beautiful setting were Easter figurines. Truly, it was a surprise; a bit of God . . . His beautiful world . . . and resurrection of a lovely day. Like God's resurrection, costing no gold, it was *priceless!*

TO THINK AND PRAY ABOUT: Consider giving small things. Ponder God's gift, His Son, bringing to us Eternal Life. Love is the key.

End-Of-The-Month Pressures

March 30
Jeremiah 17:9-10

THE MAILBOX was stuffed this morning. I should have taken the wheelbarrow down to bring in the load; but, then, I would have had to push it back up the inclined driveway—doubling the load. I had to go back for a paper sack to hold it all. As I made a second return trip to the house, my arms aching with the load, I thought of the ancient fable of one man's journey of life. He took with him something with which to meet every emergency. He explained: a mousetrap lest there be mice at the place of his lodging; a fly swatter lest there be flies; an axe lest trees block his path; a beehive lest he encounter a swarm of such insects; and a goose-down pillow lest his be straw. Now, added together, the "necessities" added up to a load beneath which he crumpled. The sad thing about the poor man's demise was that all his implements were for preventions!

Now, in a sense, pressure intensifies strength. George is always talking about the good water pressure we have which makes irrigation of our avocado grove so effective. He also saves all the grass clippings and fallen leaves and tamps them down in the compost heap. He revitalizes the soil with the peaty accumulation of the vegetation. Maybe if I had pushed the wheelbarrow back with this load of mail I would have strengthened a muscle or so. More likely, I'd have gone limber-legged, put the wheelbarrow in reverse and made tomorrow's headlines: "Local Lady Runs Over Self with Wheelbarrow." Pressures can make or break us.

Take this mail I am sorting. Often I have yielded to pressure to give to this and that: guilt-provoked. Were my contributions really inspired by love and concern? Were they to help the widow and the orphan? If so, I am growing according to God's plan. *What am I preventing?*

TO THINK AND PRAY ABOUT: As you make your April budget, lay aside a bit above tithes and offerings to send anonymously. Then think of contributions of the self: visit the sick, give a neighbor of your time, say, "I love you."

End Of An Age

LAMB-TONGUES, those tiny flowers so shy they grow in hidden places, in only a few states, have bloomed briefly and slunk away. The golden-haired dandelions have faded into weedy stalks with deeply toothed leaves. Did you grow up with lamb-tongues and dandelions—one so fragile, the other so hardy? The gentle lamb-tongues blossoms are pilgrims of spring. No matter how disagreeable the weather, one would bundle up and tramp into the hills looking for the never-failing signal that spring is just around the corner. But dandelions are considered pests. Adults know, but children do not. Children see the potential of dandelions: their fluffy heads of silver made to blow off as a wish is made.

Remember the childhood game? If all the fluffs took to the air when you set them sailing with one puff, your wish would come true. If one stuck, forget it. There was a scramble for the easy marks; and most of us were mighty puffers.

I personally was a little sad to learn that some weeds are enemies. When I learned that all our domestic plants are "tamed weeds," I applied it to the Scripture in Isaiah. Some day the animals would make friends as the plants had done. Maybe people would, too. Then there would be no more strife. It is comforting to know that the day will come, and spring seems just the right time for such a conviction.

Turning the calendar towards April I recalled the adage about March: "In like a lion, out like a lamb." I am unable to remember whether March roared in or entered meekly. It is more comforting to think of the two lying down together in peace.

TO THINK AND PRAY ABOUT: Isaiah was speaking of the restoration of Israel. Try relating the analogy to peace today, then Eternal Peace. Pray for both.

Prayer For The Face Of April

Show me your face in April, Lord,
In flowers, trees, and grass;
Whisper words for winds to sing
So I can know You pass.
Lord, take my heart where lilies are
That bloom on Easter Day;
Redeem my soul and make it gleam—
As pure—as white—as they. J.M.B.

DEAR LORD, I turn my calendar today, sensing new life in every limb of the trees that embroider Your footstool. The air is filled with songbirds, and my heart is filled with the joy of their songs. You have arranged each leaf and each feather in accordance with Your will. And You have created me, Your daughter, in Your image. I can accomplish nothing without Your vision. Come closer, Lord, I pray, so I may see Your face and rise to new heights.

Give me an April face, Lord—one that shines with the story of eternal Easter. Let me color other's lives like the first clump of flowers in spring. Let me have a smile wreathing into friendly laughter, such as one hears when the wind plays in the trees. Let me reach upward toward Your Son; let me reach outward toward others; let me be glad to be growing like the grasses and giving as You gave. Call out to me, Lord. Speak to me. Make me hear! Command the bulb of cold indifference within me to rise and shine like the lilies that symbolize Your resurrection; for others need a light to find the paths of righteousness and enter the garden of forgiveness.

Lord, I need to see Your face. Reveal Yourself beyond my fondest hope or sweetest dream. Renew my life each day, Lord. Fill my heart with faith and more faith, joy and more joy, love and more love. Then I will wear an April face, one that looks for and finds the best in others because You have found the best in me.

A Happiness Test

For lovely light You send my way:
The moon by night, the sun by day,
  Thank You, Lord.
For friendships near or very far
And memories where dear friends are,
  Thank You, Lord.
For every flower, every word,
Your matchless love, unfailing word,
  Thank you, Lord.
For surrounding me with care
And listening to this grateful prayer,
  Thank You, Lord; I thank You. J.M.B.

ARE YOU *happy—truly happy?* Just ponder the thought.
The "pursuit of happiness" has gone beyond a *right*. It has become a national pastime. Is happiness a *thing?* Things fade—youth, health and success. Things become empty in time. Is happiness a *place?* If so, do you know of anyone who has gone there? God filled the world with happiness possibilities. Grass learns to reach for the light and grow tall. Buds learn how to unfold and bloom into things of beauty. Trees learn to convert sap into the foodstuff for leafy limbs. Birds learn to sing and to soar above the earth's noise. Instinctively they know how to reach up and what to reach for. Only we, their keepers, seem confused—looking in vain for "lasting happiness." We look everywhere—except within ourselves.

Happiness begins with a thankful heart. If we praise God each day for what we have, what we are and what He gives us, a miracle takes place. Circumstances that we have tried to change "in order to be happy" either change as we change or we accept things as they are.

It was Jesus who made up the list that all the empty faces are looking for. Reread the Beatitudes. The rules of happiness are there!

TO THINK AND PRAY ABOUT: Think of "blessed" as spiritual joy and praise God.

What's On Today's Menu?

ENTER A restaurant. Wait in line. Be seated by a hostess.

Open a menu. First question: "What's on the menu for today?" All very orderly, organized and impersonal. We are there for a single purpose: food. We will order. We will receive. We will pay.

Enter the kitchen. Wait for a line. Be seated and concentrate. Open a cookbook. First question: "What's on the menu for today?" Same scene, different setting. Here again the process breaks down between grocery lists and balanced meals. The middleman gets in the way. Grocers, with a practiced eye for business, up the prices of holiday ham and its suggested accompaniments guaranteed to "make a hungry family happy."

Is either situation what Jesus had in mind when He said, "Take no thought, saying 'What shall we eat?' . . . for your heavenly Father knoweth that ye have need of all these things" (Matthew 6:31-32)? We are to take no thought of such things but rather to seek God's kingdom. He will provide.

God's plan for nourishment renews dependence on Himself. Back in Old Testament days there were fewer things from which to choose. That does eliminate confusion. However, it seems that whether we have a great deal to eat or little, the real difference lies in our total dependence upon the Lord to provide. God shows us the "clean" and the "unclean" foods, but His plan can only work if we allow it to work in our lives.

TO THINK AND PRAY ABOUT: Can you and your family find ways of getting God's nourishment in today's world? We tend to think today in terms of *paying*. Can we forget price tags and think of *praying?* God wants to provide.

A Morsel Of Bread

REMEMBER THE story of the little girl who was unable to go with her family to see Abraham Lincoln? She was weeping with disappointment when a stranger knocked on the door asking for directions. He was making the same journey. After accepting a cup of steaming tea, the man placed his hand on the child's head and smiled, "Tell your parents you entertained the President!" The Bible tells us (Hebrews 13:2): "Be not forgetful to entertain strangers: for thereby some have entertained angels unaware." I remember the happy feeling of anticipation when my mother said, "Add an extra potato to the pot we may have an unexpected guest." *Would it be the President or an Angel?*

Each day brings an opportunity to share. It is unlikely that it will be a prophet fleeing the wrath of a king; it is equally unlikely that it will be our nation's President in need of a cup of tea. But God needs all of us to serve from His table—in little ways. We tend to forget that no gift is small in the eyes of God when it is offered in His name.

A neighbor used to share a simple little account which she said changed her life. It happened in the days when back peddlers traveled country roads on foot. They had to depend upon invitations to meals for food on their long journeys. Trinkets were their medium of exchange. On that particular day my neighbor felt unprepared for a guest, having food but lacking time to prepare it. Instead of bothering she sent the elderly man on his way to the next house, where he was invited to join the family for the noon meal. The menu was collards, cornbread and buttermilk. After the peddler was on his way, the woman who had served him rushed to share with her neighbor who had turned him away: "Oh, thank you for directing him to me. It is a blessing to see a hungry man eat!"

TO THINK AND PRAY ABOUT: Even when we serve in frugal ways, we cannot be losers because we are serving God as we serve others. Pray that He will send you a hungry soul to feed.

Good Deeds Of Minnie

April 5
Acts 9:36-42

NOW THERE IS in the city of Yucaipa, California, a certain disciple named Minnie. This woman is full of good works and almsdeeds. And I am sure that should Peter be passing through, as he did "in those days," he would restore her if she were in need because she, too, is a Dorcas—and the world has need of such women.

The Scriptures tell us little about the woman to whom Peter gave new life. The other widows wept Dorcas' death. They showed Peter clothing she had made them—evidence of her loving spirit. I'm sure they were sorry they hadn't thanked her more often. There must have been great rejoicing when Dorcas rose. Surely her friends praised her openly then, for the Bible tells us that the story traveled throughout the land.

Minnie is my mother's friend; and, therefore, she is mine. When tragedy struck in our family and we lost my father, it was Minnie who stayed with my mother until my husband and I could get there. It was she who went about quietly organizing, knowing that grief is such a personal thing. It was she who sustained my mother on the long road back to a regular routine—which is probably the hardest road of all. It was she who always "just happened" to be going wherever my mother, who doesn't drive, needed to go. It was she who couldn't bear to see vegetables go to waste . . . and "couldn't my mother help use them?" Minnie did all this, while she nursed a terminally ill husband, taught a Sunday school class, held a family together and served others as she served us.

Recently my mother sent me an article Minnie had written for her church. In it she gave an account of taking two little girls to visit a convalescent home. "We forget age is no barrier to sharing, and our children need to learn during the formative years that youth is not forever." Minnie Davidson bridged a generation gap with sunshine.

TO THINK AND PRAY ABOUT: Thank God for examples set by a "Minnie" you know.

The Last Word

"If you do not wish a man to do a thing, you had better get him to talk about it; for the more men talk, the more likely they are to do nothing else."   Carlyle

CARLYLE'S QUOTE amuses me and reminds me of an incident related by a high school principal. This particular man had his share of trials and tribulations in dealing with student vs. teacher, parent vs. teacher, teacher vs. administrator, administrator vs. school board and school board vs. community. The way he handles these tightrope situations is an inspiration. "I just 'turn the other cheek' by letting them talk," he says.

On one particular day, a lady called screaming hysterically into his already aching ear, aftermath of a cold. As if the physical pain were not enough, she swore profusely, hurting his heart as well. The principal turned the other ear, as well as the other cheek, hoping the lady would calm down. Instead she rudely yelled, "And I want you to know you're just as educated as a_____!"

Most likely seething inside, the principal replied, "Well, if I have to be one, I might as well be an educated one."

The startled woman made some guttural noises, mumbled a "Good-bye" and hung up. She had the last word after all.

TO THINK AND PRAY ABOUT: Douglas Jerold said, " 'The last word' is the most dangerous of infernal machines; and we should no more fight to get it than we would struggle for the possession of a lighted bomb-shell." Must you have the last word? Ask God for a sense of humor to see you through.

Maintenance And Repair

April 7
I Corinthians 13:7; 9:10

THIS MORNING I heard a faint whistle in the vacuum cleaner. It was a sort of happy sound as if the machine was happy doing its job. I was happy it was happy, but I needed the lint and dog hair picked up as well. "Why do you suppose it whistles while it works?" I asked my husband. The question set off a siren in George. He unplugged the machine and flew out the door to the shop as if responding to a seven-alarm fire. I didn't have to worry; he'd do the thinking. "Quick! Come hold this." I couldn't believe the speed with which he had skeletonized the vacuum and laid its internal organs out for an autopsy. Today of all days—and the Home Demonstration Club meeting here tonight. The topic for discussion was "Efficiency," but I was unable to maintain my household because my husband was busy repairing my tools.

I felt myself getting more and more angry. Any minute I was going to let out a scream instead of a whistle. "Put it over there, Hon," my repairman interrupted my thoughts. "It" was some piece of foreign matter. The dining table was covered with nuts, screws and bolts—as were the counters, teacart, oven and sink. My cakes were pushed aside. The china had disappeared.

"Lord," I prayed, "give me patience in this circumstance; help me not to lose my temper." I thought about Paul's exortation of love. It "beareth . . . believeth . . . hopeth . . . *endureth* . . ." and tried to apply it to George, me and the vacuum cleaner. He said, "Isn't this fun—working together?" We began laughing, continued juggling nuts and bolts and soon the job was done. There's something about men and machines I don't understand—something wonderful. Maybe Paul wanted me to discover that.

TO THINK AND PRAY ABOUT: Prayer and laughter are enemies of "hardships."

Exchanging Burdens

" "**T**HESE FOUR WALLS are closing in . . . I wish we'd never bought this house . . . The kids are driving me crazy . . . I *have* to get away." How often we wish we were someone else or somewhere else. There's a touch of folly in such wishing to be somebody else.

There's a story of an old but not very wise man. He sacked up his burdens and headed for the market to exchange them with someone's whose were lighter. At the exchange booth, he met a man with a sack of gold. Now, no matter how heavy, that burden was worth bearing, the old man thought. Soon after the exchange he grew weary. The bag of gold was worse than before! So back he went, this time choosing a bag of silver. But the silver was too heavy also. He mumbled and he grumbled all the way back. This time he picked the lightest bag of all. He found a bag of sweet-smelling roses. How could anything so lightweight and lovely become cumbersome? For the third time he started up the hill. Ouch! The prick of a thorn can be far more painful than a heavy sack. He flung the bag over his shoulder and went down the hill, groaning in pain with every step. The old fellow had gained wisdom. He exchanged the roses for his first sack and went away whistling merrily.

It seems to be a human characteristic to wish vainly to be somebody else. We ignore the commandments and covet what the other person possesses. We think our own treasures and talents are valueless. I am often tempted to let the green eyes of envy blind me to my blessings. But then I give myself a good shaking, deliver Lecture Number 16, and pray, pray, *pray!* The sad part of coveting is that we fail to see our own blessings.

TO THINK AND PRAY ABOUT: Learn to value and use all you have. Wherever or whatever you may be, you carry a special bag of blessings. Talk to God about the mildest envy. He will understand—or He would not have included the last commandment.

How Much Do You Love Me?

"HOW MUCH DO you love me?" I used to ask my mother. "Oodles!" she would answer. "How much do you love me?" my son used to ask. "A bushel and a peck and a hug around the neck!" I answered, quoting from the then popular song. A generation lay between the questions; yet they were the same: *"How much?"* rather than *"Do you?"* So how do we measure love? For that matter, how do we define it? One thing we know about the great art is that it needs expression: poets write, people sing in the shower, teenagers go bananas in the spring. But Love, in the true sense, is neither sentimental, weak nor silly. It demands the best in us—responsibility.

When you love someone, you simply do not give up when you meet disaster or when the going gets rough. You unleash more power! Remember the delightful country bunny story? Grandfather Bunny, whom all rabbits respected, chose the country bunny to carry the beautiful, jewel-encrusted Easter egg to a little boy high up in the mountains. The child was crippled and ill. The bunny was determined to fulfill her responsibility and live up to her grandfather's expectations. The mountain was icy and the night was dark. The bunny slipped down; but she loved her grandfather so much that she thought she could not let him down. She tried again and again to take the egg up the lonely path, but it seemed hopeless. Like magic, as she wondered what to do, Grandfather brought two little gold shoes to her and she fairly flew to the top of the mountain! Of course, the story has a happy ending: the little boy received the beautiful egg on Easter morning. Somehow, some way, love brings happy endings. But for the donor it just goes on and on to generations yet unborn.

"How much do you love me?" I ask of God today. "Enough to let my Son die for you!" He replied. What then is my responsibility? I must trust Him as my personal Savior. Then and only then can I love as Christ loves.

TO THINK AND PRAY ABOUT: We learn to express love by asking God for help.

Washday Hymns

ISN'T IT WONDERFUL the way some people can sing away blues—and sing in *life* in their place?

"Aunt Em" and "Uncle Alex" were self-styled serfs, bound by choice to the bottomlands. Neither slaves, squatters, nor share-croppers, they occupied a modest house with an umbrella tree in the front yard where Uncle Alex hung a rope-swing for children of the community. In the back yard he placed an enormous black wash pot for his wife to boil the "whites" on wash day—and all the children gathered to enjoy both activities.

Aunt Em left stems in the fig preserves for us to suck on, fed us raw yams, and let us "punch down" the clothes when the pot boiled over. The higher the fire blazed around the pot, the harder the pot boiled; and the higher it boiled, the harder we punched as she sang. She knew all the old gospel hymns. There were two songs in particular she sang in a melodious voice:

"O precious is the flow, that makes me white as snow; No other fount I know, Nothing but the blood of Jesus."

As uneducated as she was, the dear lady did a good job of explaining the chorus. We could see the linens whiten like our sins being washed away. We saw a similar miracle when she sang "There is Power in the Blood." Her wash was snow-white! And our hearts were snow-white because of Jesus!

TO THINK AND PRAY ABOUT: Review the two hymns if you have an old hymnal. "Nothing But the Blood" (words and music by Robert Lowry) reminds us of the cleansing power of Jesus. "There is Power in the Blood" (words and music by L. E. Jones) tells us of the "wonder-working power" of His sacrifice. Sometimes while your washing machine jets away at the family laundry, try singing one of the old songs. Personally, my wash never comes out quite as white as Aunt Em's, but I find my heart is cleansed. Worship God with a "wash day" hymn!

Giants Of Today—Preserve Them Please

April 11
Genesis 1:29-31

WHAT HAS BEEN on earth 40,000,000 years and is considered the oldest living thing, lives to be 3,000 years old, grows 300 feet tall, never dies from disease or old age, but can be killed only by a bolt of lightning? It must be some kind of supernatural giant. Supernatural? No. Giant? Yes! What's more, anyone can find these real, live giants. "Wellingtonia Giganteas" and "Sequoias" live in the forest, but they are friendly. You see, they are redwood trees. And God trusts us to keep them safe from harm.

Visitors have nothing to fear. Indeed! It is the giants who have reason to be afraid, for people have been unkind, cutting and sawing the trees for lumber until there are few left. It is said that when a big tree falls, its heart breaks into a million pieces. Only part of the story is true. As a matter of fact, the redwood tree, unlike other trees, does not depend on its heart for life. It repairs itself by growing new bark—even though it sometimes takes hundreds of years to cover the scars. Nature tried hard to protect the trees, providing them with suits of armor two feet thick. The bark contains sap which kills insects that are enemies. Nature also left resin from the bark, making the giants almost totally fire resistant.

We visit the forest as often as we can. Once there were over 3,000 square miles of the towering trees in California. Now they live only in parks, green monuments of the past. With each visit we clutch their blessing a bit closer. Walking among them is like being inside a great cathedral. I have seen even the agnostic shaken by their majesty.

TO THINK AND PRAY ABOUT: Consider the handiwork of God. In His Infinite wisdom, He omitted a heart—perhaps to keep it from being broken. But He put us in dominion over these and endowed *us* with a heart for caring. He provided them with an armor and gave us His armor. *How great Thou art!*

There's Something Special In The Air

There's something special in the air
Before the sun is up,
When pearls of dew are strung around
The throat of each buttercup.
Sunflowers yawn and stretch once more
Before their petaled eyes
Start sun-to-sun horizon watch
Across the daytime skies.
Like silver hammocks, cobwebs swing,
Half-ridden in the trees,
As they weave a tender trap
For unsuspecting bees.
There's something, very special, yes,
About the morning air,
A time to watch His creatures small
Set out their task to do;
A time to seek strength for the day,
Which only once is new. J.M.B.

MOST OF US need peace and tranquility—the kind that comes directly from Christ. In a too-busy world, it seems that Christians seem to be as harried as those who have not met God. As a result, we often suffer the same problems. How, without a reservoir of strength, can we put a supporting arm around the needy in some dark hour? Maybe the answer for us is to store up light when the day is new.

When God created the earth, He assigned each small creature a job to fulfill. I think He had more in mind for Adam and Eve than garden-tending and keeping watch over the animals. The account in Genesis tells us God talked to them. He loved them. He loves us. Take time to be with Him.

TO THINK AND PRAY ABOUT: Try rising early. Go back to "in the beginning." Have a chat with God. The change of pace may alter your spiritual pattern. Ask for strength to meet the day. God will fill your reservoir.

Pennies From Heaven

April 13
Proverbs 10:22
Isaiah 33:3
Luke 11:10

APRIL THIRTEENTH doesn't have to be an unlucky day! You can walk under ladders, open umbrellas inside the house, and go on a six-mile hike in the cool of the evening—no matter how many black cats dart across the path. It can be an exciting day as you count the yearly "pennies from heaven."

It's called counting blessings. Friends of long standing know my husband and I look for coins as we walk, but they are unable to understand how we find them with regularity. The formula is so simple that nobody believes it: *Look, believe, find!*

Your friends will be agog when you tell them about your "showers of blessings." They will think you're talking in figurative language (and you are!), for you are talking about striking it rich—out walking.

Other people out walking are not so wealthy. Some can't see over their groceries. Some rush to get here or there and have no time to look. Some complain about the storm off Baja and the dreadful humidity as they walk along. But the saddest of all are those so engrossed in themselves and their problems, they wouldn't recognize a blessing if they met it face to face. They look neither to the right nor to the left, so they fail to recognize the blessings around them: their friends, the face of spring or the inscription on a coin "In God we trust." Trust God to show you His blessings as you walk. Go right on looking, believing, collecting—and counting. Put the year's findings together and purchase a "Blessing Gift."

TO THINK AND PRAY ABOUT: God's blessings are everywhere. Pray for the vision to see them as you pass. Make walking a spiritual exercise.

A Lovely Garden

April 14
Isaiah 40:1, 8

Make your heart a lovely garden
Ever cautious what you sow;
Fill each space with seeds of kindness
So the deeds of God can grow.
Face each path with bright-thought flowers;
Let their fragrance waft so sweet,
Unkind words, like weeds and shadows,
Feel unwelcome and retreat. J.M.B.

MILLIE likes her mornings. First, she has coffee. Second, she does one of two things—depending on the weather. If it's sunny she takes a refreshing jog around the block, alone with her bright thoughts. Then she's bouncy and happy and her family catches it. If it's raining she has her eye-opener, then sits in a mood as dark as the clouds. Just why is a mystery—even to her. The result is, as you would expect, a glum expression when the children enter the kitchen. Quickly they come down with her disease and the day's off to a bad start.

Millie laughed recalling the incident. "You're going to be a bummer!" she'd muttered to the six a.m. downpour. But before she had time to measure instant coffee for herself, she heard footsteps behind her. She was just about to yell "Back to bed!" orders when Tommy, her four-year-old in sleepers, shrieked, "Come quick! The roses are on fire and God's hosing 'em off!" Puzzled, frightened and annoyed, Millie chased Tommy down the hall. The scene was so beautiful: beneath the light of the street lamp, the roses, like crimson cups of rhinestones, were sparkling in gratitude of being "hosed off"! Soon the glory would end with the coming of day—unless she made it last. "Thank you for sharing," Millie whispered. "How about some hot oatmeal to start our day?"

TO THINK AND PRAY ABOUT: Share flowers of the day at home. Shadows retreat!

Render Unto Caesar

April 15
Luke 20:19-25
I Samuel 15:22

"THIS IS IT, folks! Twelve o'clock tonight spells dooms-day. The wolf is at the door!" The commentator meant the Department of Internal Revenue. Wolf? The intended victim must be our profit. Surely the wolf won't gobble us sheep completely—shear us, maybe, or even skin us; but our lives will be spared. Else, where would next year's fleece come from? It's comforting to know that we are never asked to pay taxes to exceed our income. Actually, the money isn't ours anyway. That was determined a long time ago—not that the decision pleased everybody. The very word "taxes" causes eyes to fix and spines to stiffen.

In the time of Christ, it was the chief priests and the scribes who tried to tempt Jesus with crafty questions: "Is it lawful for us to give tribute unto Caesar, or no?" And in Luke's account (20:25), He admonished them, saying: "Render therefore unto Caesar the things which be Caesar's, and unto God the things which be God's." Three reminders are tucked into those verses: (1) It was not the poor who complained; (2) Jesus did not suggest a Board of Appeal; and (3) He added that we are to give God that which is His. Do we complain? Do we threaten? Do we give God the proper gifts: tithes and offerings and gifts of *time*?

Benjamin Franklin said: "We are taxed twice as much by our idleness, three times as much by our pride, and four times as much by our folly; and from these taxes the commissioners can-not ease or deliver us by allowing an abatement." Taxes are heavy, but we have many other taxations—not so easily discharged. We know what Jesus decreed.

TO THINK AND PRAY ABOUT: We are aware of con-stant imposition of new taxes and bunglers who add to the old. We are aware of how taxing this is to the patience, for we all "render." But we should be aware of the mumblings of the multitudes, too, and pray for an open mind and a willing spirit to render as we ought.

Family Day

April 16
Proverbs 31:10, 27, 28

SOMEHOW I am unable to get all choked up about Family Day. For over a decade now I would have overlooked it except that merchants reminded me it was time to buy another gift. Up to now the observance has been on the first Sunday in August (good timing since there's no other gift-giving day in the month). Now I see somebody is suggesting that we celebrate in the spring instead, in one of the "fertility" months! The new day would be by *declaration* as opposed to *proclamation*. This (I can assume only) would make it into a legal holiday?

I foresee two things happening. It will become a highly commercialized situation with everybody giving everybody else something they have two of already.

And the single day holiday would stretch to a deadly three-day weekend, one in which the pure-heart intent gives way to death on the highway? Just thoughts . . . Thoughts I should have left unspoken, even to my friends—*especially* to my friends! I found myself before a firing squad.

"Have you read 'War on the American Family' in READER'S DIGEST . . . Did you read the results of the children's poll showing that from 50,000 surveyed, half preferred a TV set to a *father* . . . Families are the most important thing in our society . . . and they're falling apart?" Did they really think one day set apart was going to change that?

"Spare my life," I begged. "You see, it's just that *every* day is family day." No cakes, ribbons, cards . . . just "I love you," to my husband; "Bring your wife to dinner, honey," to my son; "Hello! Mama? We're coming over!" to my mother . . . just Family Day!

TO THINK AND PRAY ABOUT: Praise your family every day; praise God for them.

Exchange

God handed me a morning
All freshly-dipped in dew;
I said, "How shall I use it?"
He said, "It's up to you."
I baked a cake for someone;
Ran errands for a friend:
Two hours slipped through my fingers—
With roses yet to tend.
'Twas lunch time for the children;
I noted noon-high sun
And made each a specialty—
Then smiled for everyone.
I could not hold the morning
No matter how I tried;
I reached back for the dawning
But found the dew had dried . . . .

MY FRIEND says she wishes she knew how Joshua commanded the sun to stand still! We all feel like that sometimes. That's why it is hard to pray as Jesus taught us. We falter when we put the day into God's hands. "Thy will be done" is the difficult part. We know what we want and *think* we know what we should have. But do we really know what is best for ourselves and for others? Or, are we willing to trust God's will?

I confessed this prayer-flaw to my friend on one of her "hobgoblin days" as she calls them when everything's going wrong. We can cope—most days. It's those "hobgoblins" when we love and appreciate each other most. It occurs to me that it is God's will that we are around when the other's in a throe. We hold each other up on faltering days.

TO THINK AND PRAY ABOUT:

I bow my head in silence;
My glad heart hums a tune;
I give God back His morning—
He hands me afternoon. J.M.B.

What's Happening To Our Children?

April 18
Colossians 3:20-21
Proverbs 13:24; 19:18

"WHAT'S HAPPENING to our children?" The question stirred in the hearts of the entire congregation Sunday as the minister referred to the suicide problem. Worshippers were disturbed about statistics regarding the phenomenal increase in suicide attempts in the last two decades. The report's a shocker, but are the figures unexpected? What struck me speechless were the reasons cited for the suicides and the attempts by children. *Drugs and alcohol?* Those were around when I was getting my growth, and I'm trying to recall a suicide other than in adult population—and those were rare. *Economic insecurity?* Are they kidding? Doesn't anybody remember the Great Depression? *Changing values?* Values were changing then, too, as I reminded my parents often enough! *Stress and alienation?* Those factors have been with us always, but I do think they're a key. We had people around who cared—adults who weren't afraid to be "figures of authority." Maybe the questions should be: "What's happening to our adults?" Parents, teachers, ministers, law enforcement officers, judges and adults-at-large have an obligation. If we all abdicate at once, where is a child to turn for guidance?

There'a certain validity in "spare the rod, spoil the child." I recall a playmate trying to snatch a switch from his mother's hand and threatening to beat himself to death. She snatched it back and offered to do it for him. I received a well-aimed swat when I once wished I were dead. My "death wish" dropped sharply. God chastises, too. His reason? He loves us. He cares!

TO THINK AND PRAY ABOUT: "I don't believe in a future," was one goodby note. How would you explain to a child how to *make* one? And a future with God? Hopeless? Not if we love, listen, stay in command and *teach children to pray!*

Weed Control

April 19
Matthew 13:24-30

GEORGE has been on his hands and knees digging at nut grass all week. Somebody gave him a start to choke out the Bermuda grass. It did. It also choked out the rest of the lawn and moved in to live happily around every shrub, vine and perennial. Our neighbor has no nut grass. He's fighting a battle with weeds. He hoes, sprays and does all sorts of things to discourage the tenacious pests. Both men are losing the skirmishes.

"It's unbelievable that we can put a man on the moon and haven't come up with a way to exterminate weeds," the neighbor panted.

Weeds are interesting things. I read somewhere: "You can control weeds but not their seeds. Some weed seeds are able to germinate after being underground eighty years." That means that the pesky things are lying there conspiring, and the minute some unsuspecting homeowner diligently scratches the surface to put in a lawn, up they jump—rested and ready to choke the life from any domestic plant.

The same sort of weeding problem goes on inside ourselves. While we daydream, an enemy comes (as in today's parable) and seeds our lives with tares. Now, the trouble with tares (weeds called "darnel") is that they are so like wheat one has trouble in distinguishing between the two. It was near impossible to pluck out the tares without uprooting the wheat. When the wrong seeds come into our lives, we have to get rid of them before they germinate and confuse us—spoiling the harvest God has in mind for us.

We can go a step farther with the lesson. Should the wrong things be "smuggled in," and we are uncertain as to which is the right and which is the wrong, God promises to sort at harvest. Ours is to watch and pray!

TO THINK AND PRAY ABOUT: Some socially acceptable sins began innocently. Weed!

Sunday Clothes

April 20
Luke 5:36
Matthew 7:12

EMERSON SAID, "The only way to have a friend is to be one." I wish "Robert of Lincoln" knew that! The feisty fellow dropped by today to shower in our birdbath and never uttered a word of thanks. He was wearing his disguise; and that's fortunate, for he's unpopular hereabouts—with both farmers and other birds. He does nothing to improve his image. Across his face was a black feather-mask, but he's in the process of changing from weekday winter garments to his well tailored Sunday-suit for spring courting. The Bob-O'-Link will receive a welcome in his Northern home, where he is headed.

Once there, he'll don his swallow-tailed coat (with pointed feathers half the length of himself), choose a modest wife and help raise fledgling-children just like himself—excellent citizens there, questionable here! There, conservatively dressed, he is classified as "a friend of man." Seven mouths to feed is a responsibility he assumes with a cheerful "Chee, chee, chee!" as he carries home harmful insects.

Alas! When the leaves change color, so does he, putting on the dull outfit and that silly mask for his flight South—right into the rice fields. He becomes a thief and a scoundrel with scarcely a friend. It's a pity.

Robert of Lincoln is much like the parable in today's Scripture. If the bird kept on his good clothing, sang his merry "Bob-O'-Link" choirsongs, and followed the Golden Rule, he would find friends wherever his wings took him. We, too, have to remind ourselves to be the same persons throughout the week that we try to be on Sunday. We want our spiritual lives and our everyday lives to be consistent.

TO THINK AND PRAY ABOUT: Emerson's words paraphrase the Golden Rule. We know what our responsibilities are as far as our own behavior is concerned. God would have us go farther, however. What do we do to help the "Roberts?"

A Bible In My Classroom

SOMETIMES I think we need pills running around looking for diseases to cure. There are those who hear of the ills around them and do nothing about the groans except arch their eyebrows. Maybe they should arch their backs. A good clean fight is better than public indifference, administrative timidity or individual apathy when it comes to a heavenly cause.

Yes, I'm probably a "pill." I don't know how many I've cured. Unfortunately, there are no such statistics available for Christian teachers. We just go on "administering" ourselves with no real proof that we have *saved* our patients. My doctor has a great philosophy. He recommends minimal dosages of medication and lets nature take over as soon as possible. I'm restricted somewhat in public schools, but not completely; so *I administer first aid and let God do the rest.*

On one occasion I stirred up bad vibrations when a school official visited my classroom. I overheard him say (presumably to my principal): "Watch her! She's apt to smuggle a Bible in there." *Apt to?* There was a King James version in my reading corner. I found the word *smuggle* distasteful. I was well within my constitutional rights, and I knew it. So I dusted off my copy and placed it on the center reading table in full view. There were no side-effects. Apparently the gentleman backed into the corner where the Bible had been . . . .

The Supreme Court ruled it unconstitutional to conduct devotional exercises in public classrooms. The Court did *not* rule out the Bible's presence—or even objective discussions. Why then, did so few teachers seize the advantage? Recently I ran across my old notes: "No public demand . . . Parents beseige schools to provide instruction on sex, alcohol, drugs and automobile driving but apparently consider religious knowledge unimportant . . . If there were demand, administrators might remain apprehensive, fearing bigots and crackpots . . . ." I'm glad I was a pill.

TO THINK AND PRAY ABOUT: Sometimes it's necessary to make waves! Pray about it.

Cup Of Spring

April 22
Solomon 2:11-13

Green meadows fill the cup of spring
With poppies to the brim;
Like liquid gold, they bubble up
Along the grassy rim.
Bright daisies slosh along the slope
To saucer beds of clover;
A drop of dew comes sparkling through,
And springtime's cup runs over. J.M.B.

IN THIS MONTH of warmth and wetness, sunshine and showers, I long to be outside responding in merriment with the meadowlark or making daisy-chains, but I remember the berry pie that boiled over in the oven last night and the birthday cake I should make for a friend. Ah, April, when everything seems to keep time—except the clock. While I am spraying on instant oven-cleaner, the telephone rings. Do I remember that I am to do the devotionals . . .? Yes, but the oven comes first, so I can do the cake, so I can do the devotionals.

Is my light-headedness due to the spray-on cleaner, or is it the light hand of spring on my shoulder? A voice is saying, "Get up! Get out! Roam the meadows. Enjoy capricious April. Share a cup of spring." There was a time when life seemed simpler. There seemed to be time to enjoy the new-sprung plants in the waking world of April. There seemed to be more time for talking, thinking, reading.

A school principal devised a "parallel" reading plan. Everyone in the building paused at the sound of a bell and read for a quarter hour—quietly and without interruption. The quietness shared was wonderful.

Bible reading—that's a good idea for now! Even better, maybe it could be shared. It sounds impractical to suggest that we drop our work and read at an agreed upon time; on the other hand, the parallel reading might be just what we need. It might add a breath of spring to our Bible reading.

TO THINK AND PRAY ABOUT: Doing your daily Bible reading out-of-doors is something we all can do; alone or in groups. Invite God! He'll fill your cup.

Work!

RECENTLY my son and I had an argument which made us both extremely angry. Upon hearing the disagreement, my husband also became angry. The dog wisely ran under the bed through it all. "What a way to start the day, Lord!"

Our heated conversation went something like this:

"Bryce, would you run to the store and get me a five-pound bag of sugar?"

"I can't, Mom, I need to jog for an hour."

"Then jog to the market," I suggested, feeling irritated.

"I can't jog and carry sugar," Bryce replied with more than a hint of belligerency.

His logic was more than I could take. The sugar weighed five pounds, and the day before Bryce had had to carry a man his own weight 100 yards to prove he could "pack his own weight."

My blood pressure had reached the boiling point when George intervened. He cornered Bryce concerning his ill logic and Bryce sullenly admitted, "Yesterday was different. I wanted to prove my speed, prowess and cooperation with the coach."

"You now have an opportunity to prove it to your mother," George replied. "Get going!"

Bryce got. I cooled. George breathed in. The dog crawled out. Later in the day we had a family caucus and agreed that we all needed motivation in order to do a job well. Our son saw the after-school practice, stressful though it was, as a privilege for which he pushed aside other plans. He was seeking a goal. On the other hand, the errand, an easy task, was of no consequence. When we think our work important, we give it full attention, ungrudgingly. Henry van Dyke in his poem "Work" said: "This is my work; my *blessing*, not my doom!" He found the secret of contentment.

TO THINK AND PRAY ABOUT: God needs us all. What if farmers stopped farming; builders, building; musicians, playing; poets, writing; preachers, preaching; and bakers, baking. Life depends on *you*. There's no greater adventure than a job done in Christ's name. What better motivation is there?

At The Close Of A Lovely Day

April 24
Psalm 35:28

GOD HEARS much about tedium-filled days. Why does He hear so seldom about the flip-side at the close of a lovely day? Today was one of those wonderful days that makes me want to live forever—and know with certainty that I'm going to! In fact, it was like a gentle transition from this world to the next. What made it so? I want to trace my finger around the heart of it and see why it was so special.

The day began with candlelight and soft music. The coffee was strong and bracing. The morning breeze mingled sea-salty scents with delicate smells from the lime trees. The day ended with cold meat loaf and other leftovers eaten with our fingers, as George and I stretched out on chaise lounges beside the backyard waterfall. What sweet leisure—with nothing to do but look for a first star to wish upon!

Beautiful beginning, beautiful end; but the in-betweens also made the day successful. The candle that was supposed to be dripless, was. The coffee that was supposed to drip, did. The onions I sliced for the meat loaf did not get in my eyes; neither did the paring knife slice my finger. Nobody lost car keys, sunglasses or a button as we prepared to go our separate ways. At school, I talked and the children heard me. At home, my family talked and I heard *them*. The daisy bouquet kept its waxy freshness . . . nobody tracked the linoleum . . . the dog barked only when barked at . . . my mother called to say everything in her house was working . . . two chronically ailing friends are "improving slowly" . . . and I received a "get well" card and I'm not sick.

Stars now sparkle in the treetops and the moon shines in April fullness. I look back on the lovely day: Were there really no ropes binding my hands and feet, tying my tongue, making me gasp for breath? Are nooses my misuse of the lifelines God throws me? I only know today was filled with love, light, friends and flowers. I've had a taste of glory.

TO THINK AND PRAY ABOUT: Take a "better day" and analyze it. What made it successful? Perhaps God sends us model days from which to cut a pattern. In all things give Him praise.

God Has Planned A Miracle

The daffodils stopped blooming;
I stored their bulbs away
So they could rest and do their best
At spring's first crack of day.
When winter leaves my yard then
I'll plant the bulbs outside;
At first, they'll blink at light, I think;
Then open my eyes up wide.
And I shall rejoice with them,
For deep inside I'll know
That God has planned a Miracle
And I have helped it grow! J.M.B.

AS I PUT the daffodil bulbs away this morning I was thinking of what my minister had to say about miracles inside people. His "Reflections" page in the church bulletin always reflects a glorious side of life I haven't seen before. It helps me see the miracle inside myself! I praise God for such a minister. He somehow understands that I have moments when my personal resources seem to evaporate, when outside resources cannot put my Humpty-Dumpty world together again, and when even prayer seems to die on my lips.

Actually, he is much like the Psalmist. "Wait. Be patient," he advises. It is true, of course, that time is a great healer. Circumstances and our attitudes change; or, as he says, "There is a miracle within you being fulfilled just by leaving yourself to the discretion of time." But he sees a Healer greater than time.

"The miracle within is *Hope*, a living power that is within our control. To know that we are not victims of fate and fortune, the whims of the gods or astral powers, is the most powerful thing at our disposal. The miracle within is God given, God inspired and God directed. God calls us to a Kingdom of victory, power, growth, excitement and contribution. Within us are the resources and abilities to rise to any challenge if we will just have the faith to make the miracle work."

TO THINK AND PRAY ABOUT: Believe there's a miracle inside you and you will feel the stir of growth.

The Wife Of A Poor Man

"Heaven will not be Heaven if I do not meet my wife there."
A. Jackson

ONCE UPON A TIME there lived in a three-story yellow house with white trimming a little boy called "Jemmy." Each evening as he came down the narrow English-elm lined lane, Jemmy announced the end of the school day with a whistle. The merry little notes brought his little Scotch mother to the window with a smile of welcome. His mother was a great lover of poetry, old romantic tales and old ballads. The little boy's happiest moments were those spent listening. He enjoyed a rich imagination—even pretending medieval characters were walking to and from school in Cambridge with him. History was in the making—with echoes of Lord Perry's artillery still rumbling along the street—but Jemmy was more interested in "boy things": bows and arrows; whale's teeth; and a cockatoo in the village barber shop, which, the barber assured him, spoke the Hottentot language. His imagination grew.

Jemmy grew up, as little boys do, and went away to school. When he graduated from Harvard, he found himself faced with the necessity of making a decision about an occupation. He felt no interest in becoming a minister like his father. He didn't wish to be a doctor. There was law, which he chose from necessity—not love. His love was for poetry; but such thinking was folly the young man was taught to believe.

Then Jemmy met Maria White, who loved the stories his mother loved, and who loved poetry as he loved it. "I want to be the wife of a poor man!" she declared. Her declaration gave us James Russell Lowell.

While visiting the American poet's home I viewed the little cemetery where his firstborn daughter rests. From there I could see the tiny headstone; but a more lasting monument was the sorrow-painted picture he sketched with immortal words in "The First Snowfall." Looking from his study window at the tiny grave, Lowell compared the drifting snow to patience given by the hands of the All-Father from clouds of snow to bless and comfort in grief. We can be glad he had an unselfish wife.

TO THINK AND PRAY ABOUT: Thank God for unselfish people.

Keep On The Trail

WHEN WINTER buds unclench their little fists and reach like blind men towards the sun, a voice calls, "Spring!" We're tired of overshoes, colds and overheated rooms. Why not take an early trip before state parks are crowded? There is nothing wrong with that; there *is* something wrong with the behavior too many of us exhibit—something so wrong that the National Park Service pleads for our sanity.

Congress set up parks as pleasure places where we can get away from it all and enjoy God's world. We know the regulations about protecting wildlife, and we are given regulations on protecting the lives of ourselves and our families. The safety officers within the parks can only advise us; they are unauthorized to restrict guests. They allow freedom; they trust our judgment.

We let them down as the number of fatalities grows at an alarming rate. We know alcohol and driving don't mix; neither do alcohol and hiking. Yet, people go right on combining them as if willing death. We hear warnings of high winds and drive campers or pull boats anyway—and crash. We hear warnings of high waves and swim or surf anyway—and drown.

I remember a visit to Zion Park in Southwestern Utah, a park so beautiful one thinks of Zion of the Old Testament, or, metaphorically, the Kingdom of God on earth and in heaven. A grim reminder washes away such thoughts—a sign telling of the untimely death of young boys who, despite warnings, waded up the Virgin River between the narrow canyon walls. Even as the ranger posed for a picture beside the sign, FLASH FLOODS, two people, barely visible, waded into the same trap. And, now, I read that two adults toppled over the Grand Canyon wall, just a few feet away from the warning sign: STAY ON THE TRAIL. *Why?*

God gives us free will in our spiritual lives somewhat like the park officials give us in the physical world. He advises, warns, lets us know of His loving concern. Even so, we tend to destroy ourselves instead of enjoying God, His Love and His beautiful creations.

TO THINK AND PRAY ABOUT: We belong to God. The Bible is our guide. STAY ON THE TRAIL.

Waiting For Greater Glory!

MY FAMILY sees the Grand Canyon, the titanic gorge cut by the Colorado river through the high plateau region of Northwestern Arizona, as the world's most spectacular illustration of what God can do through erosion. In fashioning the 217-mile-long canyon, He saw to it that nature carved proper adornments. Along the steep walls of layered color are "temples"—some beautiful, some grotesque, all "alive with a million moods," said the late John Burroughs. So cathedral-like are some of the spirals that inspired geologists gave them classical names (Apollo, Diana, etc.). Other "temples" perpetuate Indian tribes. Still other points bear fancied resemblance to the religious temples of the Far East.

Imagine the glory of attending an Easter sunrise service there! We stood with bowed heads looking at the mile-deep floor of the canyon—carpeted with flowing waters. After the prayers, we looked up into the dome of a sky, too blue to be believed. One by one in the early-morning light great capes sprang into view. As the sun rose slowly, it etched them with golden lights against the hazy blues of the backdrop. An hour later, when the service ended, everything was transfigured! The dark capes of morning stood out clearly defined and brilliantly toned. The temples we saw at dawn were remodeled and the Great Architect pulled back the purple-gloom curtain to show us scores of others. We stood transfixed. For such beauty there could be no benediction. There could only be a thousand "Amens."

Each hour in the Canyon brought a new spectacle. As the sun announced high-noon, the canyon lost some of its charm. Walls flattened and temples fell to ruin in the dusty shadows. And then the spectacle of the morning reappeared in new glory, erasing the gray-garmented shadows with robes of royal purple. Evening brought a new Grand Canyon—more beautiful than before!

TO THINK AND PRAY ABOUT: God gives us a glimpse of His Glory to come in the morning of our lives. Let us work through our noons for the night; then the New Glory.

What Is Easter?

April 29
Luke 24:1-7

"WHAT IS EASTER?" I asked the children in my classroom one year. Their answers, as one would expect, were as varied as their backgrounds and their experiences: "A pink-eared rabbit . . . white gloves, white lilies and a prayer . . . an organ-choir in an angel-chorus . . . a new year, sort of . . . a new feel . . . early sunrise service . . . church, Mother, Daddy and me in between. . . ."

What is Easter? It is fact, fiction and fantasy. It is the mystical, the magical and the miraculous. It is all men made brothers under the Fatherhood of God. It is the melting hearts of sullen rivers, a million songbirds building nests . . . the hallelujahs of apple orchards in bloom . . . Easter rabbits with tireless legs . . . new bonnets . . . Virginia baked ham . . . But it is more—so much more!

To us Christians, Easter is the beautiful memory of a stone rolled away. It is hope through a Risen Lord. It is the hallelujah of the heart!

There is a mystique about Easter unrivaled by any other holiday. How its appointed day of celebration came about is a part of that mystique. In early times, countries observed the holiday on the same day that the Jews kept their Passover. (The word *Easter* is a translation of a Greek word *pascha*, meaning "passover.") Churches of the Western world remembering that Jesus, according to the Scriptures of the New Testament, rose on Sunday, kept Easter on Sunday following the Passover day. But far greater than any historical account is the significance of the Resurrection itself.

Reread the Easter story. Enjoy another springtime. And marvel at Life beyond life, unmarked by calendars. Praise God for life eternal that the resurrection of His Son brought to the world.

TO THINK AND PRAY ABOUT: It is comforting to know that no matter on what date Easter falls, it leaves with us new birth, new life and new hope—enough to last us throughout the year and all the years that stretch into the eternity Christ's birth, death and resurrection made possible.

The Shadow Of The Cross Is Gone

April 30
John 12:24-28

On Easter Day the lilies bloom,
Triumphant, risen from their tomb;
Their bulbs have undergone rebirth,
Born from the silence of the earth—
Symbolically—to tell all men
That Christ, the Savior, lives again.
The angels, pure and white as they,
Have come and rolled the stone away
And with the lifting of the stone
The shadow of the cross is gone! J.M.B.

APRIL'S DOOR opens wider and wider for May to step inside. April opened the windows of the sky, too, letting go of showers, sunshine and rainbows. The hills are now green, dotted with daisies and frolicky lambs.

But April forgot her manners sometimes. She blustered with winds. She grabbed at ladies' skirts. She wept until the streams overflowed. Early gardeners shook their heads in despair at April's fickle ways—and she pouted, withholding rain. *How like April we are, Lord.*

April always brings us surprises: Little teasing ones like that of changing weather but sometimes the most wonderful Gift the world has ever known—Easter, wonderful Easter.

TO THINK AND PRAY ABOUT:

Love is such a mighty urge
At springtime of the year—
Flowing ponds and bursting buds
To tell us Easter's near.
Life's as new, by act of faith,
As when the world began—
Robins sing in every branch
And lilies rise again! J.M.B.

Prayer For The Miracle Of May

DEAR LORD, I ask for the miracles of May—the simple yet vital things that keep me from going astray. I am a lost sheep in search of the Good Shepherd. Sometimes I pause too long looking in vain for more spectacular events. Or I follow a mirage, Lord, up rocky, barren places where there is hunger and thirst, ravenous wolves, and infertile ground. Then You, Good Shepherd, help me, Your lost sheep, retrace my steps down the rocky slopes, through the parched deserts and the dark valleys. Guide my steps, Lord, each day I am your ninety-ninth sheep—sometimes for only a fleeting moment; but sometimes long enough for me to be in want before I find the path back to where You would have me. When I stray I become anxious. I do not listen to others who are seeking. I become hurried, impatient—and, forgive me, Lord, sometimes rude. I even lack compassion for others who stray, perhaps because I see myself reflected in their weaknesses. Let me recognize my short-comings. Let me say, "I'm sorry." Let me reach out a helping hand to all Your flock, so that together we can find and enter the fold of Your forgiveness.

Lord, I know that You find a green meadow for me just when I am ready to give up. When I come into its lushness, I know it is a miracle. But how quickly I forget—becoming complacent, uncharitable and "at ease in Zion." Let me share, for Your blessings are not for me alone. Let me give of Your grace with a loving smile, honest praise and a willingness to help. And, Lord, let me never envy those who enter Your green pastures before me.

Teach me to lie down, Lord, beside the still waters You provided through the April showers. Let me rest. Let me meditate. Then let my soul be restored so that I can enjoy the miracle of May flowers and share a cup of cold water in Your name. Renew my faith. Make me strong. Keep me aware of Your goodness and Your mercy. Make me worthy of leading other sheep to Your fold where we can dwell in peace throughout the miracle days of May.

May's Language Of Flowers

May 2
The Acts 3:6

I LOVE THE month of May! It comes skipping across the countryside to fulfill April's promise of flowers. Yesterday's tight buds are today's coral-bells, blue salvia and wild poppies. Nature uses no geometric precision, preferring clumps, drifts and masses. Informally, buttercups, daffodils and daisies march along the unplowed fields—feeling welcome anywhere and nodding to children as they pass.

This is the month that the children and I make May baskets, fill them with fresh flowers and tiptoe to doors to deliver them, undetected. The little floral offerings say "Greetings" to receivers. The children know that literally flowers can't talk, think or reason, but we have fun talking of such ancient-court thinking. And they know that flowers have a "language." A little May basket can bring joy to the shut-in; and, of course, a word of love to the children's parents. Each child wants to prepare a lovely gift and the excitement mounts as they fill baskets with flowers for delivery.

While working on her May Day project yesterday a little girl became ill and had to go home. She put the frilly basket inside her desk and when she returned today she found the flowers wilted and limp. She burst into tears, "Nobody would want this," she sobbed. "And besides the giving day is over."

Unfortunately I had no flowers left from the day before, but I called her aside and said, "It's the gift that counts, and any day is giving day. I know a lady who received no lovely flowers—Mrs. Brannon, right here by the school. Take your basket to her."

The child was not to be comforted. "She's blind and can't *see* them!"

Another child came to my rescue. "Oh, that's good! We're not supposed to get caught, are we? Mrs. Brannon can't see you—but she can smell the color!"

The second child opened my eyes, too. Next year we will make baskets for the blind who will smell them and feel our concern. I love the month of May!

TO THINK AND PRAY ABOUT: Praise God for all the senses that make giving lovely.

A Little Bit Of My Time

THE PINK-BLANKETED bundle was still in the quickly improvised apple-box crib. I tiptoed over and touched the pudgy pink face with my index finger—the way I used to when I would awaken from a needed night's sleep and wonder if my own son had swallowed his tongue or suffocated in his zipped-up cover. It was a world revisited for me. It has been a long time since I have handled a baby. I had volunteered to help the young mother whose sister was ill.

The forehead was reassuringly warm. Too warm? I pushed aside the covers. Was Bryce ever that small; his fingers (which flailed at my touch) that wee? The baby's blue eyes, tightly-squeezed together, trembled. The lips pursed and smacked—quivering into a smile just as his eyes flickered open. I smiled back, exhaling in relief—the way I did a quarter of a century ago. As I was leaving to get back to my work, there was a wail. A safety pin? It couldn't be, they wear Pampers now. The wail stopped when the baby's eyes tried to focus on my face. Wet? No. "What's the problem, fellow?" The answer was a coo. And I turned to go out again. "Please," I prayed.

This time there was a howl. Something was wrong! Should I call the pediatrician? Where was the schedule? Was it time for the baby's formula or orange juice? I grabbed both and ran back into the room. The howl reduced to a gurgle as I stood over the crib. The sly little fellow saw me for an easy mark. Fat arms and two sleeper-clad feet went into an arc—he wanted to be held. I knew it would do no good to show him the mobile of butterflies or offer him food, but I tried.

Something triggered a memory of Bryce on his fourth birthday. He'd eaten too much birthday cake; he was tired of his gifts, and he was screaming! "All I want is a little bitta time!" I took him into my arms where he promptly fell asleep. But at six weeks old? I reached for this one with remembered skill. The tiny head drooped and the smile was back . . . .

TO THINK AND PRAY ABOUT: How many new lives, fresh and shining; how many old lives, worn and drab, are in need of a little bit of our time—and a prayer?

How Do I Pray?

"**M**Y PRAYER can't seem to get off its knees this morning! How should I pray?" It's an age-old question my friend asked. The most beautiful prayer the world has ever known, eloquent in its simplicity, came as a pattern for us when Jesus answered His disciple's request, "Lord, teach us to pray."

"Do you ever feel like this?" she wondered. Yes, I feel that prayers die on my lips when I become ritualistic. And, yes, it does happen when I have a burden on my heart and know I should speak to God about it. Dead prayers, for me anyway, come when I try to "pray" instead of "talk" with God. When I become formal, it is as if we were strangers—God and me—and yet we have been friends all my life. I must work my way back to the simple conversation He and I use.

Why does our prayer life sometimes seem dead? It happens to my friend, to me, and, I suppose, to others. Didn't God promise that if we asked we would receive? That if we knocked on His door, He would open it? I have to pause and ask myself if I am really asking—or am I going through idle motions, concentrating on the problem instead of listening for His solution. And which door am I knocking on? His door or my own—the one that I have locked myself behind?

TO THINK AND PRAY ABOUT: Are there days when you feel "locked out" or "locked in" and you can't find the key? Try being honest with God—tell Him where you're at—unlock for Him.

> God requires no flowing phrases;
> He does not take thoughts apart;
> Some may find our hearts unworthy—
> God looks only at the heart.
> God requires no polished praises;
> He looks for no special creed;
> Some may wonder at our stumbling—
> God looks only at the need.
> Aren't you glad that you're acquainted?
> He'll not think your language odd;
> Rest assured that He is knocking—
> Why not have a chat with God? J.M.B.

There's Something About The Kitchen

May 5
John 21:16
Psalm 139:7-9

There's something about a kitchen
Of which other rooms can't boast:
The scent of sweet yeast-rolls rising . . .
The brown of the Sunday roast . . .
Bright windows filled with petunias
That stand on tiptoe to see
Gingerbread men all surrounding
A freshly-brewed pot of tea . . .
Sparkle of well-scalded dishes,
Lined up in soldierly row,
Reflecting polka-dot curtains,
Starched ruffles of calico.
There's something about a kitchen
That unwinds taut springs of care—
A scented hustle-and-bustle
That begs contentment and prayer.   J.M.B.

ONLY THOSE who truly think of a kitchen as a laboratory of love can appreciate its pleasures. I believe that's the room where God and I have our best time together. We share the kitchen, with no self-consciousness. I like to sing while I cook—especially the old songs—and if I clap when I get carried away on "Give Me That Old-Time Religion," nobody notices.

Countless analogies arise in a kitchen. Can you think of God as the leavening in the rising bread? Can you see His hand stamping "Grade A, Number 1" on our meat as He did for Moses? Can you see new life in the constant renewal of annuals that bloom along your window sill? Can you think of yourself feeding His sheep as He commanded Simon? Then, you are very blest. You are serving God and your family. How easy, relaxed and natural it is to pray when one is performing a labor of love!

TO THINK AND PRAY ABOUT: Now, the wonder of it all is that while we homemakers are enjoying the company of God in our kitchens, others are enjoying it elsewhere.

Hands

HANDS ARE interesting things! Compositionwise, each human hand has twenty-seven unpronounceable bones, a palm, a thumb and four fingers. The proper bone-count in each digit is fourteen, jointed so as to allow flexing backward, forward and sideways. Tendons and muscles of the hand are interlaced and bound together by fibers which give the owner a unity of action. We can do heavy work by holding levers and spades. We can do delicate work by grasping a writing pen or an embroidery needle.

Yet the human hand (unlike that of the ape) is no organ of "normal locomotion." Rather, it is essentially an organ of touch. While hands can build or they can tear down—buildings, empires, lives—perhaps their greatest claim is their ability to "sense" objects with their nerve endings and to "communicate." "I love a hand that meets my own with a grasp that causes some sensation," wrote F.S. Osgood. Still, hands do more than that. Other parts of the body assist the speaker, but hands seem to have a language all their own. With them we question, promise, plead, dismiss, threaten, entreat and deprecate. With them we express fear, joy, sorrow and surprise. And with them, we say, "I doubt," "I believe" and "forgive me." Hands reach out in friendship. Hands clasp in prayer. It is a wonderful thing when they can do both!

TO THINK AND PRAY ABOUT:

God ever holds me in His hands—
This I have always known—
And with His hands to guide my steps,
I'm never quite alone.
Today I held God in my hands
Within a bright bouquet
Of freshly-gathered flowers
I picked and gave away.
I saw a face grow blossom-bright;
I saw a seldom-smile;
I felt the Hand of God reach out—
And shared it for a while. J.M.B.

I'm Thinking Of You

May 7
Proverbs 15:23

If, instead of a gem or even a flower, we could cast the gift of a lovely thought into the heart of a friend, that would be giving as the angels give. G. MacDonald

ONE OF THE nation's leading greeting card companies recently came out with a line of exquisitely illustrated cards with a single-sentence message: "I'm thinking of you today." Analyze the message and see if you agree that it says it all! Could there be a better example of an all-occasion card? To know you are thought about warms the insides like hot chocolate on a winter evening. It needs no sticky marshmallow on top; just being thought about is sweet enough.

A friend of mine likes cards better than flowers. She says she has no time to talk to plants and they just sit around and sulk. Another friend says people send her chocolates when she makes frequent trips to the hospital; and she is trying to lose weight. Personally, I am allergic to perfumes and colognes. As for gems, well, diamonds aren't a girl's best friend if her husband is having to pay. We all agreed that cards and letters are far more practical. Any gift is just a way of saying what the card says so simply: "I'm thinking of you."

As we chatted about the advantages of this particular card, we got around to values. Now, here is a card that covers any situation: it shares in times of happiness or sadness, on birthdays or the special occasions, and the cost is minimal. Why is it that people go so overboard to show feelings? On the other hand, how is is that we neglect to let others know we're thinking of them, even on ordinary days? Must loving concern be limited to special events? Sending a card is but one way to say, "I care." Perhaps a hand-written note would be even nicer. I like what Alice said. "I'm thinking of you" would be a nice way to open a telephone conversation. It involves the other person.

TO THINK AND PRAY ABOUT: Tell someone you care! And let God know you think of Him.

The Beauty Of Quiet Things

May 8
Psalm 46:10

Beauty lies in quiet things:
A first star in the blue,
The velvet-glow of twilight
When the day is through . . .
White lilacs in the springtime,
Wild roses in the snow;
Raindrops that tie a shower
Into a colored bow . . .
A sudden flash of color
That comes from beetle-wing;
A nest of baby robins
Before they learn to sing . . .
The zig-zag stitch of lightning
Before a summer storm;
Fall's cider-ready apples;
Fat loaves of bread, still warm . . .
A peach tree all in blossom
The pastel-pink of snow
When a winter sunrise
Sets white fields aglow . . .
Beauty lies in quiet things
And they are everywhere,
But we may fail to find them
Unless we pause for prayer. J.M.B.

POETRY IS more than flowing lines: It is the quiet between the words. And so it is with the human heart: it beats and rests, and then goes on with its flowing lines. We know we must be up and about our Father's business, but there must be moments of meditation if we are to do His business well. A heart that would be holy must be still . . . .

TO THINK AND PRAY ABOUT: Dear Lord, today is mine in terms of the five senses; it is Yours in an even greater sense. Thank you for the beauty of quiet things: in nature, in others and in You.

It's Time To Beat The Carpets!

May 9
Proverbs 31:27
Psalm 51:10

MAY WAS carpet-beating month at my grandmother's house. She waited for the "just-right" day and one always came along. One needed hot sun "to kill the winter germs," she said, "and strong wind to blow 'em away."

My grandfather always grumbled on those days as he impatiently claw-hammered the winter-rusty tacks from their moorings where the wainscoting of the parlor wall met the floor. "Women's work," he would mutter as he haunched on his knees and pried at the embedded carpet tacks. "You kids skadoodle!" he would roar as a bare foot struck near a saucer of tacks, sending them flying to hide in the cabbage-rose pattern of the rug. Actually, he had little reason to complain. Once the carpet was up (and he made good time with his temper in high gear), neither he nor my grandmother had any immediate problems left. Their two youngest sons and we two grandchildren took over.

Oh, what fun! Winter dirt flew in all directions, forming little whirlwinds. We had a variety of "beaters" from which to choose: stovewood, broom handles, butter paddles and bed slats. When it was all over, we were a mess; but the carpet when removed from the clothesline was brighter and more beautiful than the day my grandparents ordered it from the mail-order catalogue—in our eyes.

Our joy was even more complete as we rolled up and moved in the carpet that had exchanged its musty odor for the smell of sunshine and fresh air. We could feel its new life as the four of us rolled over and over to help hold the carpet flat while my grandparents replaced the tacks to make it fit snugly into the corners—in preparation for another winter.

Well, I will never hear my grandmother say, "It's time to beat the carpets!" again. That makes me sad—both because I have lost her and my childhood, but the memories last. There's a lesson in the springtime rug-beating. Now and then, it's good to roll out the walked-on carpets of our lives, shake out the dust left there by too many feet that trample on them and look at the beautiful pattern that God placed there to stay?

TO THINK AND PRAY ABOUT: Pray for a clean heart with a loving pattern!

A Day For Remembering . . .

ONE THING we all share in common is that each of us is blessed with a mother. Another is a private set of memories. Put the two together—and something beautiful emerges: Mother's Day!

Daddy always watched the rosebushes to make sure they remembered the date. There was a red one at the left side of our front-yard gate; a white at the right. "You are to bloom by the second Sunday in May!" he reminded them. I joyfully added "Amen." It seemed perfectly natural in our kind of family to talk to the flowers. We did it all the time—even before it became fashionable.

The moment of the "great pinning" (as I phrased it) was more solemn. It was customary for those whose mothers were living to wear a beautiful red rose pinned happily on the left shoulder. Those who had lost their mothers wore a lovely white one in memory of them. I had never known my paternal grandmother and it was a sad moment when my father pulled the thorny stem of a white rose through the buttonhole of his suit-coat. He must have known how I felt for he always hugged me tight after the pinning.

This year I will pin on my own red rose. My father is no longer here to do it for me . . . and I will do it in honor of both my parents. I will remember Anna Jarvis who worked so diligently to have a day set aside "dedicated to the memory of the best mother in the world—your own." I will thank God, who according to the old Jewish saying, "could not be everywhere at once and so He gave us mothers." And I will thank my own mother. Like Anna Jarvis said, she is the "best!"

TO THINK AND PRAY ABOUT: "Even He that died for us upon the cross, in the last hour, in the unutterable agony of death, was mindful of His Mother, as if to teach us that this holy love should be our last wordly thought—the point of earth from which the soul takes its flight for heaven." Longfellow

A Wilted Flower

May 11
Romans 8:32-39

ANYONE quoting "Beauty is in the eye of the beholder" must know Benny. Beauty in children is seldom orthodox. It is power needing to know itself; it is undirected strength needing a goal; it is a restlessness, a searching. These qualities make children special; a response is there somewhere if only the right challenge can be found. Response is beauty—and in beauty such as Benny's lies Truth.

Benny and I had never met until today. He saw me coming and leaned against a fireplug—waiting. He pretended to search the intersection in the consecrated way that says, "My friend will be along soon." Only I knew there wasn't any friend.

When I spoke to the little boy, he shyly returned my greeting and began walking with me. "See?" He showed me two wilting daisies.

"For your teacher, I imagine," I suggested. "Let's see, would that be Miss Brown? You must be in second grade?"

Benny's face flushed. "They're for somebody who loves me."

As we talked, I learned that the eight-year-old was new here. He had come to stay with his grandmother because "Mother and Daddy don't love each other anymore." I didn't know the circumstances. What was there to say? Sometimes a searching little fellow just needs to talk. "I won't be here long. Grandma's old—and she's poor—and nobody wants her either." *Oh, Benny, Benny, you're breaking my heart!* But "big guys" don't want to be hugged. "Benny, Somebody loves you," I said. I wondered, *"Do you know about God?"* I guess he did, for he thrust the flowers in my hand and said, "Then will you give Him these for me please?" And Benny was gone. The child had sensed a responsive chord in me; and I'd caught a glimpse of Beauty in two drooping daisies. I pressed them in my Bible.

TO THINK AND PRAY ABOUT: Today God sent two "unwanted people" into my life—one very young and heartbroken; the other very old and helpless. *How* can we help in a world that all too often doles "charity" without love? Tonight I read an anonymous quote which filled me with sadness: "Handing God a used-up life is like handing Him a wilted flower instead of a fresh bouquet." Time is a relevent thing. Let's share our time for the somebody who loves us.

Let Me Be First

"**I** WISH I'd said that!" It can be a touch of humor, bit of philosophy or soft word which "turneth away wrath." In the case of one particular couple, it's a man-and-wife game. She told us over a cup of coffee.

Maybe husbands would tease us wives less about our *klatches* if they knew we built them up in our conversation. We quote them widely and exchange the how-to's of our working relationships more often than recipes or rose cuttings. Gossip is a "no no" in our group—and that includes anything damaging, including the image of our mates.

The other morning Mary said, "You know, Joe and I have a contest every time we bicker." That drew no response. I guess the others assumed, as I did, that it was to see which could outshout the other. But we all perked up when she continued, "We try to see which one can be first to apologize!"

"The loser pays a forfeit," Mary told us, "which the winner gets to name. Joe keeps the kids while I have my hair done or he buys a fishing pole with the 'mad money' I've saved for BETTER HOMES AND GARDENS."

I don't know if the others were as turned on as I, but a number of practical ideas came out of that session for me—ideas for improving my relationships with others as well as my marriage. My excitement grew as Flo said, "You're right. Apologizing to Tom made me feel really little till I saw how big I looked in his eyes!" And Emile summed up her feeling this way: "I keep telling Fred I give him my best years because he's the one who makes them best!" Just "girl talk"? Rather significant, it seems to me.

Recently an editor invited me to do a little piece on "How I've Survived a Marriage." I wish I'd known about Mary and Joe's game. I think I might have written: "Surviving a marriage is like surviving any other encounter; always be first to say 'I'm sorry' when you're wrong."

TO THINK AND PRAY ABOUT: Is it difficult for you to apologize to your family? Friends? Strangers whom you may have offended? How important is forgiveness?

"I WONDER IF I can finish this job before the bank closes . . . It's almost lunch time . . . What will I have for dinner? . . . My husband's late . . . He's never been this late without calling . . . The phone! . . . Is he all right?"

"No lunch problem . . . George won't be home for lunch . . . and he's taking me out for dinner . . . this job's almost finished . . . I *can* get to the bank on time . . . Oh, I'm thankful for telephones!"

I paused for breath and laid my shears aside. The silence was like a noise—and suddenly I realized that a steady chop-chop on the other side of our fence had stopped, too. "Are you all right?" The voice of my neighbor asked in concern.

"Oh, fine! And right on schedule." I called back. We do that all the time—chat back and forth—in a faceless sort of style. Her voice is dearly familiar. I need not see her face.

"I thought I heard talking. Do you have company?"

Would she laugh, I wonder, if I said, "Yes, God is here."

It all began a long time ago, my little chats with God. Maybe some of it was due to my being an only child in need of a playmate. Maybe the practice sprang from my forming a strong friendship with God through my parents, my grandparents and my Sunday school teachers. Most likely it was a combination. At any rate, I found a "secret pal." I say *secret* because I was afraid then (as now) of being thought of as "different," if not downright in the "off-ox" category. I remembered "Old Aunt Jane," the spinster (back when ladies were "supposed to get married"), who kept up a constant flow of talk to herself. The children all laughed, and even the adults said indulgently, "Oh, well, as long as she doesn't answer herself!" I do *both*. Only that's not the way it is. Actually, I am telling God my problems—and repeating His reassurances. I have yet to have a prayer unanswered.

TO THINK AND PRAY ABOUT: "Whatever comes my way, give me the strength to bear it." Answer: "I will."

A Touch-Up Or A Bleach?

May 14
Matthew 7:3-5

"By common consent gray hairs are a crown of glory; the only object of respect that can never excite envy."   Bancroft

HOW MUCH the hair stylist knew about Bancroft or Paul's idea of a woman's "crowning glory," I have no idea. All I needed was a haircut—until her experienced fingers lifted my "damaged" locks. I heard the barely audible sigh, just loud enough for me to get the subtle hint that my hair was a mess. "Just a trim." This time I intended to remain firm. I have been intimidated so many times.

"Oh, yes, we do need a trim," the young operator said in the tone a patron learns to recognize when there's more to come. "I was checking the white streaks. I do believe we should re-bleach the frosting. It is so becoming!"

"I do believe we should not," I told the helpful girl. "Nature takes care of that for us." (Just why the two of us were using first-person-plural mystified me since the young thing's hair was chrysanthemum-bronze.)

She gasped. "You mean it's *gray*, not frosted? Oh, no! Then we must do a touch-up. Now, we can look ten years younger with a chestnut touch-up . . . ."

Well, I suppose that is how most beauty operators earn their daily bread. They must assume that we women are dissatisfied with ourselves.

"We want a haircut—no more and no less." *We* meant George and his wife. I'm fortunate, for George agrees with Bancroft and Paul.

Driving home, I kept thinking of the hair incident. Am I guilty of forever trying to touch up the lives of my friends—when my suggestions are unsought; my advice, unwelcome? Do I look for a "wicked streak" and try to force a bleach—knowing that only God can whiten; and I should be searching out the good?

TO THINK AND PRAY ABOUT: Let your life be the witness as you tell others of the qualities of God, and leave the decisions to them. Pressure is unwise.

Bless Me With Endurance, Lord

BLESS ME *with endurance, Lord*. Today I won a battle by losing—and I am filled with the joy of victory. I wanted to lash out at the rude man who pulled into the parking space for which I was waiting. Instead, I pulled up to give him more room. At first the driver looked puzzled; I think his life is "an eye for an eye." I saluted and moved into the traffic—leaving a bit of You there. This I know, for he waved. But can I "lose" each time I face a trivial situation? Lord, with Your help, I can.

Bless me with endurance, Lord. Today I was a peacemaker, reconciling two friends at variance over one's dog which had chewed its leash and scratched up the sprouting peas of the other. It meant taking a risk, and for a while I thought they would direct their wrath on me. Can I take such a risk tomorrow if the same dog commits the same transgression? Lord, with Your help, I can.

Bless me with endurance, Lord. Today I helped ten "needy" people who called on me (I know the number because I counted the rings of distress). One wanted a telephone number Information could have supplied; another, the recipe that appeared in last night's paper . . . a missing hamster . . . a wife who thinks her husband's love is cooling . . . You know the rest. Can I listen again while my cookies burn and my perma-press clothes wrinkle in the dryer? Lord, with Your help, I can.

Bless me with endurance, Lord. Today I served in a real emergency! I administered first aid to the child of a friend. The broken water glass severed an artery. I tied a tourniquet—even though I thought I'd forgotten how and the sight of blood made me sick. Can I serve like that again—even when I know I'll throw up afterwards? Lord, with Your help, I can.

Bless me with endurance, Lord. Today I kept a firm leash on the animal of rage within me. Can I be this gentle again when someone is unkind? Lord, with Your help, I can.

Bless me with endurance, Lord. Let me make tracks that others can follow, because I have followed Your footsteps. And, Lord, with Your help, I can!

ICUPPED THE magic flower in my hands. Flowers may be the most beautiful things the Great Gardener created and failed to bless with souls. As I stood there, holding the golden Star of Morning, I became thoughtful. God gives me the ability to place a bit of my soul inside the flower. At first it was just a morning-thought, such as I am accustomed to indulging in when I look into the face of something so beautiful. As the day drew to a close, I knew I was right.

The miracle of a day lily is that it lasts for one day only. A single blossom glazes on a slender stalk. Star of the Morning is my favorite and they come out like scented stars—a whole galaxy of them, each seeming somehow to know to appear just when its predecessor stops shining. But today's was special—the first of the season.

Alone, for a sweet stolen moment, I closed my eyes and used L.M. Child's words (committed to memory) as a prayer: "How the universal heart of man blesses flowers! They are wreathed 'round the cradle, the marriage altar and the tomb. They should deck the brow of the youthful bride, for they are in themselves a lovely type of marriage. They should twine 'round the tomb, for their perpetually renewed beauty is a symbol of the Resurrection. They should festoon the altar, for their fragrance and beauty ascend in perpetual worship before the Most High."

I was a mortal—caught up in a moment of immortality—until the telephone rang. *Let it ring; I don't want to be interrupted. Oh, I must!* The wonderful lady on the line would last but a little while longer. Young, yes, but with terminal cancer . . . still conscious . . . but . . . with tears in my eyes I plucked the lily. It, too, could last but one day, but it could share "my soul."

TO THINK AND PRAY ABOUT: Can you let go of something—or someone—precious, placing the gift in the hands of God? We each hold private miracles in our hands each day; but they, like the day lilies, fade unless they are shared.

cA Little White Lie

TODAY I told a "little white lie" and I feel terrible. After-which we had to have a conversation, the three of us: I, myself and me. *I* said, "You harmed nobody. You protected a friend. *Myself* (my *real* self) was less cunning, "You harmed *you*. You did not protect a friend. You protected you." *Me* (always on the defensive) piped up, "You weren't lying—not really—you just didn't tell the whole story." *Myself (Oh, Self, I am often proud of you!)* replied, "The holding back of truth can be just as deceptive as an untruth!" Finally the three of us became a trilogy of conscience, that piece of God placed inside my heart that determined: "There is no 'little lie' and if there were, would it be *white?* Untruth can be a falsehood; or untruth can be a silence." How easy to be deceived!

Well, I must right the wrong. The words of a certain college professor helped diagnose my case a little. More than that, they led me to a biblical prescription for a cure. "Man is never so free as when he realizes he is not free at all," the man said. That made no sense to me, until he went on to give an example. "Now, if a person is allergic to eggs and doesn't know, the allergy can finish him off. When he finds out by a series of tests, he then avoids eggs in the diet. This person is then free—more free than when he was unaware that the allergy existed." I have been tested.

I turned to today's Scripture reading and reread Paul's assurances. "My grace is sufficient for thee." God will forgive me; so will my friend; for, yes, I must tell her. I may be tempted to gloss over: "You know, yesterday I forgot to tell the rest . . ." I did not forget. I must say, "Yesterday I lacked the courage to tell you . . ." Why? Because Paul went on to say: "My strength is made perfect in weakness . . . for when I am weak, then I am strong." I feel a sense of freedom.

TO THINK AND PRAY ABOUT: Can you recall situations in which you felt a healing through awareness of a righted wrong?

Sounds Of A Happy Marriage

May 18
Psalm 15:1
Psalm 19:1-3

THE WEEKEND guests are gone. I feel both elated—and deflated. Elated? Yes, because we had such a wonderful, wonderful time. One of the many advantages of long friendships is the laughter that threads the silver with gold. "Do you remember . . . ?" one of the four of us would begin—and the remembering would double us up in laughter . . . Just one of the sounds of a happy marriage, theirs and ours: Bacher-Miller.

But I feel deflated, too. It is sad parting with friends. When will we meet again? Or *will* we? For we know life here is a transient thing. We *know* God will bring us together again. What we do not know is whether it will be a warm embrace here or hereafter. Either way, we agree, there will be laughter. We think God likes happy sounds, too . . . the laughter of June and George, Lucke and Bob, friends for forty years!

I should be changing the linens, putting away the silver and checking my grocery supply. Instead I sit quietly by the window adoring my husband as he swings back into routine by mowing the lawn. I wonder if I have smeared my mascara—and I smear it some more as I realize George is crying, too. The happy sound of the lawnmower lifts my spirits. It is a busy sound. It is a *doing* sound that does not wait for the Kingdom of God, but finds it in the heart.

I remember the countless happy sounds of our marriage, and I thank God as I try to count them (which is as futile as counting the stars) . . . The shy "I do" at the altar . . . The sound of the hammer as George nailed our first house together . . . The squeals of joy our son let out when he received his first bike . . . The gentle patter of rain on a a well-shingled roof . . . The perk of the morning coffee . . . The thoughtful ring of the telephone, "I'll be a little late, Sweetie" . . . The "Wow! Mother, you look weirdo in that dress" . . . The church bells ringing out "When We All Get to Heaven" . . . And our hearing with the heart . . . for that's our meeting place with loved ones.

TO THINK AND PRAY ABOUT: Praise God for friends, memories and His promises.

Children Are Our Buttercups

"THERE'S treasure in the trees!" I told my excited group of third-grade children. It was one of those bright May days when the sun has the same healing effect on nature after a long winter as a long walk has on me after a bout with the flu. I found the four walls inadequate to hold my attention—let alone theirs! I had heard of a rare moss that clings tenaciously to the oak trees close by the school. It's shy stuff because it seems to know that it belongs back in the Evangeline countryside. Somebody "transplanted" it here (unbeknownst to the officials at the inspection stations). It's a sort of parasite, I guess, and probably quite damaging to our type of trees. But why not take advantage of its presence and study samples beneath a microscope? We had been studying plant life—*and* oh, what a morning!

Once past the clutter of broken bottles and beer cans, we took a nature trail that led past a meandering brook, banked with moss and spring beauties. The ferns reached high enough to tempt my flock to games of hide-and-seek! I kept reminding them where the treasures lay, but each time another sun-touched head would duck behind the clumps of temptation.

We walked and we walked until at last we were nearing the end of the grove. The children were tired and their necks ached. It was near-noon and we had brought no lunches. Doggedly, I urged them on, letting them one-by-one look through George's binoculars. It seemed very important to me that we find the elusive pineapple moss—even though I knew the day was losing some of its sheen for the little people.

Suddenly, I was startled to hear one of them sobbing. "What is it, Robin?" I asked, wiping her damp cheeks.

"All the time we've been looking for this silly moss, we've been walking on the buttercups!" I gave Robin a thank-you hug and said, "We'll go a-mossing some other day. Let's look down at the beauties below as we whoop it up going back for lunch!"

TO THINK AND PRAY ABOUT: Do you sometimes busy yourself with "parasites" and miss the natural things God gives us? Pause, kneel and see the world as a child sees it—down low. Children are our buttercups. Don't step on them!

Ask Not How Long

May 20
John 16:16
16:20

THIS IS the busy-happy time of year when mothers hurry daughters to "Shops for the Young," and fathers say, "Son, isn't it time we thought of your future?" This is the time when student contests abound; and teachers, weary of unsnarling shoestrings and grammar, wonder where the young get their energy. It's near graduation time.

The ceremony can only be a milepost, for "out there" lies another beginning. For those who have reached a saturation point, it can be a rest or the end. In any event, education should be a way of life as opposed to a destination. Graduation (at any level) is a stepping-stone.

A grinning little guy named Willie left a sparkle greater than some who live to maturity. The immigrant son of a Filipino family, the boy was small for his age, but he had big dreams. No amount of practice was too much for the would-be basketball player. Wanting good grades was less of a problem, as he had a great mind. Even more, he possessed a bubbly personality which led his friends to call him "super" and his teachers to call him "superior." He cared so much he inspired his entire junior high.

His promotion ceremony was a testimonial of love. The day before, Willie sat up late memorizing every word of the polished speech he was to deliver—a speech which would be delivered by a friend: "We formally challenge sixth graders to uphold good scholastic achievements and citizenship. We hope next year's class will be proud of our school . . . and keep up the spirit. . . ." The voice of the speaker faltered and the principal rose to announce that little Willie had died the night before—suddenly. "We thank God," the administrator said, "for giving him to us for eleven and a half years."

TO THINK AND PRAY ABOUT:
Ask not how long
  But how well spent each swiftly flying minute;
"This is the day which God has made;
  Rejoice and be glad in it." J.M.B.

Virtues That Are Timeless

READING THE article, I heard imagined strains of "The Overture to William Tell," otherwise known as "Hi ho, Silver!" The Lone Ranger wore a white hat; I knew this even before TV when I listened to the original radio series. He was the good guy who chased outlaws who wore black hats. He was the masked man, for me as well as my son, who overcame evil with good. Now I know the key was more than the silver bullet—the hero always left with those whom he anonymously befriended.

The article listed "The Lone Ranger's Success Formula." The thoughts were noble then; they are noble now in a changing world. I pasted the words on the refrigerator. Maybe my family will read it. The Lone Ranger believes in:

Religion: The right to worship God in individual ways. Visualized as a Protestant, his confidants are Tonto (Indian) and the Catholic Padre;

Tolerance: The acceptance of other races through an Indian companion;

Fairness: Advocates American Tradition, which gives each person the right to choose a life work and profit in proportion to effort;

Patriotism: Love of country meant more than flag-waving and answering the call of war; it included aiding churches, serving community, preserving law and order, and maintaining a home for bringing up good citizens.

Sympathy: Chooses the side of the oppressed in need of help; demonstrates a strong man can be tender; the Lone Ranger is ever-forgiving.

TO THINK AND PRAY ABOUT: This bare-bone outline of the lengthy article shows a private set of Beatitudes which advocates high moral convictions: never utilizing sex, gore or brutality; never elevating criminals; and never implying that "Crime *does* pay." While he left us no silver bullet, he befriended us with these standards. Do you see a parallel with the standards in today's reading? Some virtues are timeless. Perhaps that accounts for the Lone Ranger reruns. Do you suppose his creators knew our Creator? Pray for the preservation of good.

Brighten The Corner

CHARMING AS the young hostess' rambling ranch-style home was, it somehow looked cold and uninviting inside. Guests were milling around at the housewarming—chatting, admiring and dropping cashew nuts on the off-white carpet. Our hostess seemed less concerned with the grease spots than what she called "the house's lack of personality. The floor's fine; but the rest is too blue and brown."

The young bride was among friends and felt comfortable discussing her disappointment. "This corner is dark. Right?" she asked.

Someone suggested it should have had a window. "We just can't go through that again—the house all finished and everything."

"A mirror would pick up the outside view." She warmed up to that. "Of course! The waterfall, ferns, jasmine—" Her eyes measured the wall.

She led us through the diningroom. "Somehow the ceiling lights just don't show the mellow wood. They look harsh even with the soft-light bulbs. It needs sunshine. As a matter of fact, it seems to me that every corner in the house needs sunshine."

"I'm no interior decorator—but—candles?" I ventured. She brightened. "How practical! Almost no investment. And just the right touch!"

Funny thing about corners and colors. Corners seem forever dark. I suspect there's a little dark corner in the heart of every human being. I always think of corners as brown or blue-toned—not dramatic browns or blues one feels, just dull and depressing. I read somewhere that there are more than 6,000 shades of color the eye can sort out and that half are browns and blues. With a light reflecting here and there they can change into soothing hues—pleasing to the eye, refreshing to the spirit. And so it is with little deeds we spread, I found myself thinking. Just add a mirror for reflecting glory; or light a candle to chase gloom.

TO THINK AND PRAY ABOUT: Brighten whatever corner you are in. Maybe a face is hidden by the shadows!

Nancy's Prayer

May 23
Matthew 18:19-20

I HAD A problem. Oh, not a big economy-sized one, but even a trial-size problem can interrupt the normal flow of joyful days. I dislike being too busy, too encumbered, too hyperactive-of-mind or too preoccupied with wrong things. Such a mood borrows of my creativity, tugs at my conscience, steals away my side-by-side feeling with neighbors and friends and breeches my oneness with God. I am like trodden grass, a bruised leaf, a barren bush . . . in need of rain to restore color and force.

Beautiful is overworked in today's vocabulary, but it is the only adjective that surfaces when I think of Nancy. Oh, it has to do with complexion, hair and hands—all the qualities which constitute loveliness; but it goes beneath the skin. Her beauty springs from inside—a way she looks at me, listening with her eyes and heart. I can sense that look even on the telephone.

"I need advice again, Nancy." I guess my voice told her I had a wrinkled soul. A friend has the restoration power of a spring shower!

"Tell me." Her voice was quiet as if to say, "I have all the time in the world to listen." She has a husband, two children, a big house and yard. She writes at her home. She helps her husband at their place of business . . . I must not keep her, although nothing in her tone made me feel guilty. There are people like that—people God sends our way.

I got to the problem and just as quickly she got to the solution. That's another nice quality Nancy has. She does not play games with indirect counseling. She never gives advice until a friend asks for it. A friend *not* in need had best ask somebody else!

"I've been there," she said when I finished. "Now, just write a letter explaining. I *know* that's the way to handle it, but I'll consult my brother (he's a lawyer)—what's more, I'll say a prayer. *You* forget it."

She advised and prayed. I wrote and prayed. Today the response came by way of a letter which resolved the matter. But our *answer* had come earlier—when, simultaneously, we put the matter in God's hands.

TO THINK AND PRAY ABOUT: Thank the Lord for helpful, praying friends.

Some Day I'll Be A Grandmother!

May 24
Psalm 39:7
Titus 3:7

MAYBE SOME DAY I'll be a grandmother! Most mothers experience that same expectation—that total (wonderful) feeling of *Hope* . . . Someday I'll be a grandmother!

I haven't decided whether I will have a granddaughter who looks like me or a grandson who looks like my husband. Children do, so I hear, skip a generation in the genes they choose. Either way I will enter the nursery that is dearly familiar, but I will wear a new face—that of a guest! And I shall put Browning's poem in past tense when I whisper to George: "I'm glad you grew old along with me! The best is yet to be!"

Together we can count the ten fat toes, unconcerned that we interrupted a nap. We can tickle and tease the feet that kick with the joy of wakefulness—for they are not ours to teach to walk; they are ours to enjoy, to race with, to skip with, to dance with . . . someday.

Together we can lift the squirming teddy-bear and bounce him/her on our laps. We can let the pink fingers twine in our hair—for the fingers are not ours to teach to hold a spoon or reach for "right" things in life; they are ours to smother with kisses and to slip lollipops into . . . someday.

Together we will discover a new relationship—that of being the "older generation," a generation that is wiser than it has been since it was in its teens! We will rediscover each other in helping our grandchild discover the first star of evening, Mother Goose and birthday cakes with too much frosting—for education and a balanced diet are not ours to cope with. We will play games of the imagination and indulge (alas!) our grandchild's first tooth with unforbidden sweets . . . someday.

Together we will be more patient—less concerned with the little things, more concerned about the great ones: seeking no perfection, asking only the perfection which God supplies . . . someday. For we have learned from our parents and from our son—the true meaning of Hope.

TO THINK AND PRAY ABOUT: Lord, it is pleasant to Hope in the future, but let us place our Hope in you above all else.

The Aching Tooth Of Wisdom

May 25
I Kings 3:5; 4:29
II Chronicles 1:7

MY MOTHER and I had such fun yesterday! It was just like "the way we were then"—back in the days when she used to tell me stories about Solomon's wisdom and some of the wise decisions the peaceful king of Israel made. He prayed for wisdom, and my mother told me, he became the wisest man in the world. The Bible substantiates her claim. God gave him insight.

I was helping her run down some reference material for a presentation on wisdom she was making to her Sunday school class. The very first quote (Rochefoucauld) reminded me of a baby-tooth incident: "Wisdom is to the mind what health is to the body." We burst out laughing, remembering my front tooth that hung by less than a tap-root, which neither she nor I had the courage to yank. Finally, Daddy (her "Solomon," she called him) tied a string around the aching tooth, inquired gently, "Have you asked Mama if we're going to church tonight?" and slammed the door around whose knob he'd suspended the other end of the string. Out came the tooth—exposing a gap in front; exposing, also, my mother hiding behind the door. We never became Solomon-wise, but we learned a lot that day.

TO THINK AND PRAY ABOUT: "What is it to be wise? 'Tis but to know how little can be known—to see all others' faults and feel our own." Pope.

"Our chief wisdom consists in knowing our follies and faults, that we may correct them." Tillotson

"God gives men wisdom as He gives them gold; His treasure house is not the mint, but the mind." Arabic

"He who learns the rules of wisdom without conforming to them in his life is like a man who ploughs in his field but does not sow." Saadi

"The wise man is also the just, the pious, the upright, the man who walks in the way of truth. The fear of the Lord, which is the beginning of wisdom, consists in complete devotion to God." Zochler

A Broken Hammer And A Mended Heart

May 26
Proverbs 19:18
Revelation 3:19

JUST WHY a little girl of three would want a hammer (particularly one with a broken handle) is something only a little girl of three would understand. But to me it was a thing of beauty—"a hammer just like Daddy's," except it fit my hand. I remember thinking happily that he and I would build a doll house for me, a birdhouse for him and a window box for my mother's geraniums—maybe even a wagon big enough for our family of three to ride in on Sunday afternoons . . . .

I was visiting with the little girl next-door, a few years older than I, as I recall. She was trying very hard to teach me to play jacks, but my young fingers were less dexterous than hers. The rubber ball bounced too high and lodged behind a trunk. It was while I was struggling to move the piece of furniture, which refused to budge, that I spied the magic tool. I squealed with delight, but my friend only shrugged. "It's broken," she said as she shoved the trunk aside and recovered the ball.

It was unbelievable, but she didn't want the hammer. Well, I did. Daddy could fix it up like new. I'd watched him replace broken handles on his tools. I would take it—and I did. There was only one problem: I didn't want my friend to know I took it. Actually, there were two problems: I felt guilty!

My mother was watching as I returned when my half-hour's stay ended. She knew I had a way of chasing butterflies and missing the yard gate. I remember a look of reproach in her eyes when I strolled up the walk, with the hammer behind me. "It's broke," I said defensively. "Anyway, nobody saw me take it." That told the story, of course.

I will always remember the way Mama handled the situation. She put me on her lap and told me about other people's property rights in a language I understood. Then, gently, she said: "God saw you." Her tone of voice said God wasn't angry, but it also told me that I must return what did not belong to me. Only after we'd returned the "taken" item (she avoided "stolen") did she and Daddy buy me a new one all my own!

TO THINK AND PRAY ABOUT: Children learn so young, don't they? I was only three, but I learned a lesson without seeing God as a Spy-in-the-Sky. I'm thankful!

Giveaway Time!

May 27
II Corinthians 9:6-11

WHEN SUMMER'S garden abundance goes beyond our daily needs, it's "giveaway time." At least, that's the way it is with my neighbor, Arlene. She has a "floriferous hand" with flowers; her three children have eight "green thumbs" with garden things; and her husband has "fruitful fingers" with the fleshy fruits. Their place is a Garden of Eden. There's always something to share.

When Arlene telephoned this morning, I asked, "What's cooking?" I intended no pun (their name's Cook!), but she laughed heartily anyway. She shares her laughter, too.

"Do me a favor," she begged. "Help me use up these plums and peaches." A favor? But that's the way she is: kindness itself—walking backwards.

So this evening we will have a wonderful meal of homemade goodness, *a la Cook*. So will everyone else within reach by telephone (including long distance). "I grow enough for the Cavalry—including the horses," Arlene admits. And the outstanding thing about my friend's giving is that she has food for sojourners. So many have food—but not for the strangers. That includes the "wetbacks" that use the hills behind our houses as a way of entry without the formalities of the Border Patrol. She's just too charitable to refuse them food; but "He who does not work shall not eat." She sends them shinnying up ladders to help harvest, serves them a square meal, then says, "Get back over that hump where you belong and enter through the right door!" They get—both ways.

TO THINK AND PRAY ABOUT: What do you share—and with whom? Do you include the needy? Do you cheer your friends with flowers, forgetting the friendless in the hospitals? For a wonderful experience, check with a receptionist at a local hospital and see if you can find a patient who has no family. Chances are that the person will be without friends, too. Share what you have—and you *do* have something: a smile, a hand or a word from God. Make every day a "giveaway" day!

Tell Me I Am Beautiful

May 28
Psalm 23: 5
Psalm 44:21

SHELLY'S mother came to see me near the end of the school year.

"What *is* the trouble with this child?" There was real concern in the sable-brown eyes—so like her daughter's, except her's smiled and Shelley's did not. "Tell me truly, is she happy here?"

Happy? I was unable to answer the question. The child was preoccupied, seemingly lost in thought, and either by choice or circumstance she seemed to have few friends. "She's so different from Sarah, who's all bounce. She just daydreams—or pouts—whichever it is," her mother went on.

All children are different, I wanted to say; but wouldn't that be pointing out the obvious? She needed an answer; and all I could offer at the moment were questions. *Do you not see her as God's gift to guard?*

"Tell me about her at home," I suggested, teacher-like.

The young mother sighed, which, I suspected, was the mannerism she used in giving any account of a daughter whose behavior displeased her. "She was born frowning, I do believe! Her face is always long. We try to make her smile every way we know. Why I remember she was so sober even in the nursery her father said, 'Hello, Ugly'!"

Jolted, my mind flashed back to myself at eight. Every night I prayed: "Dear God, make me beautiful so people will love me . . ." And I gave all the details as to how I should look, choosing the best features of every movie queen I knew. Little did I know then that it worked the other way around: *We are beautiful because God made us so. Others can make us feel more so.*

I silently plead with my husband even now—"Don't tell me I look young (for not all young things are lovely or old ones ugly!) Just tell me I am beautiful. God made me so." And he does. "I love you," he says.

Getting back to the parent, I said, "Try saying, 'Hello, Beautiful'!" And I hope she added, "We love you. God loves you too."

TO THINK AND PRAY ABOUT: Make others feel like the beautiful creation God made them to be.

To Love Many Things

IAM BLISSFULLY tired tonight. Was God exhausted when He completed our world on the sixth day? I doubt it, but I think He experienced the same bliss I feel when He looked upon Creation and said, "It is good." Van Gogh suggested, "I think the best way to know God is to love many things." That's what I have been doing as the month draws to a close—feasting my eyes on the many good things of God's good earth and loving them all. *Lord, it has been a beautiful day, filled with blessings others may have overlooked.*

The air was dreamy with clustered smells of orange blossoms—pure, pearly and virgin-white as a bridal veil, so bright they lit the dusk. I picked an armful, brought them inside and the house became like a scented cathedral. I listened to the organ-tones of the tree toads and heard the crickets tune their fiddles for the night. I walked gingerly between the volunteer peas, waxy with blooms and drooping with enough pods for the evening meal. And, yes, there was a mint leaf, just the right touch for bringing out their flavor. A scented "Ouch!" of protest came from the little herb when I trampled its bed. *That's what I mean, Lord, when I say we overlook the small things You would have us enjoy.*

I heard the knife-blade sharpness of a youngster diving into our neighbor's pool. I tingle with remembered excitement of that first plunge of spring in my childhood. The cattle pool was less sparkling, but it was unchlorinated and the breathless shock was just as great as the buoyant feel of surfacing. Each plunge was like a spring baptismal to me. *Thank You, Lord, for the memory.*

The sky is now a dipper full of stars. They light the universe with a jeweled smile from Heaven—so beautiful I find myself wondering if they dropped from Your Throne. *Lord, let me look up, as well as down when I walk; and let me look forward as well as backward—expecting another beautiful tomorrow.*

TO THINK AND PRAY ABOUT: If the many lovely things came only once in a lifetime, would you appreciate them more? Love them daily and thank God.

Memorial Day

MEMORIAL DAY, as I knew it, was Decoration Day, a day to remember all who had died, but especially those who had given their lives for their country. "Back home" in the southern states we observed the day at varying times—depending on crops or weather conditions. I remember some dates as early as April; some in May, of course; and occasionally the observances spilled over into the month of June. It was a joyful time for me, frankly. The little communities which polka-dotted our state put their collective heads together and planned Decoration Day on different Sundays so we could all get together—again and again. I'm sure now that the arrangement was for the benefit of those who had loved ones in the scattered cemeteries; but, for me, it was a series of heydays. Men with white shirts and sweating faces cleared the mounds. Ladies in wide-brimmed hats or sunbonnets unloaded trunks of chicken-dumplings and peach cobbler. Young couples strolled among the oak trees . . . while we little ones gave way to the sheer joy of being alive.

I remember recitations of patriotic poems by awkward-age boys; songs by giggling older girls who, without a piano accompaniment, confused the sharps and flats of the old hymns, and solemn readings of passages of the Scriptures by ministers who looked as wilted as the flowers on the graves. I remember a ritual called "Winding of the Memorial Rose," usually performed for a public official (up for re-election). He entwined a headstone of his choosing with the trailing vine of fragrant roses . . . and I remember vaguely someone's saying that our President was laying a wreath on the grave of the "Unknown Soldier" in Arlington Cemetery. That was too far away to be significant—then. It's closer now, because we've shrunk our nation with travel. And, yet, ironically, we were "closer" then.

Memorial Day begs us to stop taking our blessings for granted. We are heirs to a heritage because of the visions and dreams of our Pilgrim forefathers, our pioneers and our consecrated servicemen.

TO THINK AND PRAY ABOUT: Praise God for our liberty. He, too, gave a Son.

May 31
Hebrews 13:8

THE ARRIVAL and departure of a season is often unexpected or rather surprising. If we found a season one place last year, we look in vain to find it there the next. But we are unable to set a trap for anything so cunning. It never walks in its own tracks. One day it is the chirping sparrow of spring; the next, it is the graceful white-winged swan of summer.

The calendar tells us today that tomorrow will be June. The world is wet with April's rain and dusky with May's purple lilacs; and sometimes there is no sign of the first June rose. But soon the month will set itself on course. Dawns will come fresh and sweet; noons will sparkle in tranquility; and twilights will bring baskets of sudden bloom. Unpredictable as summer's arrival may be, we know with a certain certainty that it will be here because God has given us His promise of the cycle of the seasons. We accept this promise as we accept all the other good promises He makes, both in this world and the world to come. This we do because of faith.

As I turned my calendar, noting a certain spring chill, I remembered how our son used to ask, "But how do we know summer will come this year?" It was simple to point out the signs to a small child. Are our lives signs to an unsaved world pointing the way to the Savior? I made a list of questions which I plan to refer to daily with the beginning of the new month. Would you like to join me?

TO THINK AND PRAY ABOUT: Do I show tranquility in time of stress? Do I perform at least one daily service for which I know there will be no reward? Do I take my problems to God? Do I watch for "situations" that threaten to blow up into real "problems" and try to head them off? Do I keep an open, charitable mind? Am I willing to listen and learn from others? Am I a person with whom others feel comfortable? Do I love my family and friends—and tell them so?

Lord, teach me to love as You have loved us. Let my life reflect the certainty of the faith in my heart. Amen.

Today's Promises

TODAY'S SUN, nearing its summer solstice, sends the promised warmth of June. A promise fulfilled is a wonderful thing. I remember my childhood as a succession of promise-fulfilled days because my parents made life so worth looking forward to. I lived in a state of anticipation of holidays, Sunday school programs or Grandmother's visits. Suddenly I would awaken with a spine-tingling awareness: *Today is the day!* Each day, as we marked our calendar, happiness had put out a new leaf of expectancy. Finally the bloom of reality came. That childhood way of life has remained a permanent source of strength, putting down roots of hope for the joy of fulfillment.

The Bible, too, is a succession of promises. The prophets of the Old Testament knew the importance of expecting God to fulfill each one. God promised life on earth and placed a bow in the sky. He promised eternal life and sent his Son. When the angels announced the birth of the King, the shepherds must have rejoiced: *Today is the day!* It was the season of joy.

As Christians we have hope through the fulfillment of that promise. But the world remains overpopulated with people who are unaware that hope can be theirs. God is a stranger wanting to meet them.

This June first is but a fleeting moment—a transition between the joy of yesterday and the hope of tomorrow. So while the sun is high I will sow a few seeds of the joy that is mine. God will nurture them to a sweeter fruition than my expectations. I can begin by introducing myself to the new neighbors I see moving in across the street—today. Perhaps one day I can introduce them to their King.

TO THINK AND PRAY ABOUT: What promises did God make in today's Scripture reading? How do they show His concern for us? Can you make promises that will bring rainbows into the lives of others?

Keep The World Beautiful

ONE DEWDROP clings to a honeysuckle bloom. In the brilliance of the early-morning sun, the single droplet reflects the whole world in a prism of colors—unblemished as in the sixth day of Creation. How beautiful the world must have been: dewdrop fresh and honeysuckle-sweet. God created the world as a leafy bower for us to enjoy. He gave us dominion over the Garden and all inside it: the plants, the animals and all that was good.

June is one of the summer vacation months, a time to enjoy our world. My neighbors are packing their trailer in preparation for a trip to the hills. They plan a "house exchange" with some mountain-dwelling friends. My uncle and his wife plan a Caribbean cruise, a nice change from his desert abode; while nearby Palm Springs resorts find more and more guests registering at the winter haven because of reduced rates. Vacations are for rests. A complete change of scenery can be a restful experience. I am sure God would like to have us see and enjoy the handiwork of his entire footstool.

In planning your retreat, think of some ways you can help to keep the world beautiful. As you make your lists for food rations, wearing apparel and survival kits, add a list of precautions: the "do's" of guarding the forests, the "don'ts" of littering, etc., depending upon the area of your getaway. This way we can all help protect our natural resources. And remember we are God's most precious resources, so watch for such signs as "Children at Play" and "Drive Carefully"; read warning signals—and pray. One day there will be a new heaven and a new earth. One day there will be a new body . . . until then, let us keep God's premises fresh and cared for.

TO THINK AND PRAY ABOUT: Discuss vacation plans. How do you plan to continue your devotionals while you are away from your home and your church?

Whom God Has Joined Together

June 3
Romans 8:31-39
Matthew 19:4-6

RECENTLY A wedding we attended left a lasting impression. After being pronounced man and wife, the newlyweds embraced. Immediately turning from the altar, the bride went to her parents and kissed each of them as the groom did the same to his mother and father. Then, touchingly, the young couple crisscrossed and greeted their "new parents"—symbolically bringing together the two families.

The quest, the individual choice, the pledges—even the happily-ever-after—could make beautiful our earthly relationships with family, friends and strangers. The tender promises, nurtured and fulfilled, can lead to the here-and-hereafter relationship with God and our fellowmen, which even death lacks power to part.

How? Bob Hammond (From the "Voice of China and Asia" Radio Program) shared a poem entitled, "On This Day":

> Mend a quarrel.
> Search out a forgotten friend.
> Dismiss a suspicion and replace it with trust.
> Write a letter to someone you miss.
> Encourage a person who has lost his faith.
> Keep a promise.
> Forget an old grudge.
> Examine your demands on others and vow to reduce them.
> Fight for a principle.
> Express your gratitude.
> Overcome an old fear.
> Take a minute to appreciate the beauty of nature.
> Tell others you love them and tell them again, again and again.
> And pray, pray, pray.

TO THINK AND PRAY ABOUT: How can you apply the poem to your life?

The Seed We Sow

THE MYSTERIES of God surround me in the handkerchief-size garden which seemed advisable after the harsh winter. The zucchini vine covers itself with trumpet-shaped blooms, dumps its vegetables and wanders on—probably into my neighbor's yard. I never realized how much one squash vine could yield. I knew *what*, however, because I knew what kind of seed I had sown.

The same is true of deeds we do. We can measure neither the rate of growth nor the yield. Selfishly, I should like to be able to gather in an armload of proofs of my planting, but my job is to continue sowing. I may never see maturity, but I have God's reassurance that it will occur.

Philosophers have defined service as a way of life. "A man's true wealth is the good he does in this world," said Mohammed. Dr. Albert Schweitzer wrote: "I do not know what your destiny will be, but of one thing I am certain—the only ones among you who will be truly happy are those who have sought and found how to serve." These are the plantings, yes; and God tells us what the harvest will be: nothing less than everlasting life.

One of the best examples of a servant to others is my ninety-eight year old friend. Mary Rockwood Peet paints, writes and lectures tirelessly. Her step is springy. Her eyes are bright. Her doctors would like to put her vitality into packets and dispense it to their patients. Her prescription? "I live to inspire. I advise others to work hard, stay happy, help others—and hang on till they're ninety—knowing the best is yet to come!"

TO THINK AND PRAY ABOUT: We know that while physical growth will end, spiritual growth is infinite—unless diverted. Discuss ways in which we grow to full Christian maturity through the deeds we do.

Growth Is Seldom A Straight Line

June 5
John 6:35-52

What is so rare as a day in June?

James Russell Lowell

THE POET must have envisioned today. My neighbor arose from her planting-position in the garden long enough to say, "This is the kind of day that makes one want to live forever!" It's comforting to know that we can! Verse 47 of today's reading tells us so. The basic ingredient is faith.

We live in a time of instant everything: cake mixes, cameras and solid-state television sets. Small wonder we find ourselves so bombarded with manufacturers' guarantees that we come to expect instant realization of God's promises. We grow impatient, forgetting that faith is the substance which makes eternal life, good health, God's presence—and all the other things we ask for—possible. Have faith, God tells us, and these things will come.

I looked at my neighbor's planting in a freshly weeded plot. What kind of seed grows so late? My neighbor knows. She studies such things. I admire her patience. Knowing that life is inside each seed she waits—never expecting instant germination. She plants at all seasons and finds equal pleasure with the giant stalks and the dwarfs. She never shakes her fist at a puny plant; neither does she ignore it, but helps it bloom. I find a lesson in my friend's good sense. Growth, even when it is "normal," seldom proceeds in a straight line. She has a "someday" sort of faith in her garden that I can apply to God's promises. I need not be disappointed when I fail to see the addition of visible cells. The process of everlasting life begins with faith. I have God's Word.

TO THINK AND PRAY ABOUT: In what ways can we relate today's Scripture reading to our everyday lives?

A Growing Place

I'm thankful for the growing things
I touch and smell and see
Shaped by the One I oft forget
But who remembers me
And sends the sun to warm my face
And find, like them, a growing place . . . J.M.B.

HOW, WHEN and for what should we pray? Jesus tells us that prayer should be constant and natural in the secret closets of our hearts. His sample prayer is beautiful in its simplicity. By beginning with "Our Father," we acknowledge that we are children of God. We are within His Kingdom and we should ask Him as we would of our earthly fathers, for food for the day, forgiveness and guidance.

We live in a day of anxiety. We, the world's richest nation, ask for more. We worry more about the future now, sociologists say, than during the Great Depression. Business firms report that candidates for positions show more concern with retirement benefits than job descriptions or beginning salaries. Some looking ahead is healthy, but when we take full responsibility, we rob God of His right to watch over us. He feeds the birds and clothes the lilies. How much more He would do for us if through simple prayer and dependence on Him we would just open our hearts and invite Him to enter. In seeking Him if we will but remember that He is looking for us, then we will find for ourselves a growing place.

TO THINK AND PRAY ABOUT: Is it more important for a family to set apart a certain time for devotions, or continue prayer throughout the day, or both?

Expect A Miracle

June 7
John 14:12-18; 15:12-18

WHAT MIRACLES there could be if we but asked, believed and loved one another! We could reshape each other's lives.

Recently at Bible study our minister said, "I wonder what would happen if each member of our congregation knocked on someone's door to say, 'Hello! I have a gift for you. I've brought a smile'." It might work miracles, we agreed, if the callers asked nothing in return; but all too often gifts are for selling gimmicks. We use them to gain entrance. Then we spread out our wares.

"I wouldn't have the courage," someone in the group commented. "Nobody would believe us," said another. And I guess that is how it is: we no longer expect miracles; so we have stopped helping them to happen.

The discussion went in many directions: "There's a lot we can't change . . . Learn to live with it . . . Don't force yourself on others. . . ." Then someone said, "We live within our clay."

If the speaker intended that comment as resignation, she missed the mark with me. Clay is a most cooperative medium. It yields to the inexperienced hands of small children; it shapes into a thing of beauty at the touch of a potter's hand. If I live within my clay, then I can do a bit of work on myself each day. I can help others to shape their lives. And, best of all, I can place my clay in God's hands—expecting a miracle!

"I need a nice smile," I explained shortly afterwards to my dentist when I had chipped a front tooth. "Vanity, thy name is woman," he teased me, but he performed the miracle I expected. I will put the smile to good use.

TO THINK AND PRAY ABOUT: God promises that we can do great works in His name. Can you recall some of the small deeds you have done which developed into "great works?" What comfort do you find in being "chosen" to do God's work?

June 8
Ezekiel 36:26-38

MY STUDENTS complete assignments with Olympic-strides if their reward is my reading aloud a chapter from MIO, MY SON. Astrid Lindgren's charming fantasy-tale carries a symbolism they enjoy. The cruel Sir Kato, epitome of evil, possesses a heart of stone. Goliath-like, 9-year-old Prince Mio conquers the wicked knight. From the heap of stone that remains as a reminder of the fierce battle there flies a wee gray bird. Released from captivity, the bird soars upwards and trills sweet notes of a new heart.

A new heart! Remember the surge of enthusiasm which followed the first heart transplant in 1967? But the mortality rate was high in the delicate operation. Cardiologists, unable to overcome the body's natural rejection of the foreign organ, faced great difficulties. Patients were defenseless against infection. However, indications are that prospects continue to improve. The rise in patient survival stirs interest anew, offering new hope.

Following the first implant, there was a flurry of TV programs of bionic this-and-thats which dulled the sheen of young Mio. Still, my children love their hero. The removal of the hard heart and the songbird replacement are more in keeping with their sense of compassion than the cyborgs.

Today's Scripture lists a series of promises: great cities, fertile lands and bountiful harvests. But the most exciting is the new heart God offers, one which the flesh and cybernetics lack. My heart sings with the children's symbolisms. The lyrics are a wonder of redemption.

TO THINK AND PRAY ABOUT: In what ways can we become spiritual "donors?"

Setting Up Priorities

"MOTHER, WILL you type my book report?" *Yes, my son.* "Hon, will you take the car to the garage?" *Yes, my husband.* "Mrs. Bacher, will the article be ready Tuesday?" *Yes, my editor.* "June, do you have a moment?" *Yes, my friend.* I owe my mother a letter; report cards are due Monday; the utility room is knee-deep with laundry; and, oh yes, a cake to bake for Fellowship Sunday . . . At this improbable moment I leave the freeway and take an off-ramp in search of the peace God promises.

The trail I follow slopes gently uphill and my pulse quickens as I climb. My back is warmed by the newly-awakened sun. Spiderwebs spun for hapless flies gleam with jewels of dew. Buttercups open their innocent eyes like children. Soon the sun will melt the dewdrops and close the petals of the creamy flowers; their work will be finished, for they will have seen the light of day. But on an early June morning all is enchanting. I walk silently, else I will miss bird-song, bee-hum and butterfly wings. God's presence closes in around me and I am restored. Appropriately the trail is marked "Not a Through Street."

I will type while the washing machine is working. With the car in the garage George and I will walk home—talking. Mother would enjoy a phone call . . . a few report cards tonight . . . and if I double my easy-mix recipe, I can share my "fellowship cake" with my friend. I feel no guilt. God made this world beautiful for us to enjoy. On the Seventh Day he rested because he foresaw a need for retreat. Jesus sought solitude from the multitudes. What better examples do we need? I hum a song of pure delight as I make my daily rounds in my mother-wife-writer-friend-daughter-teacher-Christian role. I am made whole.

TO THINK AND PRAY ABOUT: How can you arrange a "moment alone with God" on busy days? Why do we need solitude?

God's Temple Needs Care

MY BODY IS a temple, an edifice for private worship. I have an obligation to keep it in good repair. June is traditionally the month I have my annual physical examination.

Positive thinker though I am, I confess that these check-ups make me uneasy. Weakly and meekly, I stretch out on the impersonal vinyl of the examining table, looking apprehensively at the cotton swabs, tinctures-of-this-and-that and machines that are equipped to read everything—even my mind! I try to concentrate, but the superclinical atmosphere is an alien planet. I am unable to remember what my doctor of seventeen years looks like! Intellectually, I know my temple needs maintenance and repair to cut down on depreciation. Emotionally, I decide it can wait a year. I am ready to flee in the paper gown when my doctor blocks the door. To my surprise, I recognize his friendly voice, "Well, which are you?"

Which am I? It is a standing joke between us—stemming back to when the doctor categorized his patients into two groups: the ill who are "Fine!" and the healthy who are "Dying!" I relax, recognizing my anxiety. My doctor is a skillful appraiser, but with my cooperation he is able to diagnose and prescribe more quickly.

God knows our "symptoms." He knows our needs even before we know them ourselves. Are we guilty of wondering how much to tell? Are we tempted to run away, postpone our talks with God, harbor our guilt, shoulder our burdens alone? Then let us make an appointment with God and keep it; let us pray without ceasing; for prayer is the admission that His temple needs care that only He can provide. Healing is ours but for the asking.

TO THINK AND PRAY ABOUT: In what ways do you think of your body as the temple of God? Do you care for it properly? In what ways do we often deceive ourselves?

The Greatest Of These Is Love

GIFTS WITHOUT love are without meaning. Though we possess gifts of prophecy, knowledge, angelic speech—even faith—if we lack Christian charity, we are but "sounding brass." We are hollow and without substance.

I watch the fog billowing in—typical of our marine-type-weather summers. The popular California expression of hope is: "It will burn off before noon." But for now they see only the fog. I have faith which lets me see the morning beyond. We know in part; we see in part; but greater than either the hope or the faith is the love we practice now and understand "in part." When the fog has lifted forever, we shall "know as we are known," says the Apostle Paul.

"To know" is to put love into practice; and love is a demanding master. We must be kind, compassionate, merciful, helpful and patient. We must give of ourselves so that others may grow; and, spiritually, we must sign our gifts, "With love."

Would we be more than "tinkling cymbals?" Then it is wise to evaluate how we relate to those with whom we live, work and worship—dwelling not upon our accomplishments, or even our blessings, but asking: *Do I truly love?*

Love is a growing thing, stretching from here to eternity. I chose today's reading for my father's funeral. I prefer its message to "Dust thou art . . ." for I agree with the poet: " 'Twas not spoken of the soul." Love never fails. It is a beautiful promise, knowing that we shall meet again . . . The fog will be lifted.

TO THINK AND PRAY ABOUT: What do you consider to be your greatest talent? Discuss verse 11 with children in your family. Let individuals decide how they can share their special gifts. Stress love as the motivation.

June 14
Psalm 103:6-22

TODAY IS Flag Day! As red, white and blue stripe the sky, the fifty stars shine in the June sunshine as if with pride in their dominion. Christian Gentiles and Hebrew Jews must feel their pulses quicken alike. For this we have in common: ". . . one nation under God . . ." While the designation of June 14 as Flag Day dates back to 1977 and the publication of the Pledge of Allegiance to 1892, it was in 1954 that President Eisenhower signed a bill adding "under God." While there are those who would delete the words, our country continues to declare itself under God's dominion, as the psalmist declares the whole world to be!

This is a good day for remembering. As I study the stars in their field of blue I recall George Washington's explanation of the symbolism of the United States flag. The stars, he said, had been taken from heaven, the red from England, and the white stripes added to indicate separation from the mother country; in other words, *freedom*. How grateful we should feel; how "chosen!"

Stars have denoted dominion and sovereignty from ancient times when they were symbols of Egypt, India and Persia. The blue background signifies vigilance, perseverance, and justice; red is for courage and valor; and white means purity and innocence. Today as I meditate on the symbolism of our flag, I find a new significance for my life. If I accept God as the Star of Dominion, the meaning of the colors takes on added significance. What a beautiful world we would have were we filled with the Spirit of his vigilance, perseverance, justice, courage and purity!

TO THINK AND PRAY ABOUT: Count some of the blessings we Americans can be thankful for on this day set apart to honor the flag. How are we sharing these blessings with other countries materially and spiritually?

". . . He that keepeth thee
will not slumber."

PSALM 121 offers me a warm feeling of comfort. The imagery of lifting my eyes to the hills for strength is enough to set my heart beating to the rhythm the psalmist felt. But greater than the imagery, and greater than the music of the melody are the lyrics. God is watching over me. He cares.

The need to have someone care is vital. Instinctively, it seems, from the moment a new baby leaves the womb and enters the world, the tiny hands reach out for tenderness, love and protection. Ears strain for a voice of reassurance and the heart strains for signals of love. Without these the newborn baby is instinctively rejected. Medical scientists are studying the strange phenomenon, which results in death.

A baby needs care—care for it and care about it. These basic needs remain, physical and emotional, throughout the life of the individual. As individuals and as groups, we attend more adequately to the physical comforts than to the emotional security of those around us. As a result children feel unwanted, unloved.

Recently a friend of mine was driving on a near-deserted street when a bicycle appeared from nowhere. Even with the brake applied full force she almost hit the young rider. She ran to the child. Relieved that he was uninjured, she said, "Do you realize you could have been killed?" His answer, not flippant, but filled with despair, shocked her. "Who cares?"

Who cares for *you?* God cares: physically, emotionally—and spiritually.

TO THINK AND PRAY ABOUT: What assurances do we have from today's reading that God is watching over us? Are there ways we can pass His unsleeping providence to others?

*A*s You Will . . .

June 16
II Corinthians 8:1-16

WORDS SHAPE our thoughts. Thoughts shape our attitudes. Attitudes shape the will.

An English professor said it another way: "Develop a rich vocabulary, for without the right language the soul is impoverished." Overwhelmed by some of his weighty assignments, I looked for shortcuts. I found none. He called my phrases "tired." So I piled up words extravagantly only to have him pencil in the margin: "Long on words; short on thought." I became more selective, remembering the "right language" expression. Then, one day, alongside a metaphor I chose, he wrote, "Powerful!" I had listened with the willing mind.

An arrogant young man once chose to use words as weapons. Annoyed at his inability to find flaw with the thought processes of an aged philosopher, he devised a word-trap. "Within my hand is a little sparrow. Is it alive or is it dead?" "If he says it is dead," the young man conspired, "I will show him it is alive; if he says it is alive, I shall crush it!" The man of wisdom looked at the clenched fist and answered, "As you will, young man, as you will."

Much depends upon what we *will* for ourselves and others, but first we must listen with willing minds to what God has in store. We must let Him fill our minds with wholesome thoughts that determine our destiny. We must find the "right" language of His Kingdom. Each of us must know: "I am what I think in my heart" (Proverbs 23:7).

TO THINK AND PRAY ABOUT: How do you handle unworthy thoughts? What implication does the promise in verse 12 hold for you?

Binding Up Wounds

June 17
Isaiah 61:1-10

JOE HAD HAD a bad day at school. He had seen to it that the other children in the classroom had the same kind. At recess his mood led to hand-to-hand combat. "What's the trouble, Joe?" I asked as I searched for my first-aid box. Binding up wounds is an extracurricular activity for teachers.

His face crumpled. "Gramma's not coming," he sobbed. "She didn't even write!" I knew little of the child's background except that he lived in a foster home. He had announced proudly a few days earlier that his grandmother was coming for a visit. How does a teacher patch up a hurt like that for an eight-year-old?

God makes clear our responsibility to the orphans, widows, mourners and prisoners, but we are so busy with our jobs and our families we forget something. *These*, too, are our jobs. *These*, too, are our families! Are not all men brothers under the Fatherhood of God?

It is impossible to be all things to all people. God does not require that. He gives to each enough talent which, shared, can help his Kingdom of mercy and unfailing love. Each must find a particular way. One means I use is the mail. Perhaps one reason I choose this medium of serving is the thrill I feel when I myself open magic envelopes. And how much more the mail call must mean to those in orphanages, convalescent homes and prisons!

Joe? I wrote him a little note and placed it in his school mailbox complimenting a picture of a wingless bird he drew. He tucked the letter in his pocket and smiled through his tears.

TO THINK AND PRAY ABOUT: In what ways are you able to bring peace and comfort to others? Make a list and see if you can manage to do at least one extra deed of kindness each day, excluding those members of your family and close friends for whom you would do anyway.

June 18
Ephesians 6:1-10

"**H**APPY FATHER'S DAY!" Tomorrow you may want to exchange the purple necktie, but today you accept it gratefully as a token of love from your children.

It is good to set aside a day to honor fathers, for while the prerequisites of fatherhood are low, the responsibilities are awesome. A father must be courageous enough to admit fear, strong enough to know he is weak without God, and humble enough to know that if he stumbles, it is God who will give him the power to rise again. And all this in the presence of a watchful audience. A father must lead his children; but first he must learn to follow. He must laugh with them but remember the ache of childhood tears. He must hold the past with one hand and reach to the future with the other so there can be no generation gap in family love. A father is ordained to lead his children.

Children love playing "follow the leader." Most of us recall the giant strides we attempted in trying to "walk in Daddy's footsteps." One Saturday as my husband groomed the lawn, our son asked a question that showed how significant the game can be. As he stretched four-year-old legs to reach man-sized tracks, Bryce kept an eye on shadows of himself and his father on the redwood fence. "Daddy, if you fall will your shadow fall, too? Would that make mine fall?" What a vivid image!

TO THINK AND PRAY ABOUT: *Children*. In what ways can you show your love for your father other than with gifts? Why do you think God included both parents in the commandment to honor them?

Parents: Consider the responsibilities you have to your children. What rewards do you expect? Why do you think today's reading refers to the child-parent commandment as being the "first commandment with promise?"

Greetings To A Friend

June 19
Luke 17:1-11

I AM WORKING on an exciting assignment, writing a collection of poetry, *Greetings to a Friend*. Such booklets are "best sellers," publishers say. But today my mind wandered: Why not *Greetings to a Stranger* . . . why not *To an Enemy?* I wonder if it's ever been done, or what the results would be? I mean words that heal, not sound—like "I'm sorry." We know what Jesus would have us do. Forgiveness is the key.

Who knows what words will produce? I notice the lazy peach tree has decided to bloom. Back when winter winds snarled the branches of the tree next to it, the early bloomer burst out like pink popcorn. But I know both varieties: the June-blooms will bring fruit before the March-braggarts. When offenses come, I remember the stinted growth and withhold judgment.

Betty Wallace Scott wrote in *Sunshine* magazine: "The perfect garden should be a patchwork of Mississippi sand for juicy melons, some Appalachian hillside for a homey rock garden, a piece of Imperial Valley for orchard, some black prairie loam for corn; an Idaho potato patch . . . ." Perhaps the Creator had it figured right—each doing his own thing in his own place—and sharing it with others.

We could say the same of friends, I guess. The enemy is another matter? Maybe not. The flowers and fruits of Betty's garden were once alien weeds—strangers and enemies. We are to forgive seventy times seven times. How trivial our grievances when we recall the words of Jesus on the cross, ". . . Father, forgive them, for they know not what they do."

TO THINK AND PRAY ABOUT: If you find yourself alienated from another, what steps do you take to heal the wound?

The Constant Moon

"FROM EVERLASTING to everlasting" is immeasurable. And that is how long God's love for us endures! He shows it in so many ways. For instance, observe tonight's full moon. One of God's early miracles, it holds a special mystique for us all. Only a few nights ago the moon was a thin silver slice with just a faint promise of light. Tonight it is a lantern to the feet of night-creatures. Man has walked upon its surface, but while the moon was hospitable, it remained inscrutable—retaining the mellow mysteriousness God endowed it with.

Beauty alone would be reason enough for God's including the moon in the firmament, but he planned that it should help divide the night from the day. And the moon has other work: it pulls the tides along, lights the hunting grounds for nocturnal animals, inspires by-the-almanac gardeners and glows for young love. High school literature students of Shakespearean tragedies will recall Juliet's plea to Romeo that his pledge of devotion be not based upon ". . . the inconstant moon, which monthly changes in her circled orb, lest thy love prove likewise variable." Yet, there is a constancy in the waxing and waning that Juliet overlooked. Even in "the dark of the moon," we know it is there, ready and waiting for the signal to reappear as a "new moon." We expect its "circled orb"—even if unconsciously—and the moon never disappoints us.

We have reorganized our calendars, but we have not rearranged the mysterious phases of the moon. The moon, like God's love which provided it, is always there. This is a comforting thing to know—even when we lose sight of either of them briefly! God's love will never "phase out."

TO THINK AND PRAY ABOUT: What promises do you find in today's reading? What responsibilities? Which is conditional: God's terms or His love?

DOES LIFE provide anything more precious than love given freely and unconditionally? God offers such a love. Why do we hesitate to accept His gift? Is it "too good to be true?" Do we feel unworthy? Or, do we suspect some hidden price tag?

I am a poor receiver. For instance, today is my birthday. Surely everyone must enjoy being pampered and greeted in a special way by family and friends who want to show by word and deed how much they love us. Why do I feel embarrassed? Also, I am blessed with a husband who would not let me forget a birthday if I wanted to! My gift was waiting by my chair at the breakfast table—extravagant as always. And, as always, I felt guilty. "You shouldn't have . . ." I began. Seeing his disappointment, I reminded that it's "more blessed to give." "Then let me be blest!" he said. He has a point: He asks nothing in return—except for me to be happy. An extreme, but logical extension of my inability to accept what is lovely would be to hold my breath as I pass by our roses.

Most of us grapple with the concept of God's abundant love—so abundant that He accompanied it with the greatest gift this world ever knew: His Son. Jesus came to atone for our sins, freeing us to love God, to love each other and to love ourselves. But we must open our hearts and receive the gift He offers. In hearts filled with gratitude, there can be no room for guilt or remorse. I shall accept my gifts today. Herein lies love.

TO THINK AND PRAY ABOUT: There is a difference in "accepting" and "taking." Some people seem to take love for granted. Others are willing to give love but seem to be unable to accept it in return. Where do you find yourself? What special significance do you find in verse 10?

The Cross Is Made To Lean On

June 22
Matthew 11:25-30

"And let us not be weary in well doing; for in due season we shall reap, if we faint not." Galatians 6:9, KJV

THE VERSE was a favorite of my grandmother's. I thought of Gran, her season-quotes and "garden-crosses," yesterday as summer began officially. She always said seasons had distinct personalities, but, like so many other things in life, it was difficult to separate the ending point of one from the beginning point of the next. June, of course, has a split personality—half-spring, half-summer. The fields, still green, flush hay-gold, reminding me of the mortality of grass . . . But were my mother's mother still here, she would pay it little attention. Her busy hands would have started the early canning.

My grandmother had ripe tomatoes in June while somewhat envious neighbors waited until July. She had no great love for bedding plants. You can start them in a hot house and force them along for early fruit, but the taste tattles the process, she said. So she planted them out-of-doors and staked them. Her youngest son and I were fascinated by the wooden arms she made to keep her tomatoes growing towards the light while neighbors let theirs stumble and fall. "A cross is made to lean on," she said.

Maybe we should apply the philosophy to our daily lives. How often we hear people say, "It is my cross to bear." Is a cross to bear, or is it to lean on? Sometimes we are so turned inward we fail to see some of life's "burdens" as blessings if we will lean upon the cross of Jesus. His work knew no season. He told His disciples that the harvest was now; not four months away. And as we help, we need not grow weary; we need not grow faint; for He has promised to lighten our burdens. Jesus bore our cross.

TO THINK AND PRAY ABOUT: Can you think of instances in your daily lives when you have been able to lighten your load by "leaning" on either the cross or God's promises?

What Can I Do?

"WHAT CAN I do to be saved?" asked the Philippian jailer. "Believe on the Lord Jesus Christ!" was the Apostle Paul's answer. This single question and answer neatly summarize the teachings of the New Testament.

"What can I do?" we ask our ministers and our doctors. "What can I do?" ask men caught in financial straits. Women ask the same question of their hair dressers. Parents ask it of teachers regarding their children's behavior or academic problems. A survey might show that this is one of the most common questions around. It became such a common rainy-day question in our home, I made a list of activities for our son to engage in so that he began looking forward to a storm! I made a list of stories, collected craft ideas, added suggestions for poems and Scripture passages to memorize and ended with "Look for a rainbow." The result was a happy day.

Jesus tells us that He came to earth that we might have life and have it more abundantly. How do we achieve an abundant Christian life? First, we believe with a faith so strong that the storms of life can threaten, but they cannot destroy. The abundant life begins for us here on earth and leads in natural transition into eternity. A wonderful thing, faith; a positive thing.

The positive attitude of Christian living communicates to those around us. "I am convinced," said my retiring principal after having spent over forty years in education (and an equal number of years teaching a Sunday school class), "that most folks are just about as happy as they set out to be!" He had the happiest faculty I ever worked with.

TO THINK AND PRAY ABOUT: Do a self-examination. Do you consider yourself a positive thinker? In what ways are you able to share today's simple answer: BELIEVE with others?

A Gift Of Words

June 24
Psalms 29:1-11; 84:10-12

DAVID PRAISED God for inner strength and peace of mind which neither earthly goods nor political power could bring. What we praise Him for depends upon our sense of values.

Recently an older couple was sorting accumulations, preparing to move to a small house. They decided to divide valuables between their children, hold a garage sale and discard the rest. They tossed a book aside as "just words."

A born collector—more of ideas than things—I picked up the old scrapbook. There I found "We Leave Our Children": *love*, the most precious of all gifts—familial, brotherly and spiritual; *our attention*, for one day they may not hear us; *a value system:* self-reliance, courage, conviction and respect for self and others; *a sense of humor*—for laughter is life's gyro; *discipline*—else life will be a bitter teacher, *a will to work*—for work well done brings pride and joy; *a talent for sharing*—for society needs belief in individual worth; *the passion of truth*—for truth is a straight answer, the beginning of trust; *the lantern of hope*—which lights the dark corners of the mind; *the knowledge of belonging*—impromptu praise, a soft caress; *a sense of wonder at*—the things of nature, love of friends without reciprocity and the size of God's Word, in print so small it fits inside each heart, in meaning so great it spreads over the earth.

Just words? To me they were *great* words—instruments communicating with loved ones and communing with God.

TO THINK AND PRAY ABOUT: In our spiritual lives, how do we go about sorting what to keep, sell, give away or burn? Relate this to David's choice (Psalm 84:10).

For Want Of A Nail

IF A FRIEND knocked on your door at midnight, asking a favor, would you say, "Come back tomorrow"? Reverse the situation. If you went to a friend in the middle of the night, what kind of reception would you expect to receive? These are interesting points to ponder.

There is a sort of drama in darkness. It is possible that we would meet the emergency graciously. It is also possible that by the light of day we are so busy with living we ignore the ordinary needs around us.

Recently a friend told me this experience. In conducting a series of interviews for a Christian magazine article, she contacted a paraplegic. At the close of the conversation, she invited the man to church. He hesitated and then inquired, "Has your building a ramp for my wheel chair?" He expressed a very real need. Well-meaning members from seven local churches had invited the paralyzed man to attend the worship services. The man had refused of necessity. There were no ramps.

My friend's account brought back a childhood memory of a room in the home of one of my aunts. Hand-stitched samplers were a must in those days and she had covered the walls with embroidered adages, axioms and passages of Scripture. One of the samplers impressed me so much I committed it to memory:

> For want of a nail, the shoe was lost.
> For want of a shoe, the horse was lost.
> For want of a horse, the rider was lost.
> For want of a rider, the message was lost.
> For want of a message, the battle was lost.
> For want of a battle, the war was lost.
> All for the want of a nail.

Jesus tells us to ask of Him and we shall receive. We must follow His example in providing for others.

TO THINK AND PRAY ABOUT: What ways do you personally find in which you can be of service to the handicapped?

I Believe . . .

June 26
Mark 9:14-30; 11:23-24

THE UNITED States Constitution guarantees us the right to worship as we choose. The Bible is more universal. It guarantees peoples all over the world the right to believe. Faith is a mighty power. With it, we can remove mountains; but how many, I wonder, possess complete and total faith?

I recall asking, "What is a Christian?" in a study group I was leading. A Christian keeps the commandments . . . does these things . . . does not do those things . . . All interesting answers, but answers which gave the characteristics of a Christian—not the definition. Nobody uses the word *believe*.

My mother prefaces most of her statements with "I believe." She uses "believe" as a snyonym for "think": "I believe the sun will shine . . . I believe I can finish before noon . . . I believe I feel better today." Quite unaware, she passed along a positive-thinking attitude to me. Language patterns are contagious. I notice that our son uses "believe" instead of "think." His Korean-born wife in struggling with the English language picked up the usage. I am in no position to cast a stone; and I admit that I enjoy "believing all things" anyway.

There is so much to believe in on a day like today with the water sprinklers creating halos above the lawn and the birds dipping down for a quick shower. Something I call "molecular motion" is taking place out there. This I know, although I have never seen a molecule and would be unable to recognize one if I saw it. In like manner, I do not see the hand of God, but I refuse to subscribe to the idea that God set the world in motion and left it to go its own way. He is watching over the world. He is watching over His family. This I believe.

TO THINK AND PRAY ABOUT: Read and discuss the Reaffirmation of Faith. What does it mean to you as a child of God?

cA Good Wife

LEMUEL'S (v.1) praise and properties of a good wife never fail to humble and intrigue me. One verse calls for another, like my mother's chocolate fudge. I find the praise sweet but the properties awesome. Fortunately, he brings it all together in verse 28, which is why I read it on George's birthday. It is good to pause at the "spindle" (or dishwasher) and take stock anyway. I see reminders here for myself and all other wives.

My annotated Bible has numerous references but omits the one I find most helpful as companion reading: Ephesians 5:23-33. This is a letter Paul wrote to the Ephesians from his Roman cell expressing heavenly thoughts no prison bars could restrain. The epistle draws a vivid analogy between marriage and the Church. He writes of the Church as the body and the spotless spouse of Christ. He emphasizes the Christian family because it is the symbol and likeness of the Church.

By putting the two references together I am able to put on the "full armor" and better perform my duties as a Christian—and a wife. The promise of the ideal Church is worth the efforts of the writers. And Proverbs 31:28 offers a beautiful reward for being the ideal wife—although the giving of one's self and talents carries its own reward.

Yes, I arose early this morning. I did not gather flax, but I baked my husband's favorite cake and wrote him a poem. May it be a blessing to you all in God's beautiful world.

May you know the sparkle as this day unfolds
Of precious dewdrops a violet holds;
May you see the colors of spectrums above;
May you know the blessings of friends and God's love. J.M.B.

TO THINK AND PRAY ABOUT: Can you find other ways to compare marriage and family life to the Church? Share the ideas with your children.

To Be Worthy Of God's Kingdom

June 28
Luke 9:51-60

A PROMISE is peculiar in that given it must be kept. Its paradoxical terms are binding; and yet it is a positive thing. I remember a special Sunday school teacher who referred to the Bible as "God's Book of Promises." We children liked that and made a game of seeing how many we could find. The wise teacher led us to know that God kept them all.

By beautiful coincidence my parents celebrated their golden wedding anniversary the year my husband and I celebrated our silver one. My mother and father "stood up" with us as we renewed our vows; then George and I were their attendants as the minister said, "Repeat after me . . ." Those were fragile moments.

Since our anniversary came first, we served small cakes to the guests at the reception and, for sake of sentiment, froze the white tiered one. Together we replaced our silver leaves with gold.

In the light moments following the solemnity of my parents' "second marriage," a friend asked to what they attributed the longevity of their union. Applying his farming philosophy, Daddy said, "We never look back at the crooked rows."

Jesus uses the same analogy in verse 62. If we look back, we lose a sense of direction. Our furrows become crooked. Dwelling on our failures robs us of confidence. Yesterday spoils today; today spoils tomorrow; promises go unkept. Had my parents said, "I can't" instead of "I will" at the altar or failed to keep those promises, there would have been no lovely silver-and-golden year in our family. To be worthy of God's kingdom we, too, must say, "I will," never looking back with regret.

TO THINK AND PRAY ABOUT: Discuss ways of keeping promises and commitments with family and friends. God keeps promises. Do we keep ours to Him?

Hello, Friend . . .

WHAT IS A friend? Could that beggar be reaching for friendship instead of a coin? The Bible speaks of a friendship greater than kinship. We witness relationships in families tearing apart—sometimes beyond repair. Maybe true friendship is a stronger bond because friends choose each other. Adversity seems to draw them together. But who are our "true friends?"

In a fabled conversation, a man's shadow said, "I am a friend. I walk with you by light of day. I sit by you in candlelight."

"You are not a *true* friend," the man replied. "Where do you go when the sun is down and my candle has burnt out?"

By the natural order of things lights go out; and there are dark moments in life. It would ease my responsibilities if I were a Christian Pollyanna who denied all hardship. It would provide a nice dodge, too! There are those who rationalize adversities and afflictions of others as if they were shawls easily shed: "He enjoys poor health . . . She made her own bed . . . They like the shadows . . ." This I do not accept. I prefer to open the blinds. The troubled may blink uncertainly in the eerie half-light, but eventually their eyes will adjust to the sunshine a friend lets in.

Sometimes it takes only a greeting. Recently a man I know faced financial ruin alone—forsaken, he thought, by all who knew him. He considered simply disappearing, but something compelled him to call the loan company which held a mortgage on his house. By coincidence, the telephone number differs by one digit from the Dial-A-Prayer service our church provides. The warm voice of our pastor said, "Hello, Friend . . ." The greeting changed his world.

TO THINK AND PRAY ABOUT: Define friendship and compare definitions. Who is the friend that is closer than a brother?

IT IS THE last day of June. I turn my calendar, forgetting those things which are behind, reaching forward to those things which lie ahead. My writing, like the month, has ended. I say a prayer that my words have been truly those of HOPE.

I did some self-searching before attempting these devotionals. Oh, I wanted to do them! But what did I, a lay-Christian, have to offer? Strangely, the answer did not come from my close friends whose opinions I trust, or my family who trusts mine, but from a friend in Indianapolis I have yet to meet! "God works in mysterious ways," she wrote, "Your writing has reached out and touched my life." I made my decision.

I think I have divided people who please God into two groups heretofore: those who serve Him because they know Him; and those who do not know Him and are seeking. God is not in hiding; He wants to be found. As one who knows God, it is my duty to introduce Him to those who are still seeking. But as I worked my way through these daily devotionals, I decided the division line was less clear than I had drawn it: what of those who have not heard of God's goodness; what of those who do not know how to search?

In retrospect, I know that I have grown from this experience. Little things take on new significance as I stop, look and listen for signals of distress. Only when I can empathize am I able to help. I have rearranged priorities—according to the cries I hear. Ultimately I as a person and we as a Church will be judged not by things we possess but to the extent that things possess us. May the love of God be our possessor as we press toward the mark.

TO THINK AND PRAY ABOUT: Have you become better acquainted with God? Is God still a stranger? May those who have yet to meet Him be inspired by *Words of Hope*.

My Freedom Prayer

DEAR LORD, as I face the new month, my heart is filled with gratitude that July is a dream-come-true. Thank you for the tough fibers you put into fashioning dreams for our ancestors whose vision kept them here against impossible odds—to battle death, hardship and hunger. Their iron tears were shed to free a country, plow it and hand it down. I thank You for Your Almighty Hand which led them. I thank You for the flag of freedom which waves its red, white and blue symbol of this mighty land. Ours is an estate of inherited wealth: our golden granaries once were wastelands; our scented orchards once were forests; our harnessed streams once were powerless; our ribbons of concrete and steel once footpaths. Thank You for the countless highways that knit together the cities and farmlands where once alone, but for You, the pioneers labored to build homes and hold the land. Now organizations of religion, charity, education, labor and public service unite to share the task. Gracious God, make us worthy. Make us grateful. Only then can we claim to be the rightful heirs.

Dear Lord, we become more conscious, as Independence Day draws close, that we owe a debt to this great country—one which is humanly impossible for us to repay. The freedom we enjoy was hard-bought—paid for in sacrifice on battlefields. We become more conscious, too, that You gave a Son who made the supreme sacrifice that our spirits might be as free as our earthly estates. We cannot repay. You do not ask that, but we can be obedient. We can be grateful to You. We can love one another.

And, dear God, I want to thank You for all the little freedoms I too often take for granted. I can reach my full potential, be "my own woman" because of the courage endowed in so many courageous ladies before me. Truly, You have prepared a table before me, and I say with the Psalmist, "My cup runneth over."

Let me pray, knowing everything depends upon You. Let me serve You, my family, friends and country. Thank You for making me a free woman—while binding me with chains of Love.

Togetherness

JULY IS A month of togetherness. Most of us have tender memories of family gatherings when Grandfather, the undisputed patriarch, declared it was time to do this or that. In my part of the world grandfathers said, "The harvest is white already" which translated into, "It's time to can." There were enormous out-of-door fire-pits, where great kettles of assorted fruits split their skins in tubs of boiling water. Menfolk fed the fire which had an insatiable appetite. Womenfolk sterilized jars and scolded flocks (which unscolded would have consumed the bountiful yield).

July is a month of togetherness in other ways, too. Remember fishing and camping, marching bands, firecrackers, Old Glory flying high and summer "Revival Meetings?" Those were the days when everybody attended regardless of a particular faith—or any faith at all. It was a special occasion of unique togetherness.

July is the month of togetherness in history, too. Could anything knit a nation closer than our Declaration of Independence? Unfortunately, it seems some of the closeness has melted away. It is easier for families to scatter in a travel-shrunken world; and all too often the members purchase one-way tickets. Communities have grown into cities; and cities are busy. But it goes deeper. There is a trend in religious literature to move away from "we-ness" in favor of "someone has said" or "I"—lest we sound "preachy."

We can praise God that our churches have grown; but let us hope they do not grow apart. Small committee groups for this and that are important and bring a closeness that comes "when two or three are gathered." However, spreading the warmth we share in small units to the entire congregation is important—just as we used to spread the warm glow of the single family unit to the extended family. Togetherness.

TO THINK AND PRAY ABOUT: Ask God for the restoration of unity to our churches and our world. Then, let us say, "*We* thank You, Lord!"

We Made It!

WE CLIMB all sorts of mountains every day. Our friends can help us with words of encouragement and warm hands, but only God can help us over the top. Sometimes unexpected objects and situations serve to remind us.

Today I picked up a much-used copy of SOUNDS OF LAUGHTER, and, bookmarked by small hands, it opened to "Knots in a Counting Rope," a story by Bill Martin Jr., with a special meaning.

"Grandfather, will I ever be strong like you?" the little American Indian boy asked. His grandfather reassured him, "You're growing stronger every day."

"How strong must I be, Grandfather?"

"So strong that you will not speak with anger even when your heart is filled with anger . . . That you will want to know what other people are thinking even when you are listening to your own thoughts . . . You must be so strong that you will stop to think of what happened yesterday and what will happen tomorrow in knowing what to do today."

"Will I ever be strong enough to cross over the dark mountains?"

And his grandfather answered, "You already have crossed some of the dark mountains, Boy. The mountains have no beginning and no ending. They are all around us. We only know that we are crossing them when we want to be weak but choose to be strong."

There came a day when this story took on new meaning. It came to my mind as we were ready to ascend a steep trail at Zion Park, Utah. A crippled man wanted to accompany the group, but was he able? As he deliberated, a lady, in somewhat the same physical condition, joined the hikers. "Shall we try it?" she asked of the stranger. "We shall!" And the climb began. On the way down, the lady called across to the gentleman, "By golly! We made it!" "By golly! We did!" he called back triumphantly.

TO THINK AND PRAY ABOUT: Choose to be strong and talk to God: *Dear Lord, thank You that we can choose to be strong. Thank You for the hill-climbing power You have made available to us. Thank You that You enable us to go higher and higher.*

My Declaration Of Independence

DEAR LORD, I stand beneath a flag with fifty shining stars and stripes with memories of the small colonies that put You first in their lives. It was Your cause that brought them here. It was Your hand which guided theirs as they quilled names to the mighty Constitution, that You, no doubt, inspired them to write. My head is bowed in respect. My heart is filled with gratitude. And, yet, Lord, I have a confession to make. Something inside of me rebels. As our forefathers resisted tyranny, I resist the voices that grow louder—insisting on too much autonomy. Muffle their shouts, dear Lord, before they become too forceful in cadence of anarchy.

I thank You for our nation's independence, making us subjects of no monarch, but let us not forget that we are subjects of Your kingdom. And so it is that I thank You for my dependence too. Please hear my declaration.

I thank You for creating me from chaos—as our Pilgrim Fathers created a working form of government from chaotic conditions surrounding them. I thank You for Your love, from which nothing can separate me. Though I stumble, fall or lose my way, You will seek me out and lift me up on the wings of eagles—because I depend on You.

I thank You for the love of friends who laugh with me and cry with me, then hold me when I am too weak to do either—lifting me high enough to reach Your hand. I am glad to be dependent upon them, Lord.

I thank You for those who spitefully use me. I must look to see if they are mirrors reflecting that within me which I must try to correct.

I thank You for the talents You gave me. I must depend upon You to help me channel them into ministries of Your love.

I thank You for the islands of trees and seas of grass and all the animals therein. I need their beauty. They need Your care. We depend upon You.

Dear Lord, I thank You for my independence—and my dependence too.

God's Gift

A CHILD IS a special gift from God—whether you brought your child home from the hospital or the court. The following is a letter to our son when he was two years old. May it be a blessing to you.

You are special. Every child is special, but you are *special-special*, not flesh of our flesh, but heart of our hearts—and the Spirit of God's. He gave you a wonderful body, equipped with the senses needed for enjoying this glorious land. He gave you a wonderful mind, equipped with the power of reasoning and sharing with others and with Him. He gave you the right number of fingers for exploring His world as you learn. He gave you the right number of toes for running through childhood-meadows while the wind tugs at your two cowlicks. One day the cowlicks will die down and the toes will slow down—walking and fitting into His tracks.

You are special. You have a special name, voice and set of fingerprints. We gave you the name—like we gave you other tangible things: pets, toys, clothes and friends (for we gave you no brother or sister). You gave yourself your voice from listening to the wind and trying to imitate it, listening to the church choir and letting out joyful noises while you were yet too young to mouth syllables—too unsteady on little feet to stand alone. And God provided you with unique fingerprints—just as He provided you with a heart and taught it how to love.

You are special. You belong! You are our son. You are the much loved grandson of maternal grandparents (and paternal grandparents would have loved you equally had they lived to see you). You were shortchanged on aunts and uncles, because your mother, too, is an only child; but your father gave you an aunt who also knows you're special. While you have no "first cousins," you are blessed with "seconds" and with friends. You belong elsewhere as well. *You are a child of God.*

You are special. Happy birthday!

TO THINK AND PRAY ABOUT: Birthdays are special, a time when parents receive a gift from God! The greatest gift we can offer is continued love.

Neighborhood Group Therapy

SITUATIONS are not sins. But if situations develop into problems, they can become either sins of commission or omission. Problems cause inward seething. What can we do to release the pressure valve? The idea of Group Therapy came home with me from school. There's value in exploring alternatives.

At a faculty meeting the principal handed us "theoretical" notes from his "In Basket."

"One teacher wants to leave early for a hair appointment; another teacher wants her to cancel the hair appointment for chorus practice; a teacher wants to use the money from the pop fund to purchase books for her room, as she contributes more to it than do her colleagues; a lady has seen boys bothering her mailbox; an "off beat" group wants to meet in the auditorium; a parent claims her child has been sent home with a cold to change from pants to a dress, and now she has pneumonia; two teachers were in an accident at three o'clock in a supermart parking lot (and what were they doing out of school?); a child has been stealing lunches; a teacher wants the principal to let her circumvent the rule on required college hours for next semester (because he is "more fair than the superintendent"); and there is a letter from an irate parent who claims there's a picture of Christ in a room."

Written down, the situations sounded humorous. Yet, each was potentially dangerous unless handled carefully. In the brainstorming, it was stimulating to get opinions of others, as each sought solutions. It was also comforting to know that other people floundered as each of us did.

Each of us has an "In Basket" of concerns—concerns which involve our associates. We have to remind ourselves we're surrounded by streams of feelings, tribulations to a sea of problems unless we stem the flow. How?

TO THINK AND PRAY ABOUT: God reassures us that He wants to hear our problems. He also points to the value of confessing our sins to each other. Consider the excitement and fellowship of neighborhood therapy—examining situations before they're problems. God meets with small groups.

Full Measure

He borrowed a bushel of wheat from my bin,
Then asked for a basket to put it all in.
He went to the miller and had some grain ground,
Then shared with his neighbors who lived close around.
He planted the other and toiled in the field
Till wheat heads grown heavy turned golden with yield.
He brought back my basket as good neighbor ought,
But its weight was heavy— so much he had brought!
The basket ran over, for wheat he had ground
Had doubled the measure of friendship we found. J.M.B.

"DOUBLING" was a nice, old-fashioned custom. When one neighbor borrowed from the other, the borrower repaid the lender in double. Ironically, now that the fat years have come, neighbors are closer together in the urbanized world; but people in a land of plenty have grown farther apart.

Recently we visited "back home" places—where days were twice as long, everything was twice as funny—and people returned twice as much. As a former classmate chatted, she poured homemade jam into a container and asked her husband to return the glass to its owner. That was another quaint practice, refilling a glass or dish with some "specialty of the house."

"You know," she said, "I can't buy something our minister said Sunday—that we no longer need each other. We need each other now more than ever. We've gotten away from God and from each other. We're all too lonely."

God's words are timeless. And He makes it very clear what our relationship with others should be—long-lasting and giving as well.

TO THINK AND PRAY ABOUT: I like to think of neighborliness being the warm cloak God offers until He hands us our heavenly robes!

Correcting The Carbon

"Some of the best lessons we ever learn we learn from our mistakes and our failures."   Tryon Edwards

"ISN'T THE new carbon paper intriguing?" My friend looked at the package. "Actually," the clerk continued, "it's copy film and keeps renewing itself right in the package."

Wonderful! No more dim second copies. No more smearing and smudging. No more constant buying . . . .

And the copy film lived up to its name—and more. What she didn't know, of course, was that the second copy would be so bright and so near-indelible that it was almost impossible to erase.

She decided there was no need really to bother erasing the second copy. It was only for her files. What value was there in correction tape for the original if she had to stop constantly and correct pages nobody else would see?

She knew what she had written. If not, she could guess from context. Under what conditions would she need to quote *verbatim*? She soon found out.

There are no synonyms for numbers; and IRS would like to question Page 3, Section C, Line IV, Subhead *a*. She strained to make out the figures. Poor Sheba. *How* she strained to make out the figures! There was no way. She tried to erase, but all efforts served to blend together the errors and the corrections. Eventually, of course, she was compelled to refigure the entire form and retype the income tax return. It took her hours. It strained her patience. And all the while she was painfully aware that it resulted from carelessness.

"You know," she commented when she finished, "I think life's a lot like that—'one original and from one to six carbons to correct'!"

TO THINK AND PRAY ABOUT: Sometimes we try to cover over our mistakes with *superficial things*, but what about the heart underneath—deep down? The heart belongs to God. He sees inside it; and one day each of us is to give account of his uncorrected mistakes. Maybe we'll realize then that what's underneath is what matters!

A Garden Plot

July 9
Luke 21:36
Jeremiah 29:5

A garden plot's a healing spot;
Just how I do not know,
But as I watched my mother work
Her eyes just told me so.
When she was troubled, I could tell:
She'd take her spade and go
To her own private piece of earth
And dig it row by row;
And then she'd kneel and take the soil
To sift it here and there,
Talking softly as she worked—
Perhaps it was a prayer.
A garden plot's a healing spot;
I know the feel of sod
Was my dear mother's way to say,
"I've touched a bit of God." J.M.B.

ONE OF THE pleasures of the Southern California climate is the sunshine winters here. That means we can have year-round vegetable gardens.

For winter harvest here, gardeners sow seed and set out transplants in summer. God saw the Genesis-world as "good," which means He scattered blessings everywhere. California's blessings come in fertile soil, wrapped in sunshine; and good-neighbor states share their blessing of water. So, here at the outset of winter, we are able to choose from a wide spectrum of such thrivers as peas, cabbage and all its cousins (cauliflower, broccoli and brussel sprouts), carrots and lettuce. Children, who enjoy immediate results, plant mini-gardens of seed which germinate quickly. Radishes must understand children; they respond at three-week intervals. Letting children experiment in gardening is an exciting way to introduce them to God's miracles of growth. We used to have little "radish prayers"—reasonable requests like "Make me thankful today, dear Lord."

TO THINK AND PRAY ABOUT: Even a window garden lets you "touch a bit of God!"

Singing Together

DO YOU FEEL a spiritual lift when you join the congregation in singing a great hymn of praise? Singing together unites hearts as well as voices. Christian songs are powerful. They can release us from the prison of our fears, untie our tongues and lift up our souls.

There used to be old "singing schools" on Sunday afternoon. People of all ages gathered to "sing the scale," have their voices tested by a tuning fork for pitch and to study the historical background of composers. Somehow the "singing schools" gave way to more formalized choir practices and music appreciation courses (fine—except that it left those who used to sing by rote instead of note at a loss). Now, the young people seem to be going back to the old practices in new ways. Guitars are replacing pianos and organs; folk songs and spirituals are replacing the hymns. All the same, they are singing together.

I was a teenager belonging to neither the older nor the younger generation. Maybe that accounts partially for my appreciation of the hymn explanations our church organist inserts in the bulletins from time to time, the most recent being on "Love Divine, All Loves Excelling" (words by Charles Wesley, 1747; music by John Zundel, 1870).

Who is the "Joy of heaven, to earth come down?" One assumes that the hymn extolls the love of God, but it is Jesus Christ who comes to make our hearts His humble dwelling in "pure, unbounded love"—the love of God incarnate made manifest in the flesh. "The hymn," Jackie wrote, "is a prayer to Christ who is Love Divine."

What is the "second rest" mentioned? The early Wesleys believed that after conversion there was a second experience for the Christian—a time of total consecration when the heart is cleansed from all sin. Afterwards came rest—or liberty in Christ. She defined it as "wholeness," a personality balanced by virtues and strengths in body, mind and spirit.

TO THINK AND PRAY ABOUT: Spiritual "wholeness" or maturity is something we all desire. Seek it in prayer.

Walking A Summer Road

July 11
Psalm 100:1-5

WALKING a summer road gives me an opportunity to take inventory. The breath of the morning is sweet and I find that I am wealthy in my todays, yesterdays and tomorrows: real, remembered and prayed for.

To the right stand soldierly rows of corn in green, tasseled uniforms. "Shoulder-high by the Fourth of July," I recall my grandfather saying. I pause, remembering the slender corn-silked ears which fattened to fill fall's granary with gold; reflecting, as I stand, on Elizabeth Browning's "Out in the fields with God." In His fields I give thanks that I am more than a graduated animal, that I am gifted with the power of memory and a happy-ever-after conviction made possible by Jesus Christ.

To the left the sunflowers, their golden-rayed heads too heavy for their stalks, tilt towards the July sun—like a sleepy child in church. The leaves are enormous, rough and somewhat heart-shaped—like my thoughts. Such practical things, sunflowers. My mother used to plant the bright ornamentals to conceal unsightly fences. Worshiping the sun as they did, they grew tall rapidly, furnishing quick shade where the chickens could dust themselves. They gave off a nose-tickling aroma. Bees gathered their gold-dusted pollen in summer; birds gathered their copper-toned seed in fall; and I pressed a few spikey petals in my poignant book of memories.

The road twists and bends, like the years. Ahead lie the little hills, still rounded with their own green growth in the "middle-child month" of summer, and still waiting to be climbed—as hills always are. Beyond them lies the tracery of purple phlox, flushed hollyhocks and one yellow rose twisting its vines round a garden gate like a lady's hair on curlers. That gate at home would swing open if it were there anymore, for it enjoyed the pleasure of summertime company. It squeaked with a "joyful noise." My father was always going to oil it. I am glad he never did. I like to remember it that way.

TO THINK AND PRAY ABOUT: Take a walk—real or imagined. When the magic of the morning's gone, remember that shadows are short at a summer's noon. "For the Lord is good . . . and His truth endureth to all generations."

Why The Big Rush?

THE MAGAZINE article declared one is able to cook a nourishing meal in thirty minutes. I should have been wise enough to ignore "This Timetable Can't Fail"—then I could have avoided a disaster. Could the author of the article possibly realize that this particular reader has been known to shrink a sweater in Woolite, and bake a pound cake with a Swiss cheese texture?

Thirty-minute beef-stew—simple. right? Wrong! Waiting until the allocated 30 minutes before dishup-time was the first pitfall. The main course recipe proceeded to tell how to coat meat cubes with salt, spice and flour; brown in Dutch oven; remove from pan; prepare vegetables; stir in fat; add broth; return meat; add rice; and cover. What they neglect to mention earlier is that one doesn't start counting until this point. Now with dinner already destined to be an hour and a half late, one has to set the table, toss the salad, perk the coffee and take care of any other incidentals: such as husband's telephone-question, "Dinner at the usual time?"; or having to haul the meat-smelling dog outside.

Maybe the *timetable* didn't fail, but *I* did. Anyway, why the big rush? Today's suggested reading says nothing about stew, but the writer stresses patience. God promises, God fulfills; but He works on His own timetable—not yours, mine or the article's. He is not in a hurry like we are. He is willing to work with His design for our lives (in ways we cannot see) until He has produced that which is perfect in His sight.

Examples of God's plan and how He achieves them are the total thesis of the Bible. Undoubtedly Sarah and Abraham were anxious for their promised son. God sent the child when the time was right. Think of how long Israel waited for the Messiah; and when God's Son appeared, few recognized Him in the simplicity of His Father's design.

TO THINK AND PRAY ABOUT: Slow down . . . wait . . . pray . . . rushing can be hazardous to your health.

The Warmth Of Loving

DO YOU FEEL it: a certain sense of warmth? True, it is midsummer and the July breeze is twisting into hot-breathed whirlwinds that dance across the pickle-making cucumber vines. The sun heats beaches to sandy ovens, bronzing bathers along the shores. But it goes farther than the garden and deeper than the skin. It's the kind of warmth that penetrates the heart—the warmth of loving.

When we Americans say we love our country, what do we mean? The Deep South when azaleas are in bloom? New England when autumn kisses the sugar maples? Wheat fields glistening in the sun . . . pine trees . . . sea foam? It is all of these—and more. Henry van Dyke came closest to expressing a national feeling perhaps when he called America "The Blessed Land of Room Enough" and described it "where the air is full of sunlight and the flag is full of stars." We are a large country with a large heart, where there is room enough for all codes and creeds. The air we breathe is an inner air in which we can inhale the breath of freedom and self-respect.

When we Christians say we love God, what do we mean? That we believe in a Creator who set our world in motion? That He continues to populate it with His Images . . . seed it . . . harvest it . . . repeat the process? Or isn't it more—*much* more? Jesus said that unless we are willing to renounce all for the sake of the Kingdom of God, we have no part in it. This means a total commitment of our lives to Christ. This means accepting Him as our personal Savior. Jesus opens His arms even wider than America can swing open the gates to welcome the stranger to our shore. If, as Americans, we can breathe the inner air of freedom, let us, as Christians, see with the inner light of love. That is the sense of warmth I mean!

TO THINK AND PRAY ABOUT: Are we people who hesitate to get involved, make sacrifices, correct injustice or heal wrongs? We can turn the negativism in this statement into something positive. Let us pray: "We know our problems, Lord. Give each of us a share in the solutions." The cost is high. Can you pay? Jesus did. Our patriots did. We can!

Winged Thoughts

The little bird flew down to perch
Upon a fragile limb;
It swayed beneath the tiny weight,
'Twas much too small for him.

And yet, as it bent towards the earth,
The bird had notes to sing:
A message for the world to hear;
It, too, must trust its wing.

I found the place inside of me
Where wings of faith must start;
Then hope came by to sing a song
And perched upon my heart. J.M.B.

"IF I KEEP a green bough in my heart, the singing bird will come," says an ancient Chinese proverb. If our hearts wore "Welcome" signs, what birds might we attract?

Perhaps the first bird to arrive would be that of *Kindness.* A song of kindness comes from a heart filled with love. It does not long for a larger limb where it can do great things. It sings a song of kindness in its own little green bough; and that is true greatness.

Would you suppose the next guest might be the bird of *Enthusiasm?* Enthusiasm sings with a sparkle in its eye. It sings of the zest of life. It sings of faith, hope and charity—never complaining about its job, but ever begging for more work to do.

And here comes the bird of *Generosity!* It shares its song—with or without talent. It loves and is loved because its secret is happiness. Its song is so service-filled that all doors open to hear its words.

The little bird of *Humor* slips in on unseen wing. It is so accustomed to goofing around it's not even sure it has found the right bough! But its notes ring with laughter even when the words tie the tongue. We need *Humor!*

TO THINK AND PRAY ABOUT: Lord, most of all, send our hearts the bird of *Gratitude* that we may thank You and those around us.

What If?

WHAT IF YOU, *an adult, received this letter from a child? Do a bit of role playing: be the mother, grandmother, aunt, older sister, teacher—or any other authority figure. When we are "figures of authority," we accept that children look to us for guidance, but are we aware that—title or no title—we are the patterns that they follow? Are we vigilant? Do we wear our crowns gladly? Read the letter carefully. Consider how you would respond.*

Dear Dad and Mom,

I trusted you so much and you let me down. Today I am in Juvenile Hall waiting for whatever they have to dish out. It doesn't matter much because it'll be coming from the wrong person—and too late. I am a number now—an "offender" they tell me. But whatever punishment I have coming should have come from you. Why didn't you see that? I did. But kids don't have the courage to ask for what they know they need and think they don't want.

Why did you fly into a rage at little things and let the big ones go? What difference did it make which fork I used? What really bugged you was the company I chose, wasn't it? Why didn't you say so? You knew their parents were strung out on booze. You knew the kids would be just like them. "We don't do that in our home," you said. Maybe you were right saying it was their business; but I was *yours!* I got the feeling you didn't really care.

Were you afraid of being strict? Did you think you'd lose me? Well, better there than here. And why weren't you consistent? If it wasn't okay for me to stay out late on week nights, what made those Saturday night parties so different? If I was supposed to mow the lawn, why didn't I? I tested you. And you flunked. And didn't you know how I felt when you giggled and carried on like one of my crowd when I brought friends home? I wanted to show you off, not have you show off. Why didn't you shake me till my teeth rattled when you caught me in that first lie? You knew the little white lies would grow into big black ones. You let me win. And I didn't want to. There's no victory behind bars. You went to church on Easter and Christmas, then sent me out alone to find God.

TO THINK AND PRAY ABOUT: *Stand firm! Somebody who loves you is watching.*

Have You Heard From God Today?

July 16
Luke 13:34-35

GOOD MORNING! May I come in for a little chat? I am in your neighborhood and thought I would see if you have need for repairs. Your heart, maybe? Is this as wide as it will open? Perhaps its hinges are stuck.

Now, now—leave things as they are. Just talk to Me as you talk with the others who love you. We have mutual friends but some of them forget to call on Me when their households fall apart. I hope they have shared with you. I came prepared with My tools—prepared to heal the sick, feed the hungry, clothe the naked, give water to the thirsty and bind up hearts that are broken. But isn't there more for Me to do? Hasn't anyone spoken of a soul that needs cleansing? I have the ingredients for purification, just in case. They call other repairmen. They call their physicians. And, yet, My office is less crowded, My schedule more flexible and there is never a waiting line. Why, then, do My children not call on Me daily? Are they ashamed? Do they feel unworthy because of self-pity, unkind thoughts, oversensitivity or procrastination? They need not worry; all information is strictly confidential. There is no reason for shame. All have sinned; and those who bring their problems to Me are healed bit by bit. Not only do I forget the errors of the past, I offer day-by-day suggestions for self-improvement.

What are your building plans? Have you any ideas for adding another room? It is good to expand. In a house with a larger heart, perhaps you will find a place to entertain those who have forgotten Me. I will bless you as you meet in My Name.

Incidentally, the lighting is poor in several corners here. May I shed a little more light for you to read by? I see you have a copy of My Book. More reading will help to spread the light and get rid of some of those fears you told Me about. Trust Me. I do all things well.

TO THINK AND PRAY ABOUT: God is talking. Are you listening? He longs to gather His children to Him. Invite Him in to bless your house.

What Is It That God Cannot Do?

July 17
Mark 10:27

IN A HIGH-VOLTAGE discussion of the Gospel according to Mark, our minister posed the rhetorical question: "Can God create a stone so heavy He can't lift it?" The idea blew a few fuses, which he replaced effortlessly by explaining that such a question imposed our human limitations on God, and that he asked it for the purpose of initiating discussion.

In the charged atmosphere of our Bible study group, some shocking comments came (just as our leader intended!): "Why, that's Pharisee-questioning . . . No! It's Satanic . . . Wait! Remember here in the book of Mark, the disciples, themselves were questioning Jesus . . ." It was a senior member of our ladies' group who threw the switch with a gentle touch, "No need for getting excited. God could if He wanted to."

Don't those simple words sum up God's Power? The discussion sprang from the story of the rich young ruler who wanted to follow Jesus but was unable to make the sacrifice. It was then that the Master commented sadly, "It is easier for a camel to go through the eye of a needle than for a rich man to enter into the Kingdom of God." Jesus did not say it was impossible; He said it was hard. I believe we will meet some rich saints in heaven; and we will know they fought a good fight.

Actually, we are uncertain as to the exact interpretation of "eye of a needle." Those of us accustomed to mending think of the needles as an instrument of sharp steel, pointed on one end, with an eyehole for thread on the other. Once, however, I heard the needle's eye explained as a low arch through which camels crawled—difficult but possible. Either way there is an element of difficulty. Personally, I would be unable to push a thread through (let alone crawl!) without my reading glasses. With them, the task is easier; but with God, *all* things are possible!

TO THINK AND PRAY ABOUT: Can God repent for us? Can He believe for us? As my dear Christian friend said, "If He wanted to." But the conditions of salvation are repentence, trusting and obeying. These we must do for ourselves.

Keep Mowing Your Lawns High!

July 18
Jeremiah 17:7-8

THIS WEEK'S *Notes To The July Gardener* suggested: "Keep mowing your lawns high. It will help keep the roots cooler and the grass happier during the heat." Lawns around here when close-cropped look like the velvet pile of an Oriental rug, but they lack its durability. Within a matter of hours the tender green fades in the sunlight. One would suppose that with the next mowing the emerald tones would surface, but grass hereabouts is shallow-rooted. It will be next year before the lawns are lovely again—if they survive at all. So, pleasing to the eye as an Oriental cover may be, a "shag" is more practical. So take the good advice and set mowers high.

Any time roots are impaired growth is stunted. In Tokyo, Japan, there grows an ancient pine—a tree so old that nobody remembers its age. Some say that it was over four centuries ago that a gardener planted the pine tree in a temporary dish. It was much too shallow and the man planned to transplant it into his garden, but he loved the pungent needle-scents and kept the tree as a companion until his death. His descendants, in an effort to please their ancestor, trimmed each root and pruned each bough as the tree tried to outgrow the inadequate dish. Today, in the original container, the tree stands—having long ago given up any effort of growing. What could have been a towering landmark is a dwarf—twenty inches high. Held captive, no growing thing can thrive.

I guess what it all amounts to is that we have to make a choice in this life: Do we want to produce lawns and shrubs that make a temporary showing, like the grass, only to wither and die because of our vanity? Do we want to withhold growth by making a tree into a shrub, because of our selfishness making it into something nature did not plan for it?

Let's apply such practices to our personal lives. What happens when we expose our "roots" to the wrong things, without a shield of God's protection? And what about dwarfing lives (ours and others) by cutting ruthlessly?

TO THINK AND PRAY ABOUT: We grow through God's love; others grow through ours.

Who Am I, Lord?

IT WAS A CONSTANT source of irritation to me when everything I did wrong in school (more times than I choose to recall) was attributed to my being an only child. Having no brothers or sisters made me "different"—in the wrong way. And there was simply nothing I could do about it. Labels can be dangerous, even when issued by the Surgeon General. Hang a label around the neck of a child and, ironically, the child becomes exactly what the label claims. "A little bossy . . . sort of self-centered . . . tendency towards laziness . . . a wee bit underhanded . . . you know the way 'only children' are." Maybe I was able to conquer the only-child stigma in my adult life; but why do authority figures not see what they're doing? Stereotyping may be hazardous to one's emotional health. Another person can encourage a poor self-image that never allows one to become the "somebody" God intended.

Outwardly I shrugged off my label but inwardly I cringed. Little did I know that most of my classmates were experiencing inferiorities right along with me—until, finally, one by one, we made full confessions. One was the oldest; another the youngest. Then there was the middle child . . . one girl among all boys . . . the twin . . . the tallest . . . the shortest . . . the smartest . . . the dullest . . . all "*You* knows."

I learned a valuable lesson young. Just leave the labels off. Forget the *clichés*: "Like mother like daughter . . . birds of feather . . . spots on a leopard . . . book by its cover" . . . the works. Red or yellow; black or white; Jew or Gentile; rich or poor; beggar or thief, let each stand on his/her own merit before God.

Now, who am *I*? The lesson I learned added stability to my own life, too. It is as if the Lord speaks to me saying, "You are a special child of Mine, one of many—but you are unique!" "Thank You, Lord," I answer, "that I am different—in just the right way." How do I know? He created me so.

TO THINK AND PRAY ABOUT: Do you torment yourself for fear of being different? Praise God that you are different. He has a plan for you!

Jesus Loves Me!

July 20
I John 4:10

Jesus loves me! This I know;
For the Bible tells me so.
Little ones to Him belong;
They are weak but He is strong.

DID YOU SING this children's song when you were small? I sang it long before I knew the definition of some of the words. I only knew Jesus loved me, and I knew *how* I knew. That's the wonderful thing about learning of the Savior in the days of our youth.

I remember a rural preacher at a "tent revival" saying: "Brothers and Sisters, you are like hogs eating acorns under a big oak tree. You never look up to see where they're coming from." It is important that we teach our children to look up and *see* where their blessings are coming from.

In these push-button days when noise flows into the home like a broken fire hose, how much do children *hear*? We have to practice listening to God and teach our children to do the same; for listening is a learned skill—not an instinct. Would you believe that educational psychologists say that according to research we learn seventy percent of what we know by listening? That's how we learned to talk. That's how we learned to sing:

Jesus loves me! He who died,
Heaven's gate to open wide;
He will wash away my sin,
Let His little child come in.

Do the children know the gate is open? Yes, if we teach them, tell them who opened it and invite them to enter. But, first, perhaps we need to review the rules again: We only know the gate is open if we look up to *see*; we only know we are welcome if we *hear* His Voice.

TO THINK AND PRAY ABOUT: Jesus, take this heart of mine, Make it pure and wholly Thine; Thou hast bled and died for me; I will henceforth live for Thee.

Extended Families

TODAY'S QUOTE seemed out of context for a family gathering, but there was no sign of teasing in the face of the friend who used it to describe the gathering of the extended family. "Time was," she said, "when the clan joined together at the drop of a hat. The big family saw no reason to wait for holidays. They held reunions at peculiar times and places: fishing the rain-swollen creeks in spring; hunting in the autumn-touched bottom lands—even gathering to butcher in winter and to can from the summer garden. There were fish fries, campfires and all-night talks."

One supposes such things go on forever. They don't, of course. The unifying presence of grandparents is usually first to go; then, sadly, one by one, parents. "Extended families" scatter; and we tend to think the remaining relatives have little left in common.

"Not so!" said my friend, who arranged a "getting together" during Christian Family Week. "We have a common past and a whole new generation to share. Never mind the deadly statistics of broken homes, large population of single adults and all that. We proved we could bring ourselves together in the flesh!" Hooray for her!

There are other ways of keeping in touch. One family I know prepared a cookbook utilizing the favorite dishes from generations as far back as they could trace, bringing it up to date for the youngest members. In several instances, families were reunited in visits motivated by the recipe gatherings. In others, correspondences were revived.

Once there's an icebreaker, everything else seems to fall into place. Big dinners with relatives from all parts of the country (like my friend's) are great; but even tacos together would be fun—if that's all a schedule would allow. Telegrams, cards (*with* messages!), phone calls during 'rate hours' . . . There are limitless ways to gather. It is a very special way of perpetuating love from one generation to the next. Our children need to see love work overtime, "As He loved us."

TO THINK AND PRAY ABOUT: God put together the first family. *Let us perpetuate family life, expressing appreciation to the members and to You, Lord.*

Over The Backyard Fence

July 22
Jeremiah 20:10
Psalm 41:9, 12

How nice to have a backyard fence
Across which neighbors chat,
Exchange a cookie recipe—
Or speak of this and that . . .
Someone who'll reach to hold your hand
When you are feeling sad,
Or double-twice your happiness
When you are feeling glad!
Today my neighbor called to me,
"Come see my summer rose!"
And as we chat her coffeepot
Boils up and overflows.
We laugh together and she says,
"Oh well, come in for tea."
We share a fence, a rose, a cup—
And, oh, how blessed are we!

"**A** FENCE CAN bring neighbors closer together," reads a building products ad. They have a point. Good fences can make good neighbors, because sometimes it's the little things that cause the big problems: a dog buries a bone in your prize begonia bed; *your* child picks the first rose of the season for you—from someone else's garden.

Think of it this way. You are fencing out problems, not friends. Hazlitt turned the phrase neatly: "Familiarity may not breed contempt, but it takes the edge off admiration." Our human frailties crawl through when there are holes left in the hedge. We hear too much, see too much, and understand too little. I don't want to be seen in curlers even in my backyard. And when George steps on the rake prongs-up—I just think it's best the entire neighborhood doesn't have to hear what he has to say. But there are two essentials to a fence: 1. Leave the gate unlocked for neighbors; 2. Leave the heart unlocked for God.

TO THINK AND PRAY ABOUT: Vibrations leap fences! Do others hear Jesus in you?

Midsummer Night's Scream

THE BETWEEN season ho-hum creeps up, marked only by a slight headache, low-grade fever and feelings of irritation over little things—then, wham! It is at an epidemic stage; it's most contagious. Hard as it is to admit, we homemakers may be the carriers! Our family members develop the disease by just looking at our faces or listening to our voices. "I don't feel like going to the beach . . . It's too hot to barbecue . . . I'm tired of picnics."

Rest assured it's not in your head. You need a change of pace. Read Psalm 146. If you aren't stimulated, see your doctor!

"Praise ye the Lord." How long has it been since you sang? Gather around the piano, turn on the record player or bring out the guitar—then, clap your hands or stomp your feet *together*.

"Happy is he . . . whose hope is in the Lord." How long has it been since you've thanked the Lord for the hope you have in Him. He has given His children the hope of eternal life in heaven and the hope of abundant life on earth. Your offering will be received even if it's only "Thank You, Lord."

"(Happy is he) who giveth food to the hungry." How long has it been since you invited a stranger or a poor acquaintance to eat with you? Or how long has it been since you sent the children out with cookies for a shut-in? Doing some unselfish deed for one who is unable to return the kindness does indeed bring happiness.

"The Lord raiseth them that are bowed down." So there you have it—the ingredients for happiness: a heart full of praise to the Lord and a willingness to give to others from the overflow. Praise ye the Lord!

TO THINK AND PRAY ABOUT: Think about, then write down, all the things you have to praise God for. Then make a list of how you can share the praise in your heart with the needy.

Do Hummingbirds Go To Heaven?

July 24
Luke 17:2

MY, MY, MY! The questions children do ask. It would take King Solomon before Delilah styled his hair to answer some of them. "Whose child would I have been if you and Daddy hadn't married?" "How does the water keep from sloshing out down in China?" "What color are God's eyes?"

Child psychologists advise: Keep all answers at the level of the child's understanding" (But what about my understanding?). "Don't talk down to them" (Down? The questions are more "up" than my answers are likely to be!). "Don't over-explain" (Chances are ten to one I won't explain at all!). "Appear to think the child's question over" (Now, that one I can do without faking!).

The question posed to a young mother recently and her answer (solution, really) was so inspiring. "Do hummingbirds go to heaven, Mommie?" The tot was soberly watching a ruby-throat whir from one hibiscus bloom to another. His mother squatted down beside him. "The Bible doesn't mention hummingbirds," she answered honestly. She waited, but there were no more questions—temporarily. Then other hummers gathered to feed from the single bush. What's coming next? she wondered.

"They have propellers like airplanes on their wings. They could fly to heaven—if it isn't too far." The four-year-old's mother quoted what her son seemed to be talking over to himself. "Look!" he cried suddenly. "They can fly backwards. If God didn't want them there, He could send them back." A sudden war between the hummingbirds saved the day for the mother. There was bickering, indignant twittering and finally disorderly retreat—all over a single flower.

The child shook his head. "They won't get to go to heaven; they're bad—they fight. He was sad.

"They're not bad, honey," she consoled. "They're hungry. I have an idea. Let's build them a heaven in the yard. God wants us to care for all His little creatures." The child was ecstatic as together mother and he hung up separate feeders to avoid competition and nasty arguments. Soon the backyard was a heaven for many contented hummingbirds.

TO THINK AND PRAY ABOUT: Children's questions are often creative. How creative are your answers?

Strength Born Of Weakness

July 25
Psalm 71:16

L OOK AROUND you today and you may see a world concentrating on its weakness instead of seeking strength to
overcome.

Look around you again and be comforted. You will see excep-
tions to the rule: those trusting people who refuse to focus on
the negative, defeating things in life which so distort the view-
finder. God strengthens them in their weaknesses.

I know a writer. You know her work. But her byline is less important than her lifeline. She receives it from God and tosses it
out to others on the printed page. Readers don't know of her
handicap—which is exactly as she wishes.

"In sickness and in health . . ." was just a get-it-over-with
phrase when a dreamy-eyed sixteen-year-old bride exchanged
vows with a twenty-year-old hero who was poised for flight.
How could he have known he was to be grounded by a wife
declared "totally disabled?" How could either of them have
known that "to love" meant to cheer, to encourage—truly "for-
saking all others?" They held hands and trusted. They still do.
Actually, "hands" is the key word.

She saw her hands as square, blunt and ugly—until her husband's tender touch made them seem beautiful . . . saw both
hands white-clenched in a hospital labor room . . . saw them
tough enough to join the work force to supplement the family
income while diapering and feeding two growing children . . .
gentle enough to wipe away grandchildren-tears when one
child's marriage fell apart . . . determined enough to reprimand
when necessary . . . compassionate enough to uphold a husband
in gentle love and commitment . . . and beautiful folded in
prayer.

Then those capable hands drew from God's reserve and
doubled their work, typing by day, occasionally massaging a
limp leg and adjusting back braces, and holding Bible
storybooks for grandchildren by night. They gripped crutches
with such authority, the crutches surrendered to a cane. God
found no fault with those hands!

TO THINK AND PRAY ABOUT: Faith in God and
love for each other offers new strength daily.

Rooting For The Underdog

July 26
Romans 8:28

THERE THEY sit—eyes glued to the screen. Are they rooting for the underdog in the World Series? Most likely. This is a favorite time of year as many men exercise their powers as "king of the castle," demanding meals on TV trays and getting them. But we homemakers need not feel like the underdog—we win by giving.

If chess is a game of war, and golf is a "sudden death" play, maybe baseball is a game of life. (Certainly it can be lively with runner and pitcher colliding at home plate; manager and umpire doing verbal battle on the field; and fans fist-fighting it out in the stands—which, I guess, makes it all the more lifelike.) The struggling new team outclassed by the "aristocracy" of the national favorites rings a patriotic bell, doesn't it?

The Statue of Liberty in New York harbor bears these sonnet-phrases on a bronze tablet on the pedestal:

". . . Give me your tired, your poor,
   Your huddled masses yearning to breathe free,
   The wretched refuse of your teeming shore;
   Send these, the homeless, tempest-tost, to me,
   I lift my lamp beside the golden door!"

Maybe our game-watchers identify with the historical parallel. Many of them are veterans who helped us, a "nation of underdogs," keep our freedom. Memory or a history book can replay World War II's dramatic conversion from a peace-loving people to a nation in uniform—united for a common cause in which we believed. Teamwork did it.

There's a spiritual parallel here, too. Just look at the people around you who depend upon God, team up with Him, then draw in all the talent they can scout—working for a common cause. And the exciting thing is that everybody can play the game. God uses the handicapped as well as the able-bodied. Sometimes He can coach them even more effectively, for they know the odds are against them and push a little harder. God has no losers—just winners!

TO THINK AND PRAY ABOUT: Trust God as your manager. Never wave the white flag of surrender. Instead, lift high His royal banner!

Swinging A Hammer

I 'M NO "mechanical woman," but now and then something comes up that—well, has to be hammered down. I needed a just-right hammer. Tell me, have you ever weighed a hammer? No? Then try it and you'll be able to have seconds on desserts afterwards. The common household type weighs at least a pound—usually more, say from twenty to twenty-four ounces. (No, I didn't weigh them; they don't come by the pound; the weight was stamped on the head—and didn't include the handle!)

After I read an article on how to choose a hammer just right for swinging, I decided to buy one for myself. The writer advised the shopper to pick up said object and swing it full force as if hammering a nail into wood (or was it concrete?). "Do it again and again, no matter how many persons in the store are staring at you. Don't buy unless it feels right. If you are a golfer, you know well how a difference of an ounce or two in the weight of a club can affect your swing." I know nothing about golf, but I know a lot about hammer-weights—now.

While I swung (with a good audience as predicted), it occurred to me that we use hammers of different sorts throughout life. There were so many hammers in the hardware section—any of which could perform great feats: building up or tearing down; damaging or repairing; beautifying or defacing. Imagine a claw hammer in the hands of a wrong person. The looks of the tool are enough to send you underground; and yet those physical blows might prove less of a threat than claw-hammer words. The tool could strike a glancing blow; words, unfortunately, seldom miss their mark. They smash the heart.

The same article had something to say about handles. My hammer's new now, but I want to file this away for future reference: "Get into the habit of inspecting the handle before each use. The trouble is that most persons never discover there is anything wrong until there is an accident." Isn't it the truth? Few people really want to hurt each other—for keeps. But we are careless and hurt others in our thoughtlessness.

TO THINK AND PRAY ABOUT: Choose words wisely. Follow Christ's example.

What We Can't Have

July 28
Psalms 73:12
49:1-3, 14

SOMETIMES LETTERS TO THE EDITOR can be more revealing to a reader than the articles themselves, can they not? Recently one of the leading women's magazines carried the results of a poll taken among motion picture stars, all of whom were Academy Award winners at one time. The results were the usual: bored, lonely, misunderstood (real or feigned). Reader responses in the following month's issues were very interesting:

"What is it money can't buy? Reading their problems makes me think they think their problems are different from mine. It ain't so. There's not a woman alive who doesn't feel bored and misused. Why do movie stars think they have a corner on these emotions? We all feel we have to live up to images somebody makes us into—no matter who we are or where we are. What's beauty, status and money got to do with that? I have to go here, go there, say this, say that, just like them. I get lonely, too, but it would be better to be rich-lonely than poor-lonely; and lonely-beautiful than lonely-ordinary. They depend on us to keep them on that pedestal. They needed an image. Don't they got no 'preciation?"

"Thanks a lot, Ms. Editor and Girls! You're right, you know we all agree with you. Women's Movement got us in more trouble than it got us out of. Pie in the sky, my eye! Women are going to have to make their own contributions and affect the world in their own way if they want it changed. Do we want to live in a world man created?"

TO THINK AND PRAY ABOUT: These reflections are pretty earthy, but they're worth thinking about. Analyze them, then come up with some answers that fit your thinking. Ask yourself what God would have you do. Look at the first writer's comments. How much stress do you place on money? (Be honest!) If you feel bored and misused, do you attribute it to your being a woman? What do you do about it? Talk to your husband? Talk to God? Define beauty. Could God create anything *unlovely*? Or, do we make ourselves so? Look at the second piece. It's loaded! Did "man" create our world?

Bargain-Buying

July 29
Hebrews 11:6
Matthew 6:19-21
II Timothy 3:1-5

"SUMMER CLEARANCE SALES" filled every inch in last night's edition of the local newspaper. You're familiar with all the pitches.

But do you know the pitfalls? Two of them glared out at me. One merchant suggested: "A smart shopper keeps watch for bargains throughout the year at our store." I'm not a smart shopper. I watch—but with a suspicious eye. Anything on sale is bound to be a "second," going out of style, giving off radiation or shopworn. Else would it be reduced to sell? Anything *not* marked down is too expensive, so I am reasonably sure I'm being duped. The second thing that caught my eye was a stamp of approval put on sales promotions. "Monthly bargains add up to substantial annual savings," the bank manager's message read. The dissertation that followed was on depositing the savings in a way to insure maximum income. "We are merchants. Our product is money." Have you ever tried to find the money you save on sales? It's as elusive as the whooping crane.

What *is* a bargain anyway? Actually, there are two major concepts to bear in mind. First, there is the "bargain counter" displaying all sorts of merchandise which the shopper can purchase at reduced prices. Sometimes (in certain departments such as hard-to-sell foodstuff or closeouts on cosmetics), you can get a free sample. Second, there is the bargain in terms of an agreement (such as banks offer). The business transaction settles what each shall give and receive. Think of this in relationship to God.

TO THINK AND PRAY ABOUT: Does God hand out "sample" blessings? If so, are any "buying obligations" attached? Does He reduce quality or change models? When Jesus said, "It is finished," God had given. Have we received, then given? Answers lie in today's reading—and in prayer!

Running For Your Life

July 30
Psalm 19:1-7

"**R**UN FOR YOUR life!" used to shout disaster. We fled on such warning. Remember? Now, for the most part, the message applies to fleet-footed joggers. You know its claims; maybe you've collected some: loss of weight, improved cardiovascular system, strengthened muscle tone, emotional balance and companionship. The latter is moot, isn't it?

What I didn't realize was that running supposedly took special shoes. I thought any comfortable shoe would do. As for shoes, as long as they don't cramp the fifty-two bones in the runner's foot, replacing psyche with bunions, they're adequate. Right? Not according to a "Training Shoes" article. One needs training flats (a heavy basic shoe) and racing flats (for the big getaway, obviously.) "Women's shoes should be somewhat lighter," the writer pointed out. That would make them cheaper. Wrong! I tossed the magazine away, perfectly content to continue running in "improper shoes."

We should have known it wouldn't be long until some *entrepreneur* came up with a scheme that would make adults self-conscious to walk, run, creep or crawl in canvas shoes and children sulk if they're denied proper gear like *all* the other kids wear. Such a short time ago magazines were action-packed with praise of this "no investment" exercise. Now, who can afford to run?

Two suggestions in the article were sound, however: 1. There should be little distance between the toe and the shoe; and 2. There should be no stress anywhere at any time. That's good advice for the purchase of any shoe, but I was thinking of a little anecdote that had nothing to do with shoes. One little girl said to another (about a mutual friend): "You'd better quit telling her your business. She runs to God with everything!"

What better destination? And the practical part of running to God is that prayer needs no investment. The claims are sound indeed and better than any entrepreneur's—just about the same as those for jogging: physical and emotional strengthening with a spiritual thrust! Let's run for our lives!

TO THINK AND PRAY ABOUT: Let there be no distance between you and God—and no stress.

Our Togetherness Prayer

ALMIGHTY GOD, as we turn our calendars forward, let us look backward upon the history of this great nation with grateful hearts. You, Lord, have brought us to a land of promise and helped us make it into a Promised Land.

Thank you, Lord, that You have blessed us with bountiful harvests—enough for our families, our neighbors and our brothers and sisters all over the world. Here there is opportunity for all. Here there are resources untapped. And here we can earn and learn in an atmosphere of peace. Abundance is ours through our efforts and Your answers to prayer.

Thank You, Lord, that You have made us free. Freedom is a state we must continually protect lest we lose it. We earned it through sacrificial blood of our patriots. Please, Lord, keep us as hospitable as our forefathers, but as progressive as we are today—our bodies filled with their courage and optimism; our hearts filled with Your hope and love. Let us put away all hatreds, lay aside all grudges, *now*.

Thank You, Lord, that You have made our land truly "America, the Beautiful," a panorama of majesty put together by your caring Hand. Here those who came before us faced perils we cannot know. But they conquered and built homes for themselves. Give us the same courage You gave them. Let us face today's perils, conquer them and build for ourselves spiritual homes such as architects are yet unable to envision.

Thank You, Lord, that You joined the fifty states together into one nation, under God, indivisible. Thank You for the well-planned cities, the wheels of machinery that turn our industrial world and the yet unspoiled refuges You helped us maintain.

Thank You, Lord, for religious liberty. Teach us to use it in a way that is pleasing in Your sight that others may see the light that leads to ultimate freedom in You.

Thank You, Lord, for grateful hearts!
Amen.

Prayer For Preservation

DEAR LORD, You hold all the gifts of earth and heaven in Your storehouse. I have come to You today to ask but one: that of preservation. If You will bless me with this one gift, much can be acccomplished in Your name.

Preserve the talent You gave me for seeing beauty in the smallest things. Keep the desire within me to share in whatever way You think best. If it be with words, let my symbols shine to reflect Your glory. If it be with song, tune my ears to right lyrics; give loving pitch to my voice. If it be with vision, open my eyes wider; let there be less mystery and more wonder. Unlock my heart, Lord. Fill it with greater love. Let me share it, knowing that only through sharing can I preserve love at all.

Preserve in me the small fragments of Your wisdom, Your truth and Your love. Let them grow so that some way, somehow, I can touch some lonely heart. Your power over our lives enables us to be victorious when we find ourselves complaining about the summer heat, the too-early rain that spoiled a garden or the guests who left our house in shambles. These can be repaired, Lord, so much easier than my fault-finding pettiness and narrow attitudes. Preserve in me the awareness that unkind words cut closer to the bone than serrated knives; that an uncaring shrug can bring greater pain than a bee sting on a bare foot. No packaged balm can ease such pain.

Preserve in me the strength to conquer the anger I feel at small deceits, for they are with us, Lord. You know how hard it is to shop when candy bars are reduced in size and raised in price; when "Special Purchase" items shrink at first laundering; when there are fewer tissues in each box I buy. These manufacturers have broken no laws, Lord, but they have broken faith with me, their customer. Let me learn by such subtle dishonesties. Let me be open and honest with all who cross my path. Preserve my patience when they are less honest with me. Let me show others that nothing "downsizes" Your care.

And, Lord, preserve in me most of all my complete dependence on You. Only then can I serve others with an enduring courage in the face of pain or agony of death . . . only then can I be Your ambassador of laughter, Your earthly shoulder for the release of tears from Your children. Lord, I need Your preservation.

Summer Mood

SUMMER HOLDS its breath. The speckled leaves of the oak are still. Still, too, are the once-lovely voices of the nesting birds which built a parish in the oak tree's boughs. There is only the complaining caw of the crows which know that the early grain is gone and are in no mood to wait for another harvest. The sun rises crimson in a sky, bluish and hot. The flowers droop as if in mourning—except for the zennias, which blaze in such glory they seem to add to the heat of the earth, which has been absorbing the heat of the sun since the June solstice. Now it waits for a north wind to bring relief from the polar circle where the ice is thawing. But in August there is no wind, just breathless heat—determined to stay until the September equinox. The tinkle of a distant cow bell suspends in midair as if too tired to move on. A few rusty needles fall from a dusty pine as an irate squirrel, the absolute monarch of a dozen acorns, spots a bandit jay. Then all is still again in solemn lamentation—a pathetic sense of old age. Summer's eye is pale and bleared—as is the weary watcher's of such scenes.

But let's not get caught up in the discomforts of the month. Instead, rise up; the garden needs your attention. People need it, too. This can be our time of waiting on the Lord as we minister for Him.

Solomon was right, wasn't he? "There is no new thing under the sun." We just rediscover the past, which is good when it brings us back to God and the way He made the world a garden place. The wise king kept posing the questions, "Can the world without God meet our needs? Can we truly live without God?" He answered his own question with "All is vanity" if we delude ourselves. God alone is able to bring lasting relief like an unexpected breeze in August.

TO THINK AND PRAY ABOUT: Seasons are too brief to dwell upon discomforts. Around us people are in need; maybe time's right for us to give.

Three Coins In The Fountain

WHILE THE rain that hit the San Joaquin Valley this week may prove disastrous to grape and fig growers, it was a boon to the valley's olive crop. Tenders of the vineyards and the fig groves were scratching their heads and saying (rightly) that the downpour was "unusual." Olive growers were singing in the rain. Maybe lettuce growers, for example, cared little either way since they regulate their precipitation with irrigation systems. There is no report as to what, if any, effect the unseasonable storm will have on the citrus crop. The situation has the familiar ring of some parable, doesn't it? What if these were our "husbandmen"?

How are the prayers of godly men heard? They have served their Master and they have families for whom they must provide. All of them pray regularly—asking for only what they need. We know that those depending upon the grapes and figs would ask that God withhold the rain. Those depending on olives would ask Him to open the windows of the clouds to irrigate the thirsting groves. Perhaps the other agriculturalists would make no mention, interceding for neither side since they would be unaffected. Which prayers would God hear and answer? Supposing, for that matter, they were unjust. Would God hear? Suppose for a moment that the olive growers, who received the blessing, were less deserving. They were expecting a good crop this year, but now the rainfall will add size and encourage even quicker maturity. Size is a second blessing; and maturity is a third. Quicker maturity allows growers to harvest early and avoid the usual problem of finding adequate labor. In normal years the citrus harvest begins simultaneously with the olive harvest and there are seldom enough workers for both crops.

What will the Father do? Do you suppose the losers are asking, "Why me, Lord?" Of course, but are we rewarded or allowed to suffer hardships according to how "good" we are? God allows blessing and calamity to fall on both the just and unjust. We are challenged to rise above "poor me" feelings.

TO THINK AND PRAY ABOUT: Live above your circumstances, not under them.

"Good Friday" For Someone Dear

August 4
Romans 15:13-14

CHRISTMAS AND Easter are the two Holy Days that Christians celebrate all over the world. We continue to celebrate the birthday of Jesus with great joy. Easter is our greatest Christian triumph—triumph over death, sin and the grave.

But before either of these great events came to pass, there were less joyous times. The entire hope of the Old Testament is the hope of the arrival of the Messiah, as promised by the prophets, who would redeem the lost world. Jesus (born to die for us) is the Messiah of the New Testament (John 1:41; 4:25). Then when His mission was finished, before there could be a Resurrection, there had to be the Crucifixion for harmony of the Gospels. We keep that sad day ("Good Friday") in various ways according to the mores of our churches and communities. We all have "Good Fridays" in our lives—days when we relive the pangs of sorrow and remorse we felt at the time of the loss of someone dear. Does it sound strange to share with you that today (the "Good Friday" of my father) I remember with an unexplainable joy?

Does it occur to you to observe the birthdays of those you have loved and lost in their absence? I thank God that somehow through all our shared laughter I realized that life as "Daddy's girl" could not go on forever. First, I went away to school; then when I was married, I was forced to focus on my own family; but our love went deeper. I was aware that only in eternity is there a "forever after." And so, I prepared his favorite dishes, and said and did the things that brought him happiness. Today, I held a little memorial service in my heart.

Such practices can teach us a better way of life. Life is comprised of small things that are greater than the big ones: a family member's favorite omelet can bring more love and more comfort than great sacrifices or duties performed for duty's sake alone.

TO THINK AND PRAY ABOUT: Today is the day to "indulge" your loved ones—within the family or outside the family circle with a lot of love and a lot of forgiveness. We can never equal God's gifts, but we can show appreciation.

Trying To Please Everyone

"**I** CAN'T GIVE you a recipe for success, but I can give you one for failure—just try to please everyone!" The fact that the statement was not original with my friend made little difference. It brought about a brainstorming that proved "Laughter is the best medicine." And God is our cure!

"If you're talking about the kids, I'm with you," Ardith chimed in. "I've had it. One grandmother says I'm a dictator; the other says I'm permissive!" Taking a stand takes courage, we decided.

"She's talking about husbands, I think. If I laugh at his description of the day at the office, he says I don't understand; If I don't, he says I've lost my sense of humor." This calls for understanding, we agreed.

"You're both wrong. She's talking about neighbors," a third voice claimed. "When I report my activities to the paper, they say I'm trying for the limelight; if I don't, I'm hiding under a bushel." Needed: balance!

Alice is a principal's wife. "I think she's talking about administrators. If Josh calls a teachers' meeting, he's just trying to get new ideas to take to the superintendent; if not, he doesn't appreciate the democratic process." We must have faith in each other and ourselves, we determined.

Ann grabbed onto that. She's a teacher. "If I even say 'Good morning' to the principal, I'm bucking for a raise. If I ignore him, I'm disloyal." By then all of us were laughing. One by one, each of us came up with some sort of thesis-antithesis which led to no synthesis—just dilemma.

Our first speaker, whose voice had been drowned out by problems-gone-funny, finally got in the bottom line: "I didn't mean to stop there. I was about to say maybe we need stumbling blocks to make our legs strong!"

TO THINK AND PRAY ABOUT: It is far better to try to do God's will than be "people pleasers." Pray for "strong legs."

A Million Dishes To Do!

"THERE'S SOMETHING so special about a big company meal like this!" said the hostess of about thirty of us guests.

"Yeah," said her teenage daughter, "the dishes!"

"Did any of you bring dishes?" her mother laughed. "I am sure I don't *own* this many!"

The daughter gave a last gasp before clearing the table—not that I blamed her. "Scraped and stacked, they'd still be higher than Mount Everest. I'll have to preserve my strength."

"Now, dear, remember our rule for doing a million dishes."

"Yep! a tick at a time. Still I'm going to rest at 20,000 feet!" Both of them were smiling. The rest of us were puzzled. Then as we all rolled up our sleeves to help, the girl shared the "tick at a time" phrase.

It all began many moons ago (when clocks were first invented the girl surmised) that the town clock broke down. Now, this was a great tragedy since all the townspeople depended upon the big instrument to tell them when to retire, rise, eat, work and play. Everyone was confused and so they summoned the clock doctor who lived many miles away. He examined the ailing instrument and said it was in a "general run-down condition" brought about by stress. Now the kind of stress he meant had nothing to do with main springs or too-tight coils. Would you believe worrying? The clock began counting its ticks, second by second; multiplying them by minutes, hours, days, weeks, months and *years*. No wonder its mind was boggled!

The doctor gave an understanding nod and gave a prescription. "Just take it a tick at a time. It's a nice rhythm you have, so hum on each 'tick' and pray on the 'tock'." The clock recovered and "tick-tocked" happily forever after, serving others with a prayer and a song!

And what do you know! We'd reached the top of Mount Everest.

TO THINK AND PRAY ABOUT: Wouldn't our jobs be depressing if we calculated the number of dishes we had to wash in a lifetime? Dish by dish, it's easy—especially when we all work together with a prayer and a song. And one day at a time is all that God requires. Can you plan His work that way, too?

Why Beg?

T WO LITTLE girls were talking as they passed our house this morning on their way to the Summer Parks and Recreation Program. I learned something!

One of the children said, "Can you come?" Her voice was breathless.

"I'm not sure," her friend answered.

"Why, Mary?" the first child persisted.

"My grandmother's coming and I don't know for how long—" It was obvious that Mary wanted to go wherever it was they were discussing, but there was no bitterness or sadness. (It seldom works that way in our family!)

"The slumber party's for my birthday! You can see your grandmother any ol' time!" Her voice had been urgent at first. Now she took on a whine: "What excuse did she give for saying 'No'?"

Little Mary ignored excuse and went right to the no. "She didn't say no, Bella. She said we'd see."

Bella then said the whimpering words that brought a response worth remembering. "Why didn't you beg?"

Mary showed emotion for the first time. Her face registered genuine surprise. "Because my mother knows what's best for me. And because she always answers. I don't have to beg—" The little girls were out of earshot, taking their voices with them, but leaving me with a question: How do I pray?

Mary had a deep trust in her mother. Do I trust the Father that deeply? Do I believe he has only my best interest in mind?

TO THINK AND PRAY ABOUT: Is it hard to say, "Thy will be done," when you feel you know your needs? Do any of us really know; or do we just think we know? The little girl knew what she wanted, but she trusted her mother to provide the right answer. Are you willing to pray—without begging—and wait on the Lord to answer? Waiting is difficult. Perhaps we should pray for patience to wait until His answer comes.

Cleaning Out The Clutter

DO YOU DUST the piano, arrange an eye-catching centerpiece, maybe even Mop & Glow the linoleum — and leave closets filled with skeletons? I'd believe anything about what may be found in closets, especially after I cleaned out our front closet: clothes that haven't been worn in years, a tennis racket without strings, old Christmas decorations, a tuba that no one mastered playing and an overabundance of coats.

Cleaning a closet can be sort of fun, once one gets started. Doesn't it make you feel good inside and make you wonder if the closet feels the same way? Doing a project I have been neglecting a long time gives me a sense of satisfaction. There's another plus when the project's a closet—you can be alone. A closet is a nice place to sort out thinking. At least it worked that way with me when I cleaned out the front closet the other day.

I went over a list of burdens I'd been shelving, most of which I didn't need; and some I'd forgotten I had like "dead men's bones." In the corner of the closet—and in the corner of my mind—I found little cobwebs; which made me realize I needed to dust off my thoughts so they can be pure in God's sight. As I cleaned and sorted out the closet of my mind, I gave the clutter to the Lord. And He took it—what a wonderful feeling!

TO THINK AND PRAY ABOUT: Do you find yourself letting things "just hang on" that perhaps should be given to the Lord? Dig into your heart and mind—be honest with yourself; and give God the clutter.

How Did Your Day Begin?

EVERY DAY deserves a good start. God made it for us and what He makes is perfect. How do we botch things up? Maybe if we knew the answer to that, we'd be able to prevent the misery that failure brings.

The new bride who came running across our lawn this morning looked half-drowned. She was crying so hard I doubt that she even noticed the sprinklers were going full blast. I was peeling pears.

"I feel awful. I'm a failure. I've ruined it all!" The jerky sentences came without the preface of a "Good morning" greeting. Poor dear! For her there was nothing good about it.

"I broke all my vows. I was supposed to make him happy. I promised—and still last night I ruined our marriage!"

"Do you have just a minute—*please? I have* to talk." When her uncontrollable sobs dwindled into little whimpers of self-pity, I let her talk. Her husband had been detained at his office and neglected to call; the chicken casserole dried out; the lettuce wilted; and her temper took over. She met him at the door screaming. She accused him of no longer loving her. She implied that maybe there was somebody else in his life already—and the honeymoon not yet over.

Her sobbing began anew. "He didn't stand a chance. I grabbed a blanket and ran for the couch." I ached for her as she continued her story. The husband who didn't love her had cleaned the kitchen and left a note of apology. That turned her anger to guilt; but, instead of apologizing, she'd given him the silent treatment at breakfast—running for the bathroom rather than saying, "Forgive me. I love you!"

"But I will tonight—no, I will right now!" and she ran for the phone. I'm glad. Is there a wife who hasn't been through this to a greater or lesser degree? Insignificant hurts add up to big grievances until we learn!

TO THINK AND PRAY ABOUT: How do you preserve peace and love? Do you let God help?

Count Your Blessings

IF EVER THERE is a blessing-time of year, it is in late summer when all the joys of our work pile up their bountiful rewards. Does it ever seem to you that our parents gave more praise than we? I think of what my mother called her blessing song: "When Upon Life's Billows," (words by Johnson Oatman, Jr.; music, Edwin O. Excell). She often sang the lyrics as she hurried about baking fat lemon pies or spading her garden where she taught onions and petunias to live together peacefully: "Count your blessings—name them one by one; Count your blessings—see what God has done."

My mother is eighty now—looks twenty years younger without professional manicures and facials; and would laugh at anyone suggesting a physical fitness course. If beauticians could bottle the formula for youth, she'd be rich; but then you don't put a song in a bottle—so she's "rich" in her own way.

Doctors tell us an active life is a factor in maintaining our youth. Exercise is important; so is excitement over learning or doing something new. Neighbors tease my mother because she's the first to try every new product; she changes every recipe she reads; she sprays herself with sample bottles of cologne in drug stores; and she teaches flowers and vegetables to be friends. But, youth is even more, isn't it? It's more an attitude of happiness—no, *joy* is a better word—joy in the little things God provides.

Do you count your blessings daily? If not, it's the best exercise there is! How high can you count? It's sure to surprise you what the Lord does for you daily. I am sure I have more blessings than any other person alive!

Isn't it refreshing to encounter a person who tells God (and you) of all life's joys and who claims to have received more than anybody else? It is a worthwhile goal for us to set for ourselves; for the world is overpopulated with those who are convinced that "Everything bad happens to me!"

TO THINK AND PRAY ABOUT: How we see life and how often we count our blessings may leave a blessed heritage with our children. It strengthens us, too!

The Art Of Living

"LIFE BEAUTIFULLY lived is an art," said the sculptor as a group of us viewed her work. That quote is familiar, but it took on a new meaning in the conversation that followed beween the two women.

The sculptor, instead of picking up one of her own works of art, opened a magazine and showed us a centerfold reproduction of Michelangelo's work.

One viewer exclaimed, "A painting."

"No, a photograph of one of the master's Renaissance sculptures," the sculptor replied.

The spectator looked uncomfortable. "I'm no sculptor, so I guess I can't appreciate art properly."

The other lady said, "*All* of us are artists. Now Michelangelo could see an angel in a rough stone and liberate it."

"I wish I could do that," the viewer said wistfully.

"You can!" said the other enthusiastically.

The viewer giggled then; and I joined her. If you don't sculpt, it will be easy for you to imagine the strange monstrosities the two of us thought we might liberate. "Only somebody with a sense of humor would appreciate what I would share," the visitor said.

And that's when the artist replied: "What wrong with that? The world needs a laugh. You just furnished me with a smile when I was down. My show hasn't been going well."

The two looked as if they were about to embrace each other. The viewer (unintentionally) was an inspiration to the sculptor. It gives one a lift for the day, doesn't it? Think of taking a shapeless mass of problems and seeing a smile inside them that needs to be liberated! Put like that, life *is* an art; and all of us are artists.

TO THINK AND PRAY ABOUT: Let us thank God for daily opportunities of making life happier for others. He molded each of us for service—no matter how small it seems to us at the time. Even a smile can make a day for the person we think contributed more!

Lord, Send Me Another Mountain

MOUNTAIN CLIMBING was a popular sport as far back as the sixteenth century, according to GOOD READING. The little item said that Leonardo da Vinci took expeditions up the southern slopes of the Pennines. The article appeared about the time the world was watching "Wide World of Sports" when those two adventurous men were shinnying up Mt. Angel in Zion Park, Utah.

Heights make some people dizzy. Count me among them. My feet tingle when I stand atop tall buildings and look down on toy-sized cars. I was puzzled by the lady who prayed, "Lord, send me another mountain." In a way, I guess, the real significance of her prayer sank in when my feet tingled familiarly and I made the analogy at seeing victors stand on a peak. She admitted being terrified at points, but then announced her intentions of looking for even greater heights to scale.

Curious as to why this mountain-praying lady kept wanting more to climb, I asked (as children will): "What's on the other side?" Her answer was even more puzzling, "Another mountain—probably higher."

"Won't your legs be tired!" I asked.

"No, just better equipped for another mountain," she replied.

Maybe high altitudes make us all pant a little—whether it's climbing a rise in the terrain or ascending to the peak of a problem. Would you choose mountain climbing as your sport? There must be a feeling of exhilaration that comes from reaching the top. We experience success or failure every day, don't we? It may be a little slope or a circumstance. Come to think of it, one does feel like tackling bigger things after conquering small ones. Climbing takes practice and faith. Those mountaineers must have combined the two. It's unlikely that they doubted reaching the top. Neither did the lady who wanted another mountain.

TO THINK AND PRAY ABOUT: Do you see climbing as a challenge? Do you welcome the opportunity? If we keep our eyes on the peaks God would have us reach, He will take care of our feet. We need have no fear of falling in our daily lives with God as our guide. He waits to be invited through daily prayer. Do you have the courage to ask for another mountain?

Lord, I Am Not Eloquent

"I CAN'T!" Each of us wanted to cry out when the request came. Two of our dear friends and neighbors had lost a daughter. Would we write the eulogy? We all felt too close to the situation. Vickie had been a student of mine as she recuperated from open heart surgery. After the teenager recovered (we thought), graduated from college and accepted a teaching position in Australia, all of us women felt a mother-glow of pride. How could we comfort parents when news of her sudden death came?

It was then that we talked about Moses—and I, personally, sorrowed for him in retrospect. What an awesome thing God has asked him to do, lead the children of Israel out of Egypt! He lacked confidence in his power of speech. We lacked in the power of our pens. We just couldn't do it; and the hardest part of it all was that the group asked me to call and explain our decision to Vickie's mother.

When my friend answered the telephone, she said, "Oh, I'm glad you called. Friends are such a help." Her voice was disarmingly serene. "You will know what to say . . ." and she left no opportunity to explain the way Moses had. What have you done in similar situations?

Two thoughts came simultaneously. One was God's reply to Moses and the other was a positive-thinking line Dr. Norman Vincent Peale had written. God had said to Moses. "I will teach you what to say." And Dr. Peale had written, "Never have any doubts that you are able to carry out God's plan." Nothing compares with the joy of serving. God has a plan for us!

There are times in our lives when we have to crawl out of our self-made corners and do the work cut out for us. Our grief turns to joy in helping others. And so it was as I made notes on the little ordinary things that would help and comfort the family. When we turn the problems over to God, He leads us to move beyond ourselves. God tells us that with Him all things are possible. We must believe.

TO THINK AND PRAY ABOUT: Do you find it difficult to offer words of comfort when you, too, are grieving? It is a feeling we all have at times. Let us remember that when God calls us to work, He can give us the strength.

A Memory Verse

WERE WE HEARING right? "Thank God I'm blind," said the young Navajo Indian visiting our pulpit from Burnt Corn, Arizona. How could anyone so obviously bright make such a statement?

Then Jackson went on to explain how in his affliction he could see—*truly* see—for the first time. "I was twelve years old when I lost my vision," he said, "so I remember color." That was good, for he wore a maroon shirt and the true-blue turquoise beads and rings that only Indians seem to put together properly. "I can see you all out there with my inner eye; and you are so close, my Brothers. I see with the power spoken of in I Corinthians 9:12, a verse I learned at Boys' Camp before I went blind. I didn't know its true meaning then. It was just a memory verse until I lost my sight."

The congregation listened raptly as Jackson told how the witch doctors and medicine-men tried to heal him; and how there came a missionary to the reservation who told of inner healing. "But that, too, was hard to understand," he said. "The missionary told of all-forgiving love, but my people did not understand. They felt they were unacceptable until they moved from hogans to houses, put on shoes and stopped chanting songs at twilight." In other words, they thought they had to become "civilized"—confusing Christ and culture.

"I did not understand either," the young man said, "until I realized that I was incurably blind, but I could be 'healed' by Jesus on unconditional terms."

Jackson's clasp was firm and warm as we shook hands with him; and I felt warmed inside. Can we look out and see as clearly as we should—even with two good eyes? Do we shine love and allow others to see good in themselves, accepting them just as they are because Christ made them so?

TO THINK AND PRAY ABOUT: Let us pray for the strength to leave the changing of others to God. We need God's Light to shine through in our words and deeds so that others may see Jesus in us—and follow. Then, there are none "blind"!

Seeing With The Heart

SEVERAL SUMMERS ago a friend shared this account with me, following a telephone call from her principal giving her a special assignment at school.

"I can't do it. You know there are other teachers better qualified."

"I choose you." The man's voice was calm. Hers, she said, was shaking as she offered all the *why-not's* (each of which he said was no reason—just an excuse). "Before anything is settled," the principal said, "I have a book I want you to read." After she read THE LITTLE PRINCE by Antoine de Saint-Exupery, she was hooked.

That little dignitary lived on an imaginary planet where day after day he tended a rose he loved very much. It was the most beautiful thing in the world—until the prince reached Earth and saw thousands of roses. His rose no longer seemed special, and he was sad.

The prince met a fox—no different from any other fox, actually, until he tamed and cared for it. Now the fox was unique! With new insight, earth's visitor went back to all the roses and said, "You are beautiful, but you are empty. One could not die for you. To be sure, an ordinary passerby would think that my rose looked just like you . . . But in herself alone she is more important because it is she that I have watered; because it is she that I have put under the glass globe; because it is she that I have sheltered behind the screen . . . because it is she that I have listened to, when she grumbled, or boasted, or even sometimes when she said nothing. Because she is my rose." And Little prince went back to say goodby to the fox, who told him the simple secret of life. "It is only with the heart that one can see rightly; what is essential is invisible to the eye."

That friend was forever grateful to a school principal who knew her for what she was and what she was not; who had loved her and watched her grow; and who thought she was "special" enough to do a special assignment.

TO THINK AND PRAY ABOUT: How much greater is God's love for us—even when we boast and grumble. He sees in us what is invisible to the eye and He chooses us to serve.

I'm Glad To Know You!

August 16
Matthew 6:33

OUR FRIEND sets up her priorities: God first, friends second—all else later. Six o'clock is early for calling even from a friend—but she knows we're all early risers. "You're first on my list," she'll sing out. A grump wouldn't appreciate her tune, but we're no grumps. Who could be when she invariably adds, "I'm glad to know you, Friend!" This poem describes her:

> A friend is one who shared with me
> The bright sun or the gloom.
> A friend is one with love to spare
> Because the heart has room.
> A friend will share a silver thought,
> Discuss a golden dream,
> Or hold my hand and understand
> The silences between.
> A friend is one whose faith in me,
> Like yours, will never end,
> And so, today, I proudly say,
> "I'm glad to know you, Friend!" J.M.B.

My friend explains it this way: "Each morning I ask myself what's the most important thing I have to accomplish; then I make it the first task of the day."

You should see her household: a busy-executive husband, three children, assorted animals and a big family-size house with an acre of roses. Then, she's enrolled in Bethel Series and teaches an Adult Ed class, keeps books for an oil company and is writing her second book. Yet friends are Priority Number II with her.

When I received one of those welcome calls today, it was like a ray of sunshine that hadn't come through the avocado grove yet. That call broke into her busy day—just a minute or so—but she'd have taken more time if necessary. Once she said, "My priority may take *all*. So? I have the satisfaction of meeting that one goal."

TO THINK AND PRAY ABOUT: In the rush of a busy morning, could you spare a moment for a friend?

Prop Me Up

WHEN I WAS a child of nine, I had a bout with rheumatic fever. To have to stay in bed so long was just about as aggravating as the illness. No amount of nagging swayed my mother. Then one day I overheard the doctor say, "Prop her up a little. It'll help her disposition. Increase it day by day until she gains her strength."

No matter whether it's with an illness or a crisis in life—strength comes gradually. If we would just take life a day at a time, each day we would be able to "sit up" longer. Each night we can ask for added strength.

Family members or friends often serve as props until we're able to stand alone: the shoulder to cry on, the hand to grip, the ear to listen. But they can also be the ones to pull the prop right out from under you. They tell you of the danger of hepatitis right before you're to have a blood transfusion. Or they talk about medical insurance that won't take care of the bill; so now you can worry as well as hurt. A small prop can support or give way—what kind of support do you give?

But even though family and friends can be used in support, we still need the sustaining support of Jesus. If others fail you just say to God, "Lord, prop me up." Does it work? Yes.

Just as a child easily rests in the arms of his father, so can we rest in the arms of our Heavenly Father. And after a time our friends will come to us and say, "you look rested!" And you'll reply, "I am, I've been propped up."

TO THINK AND PRAY ABOUT: Give some thought to the things you think will be most helpful to the person you visit. Ask God to be your stay in time of weakness; to appreciate your recovery; and to help others when they're in stress.

August 18
I John 4:11

Have you had a kindness shown? Pass it on.
'Twas not given to thee alone; pass it on . . .

WERE THOSE lines a part of your school-days? Well-meaning teachers taught us the song and its meaning, only to see it misused. Do you remember "Pass It"? It was difficult for a teacher to locate the culprit who initiated the game. There was a pinch, then a whispered "pass it," and around the room *it* traveled, causing disruption in general—ending suddenly.

The superintendent, a big WWI veteran, said, "Now, we can play 'Pass It' as much as you wish—with one understanding. It's to be a smile instead of a pinch. Woe be unto the one who goes back to the pinch. That offender will stand before this room and sing 'Pass It On'!" The girls enjoyed learning the song—*and* the penalty: watching half-grown boys with changing voices standing in front of the room red-faced, forgetting the words and the tune! But as the superintendent predicted, childish things were put away and more appropriate things were passed from person to person.

The practice took on a new meaning for one of my acquaintances when she and her husband arrived in British Columbia. They had forgotten that the country was planning a national celebration: Queen Elizabeth was coming; and every hotel and motel was taken. They were on the ferry, car and all, before they found out. A couple of strangers—what were they to do? A snow-haired lady with round-apple cheeks, looking like the fairy godmother she was, approached the couple. "I have this little apartment . . ." They couldn't believe their good fortune, and when they tried to pay her at the end of their visit, Ana said, "Pass it on and God will bless."

TO THINK AND PRAY ABOUT:

Let it travel through the years;
let it wipe another's tears;
Till in heaven the deed appears;
pass it on!

A Son's Wife

August 19
Ruth 1:16

HOLDING OUR tongues can be a help in keeping family unity. But there are other interferences. Sometimes "withholding" is a problem.

"I think she dislikes me because I can bake an apple pie the way she can—even better!" Lil was speaking of her mother-in-law.

"Apple pie! If my problems were *that* simple. My mother-in-law's a battle-axe. Know what she did? Went through all the kids' comic books and burned most of them," Ann answered.

Millie seldom says much at sewing club where we exchange patterns, ideas, darn sox and mend family spats. But today she ventured, "Well, maybe some of the comics needed sorting—"

"By *her?*" Ann was building up a head of steam.

"Well, I mean, some of them are, well—" Millie faltered. "Some are O.K."

"Comic books or mothers-in-law?" Ann's quip brought a laugh that broke the tension and the group settled down to in-lawism. They agreed that mothers-in-law just weren't everybody's favorite relatives—also that nine times out of ten the good ladies don't get a fair trial. Granted there are dillies; but none, as far as they knew, carried buggy whips or rolling pins—except in the case of the latter for making apple pies. And (as they mellowed) didn't Tom, Dick and Harry deserve Mom's pie now and then?

I lost my own mother-in-law some time ago and I still miss her. As we talked, I recalled what she said the night before I married her son: "You are part of the family now. Please stop me if I interfere. Just remember you and I have something in common: we love the same person."

Millie set our thoughts in another direction again. "I think we should leave off the title anyway. I introduce Ethel as my husband's mother."

Now, there's an idea worth remembering. Now I say, "I would like to have you meet Sun, our son's wife." I read appreciation in her eyes.

TO THINK AND PRAY ABOUT: Let us ask God to remind us that we are one family—under His Fatherhood.

What A Friend!

"WHAT A FRIEND we have in Jesus, all our sins and griefs to bear . . ."

Do you thrill to the words of George Scriven and music of C.C. Converse in the old hymn? It is exciting to hear the songs we learned in childhood after sleeping in some corner, awakened, then reused.

What is a friend? Some say it is a person who knows all about us and loves us just the same. Maybe that would disqualify a few! Henry Brooks Adams said: "One friend in a lifetime is much; two are many; three are hardly possible."

Maybe they're both right. If our acquaintances really knew us, would they cease to be friends? Do you feel free to lay open your inward self—your insecurities, prejudices, fear of failure—for fear your circle of friends will diminish? As a matter of fact, if we *really* revealed our thoughts, would we have but one friend left? Probably the late Mr. Adams didn't refer to Jesus, but the author of the old song did.

Recently I ran across an item about the writer. "It seemed that Joseph Scriven was destined to go through life alone, knowing only the friendship of Jesus Christ. Through much of his life he experienced loneliness, meager pay for menial work and a great deal of physical illness. 'What a Friend We Have In Jesus' is his testimony that prayer does not necessarily eliminate trouble from our lives. But, in the midst of tragedy, temptations and weakness, Christ will be our ever-present Friend who will give us peace, 'take and shield us' and carry our 'load of care'."

What kind of a friend am I? Now and then, it is good to conduct a self-examination. Like marriage, there is a lot of "give and take" in friendship. Rebuffs (real or imagined) are the hardest to take. When friends fail to respond properly, do you take it well and go on being the real *you?* I admit I find myself suffering withdrawal into the other *me.*

TO THINK AND PRAY ABOUT: We are to pray for our friends. Do you keep them in your prayers before a real "need" arises? And let us praise God daily that knowing us, He accepts us as we are and loves us **anyway!**

Thank You For The Pepper

I F YOU ARE in the process of bringing up a child, you can identify with this account. If you've *been* through it, you can be grateful.

A bulky questionnaire came in the mail. Somebody is writing a book "Parenting Made Easy." Glib title! The writer needed "random samplings."

The writer is methodical all right. With a questionnaire that made me gasp. The prologue scared me. "Each child is a blessing." (Did she know about the baseball mine put through the neighbor's bedroom window; the gate he sideswiped when learning to parallel park?) "Every parent can cope," I read on. "These anecdotes are from successful parents." (She should have seen *me* when those incidents took place.)

Bravely I read on and the fog lifted beyond the introduction. Could I recall an incident when prayer helped? That was familiar ground. Who could survive without it?

Be specific, the paper admonished: "Did your child's methods of prayer ever present a problem? How did you handle it?"

Are we parents always unwilling to lay ourselves open to criticism? It seems that most of us are most of the time (and for good reason). Anyway, the way I handled the incident was to do nothing—and I'm still glad.

Our son was having no part of a ready-made prayer. The "Lord, make us thankful for this meal" was not for him. He was specific, looking the table over and thanking God for everything he saw. It got out of hand one evening when friends had dinner with us: "Thank You for the bread, butter, jam, potatoes, gravy, salt, pepper . . ." and seeing our guests were amused, he stopped to set them straight. "Put your heads down unless you're not thankful for the pepper!"

TO THINK AND PRAY ABOUT: How do you handle similar situations? Which is more important: the out-of-hand prayer of a child or what guests may think? How and when would it be best to discuss prayer with a growing child? It is good to remember that children carry a special insight. It is good to be grateful for all things—great or small.

I'm An Average Christian

August 22
Matthew 5:48
II Corinthians 12:7-10

"**I**'M AN AVERAGE Christian," the speaker was saying. Did others wonder as I wondered what an average Christian is?

Use of the word "average" immediately triggers the question: "What is the norm?" followed by "How many are above the norm?" "How many below?" But to be so measured in terms of Christianity—even when measuring oneself—sounds risky.

We hear so much about the "average citizen," which perhaps means the middle class—although it may not; and, of course, average rainfalls, snowfalls, etc. are helpful statistics, but somehow I never exactly wanted to be average in important things in life. Being an average wife and an average mother just weren't good enough in my definition to deserve the love of so special a husband and so "above average" a son!

Yes, others *did* wonder what the speaker meant! At the close of the meeting, several gathered around him when he invited questions. He made mention of dedication to his work, being temperate in all things, observing the law, preserving the right to worship as we choose, supporting those who have rule over us and abstaining from violence—that sort of thing. Does this strike you as a description of the average citizen?

Just what is a Christian to you? Isn't it the person who believes in the Lord Jesus Christ and all the truths He taught? And didn't He teach that we were to press toward the mark of perfection—knowing that we could only reach it through faith? We are created by God; we are chosen to do His will and spread His Word to others. God asks for more than the medium, the fair or the mediocre. Just being *His* makes us more than average.

TO THINK AND PRAY ABOUT: Discuss with family and friends how you can become a greater Christian. Surely our first priority is a life of constant prayer.

I'm A Great Believer

YOU'VE BEEN through it: the dry mouth, wet palms and butterflies in the tummy; the desire to laugh, cry and run simultaneously. Remember your first "in class" writing assignment—ad-libbing on paper? My assignment was: "What are you afraid of—and why?" I was afraid of failing!

We all have fears; it's how we handle them that counts. Recently I saw Lawrence Welk walking towards a local bank. There was a time during the music-maker's career when things got kind of shaky. Yet, now, past seventy-five, his squeaky-clean program is more popular than ever. What did he have to be afraid of, you ask? He was shy and he feared ridicule in his youth. The more polished band leaders could out-talk him; but could they out-play him? He knew what he wanted: a clean, family-type program. Number one: he wanted to succeed. Number two: he believed he could do it. Welk, brought up a Christian, screened his "musical family" as if he wore spiritual bifocals! There would be no trash. All looked good for him for a time; his popularity grew year after year. Then, suddenly, ABC network bumped him. He picked himself up, realigned his instruments and said, "I'm a great believer." He made a fresh start, using the same format he'd used for forty years. As the more "permissive" shows crumpled one by one, his viewing audience grew to over 36 million as an independent program.

My writing assignment? Seeing Mr. Welk reminded me of my decision in class that day: "Good, poor or in-between, nobody will write quite like me. I'll do the best I can—family-style: God and me." Only when we truly believe are all things possible, God takes over from there.

TO THINK AND PRAY ABOUT: What are you afraid of and why? It is an important question. One of our greatest enemies in life is fear—even fear of fear! God can take care of our fears if we hand them to Him and allow Him to deal with them and with us in His way in His time. Begin each day with "Lord, I believe."

See Life Before You Paint It

August 24
Psalm 116:7-8

THERE WAS NO answer when I rang the doorbell. My Chinese friend is a painter and often works in the backyard in the cool of the morning. I looked through the hibiscus hedge and saw her seated by the rock garden, her painting materials lying on the grass. "Hi!" I said informally. There was no response. She had heard, of course.

Understanding one another's culture can bring about a warm and loving relationship. You have probably experienced it. That kind of understanding lets you sit down quietly and wait, knowing you are no intruder. That's how I felt. She would get around to me to share a cup of Oriental tea and a Moon Ball, her father's specialty.

Meantime, my gaze followed hers. Mai Ling's head was tilted back and her eyes were fixed on a giant magnolia blossom almost overhead. I studied it—not from an artistic point of view but as the lovely thing of nature it was. How wax-like each petal, all put together to form one giant bloom: fragile yet strong. Was this the "form" she had spoken of? "Form has three elements," she tells her friends. "Somewhere there has to be the solid, the vapor and the liquid." And there with the deep blue solidity of the sky in the background, the rainbow mist rising from the fountain and the rushing waterfall, the subject was traced across the background. Mai Ling's painting would be more than a magnolia in bloom.

Such awareness and sensitivity may not be a part of our background; but such concentration carries a message to our busy lives. "Never do I paint till I am still and see the essence of life; then the subject lives."

TO THINK AND PRAY ABOUT: There is so much around us that needs doing. Do we fail to see it? Or do we see and in our rush "to do" neglect to pause for an awareness that would lead to a greater understanding? Can you apply a little of Mai Ling's "aesthetic pursuit" to your daily life? "Let me be still, Lord," is a good place to start.

The Left Hand Of God

ISN'T IT GOOD to have someone nearby as an inspiration on the hard-to-handle days? A someone who knows (and makes you know) that God is your right hand in time of trouble? Here is an example of a friend who had to let God be her right hand—literally.

"You're about up to snuff," her doctor said. "Gradually resume normal activities." Sweet words after surgery—only there's nothing "normal" about this person's activities. Daily she comes out punching with a right uppercut and a left-hand cross. And with the doctor's announcement, her mind busied itself with the strategy of attack: "messy house, bulging laundry chute, husband fed up with TV dinners, son going to flunk English without my help . . . but, first a walk. Oh, to see the world," she thought.

Then, as her husband locked the garage, she leaned to snap the leash into the dog's choke chain. In the boxer's excitement, he leaped forward playfully—taking her with him, her right hand caught in the chain. "It would have been a comedy of errors, had my wrist not been sprained, one fingernail all but removed and a blood vessel broken in the index finger," she recalled. "Skip the discomfort. Make it despair!"

Her account interested me. How does anyone as right-handed as she do the things she's sure have to be done? "How will I carry on?" she wondered.

One can end it all; one can scream; one can weep. "For one split second, I wanted to do all those things out of sheer desperation," she admitted. "Fortunately, we own no weapons; the scream I repressed came from my son; and there were tears in my husband's eyes." So she prayed: "Dear God, pull me together for them." The moment she spoke her internal gyro set her back on course. A burst of energy replaced pain. "I'll forget the messy house . . . order Chinese food . . . and type with my left-hand cross."

TO THINK AND PRAY ABOUT: Sometimes trials can remind us of the power of prayer.

Be Prepared!

YOU HAVE JUST started traveling. Enjoy it: it's the best scenery you've seen in ages. It takes your breath away as does the clean air. The children are sitting like angels with folded wings. Dad already looks ten years younger. You are relaxed for the first time since the last family outing. The car's purring like a kitten. Eight a.m. and all's well. A fine place to be!

Two hundred miles later, Junior says casually he left the shower running—on "Hot" to clean out the fungus "the way you taught me." You're wondering if you notified the newsboy to hold the papers, when your husband asks if you cancelled the three-quarts-a-day with the milkman. You gulp. It's turning chilly and you brought summer clothes. Air conditioner off, heater on—the heater is broken. What's this? The weather report on the car radio says the heat wave back home will dry all lawns that are not deep-watered immediately. "I think I'm going to vomit," Junior says. Great!

Sis left the house key beneath the Welcome Mat (which thieves take literally); and "Anyway," she pouts, "I forgot to lock the front door. *He* (Junior) was hurrying me out of the bathroom." The very suggestion brings about a pit stop but there is no rest for your mind. You split a Pepsi five ways . . . and head home. Vacation ended before it began.

It doesn't have to be this way. Talking things over, planning ahead, putting each person in charge of designated duties and making use of suggestions from police and friends can avoid disappointment. Isn't it amazing how much we take for granted? We assume everybody knows; and nobody does. Or one tries to shoulder the entire burden and the others feel left out. You can think of other combinations that kindle the fire of bedlam.

And doesn't the same apply to our Christian lives? God understands us better than we understand ourselves, and yet we take on His work; or we take it for granted that all good gifts are ours, but we forget to ask—or to thank Him. And this is far more serious than little domestic crises.

TO THINK AND PRAY ABOUT: If unseen problems (therefore, unavoidable) arise, it is wise to make a U-turn, repair the damages and make a fresh start. God is just a prayer away! Talk over the things you're unable to handle alone.

Coming Home!

Sometimes feet are prone to wander—
Treasures they must seek and find—
So they travel to far places
To some pictures of the mind.
Open roads will always beckon;
Lure of unseen never ends;
This is only as it should be—
But, for me, I miss my friends . . .
So each time I seek adventure,
Letting soul and body rest,
I return refreshed and thankful
For the place I love the best.
Could it be the friendly handclasp
That new places seem to lack,
That makes pleasure of my travels,
Lie in joy of coming back? J.M.B.

PORCH SWINGS were for lying in and thinking in. Like grass blade chewing, these are forgotten arts—mostly because: who has time? Skies we used to watch for cumulous-cloud-animals are now smogged; grass we used to chew, tainted with insecticide. So our feet are prone to wander . . . say, to "Innisfree." Innisfree is anywhere the mind will wander. We could find it in our own backyard, if the push-pulls of our lives would let us rest. Instead we go: in big cars, little cars, campers and vans—only to return, saying, "Never again" (true until next summer).

Of course, some of us can circle the globe and see little; others can remain in the backyard and see God's handiwork. "Innisfree" like happiness is a state of mind, but no matter what our philosophy, one thing is certain: getting back is wonderful.

Sometimes in our Christian lives our feet are prone to wander, perhaps in the wrong direction. We become so wrapped up in routine that before we realize it a change takes place in our lives. We find ourselves praying less. It is then that we must turn back! And isn't it good to be home?

TO THINK AND PRAY ABOUT: Vacations are necessary, but not without God. Pray!

August 28
Psalm 46:10

THE CONVERSATION took place at Neighborhood Watch, a crime prevention program. On our street we watch out for each other's needs; this has to do with property, protection of—with helpful hints from the local law enforcement officers. During these summer months, with so many on vacation, our Watch proves most valuable. Guest speakers do a nice job with dead-bolts, night-lights, newspaper collection—some new suggestions, some review, but all helpful. This particular night the conversation swung to the favorite topic: vacation!

"This year, no work! I'm leaving my briefcase at home," said Charles, the lawyer.

"I just hope he doesn't overwork *beforehand*," his wife commented.

Marge, a teacher, sighed, "I just wish the whole family didn't descend on us each summer. Family visits are not vacations."

Joe appeared to be thinking. "You know," he said slowly, "sometimes I think we look at this whole thing wrong. Why do we have to travel on a crowded freeway? Does vacation have to mean *go*—or can't it be doing something that's entirely different from the usual routine?"

The group kicked around the idea and Marge's husband replied, "Problem is I can't relax doing nothing. I'm so used to puttering around in the greenhouse . . . ."

However, Joan's remark caught everybody's ear: "Well, no matter what we do, I'm not rushing back to the office. I'm keeping one day to rest up from vacation." *Cliche?* Is going back to work a culture shock after you've spent precious hours in your private haven? Are you rested in body, revived in spirit, restored in soul? *A re-entry day:* a day to rest and give praise to God for bringing us home safely—a day to thank Him for the peace He gives when we are still.

TO THINK AND PRAY ABOUT: Be our traveling companion, Lord; then teach us to rest in Your peace.

The Beauty Of Growing Older

A S A MONTH nears its end, do you think of it as dying? Or, are you able to think in terms of all you have accomplished and look forward to a new month with anticipation? And how do you look at life and its years?

I, for one, am weary of the how-to books on "growing old." You know: no whining, sniffling, feeling neglected, demanding attention, interfering, taking sides, criticizing, being nosey, bossy, *ad infinitum*. Why am I weary? Because all these ugly little traits seem to be characteristic of only those past forty. Still, there are some such characters—at any age—I suppose.

Take the two letters from old (correction: *long-time*) friends. Gert's letter ached with health problems; and, for good measure, her neighbors' were thrown in. Each "catches" everything the other has; and, somehow, it never occurs to them to stay apart. Comparing symptoms won't allow for that. The way she told it was significant, too. Gert doesn't "have" a headache; she "dies" of one. She must die a million deaths, or her expression is indicative of her attitude toward life. Philosophically, her letter ended: "But at our age, what can we expect?" I wish she'd leave me out of it.

Now, Jean's letter was a side-splitter. She's as unaware that she's spreading sunshine as Gert is that she's enshrouding her readers with gloom. Of the two, it's Jean who has the problems. How can she laugh and make the world laugh with her when the doctor told her that both she and her husband have diabetes—breaking the double-barrel news at a single consultation? The way she described the rigid diets, the insulin shots and their exercise program makes a couple's having diabetes together sound inviting! "Why, Jack and I dare not kiss each other 'good night'—have to limit our intake on sweets, you know." Isn't it good that both letters came on the same day? How does your attitude affect others?

TO THINK AND PRAY ABOUT: Let us close our mouths against little pains that everyone alive has now and then. Yes, we want to be beautiful (what woman doesn't?), so let's make life beautiful for others. Do you agree that we would please God to take that attitude? The "how-to" lies in prayer!

Second Summer

DO YOU SENSE it? There's a feeling of fall in the air. A yellow-smoke haze fills the atmosphere and a filmy mist rises to line the day with silver. A breeze whispers and then romps away like a playful kitten on colored feet. The pale heat of summer is gone and the blush of spring returns—not to the rose but to every leaf in the forest, every creeper and every blade of grass. Every shrub looks like Moses' "burning bush." Hearts are aglow and God seems very near. The world seems of a "like-mind."

Old-timers used to call it a "second summer." And in a sense it is nicer than the first one; it is more mellow. The orchards steam with amber spice. The meadows smell of new-cut hay. The woodvine berries are luster-glossed. And once more the air fills up with bird calls as something tells the wild geese it is time to go. They leave their roofless dwelling places in search of a sun that the world has thought heartless, torrid and interminable. The geese must have seen the late-summer shower rinse and polish leaves in scarlet-yellows of approaching fall.

Maybe you knew the short season by its Indian name, "Squaw summer." At any rate, it's that first cool spell preceding the Indian summer of autumn. Its smoke signals are brief as if saying, "Enjoy it!" for soon will come the melancholy russet leaves followed by the rime of ice . . . .

Our versifying friends call spring the child of winter and autumn the child of summer. Summer, then, is nobody's child. Why, is it, when the orphan-month of August exhales near the end, that everyone seems to ask, "Where did the summer go?"

We hear the same question at the close of day; and again, as people grow older. "Where did the day go?" "Where did the years go?" I guess the day-question will be with us always as we build our nests, feed hungry beaks and teach our fledglings to test their wings. But the year-question has put on a new fall face! Isn't it marvelous when the older generation counts its blessings and shares them with us? Truly, God has seen to it that their "second summers" are richer; and ours are made richer through their service.

TO THINK AND PRAY ABOUT: God uses us through every season. Let us be of "One Mind."

Just In Time

SUMMER'S ending—just in time? Be honest! Won't it be good to get back in the swing of things? Join the crowd if this sounds familiar.

The dishwasher balked in mid-cycle from an overload and the door's jammed. That's unfortunate, since all the drinking glasses are in the machine. The carpet leading from the refrig to the bathroom is tracked with peanut butter and the rug jet-cleaning service is closed for vacation . . . Tomcat's having a romance which keeps him out nights and *loud* nights; consequently, the neighbors are overdosing on sleeping pills. Someone mistook the electric heater switch for the fan in the guest bathroom; it has been running a week. The refrigerator reeks of sardines, onions and overripe Limburger; when was baking soda changed and is the price up again? The dog has gained five pounds which means Husband isn't walking enough. None of the children want to bother shopping for school clothes, except the one too young to go. Sound like some things you can identify with?

Most of us feel a little guilty to be calendar-watchers. But should we? We've run shuttle service all summer, entertained our children's friends, spent two weeks packing for a vacation and two weeks unpacking, answered phones, cancelled our appointments for their booster shots, umpired games and settled squabbles while the strawberries went unjammed and our nails were bitten off instead of filed. August-going-on-September assures us "equal time." Now we can be wives again. We can give the house an overdue cleaning during the daylight hours. Now there will be time for the Children's Hour, the after-school snack and the account of their hours away. We need the chance to love them at a distance, and they need to fall back in step with the world outside the home. Strangely, as we urge them back and they grumble, it is we mothers who will be more lonely!

TO THINK AND PRAY ABOUT: Let your summer tensions slip away and enjoy the tired-but-happy feeling. This is a healing time of year God prepares for us.

My Autumn Prayer

DEAR LORD, the things I ask are very small. I have them already, for You have given them to me. And, yet, my prayer is very large. I want to share what You have given me with others. Lord, show me how to teach bright-eyed children that You have a purpose for everything that will come to them in this life . . . and, Lord, help me to remind those who are older and have seen many Septembers that they have achieved a purpose already. Hopefully it was Your purpose. There is nothing new under the September sun . . . there are only beginnings, endings and blendings . . . in the seasons and in the lives of us all. In Your eyes little things are not ordinary or without purpose. My prayer, Lord, is that I will share those special (little) things You have given me with others.

If I would show, then I must see, Lord. Let me look at Your autumn treasures anew: tall fires and white-barked birches from the first fall rains . . . velvet cattails on reedy stalks . . . sheaf-ready grain . . . the first flush of the maple trees. And seeing this beauty about me, help me to release my grip on summer. But, Lord, let me not think winter-thoughts yet—until the time is right. Let each day be a blessing unto itself.

Lord, there was rarity in June days. Later there will be December's chill. And between the two, the air will be filled with leaves—for such is life. Today let me see Your innate goodness in the clean air of a changing season; let me find new meaning; add bold horizons to my faith; lend me the strength of the hills; bring out the autumn-best in me to share. For there is excitement in September. It is a time of "new studies" whether we enter the front door of buildings or recall an exit. Life and learning go on, for You keep us growing.

Make my steps more certain, Lord; my destination more purposeful, that I may help guide unsure feet. Keep Your instinct of endurance alive in me that I may build it in others who are groping towards Your right path.

We are all teachers, Lord. Use us! Let us remove the motes of irritation and frustration from our eye before trying to enlarge the vision of others. Bless us all with Your patience and Your wisdom that we may share the many reasons of Your love—that they may shine like brilliant autumn!

Scripture Cake

September 2
(See recipe)

SUNSETS FLICKER briefly. Evenings are longer and spiced with a growing chill. There is something about the earlier nightfall, chillier air and back-to-school atmosphere that says: "Batten down, bring in and gather round!" Lagging summer appetites pick up with wanton winds—as season meets season head-on. It is time to get out the cookbooks and put together concoctions that summer did not invite. It is time to be indoors more. It is family time!

While restaurants or fast-food emporiums fill a real need for those wishing a change now and then (and who doesn't), home-dining is still American style! And home-cooking, whether by fast or slow method, simple or gourmet dishes, is the most precious way for "breaking bread" with those we love and cherish. There's something about food that invites fellowship, and don't we all agree that's what the world needs now?

Now if you are busy wearing the many hats of half a dozen careers, any one of which is a full-time job, you *can* have your cake and eat it! No time for family devotionals? Why not plan for moments together that will be so delightful you will leave every member rising up to call you blessed—and begging another crumb of what you have to share?

Have you an old cookbook lying around? Most of us have; and let me tell you that Grandmother knew some wonderful things to do with food—and God's Word. She knew how to administer both. For instance, Grandmother's Scripture Cake:

½ c. Judges 5:25 (last clause)   Some of each II Chronicles 9:9
2 c. Jeremiah 6:20   Pinch of Leviticus 2:13
2 Tbsp. I Samuel 14:25   ½ c. Judges 4:19 (last clause)
2 c. Jeremiah 17:11   2 c. Nahum 3:12
1½ c. I Kings 4:22   2 c. Numbers 17:8
2 tsp. Amos 4:5   2 c. I Samuel 30:12

TO THINK AND PRAY ABOUT: Let members of the family help by looking up and reading aloud the references. After you have finished blending the ingredients, bake it in prayer and song. Eat it slowly and use the rest of the day to digest it.

HOW DO YOU view a changing season? A new month? A new phase in your life? Do you find a change of pace is good for the soul as you take off the old and put on the new? Scientists tell us "Matter is never destroyed; it simply changes form." Take comfort: all you cast aside, if it is worthy, will rise up in new form—to meet you, greet you and grow a new body.

One of the columnists in the local newspaper bade readers farewell recently. Her column, "Ten Years Ago Today," gathered tidbits of activities in the area from years past. Old-timers enjoyed reminiscing through the poignant stories; newcomers familiarized themselves with the area's history. "But, the editors felt that the column had run its course, and it's time for something new. . . ."

Do you remember Gladys Tabor's "Butternut Wisdom" column that appeared over a period of years in a leading women's magazine? She had a way of elevating little everyday incidents that made readers feel such beauty could happen only in New England. Suddenly her colorful chatting stopped. "Why?" Her followers asked. And the reply was the same as that of the local writer's: "The column has served its purpose." Temporarily, perhaps it had; although those who enjoyed the inspirational pieces were unconvinced. And now her reprints are back—just as beautiful, just as timely; but perhaps more mellow in their distant view.

In parting, our lady-writer said: "I have told you a lot about myself—how I felt about being a working mother, or being a parent, period! Somehow it seemed to help other mothers know that you can have a son who steals gum from the grocery store or a baby who tries his first artistic talents on your freshly painted walls and there is going to be a tomorrow. The tomorrows are usually brighter . . . I simply cannot be a prophet of doom."

TO THINK AND PRAY ABOUT: People who share themselves with us always leave a gift—or return to bring an even greater gift. Christ did both. He built no building, wrote no books, left no money and erected no monuments. Yet He left words no prophet of doom can destroy: beauty in today and hope in tomorrow. What more beautiful challenge than that we be ready for His promised return?

Reaffirmation Of Faith

LOOK AROUND you this autumn day. It is interesting to note how numerous are Jesus' use of secular things to illustrate spiritual values.

I believe God shows His face in every little flower and its sheer joy of sharing beauty for a single day—gloriously unconcerned with tomorrow.

I believe God shows His hands as He sets every little bird to flight, teaching each to trust its wing, trusting Him to provide.

I believe God reveals His voice with each little zephyr which says, "Fear not: I am with you."

I believe God shows His universality in the vagabond-clouds, which momentarily obscure the sun, shielding us from His light, only to reveal it with greater brightness—as He moves the clouds some other place.

I believe God shows His caring with each silver drop of rain, using raindrops like teardrops, to lift up the fallen spirits after a storm.

I believe God shows our need for rest in the purple hush of twilight. "Have faith," He whispers as the sun dips down below the world's horizon.

I believe God shows Eternal Life with each dazzling sunrise! Each day is a resurrection. I stand still and marvel; words are inadequate tools; I reaffirm my faith in God the Father Almighty in a way He understands.

TO THINK AND PRAY ABOUT: No matter how busy life keeps us or how informally we speak with God, it is good to reaffirm our faith. The Apostles' Creed is an ageless reaffirmation: *I believe in God the Father Almighty, Maker of heaven and earth; and in Jesus Christ, His only Son, our Lord; who was conceived by the Holy Ghost, born of the Virgin Mary; suffered under Pontius Pilate; was crucified, dead and buried . . . the third day He rose . . . ascended into heaven, and sitteth on the right hand of God . . . from thence He shall come to judge the quick and the dead. I believe in the Holy Ghost; the holy universal church, the communion of saints; the forgiveness of sins; the resurrection of the body; and the life everlasting.* (Praise God!) Amen.

Short Summers

September 5
Ezekiel 18:20-22

The August heat has dwindled
To autumn-sort of mild;
Vacation time has ended—
Too short . . . Ask any child.
What happened to the fishing
That each one planned to do?
The space ship's hardly started;
The tent's unfinished, too . . .
It's "Eat your breakfast!"
And "Hurry, comb your hair,
The bus is at the corner . . ."
Does any adult care?
Ah, yes, we care, dear children,
But you're too young to know
That as the years march faster,
How short the summers grow. J.M.B.

BABIES OF yesterday, suddenly grown tall, will head for college this month—some of them for the first time . . . some of them for the last. . . .

What in the world is this disease one reads about called "College Blues"? "Inner conflict," "peer group pressure" and "loneliness" would be funny answers were it less serious. The predicted 78 percent who will suffer symptoms of depression don't worry me (chances are that it's higher than that among housewives!) But the projected figures for expected suicides are no laughing matter. What is bringing on the dangerous kind of melancholy that makes those who have everything going for them want to end it all? *Do they know of God's love?*

Sociologists are saying it is removal of established support systems. Just a short while ago, we were reading of rebellion against establishments and systems. Is it possible that they didn't reject us, but that we rejected them in letting them get away with it? Why didn't we follow the dictates of our upbringing and call their bluff? Giving our children something to press against may mean giving them the proper kind of love.

TO THINK AND PRAY ABOUT: What can parents do? *How well do you know your child?* Start with the cradle and never let down!

Dead Ashes Or A Glowing Ember?

THERE COMES an evening when you know the time is right to light the neatly laid fire which has remained intact all summer "for appearances sake." There's the crackle of logs and a hoop of smoke as the wind swoops down the chimney . . . Nobody minds, for spirits leap as high as the flaming logs. . .

But there was a time when fireplaces were more than things of beauty and places to warm the heart. They were necessities—in most cases, the only means a family had of heating a room. Every coal was valuable—so valuable that the occupants carefully covered the embers with ashes each night before retiring. The coals, shut away from air, retained the spark for tomorrow's fire. Such is the setting of a little story which illustrates how uncovered, neglected, exposed and alone our lives can become. We are keepers of God's fire.

A man and his wife were members of their church in-name-only. "How long has it been since we last attended a service?" the lady of the house asked.

"We are about to be told!" replied her husband who had seen the minister dismounting his horse at the front gate. "I dread this! He will use Scriptures like I use the poker, no doubt! Yep, we're sure in for it."

The minister entered, warmed his hands by the open fire, seated himself, and then, with the fire tongs, removed a single coal and laid it on the hearth. At first, the couple sat tensely awaiting their scolding. Then gradually they relaxed as the visitor discussed the weather, crop prospects and the beauty of the first fall snow. Suddenly, with a warm handshake, he departed.

His hosts scratched their heads. What had he come for? What was the significance of the coal on the hearth? Puzzled, the man turned it over. It was dead. Alarmed, the man remembered he'd neglected to add a log. Had the other coals died? He poked at the ashes, and there huddled close together were glowing embers. The minister made his point. "Next Sunday?" the man asked. His wife nodded with a smile.

TO THINK AND PRAY ABOUT: We can be the spark that lights another's life.

How To Avoid Wasting Time

September 7
John 6:12

WITH TIME at such a premium, do we waste it? Chances are that most of us fail to realize how much time we *do* waste; what's more, we work ourselves up into a lather because of delays. Our appointment with the doctor is at ten o'clock. At eleven he is still in surgery. Our appointment with the accountant is at one o'clock, six people are ahead of us; and the computer breaks down. The only possible way we can waste such precious time is in fuming. There is a way to use "dead time" constructively, reduce frustration, lower blood pressure and minimize boredom to zero.

Do you seldom get around to reading your church magazine, the Bible, your favorite old poems or the latest issue in "Book of the Month" club? Take it along and you'll find yourself resenting it when your turn comes!

Are there people to whom you owe letters, but your busy schedule simply won't allow writing time? Here it is built in for you.

How long has it been since your checkbook balanced? Here's a chance to find your error (or the bank's—it could bring in dividends!).

What are you having for dinner tonight? Or for that matter, tomorrow night—make it all week? Make use of leftovers in your mind. Save time!

Is your grocery list made out? That logically follows menu-planning.

Are you waiting to visit a sick friend? Make a list of all the pleasant news you can tell.

Are you waiting for an interview? Jot down your qualifications and be prepared to land the job.

Are you waiting to see the doctor? Now, *here's* your chance to get even with the world! Make a list of your ailments; he's the only one wanting to hear!

TO THINK AND PRAY ABOUT: Our grannies and aunties did embroidery and made lovely gifts. Maybe some of that rubbed off on us and we feel guilty—waiting. Let's put our minds to work constructively (that lets tongues rest, too!). And, simultaneously, we can turn waiting into a productive time!

A 10-Day Spiritual Fitness Program

NOW IS THE right time to shape up for fall, since spring's resolution to shape up for summer never materialized, and the flab remained intact all summer. Let's leave gathering to those who sowed and weight-losing to those who are overly endowed and get down to a 10-day spiritual fitness program. This is practical for us all.

First Day: Today I will dine on gratitude—thanking God for the life He gave me and seeing that my "helpings" are generous. I shall share, saying, "Come to the table of the Lord; taste, cherish, enjoy!"

Second Day: Today I will skimp on pessimism, substituting optimism. I shall pray for "sweet things" and know that they will be served!

Third Day: Today I will go on a liquid diet of cheer, sharing a cup of joy with everyone I meet. I shall experiment with flavors of sunshine and song.

Fourth Day: Today I will nibble away until I find something good in each member of my family and friends. I will sift and sort until I find it!

Fifth Day: Today I will drink from the cup for forgiveness—even when the dregs are bitter. I will discard every grudge—no "snacks" allowed!

Sixth Day: Today I will indulge myself in prayer! I have worked very hard on this program and I must rest and ask for new energy.

Seventh Day: Today I will clean my pantry, removing self-pity and selfishness. I have been gluttonous and these must go! *Lord, let me not be tempted.*

Eighth Day: Today I will discard all of yesterday's leftovers, letting today be sufficient unto itself. A "warmed over" past can spoil my day!

Ninth Day: Today I will serve low-budget "happiness food," remembering that a tender touch, a pleasant smile, a call are great nourishment.

Tenth Day: Today I will fast—refraining from complaint; listening to others.

TO THINK AND PRAY ABOUT: Now, try putting all these together! Have a good day!

The Prayer Of A Handicapped Person

IF YOU ARE a handicapped person or you know a person who is handicapped, perhaps this prayer will be a blessing:

"With the Psalmist I pray, 'God is our Refuge and Strength, a very present Help in trouble; therefore will we not fear'. Lord, there are times when I am fearful because of my condition. I am not able to do the things I would like to do. At times people either make fun of me, deride me or just seem to feel sorry for me. Lord, I don't want any of that. Rather, Lord, take all fear from my heart and give me courage to face the realities of life with determination.

"Lord, I see some perfectly healthy people wasting their lives. This makes me feel sad, because I feel they could do so much more than they are doing. Then I see some other people who make the most of their lives. It seems when a person has lost the sight of one eye, he is much more thankful for the one he has left. When a person has lost one arm, he seems to be able to do so much more with the one arm he has left. Lord, there are many handicapped people in this world. At times I realize how many people there are worse off than I. Lord, help me not to feel sorry for myself. Lord, grant them help and courage likewise.

"Now, Lord, help me to develop the abilities that I have and let me be thankful for what you have given me. Grant me grace to accept my situation and find joy in being able to accomplish the things I can, so that perhaps I also can give courage and hope to others. Grant me love and joy in serving You and my fellow man. In Jesus' name. Amen." (from The Lutheran Prayer Book).

TO THINK AND PRAY ABOUT: We are all handicapped in one way or another, are we not? Perhaps you call it by another name: "restricted, disadvantaged, hindered, tied down, uneducated, slow of speech, self-conscious, shy, unattractive, impoverished" (some real, some imagined, some self-imposed). Whatever the condition or the reason behind it, let us pray for release in order to serve with the blessings which outnumber the stars! God can heal.

Here's To Grandparents!

September 10
Deuteronomy 4:9-10

"Do you miss the old home town? Will you go back
  sometime?"
Ah, my dear friends, how can you ask—of memories
  such as mine?
Why I return most every day to that familiar door
Where roses rambled round the porch and spilled
  along the floor . . .
I see the garden full of pinks that pushed the peas
  aside;
I watch Grandmother's smiling face . . . see her arms
  stretched out wide . . .
I hear Grandfather's hearty laugh as he feeds the
  mules;
His voice is filled with welcome and his hands are
  filled with tools . . .
I hear the sound of sleepy birds and know the hour
  grows late;
From orchard-nest behind the house a lover tells his
  mate.
I do not have to pack a bag or plan how long to stay;
I do not miss "Grandparent ways" . . . They never went
  away!   *J.M.B.*

GRANDPARENTS are taken for granted. Somebody should do something about it? Somebody did. President Carter issued a proclamation designating Sunday, September 10, 1978, as National "Grandparents' Day." Ideally, of course, every day should be a day of recognition to the patriarchs and matriarchs of our families—if we are fortunate to have them. If not, let's hope we were exposed to the kind of goodness that comes from godliness; that we keep teachings—and, yes, "preachings"—and hand them down!

While not all of our older people are grandparents, some wonderful programs make it possible for them to become "instant grandparents" in church, school and community programs. Many children have never known the joys of grandparents, either, so it's love at first sight. What a blessing!

TO THINK AND PRAY ABOUT: Let us give praise to—and for—our older people. Let us draw closer together.

The Dignity Of Work

MAYBE THE poor have an edge over the rich after all. Working is a fine thing! It toughens the muscles, strengthens the body, makes braver the heart and seasons life in general with patience and courage. Ancient peoples said "Labor is the price which the gods have placed upon everything worth having." Actually, our work history goes farther back, to Genesis, when God decreed that mortals should eat bread in the "sweat of the face." Time was when the caste of people was recognized by the appearance of their hands. Those with smooth, white hands were called the "idle rich"; those with callous palms were called the "gentle poor." Such trademarks are outdated in our world, for the working class makes use of the mind as well as the body.

The "right to work" was a big campaign issue during the days of the Great Depression. After World War II labor took on new dignity. Labor Day itself, celebrated by parades as far back as 1882, is now a legal holiday set the first Monday in September. Holiday-oriented as we Americans have become, it is a good time to look back over labor measures which offer security, compensation and indiscrimination in employment. This is something for which we should be grateful; for even when the pendulum swings too far and we know that violence cannot be tolerated in our society, we know that we are a free nation. Let us count dignity of work among our blessings.

The quest to get-rich-quick is an age-old adventure. But rest assured that somebody, somewhere along the way, worked. Somebody, even as the saying goes, had to "make a better mousetrap." Sooner or later the world has asked: "What can *you* do?" And sooner or later God will ask: "What have you done?" Surely a "Well done" from the Creator of us all would be a thrill beyond compare!

TO THINK AND PRAY ABOUT: In what ways can we share God's love on the job?

Summer's Lease

Summer's Lease hath all too short a date."

William Shakespeare

AN ARTIST sees autumn, as well as spring, as a time of creation. A teacher is an artist into whose hand we commit our young.

Dear Teacher: As summer's lease ends, we release our child into your keeping. All summer this child has been King of the Mountain, and we have appeared to be his slaves. Now he has need of a master who can love him more objectively. Will you help us instill the values we left out, while helping to retain the values we imparted? Will you be gentle yet firm when he rebels against your authority? For there will be times when he will press against you as he has us—unconsciously wanting us to stand fast. And when you need to, will you release him, as we have—to God's world out there?

You need to know our child in order to help him grow. May I share what we have tried to teach him so that together we can help him acquire the love, faith and courage he needs for a future, which may seem to hold more defeats than victories? To get a proper perspective, he must know it's a balanced world of: villain-hero; wickedness-in-the-high-places and goodness-in-unexpected-ones; enemy-and-friend. Only great persons can tilt the scale in right directions. If you can tilt the scale for him, perhaps he can help tilt it for the world. You see, Teacher, what dreams we hold?

He loves books. Through them he has learned to ponder the eternal mysteries of the universe. He has found heroes who chose failure rather than dishonesty; and heroines who had faith in those they loved even when the world let them down. Is there a quiet corner where he can read?

We have given him responsibility. He needs it to keep him strong enough to stand for what is right: hopefully reasoning—fighting if he must. We believe in praying at our house, so we'll be asking God that you help him become a man.

TO THINK AND PRAY ABOUT: Could you sign this letter? If so, you can work with your child's teacher helping your offspring to sell their services, but save their hearts for the only Master they are to serve. Our "lease" has expired.

In Stature And In Wisdom

"WHY DO THE leaves change color?" Each September as we fill the classroom with armfuls of autumn's glory, the children pose the question. And, annually, their inquisitive minds lead them to search out answers in the books I suggest.

It is so wonderful being a child. I remember imagining that elves splashed leaves with scarlet and gold in autumn; and "Jack Frost" did painting in winter. Even after I outgrew the fanciful stories, I heard old-timers say, "Early frost, brilliant autumn."

Actually, I was as surprised as the children when I discovered the secret of the bright leaves. It was hard to believe the unleashed color was there all along—even when the leaves were June-green. The reason for the color-change, we read, is the shortened daylight hours of fall. Sometimes slowly, sometimes dramatically, the green chlorophyll fades and the autumn hues become visible.

"But this year they're late changing," a child observed one year. True, for it had been a long, late fall with lots of sunshine.

Each harvest season I watch with awe the miracle of golden aspen, crimson maple and speckled oak. I watch, with equal awe, the miracle of discovery in the eyes of children.

And never shall I forget the words of one child who brought me a beautiful insight. With a wisdom that transcends knowledge, the eight-year-old said, "I guess trees are like us. They need light to change them. We need love." *Wow!* I thought, *I hope I can remember that.* How much, how very much, color must lie beneath the surface of other people—beauty I will never see unless I offer love as God would have me do. Truly, a little child had led me.

TO THINK AND PRAY ABOUT: Look for the beauty of the earth, as seen through the eyes of children. Look for the beauty inside every person you encounter today. *For this insight, Father in Heaven, we thank You. Amen.*

Winding Down

September 14
I Thessalonians 4:11-18

THE SWELTERING, melancholy days of summer-winding-down are upon us. It is that unreal, limbo period of the year, wedged between the frolic of freedom and the hustle-bustle of one more holiday. The sun hangs low in the afternoon, making the streets shine and the trees stand out in silhouettes. It is a strange time for children—the end of a summer they thought was endless. Now with school starting one of these soon-Mondays, boys and girls are anticipating the pinch of new shoes and the brassy bray of an alarm clock. It is truly alarming—a time for grownups to be patient.

Let's not delude ourselves. Youngsters read us like the books they are soon to open, often seeing the telltale signs with greater clarity than the abstract words on printed pages. A sense of urgency surrounds them. Mother is shopping more frequently, mostly for *them*. Mother tells friends, who know already, that school's about to start—and isn't there a sort of sigh? Mother waves more enthusiastically at teachers as they appear out of nowhere hurrying here and there getting ready for school to start. Is there a secret message between them? Is there a conspiracy?

Remember the mixed emotions you felt? On one hand there was the anticipation of seeing old friends and having new experiences. Those were the welcome smiles of fall. But on the other hand there was that certain sense of despair: a despair that the carefree days of summer had slipped away; and, as you grew older, you realized that particular summer was gone forever. You sought a refuge—a place to escape and think, to savor the lost moments of sweet vacation, and pray, lest anybody know you were scared . . . or suspected your parents wanted you gone . . . or that you wanted to laugh and cry at the same time. I remember lying, shoeless, listening to the faint hum of faraway traffic and the uncontrolled giggles of neighborhood boys as they swung from a rope suspended from an ancient oak into the pond for one last swim. It wasn't much of a prayer—so vague, so general, but so comforting! "Dear God, let it all turn out right for everybody."

TO THINK AND PRAY ABOUT: Reassure your children of your love and their need for an education as they move towards independence. Let them know God cares!

The Staff Of Life

My hands are rough; the knuckles red;
The nails are split from kneading bread.
I think of how they're used, abused,
Then muse that "Breadcorn must be bruised."
Perchance, one day, my thoughts will stray
To blender, bought, and stored away . . .
It's newer, better, so they say.
Alas! Instructions I've not read;
God needs my hands to knead His bread.
And I feel so much nearer heaven
Touching loaves He helped me leaven. J.M.B.

IF YOU WERE fortunate enough to grow up in a "Bread is the Staff of Life" kitchen, you will remember the yeasty-smell of the rising dough; the golden goodness of the fresh-from-the-oven loaves; the tenderness that combined lightness of texture and joy of sharing. Chances are that you fell heir to some ancient cookbook—and maybe you cling to some of its ways.

Bread symbolizes so many things. It was a staple in biblical days, which makes the numerous references to its sustaining qualities much more meaningful. Let's dip back into the Bible for the deeper meaning, as we delve into the old recipes and find buried wisdom there.

One must use one's hands to do God's work (one task being that of breadmaking); and if they were bruised, so be it! Like the wheat that had to be bruised to become flour, hands could only serve the "holy cause" when they suffered a bit. I guess even today I would feel guilty if I used a mixer. Dishonest bakers who cheated in little ways were thrust into the baking ovens along with the bread!

TO THINK AND PRAY ABOUT: Jesus used bread to represent His body and invited all to gather that they need never hunger again. But preparation is required and it may require some bruising of self. Can you think of ways you have been bruised in serving? Seek a new leaven of sincerity and truth.

September 16
Genesis 46:1-7

"SIGN HERE, and the transaction is ended." Is it? Or is it just beginning, once you have sold your old home where so many memories lie? Maybe this is where your husband carried you across the threshold as a bride . . . or the new home you built together . . . the old house you bought and remodeled . . . the "old home place" that generations before you occupied. Houses take on special character when they put their wooden arms around us to comfort us, shield us, echo our laughter and wipe away our tears. We sprinkled a lawn, planted a rose bush and added a room. We put up swings and took them down as the children grew up and left. The grape arbor was a haven of rest in the summertime—our leafy bower, no matter how barren. Surely we have all experienced the pangs of remorse moving brings.

But there comes a time when we must move on, leaving the hickory nut tree, which to us was a miracle of sorts; but the new occupants may see it as a littering autumn nuisance. Would they dare saw it down? Perhaps, for it holds no memories for them. You hold no claim to its future, but you *do* have its past. Pack those golden-leafed, nut-sweet moments into your moving barrels. They belong to you. But they are souvenirs—not a past to live in! See moving as a challenge, an opportunity to start afresh, and you can recapture the excitement you felt in this house. Until we are "of age," we must follow where the work of our parents takes us. As working singles, we must go where our own careers offer advancement. And, then, when we are wives, we must be the willing helpmates of the man whose name (and often children) we bear. We must grow. The stage of our lives and the conditions we live in have little to do with growth—we, ourselves, determine it.

Leave the old behind as you bring positive memories into a positive future—choose growth! Have you ever noticed how some people move into a neighborhood and there is instant acceptance? Others feel rejected. Maybe they left God back in the old house!

TO THINK AND PRAY ABOUT: Discuss how you can grow as you anticipate new things.

Why Lose A Sale?

THE ENTERPRISING young salesperson had a point. She knew that the best way to make a sale was to stop pushing the merchandise.

A patron stood before the three-view mirror of the ladies' department store. She turned round and round examining her reflection as she modeled the smartly-tailored fall suit.

"Are you sure this will wash?" she asked the clerk.

"Oh yes! It's a blend of polyester and cotton."

"It looks like wool."

"Yes, ma'am. That's one of the advantages of 'miracle fabrics'—that, and the fact that they're easy to care for."

"It feels like wool. Wool makes me itch. Are you sure this isn't wool?"

The salesgirl smiled understandingly. "Wool makes me itch, too. The suit looks lovely on you."

"I like it, but—"

"May I put it on your account?"

"Yes, I think it will do." The lady handed over her credit card and turned to the dressing room. A few minutes later she emerged wearing her own dress and holding out the suit she wished to purchase.

"There's a label inside that says 'Polyester-cotton blend'. You knew it was there, didn't you?"

The young lady nodded. "But I didn't wish to press you."

The customer looked puzzled. "You could have lost a sale."

The girl took the proffered suit. "Either way," she said confidently.

TO THINK AND PRAY ABOUT: Do you find yourself pressing your point with the children, your husband, parents, friends? It is so easy for them to push a little button and turn us off, isn't it? I find myself tending to over-explain when a sudden silence is much more effective on occasion. One of our greatest mistakes is that of pressing in on others whose point of view differs with ours; or perhaps approaching the unbeliever or the stranger too quickly as if pushing our wares. Sometimes a word or deed speaks more of God.

Migratory Workers

WHEN THE HARVEST is ready it must be gathered quickly. A sudden burst of heat, a lightning storm, a heavy rain, a high wind or an early frost can wipe out a year's work in the twinkling of an eye. It is then that farmers must send out a call of distress to the employment bureaus, hoping that field hands have arrived in time to save the crops. What a welcome sight to see them come flocking into the orchards, groves and fields! How we need their services. These migratory workers do their job and then move on to another awaiting harvest field. It is impossible for them to settle down or to become a part of a community, for their time with us is short.

Three thoughts we can gather from the migratory laborers who come to the aid of farmers. First, what sort of provisions do we make for them? Do we welcome them into our churches, schools and community as the farmers welcome them into the fields? Here is a built-in "harvest" for us! And I'm afraid we neglect them. Here is food for prayer. Second, do we appreciate them as we ought? We let their services go unpraised while we work within our own tight-knit little groups. Has it ever occurred to you to ask one of them to attend church, prayer service, a Bible study even for a visit? Third (and how important this is!), do we recall that Jesus was an "itinerant preacher" who went about healing and raising others from the dead? What is it that blinds us to the service of others—when we're all sojourners?

TO THINK AND PRAY ABOUT: He was only a migrant worker seeking labor from place to place . . . . Another unskilled and unfulfilled might have worn a frown on his face . . . But this man was magically happy, with his faced creased in a constant smile, as ambling along he'd burst out in song . . . and others were cheered for a while. How often his heart must have been broken—untidy and quite out-of-date . . . for few understand the kind of a man who'd rather be good than be great . . . Without fanfare the sojourner left us . . . and none of us knew 'til he'd gone that he saw a need and planted a new seed of love that bloomed after he'd gone . . . J.B.B. *Welcome all with open arms into the house of the Lord.*

Take Time To Be Holy

"SINCE WE are of the same vintage year," a booksender wrote my friend, "I thought GEE WHIZ! I'M OLD might be helpful for you to read." My friend's reaction was to leave the rest of the letter unread, she said, and to discard the book as well. Now, she's glad she didn't.

"There's a section called 'Prescription for Growing Old Gracefully' that I like," she read on as the book review proceeded. Her spirits lifted as she read: *Sniffle?* (Only during hay fever season, she said); *Feel neglected?* (Would that I were!); *Demanding attention?* (Avoiding it!); *Interfering when grandchildren are corrected?* (Have none). Somewhat smugly, she read on: *Taking sides in family disagreements?* (Ouch! I most likely start them); *Critical?* (Well, not . . .)

The real rub came when my friend got to the appearance thing. (Lives there a woman who doesn't care?) The book's going to tell her that hair dye (which she doesn't use) and tight foundation-garments (which she doesn't need) won't help. But cosmetics? She recalled the words of one of her ministers when confronted with the question: "Do you object to our use of makeup?" He replied, "The Lord knows you need it." Oh, well. By then she was to the point that, according to the book, there was nothing she could do to improve herself but to keep fit.

Her account was amusing, but the "keeping fit" does have something to say, doesn't it? Diet, exercise, rest, yes; but an inner fitness, too. The book title should delete the "old" and let it be a prescription for *growing*—something which has nothing to do with age! Maybe the friend who sent her the letter realized that; for at the close of the letter, she wrote: "The writer tells us we grow closer to God if we take time to be holy. Say, do you remember that old song?"

TO THINK AND PRAY ABOUT:
Take time to be holy, speak oft with thy Lord;
Abide in Him always, and feed on His Word.
Make friends of God's children; help those who are weak,
Forgetting in nothing His blessing to seek.

(Words by William D. Longstaff;
music by George C. Stebbins)

Handle With Care

LAST WEDNESDAY at 3:30 P.M. the Old Dutch Clock in the kitchen stopped in its tracks. It's been half an hour ahead or behind—depending on the weather or its mood for a year. Most would have taken it to a Swap Meet long ago. There are beautiful new clocks that wake one up to music, right themselves automatically if the power goes off and know all kinds of tricks; and they're guaranteed, manufacturers say.

Maybe. But, you know, possessing something that requires tinkering with is an extravagance one can enjoy. Houses can come alive with relics that constantly cry for help; and each has a set of memories.

This clock used to be the Bacher household's call to arms. It told the youngsters how long they had until school-bus time, sent their fathers to milk the cows and set their mothers to beating buckwheats. All those little weights and chimes of childhood are worth preserving.

But what a nice surprise to find a repairman who'd fall in love with an ailing clock. The man was old, articulate and very philosophical. "People who understand clocks understand each other," he said. "You know, we all sort of run down with the years. With clocks now it's up to the owner to see that they age gracefully."

The great gentleman moved some mysterious innard of the clock's insides. The twinkle of his eye spelled success, and he went on talking: "If these old friends are neglected, they grow old and useless. They stare at us for a time, then they cover their faces with their hands."

Isn't it good to meet an understanding human being who knows what the trouble with ancient things is—and repairs it so tenderly? None of the replacing, refurbishing or repainting promised for the newer models would require the same virtue. And we can do that for each other!

TO THINK AND PRAY ABOUT: Creating the new and recycling the semi-new are important, but so is maintaining original objects. We can help God maintain happiness by letting others know He does not forsake the aging!

Are You "Just A Housewife"?

September 21
Psalm 145:1-5

OVERUSE OF THE word "just" with a wrong connotation bothers me. It underestimates any word, phrase or clause that follows. Women who are "just housewives" are apologizing for outworking from three to four paid-by-the-hour-people—and what is their salary scale? Recently some statistics appeared in the newspaper that were startling. The homebody serves as nursemaid ($2.65 an hour); housekeeper ($4.00); dishwasher ($3.75); and laundress ($3.75). From there the staggering figures went into services performed by the day, the week, the month and the year! It added up to $351.59 per week—or $18,282.68 per year. Wow! I was ready to apply for a job—only it doesn't pay that, does it? And who wants to be "just a housewife"? Do we really see ourselves as servants of loved ones?

If you find this nonsense, you aren't alone! Since when do we charge our husbands and our children for *loving* them? And then it occurred to me to ponder the greatest service of all, that which God does for each of us every second as we walk through this life. There is no way we can buy God's services; there is no way we can earn them. He gives them to us freely. Do we, I wonder (those with minds greater than mine), calculate what we would owe Him for His care—if such thinking were not utter nonsense?

Comparing God's work to the work of the homemaker can be a humorous experience. Granted she goes unrecognized and unpraised, but her work is easy—even at its hardest compared to God. Let's say her work day starts at five (unlikely). She feeds and rushes the children to school and drives her husband to work. Let's give her a long day (twelve to fourteen hours). There's still a little time left to sleep; and although there is no "paid vacation," most wives take them. And with God working overtime, how often do we praise Him? He doesn't want us to be martyrs; He doesn't want our sacrifices; He doesn't need our money; He wants our love. And, come to think of it, that's all our family *really* wants of us!

TO THINK AND PRAY ABOUT: How do you see your role? Discuss it with your family.

Why Bother With A Garden?

September 22
Psalm 126:5-6

THE GARDEN looks as rumpled as clothes left in the dryer too long. It looks at you with the same accusing eyes. Enough beans remain for tonight's vegetable dish, but in this unpredicted heatwave isn't it easier to take something from the freezer? The weeds are taller than the chard. Hornets swarm around the year's remaining melons . . . Why bother? As a matter of fact, why did we bother to plant this year? But we'll go on planting . . . .

There's a primal urge to gardening. Our ancestors planted and reaped in due season in order to sustain human life, but I believe it goes deeper—as far back as the Garden of Eden. We are created with appetites, to be sure, the kind that demand food for fuel, but I think we are hungry for more: an appetite for that which is beautiful and holy. In a little secret corner of the heart's garden plot, we dig for beauty and holiness.

"It's good exercise," you told yourself last spring. You were right—two ways. There's nothing that straightens out the emotional kinks better than breaking up clods and wrestling with Bermuda grass—or brings on a better night's sleep once you've moaned in the shower and groaned with a brisk rub-down. But working in the garden offers another kind of exercise—an intimate contact with God through the earth and its power for growing things. Since we no longer grind our own grist, let's say we do not live by radishes, cabbage and green onions alone. A garden feeds more than the stomach; it feeds the soul.

If there's one among us who has never known the thrill of growing things, try it! You have no need for a course in botany, biology or chemistry. Just read the seed catalogues, the directions on the seed packets (knowing they are exaggerated!), start digging, raking, smoothing and praying. There! Do you feel the surge of life beneath your hands? You are helping this earth (that God Himself planted in the beginning) to perpetuate life. Something happens between you and God that's very special and very intimate. Then, with the harvest, there comes a certain knowing that you have been in direct touch with the Creator. *What joy!*

TO THINK AND PRAY ABOUT: Can you see a comparison in the patience required for gardening and that required for working with others? "Contact" is the key!

Light And Darkness

TWO TIMES each year, in spring and in autumn, the sun is directly over the equator. With the sun in this position, the horizon of every place is divided into two equal parts of light and darkness. The autumnal equinox generally occurs on September 23, a time when fall rushed in to shorten the days and lengthen the nights in the northern hemisphere. The opposite takes place in the southern hemisphere, where inhabitants welcome spring. On March 21 there is another "changing of the guard," and spring returns as autumn hurries to the lands below the equator. Only at these two times, the vernal equinox and the autumnal equinox, does the sun play no favorites. So today it blesses us all alike with golden equality!

Our lives are rather like that, are they not? We meet people who seem to make everyday living into "long dark nights." Such individuals live "polar lives"; for without sun, there is not light; and where there is no light there is a coldness that penetrates the marrow. We meet others who seem to balance their light and darkness as if they were suspended above the equator; they have their "up days" and their "down days." I suppose they are what modern psychologists would term "well adjusted," and we can't quarrel with that.

It is the "long night" people we need to help, lest we become like them. They overcast the sky and make life's landscape into depressing things: no shadows, no light, no dimension, no vigor. All is flat!

But isn't it wonderful when you find those sunshiny people who somehow give off reflected light, like the moon, even when the sun has left with the cycle of the seasons? Now these people make no false claims that life has no shadows. They find shadows interesting! After all, there can only be shadows where there is light. They take shadows and do interesting things with them—reshaping them with their own reflected light or making them dwindle to noonday proportions when the shadow-makers stand directly beneath God's Light.

TO THINK AND PRAY ABOUT: We live in a world of artificial light; and we can appreciate its controllable factors as one of our blessings. However, there is a greater light, that which God gave and made it possible for us to reflect.

I Have A Need

"I HAVE A need." How many times a day do you hear it as you help your family and friends over the bumps of life? Is your telephone ringing throughout the daylight hours to let you know your vote is needed—or your service, presence, donation? Even the inanimate objects in my house seem to have voices: "Fix us . . . find us . . .turn us on . . . off . . . clean us . . . fill us up!" Do any of these, living or non-living, know of *my* needs?

I need to be alone. I need time . . . I need—but why go on? Need is a common denominator of our lives, isn't it? Many of the needs can be filled with loving arms of family, understanding of friends, services of our hairdressers, doctors, lawyers, florists and butchers. But there's a greater need: I need Christ—a great Christ; and I have a great Christ to fill my need. How futile all these other things would seem without Him to lead me, guide me, keep me on course. The mind's-eye of my mortal being is so short-sighted, it is difficult for me to envision the greatness of His power, even when I acknowledge that without Him I can do nothing. Can you think of One who controls things: the ability to heal the sick, bring joy to the lonely, rest to the weary, new life to the dead; and yet has need of us? Too often I forget that Jesus, who is all confidence, power, commitment, love and the giver of the Kingdom of Heaven, still needs me to carry on in my own way to spread His message—by word, maybe; by deed, probably; by example, *always*.

When we think, "I have a great need; I have a Great Christ for that need. Christ has a need of my service," then small frustrations of the day become nothing. And while the big ones may stick around to discourage, frustrate and disappoint us, we find that we can bear them.

TO THINK AND PRAY ABOUT: Reflect on the words of the old hymn, "I Need Thee Every Hour" (words by Annie S. Hawks and music by Robert Lowry).

I need Thee ev'ry hour, in joy or pain, Come quickly and abide, or life is in vain. I need thee, O I need Thee;
Ev'ry hour I need Thee! O bless me now, my Savior,
I come to Thee.

When Tragedy Comes

TRAGEDY struck in the North Park neighborhood of San Diego, California, on September 25, 1978. The fiery collision of a Pacific Southwest Airlines 727 jet and a four-passenger Cessna was proclaimed one of the worst air disasters in the history of aviation. As officials continued to sift through the rubble for more victims, clues to the unexplained crash and ways of preventing a similar catastrophe, survivors sifted through the gamut of their emotions, inspecting things within their innermost selves to determine what stuff they're made of.

Why is it that tragedy such as this one brings out the best or the worst in us? Does it take such a holocaust to show us who we are, what we are, what we can become when circumstance turns our world upside down?

Symbolically, there was no breeze to lift high the stars and stripes, so the nation's flag hung limp at half-staff. The sky was bright—too bright—as often is the case in a California autumn. Visibility seemed to go on forever that dreadful day, which, ironically, may have contributed to the disaster. With no fog and no wind the pilot of the fated plane probably thought the plane was safe to land at Lindbergh Field; but it could have been the roofs that gave back a blinding reflection. It would have been easy to blame nature for obscuring the small plane; it would have been easy to blame this or that; but "blame" was not the greatest issue. The victims were gone. The aftermath was in the hands of the rest of us.

The looters moved in like vultures descending upon carnage. With no visible signs of conscience, their first thoughts were to rush in and salvage what they could from bruised and broken bodies: jewelry, wallets, purses, luggage—pieces of the wreckage, some of it human flesh. One can only pray, "Forgive them, Lord; they know not what they do . . ."

But, oh, the incomparable joy of those who rallied with charitable, faithful and stable services to help restore a degree of normalcy: flocking to blood banks, bringing food and clothing, volunteering to assist Crowd Control experts, setting up tables with lemonade for parched throats—serving God.

TO THINK AND PRAY ABOUT: Rally for Christ when tragedy comes. We need each other.

Something Very Special

There's something very special
And I know where it grows:
I've seen it in a lily;
I've seen it in a rose.
I've seen it in a rainbow
Across an autumn sky;
I've seen it in a dewdrop
And in my mother's eye.
There's something very special
And each of us has part:
A little glow worth sharing
God planted in each heart. J.M.B.

IT IS AN exciting thought to try to imagine a movement in this world which would banish all hate and replace it with love: love for God, love for each other, love for everything that is good and beautiful—and yes, love for the unlovely. For beneath the exterior of the unlovely may be something God has placed there—something which can be unleashed only by love. God placed within each of us a certain unique power—a little glow we can share each day. It takes so little to turn a frown into a smile—just a twitch of a muscle. It's challenging to know you have the power.

"A Stoic's Prayer" It is worth reviewing:

"May I win no victory that harms either me or my opponent. May I to the extent of my power give all needful help to my friends, and to all who are in want. May I reconcile friends who are wroth with one another. May I never fail a friend in danger. When visiting those in grief may I be able by gentle and healing words to soften their pain. May I respect myself. May I always keep tame that which rages within me. May I accustom myself to be gentle, and never be angry with people because of circumstances. May I never discuss who is wicked and what wicked things he has done, but know good men and follow their footsteps."

TO THINK AND PRAY ABOUT: God gave to Christians a special sort of shine. I like to think it bounces off the Halo of His Son.

How Great Thou Art!

WHAT IS GREATNESS? Only God is great in the true meaning of the word. However, He placed within each of us, no matter how small we feel we are, an ability to do great things—through doing the small ones. The collected pleasures of life fade like the summer grass unless there is at the root of them the gladness in serving—the gladness of having done something that made someone happier in His Name. ITEM: Seek no recognition!

The following, author unknown, depicts greatness at its best: "Here is a man who was born in an obscure village, the child of a peasant woman. . . . He worked in a carpenter shop . . . and then was an itinerant preacher. He never wrote a book . . . held an office . . . owned a home . . . had a family . . . went to college . . . put His foot inside a big city . . . traveled two hundred miles from the place where He was born. . . . While still a young man, the tide of popular opinion turned. . . . His friends ran away . . . one denied Him. . . . He was nailed upon a cross between two thieves . . . His executioners gambled for the only piece of property He had—His coat . . . Nineteen centuries have come and gone and today He is the centerpiece of the human race . . . One solitary life."—which left us Life Eternal!

And, while no mortal can compare with our Risen Lord, it is good for us to note that He left with us His power over many things. Have you read "This Man Lincoln" (T.V. Smith)? Here is a sampling: "No man made great by death offers more hope to lowly pride than does Abraham Lincoln; for while living he was himself so simple as often to be dubbed a fool. . . . This Lincoln whom so many living friends and foes alike deemed foolish, hid his bitterness in laughter; fed his sympathy on solitude; and met recurring disaster with whimsicality to muffle the murmur of a bleeding heart . . . . He pitied where others blamed; bowed his own shoulders with the woes of the weak . . . and won through death what life disdains to bestow upon such simple souls . . . peace . . . ."

TO THINK AND PRAY ABOUT: We are not called upon to die for Christ; we are called upon to live for Him!

Help Me Help Her, Please!

DEAR PARENTS: I looked over in a bright corner, and there she sat. She looked so ready for what I wanted to give her that I knew this child had special parents who cared very much.

Today she looked a little scared, and I am scared, too; for while children are my business, I am often awed. I am prepared to teach children, my credential says, but your child is special. We both know that. As the day wore on, her blue gaze became more trusting, and tonight she may come home to tell you, "My teacher says" in a tone that says I hold all the world's wisdom in my grasp. Deal with this gently, even when the ideas she brings home may conflict with yours. You see, we busy teachers may be thinking one thing and communicating quite another. And, indeed, we may be wrong. Please give me a chance to right whatever I have done or said that upstaged or downgraded you and your teachings in any way; because, you see, she loves you even more.

How often will I hear as I heard today, "But my mother said!" Maybe if I share with you what I hope to instill in these young minds, we will understand each other better. As the year wears on, your little girl's curls will become snarled and her shoes will become scuffed. My nerves will become frazzled and I will no longer seem like a goddess, but rather "a mean teacher who gives too much homework!" Ignore it; let me become mortal to her.

I want to give them each a dream and inspire them to capture it. I want to teach them to compromise in small matters, but to be uncompromising in matters of the heart, soul and conscience. I want to encourage them to have inquisitive minds which lead them to know the truth. If you will but help me, we can lay the foundation for her life.

TO THINK AND PRAY ABOUT: Would you enjoy such a letter? Remember, teachers want your help. You have something very precious in common!

Blooms That Go On And On . . .

HERE AND THERE a single rose lingers—looking lonely, since most of its companions have faded and gone. Not so with the very-double petals of the grimly determined floribunda. Thousands of fiery red blooms come on and on and on . . . covering the bushes with giant clusters of blazing color, daring the autumn leaves to try to outshine them. I wish I could remember the name of these faithful flowers, so I could share their availability as they share their color. The nursery offered them as "ideal hedges against hard frost." Almost everyone could share in the most spectacular show in the world if I but knew the name. But isn't that the way? We see some face, experience some small event, little realizing what impact it will have on our lives. Each has served a purpose. God has a plan.

If you are a rose lover, you know their advantages already. Roses say what words cannot in times of great joy and great sorrow. They mend quarrels; they strengthen family ties; they win "fair lady" when "faint heart" cannot; and, on the more practical side, they attract attention from a film of dust when the busy homemaker banks the house with garlands of bloom. They are a gardener's dream come true . . . a poet's favorite subject . . . and so on. But roses serve with more than their beauty and their fragrance. They furnish pollen to the hungry bee; and with that same fine, yellow dust they serve each other. Do you know how these hybrids came to be, besides by grafting?

The Pennsylvania Dutch, so noted for their fascinating tales, have one about the gradual changing of an ordinary rose to a thing of rare beauty. It began with two bushes; one very fair but delicate; the other of insignificant blossom but sturdy of stock. Farsighted horticulturists (with little formal training, but an abundance of imagination) let the fair rose bloom in its brief season alongside its less attractive friend. The sturdy plant they allowed to bud but not to flower, lest it give off pollen which would mingle with the beautiful blossoms and gradually change their design. As the years went by there was a gift-exchange. Perhaps my rose which sets a small world on fire is a result! That's what happens when we share the gifts God gave.

TO THINK AND PRAY ABOUT: What gift have you to share? We are of one Body: Christ!

September's End

September's arms are filled with wheat;
A goldleaf's in her hair;
She seems to hold her breath sometimes
As if in autumn prayer.
September's led a lovely life;
She does not dread her leave
But pauses, saying: "Thank You, Lord,"
For all she helped achieve. J.M.B.

FIRST WITH a trial splash, then with a brilliant stroke of color, September has blended into autumn. Fat pumpkins seem to jump out of hiding as the leaves wilt on the vines around them and corn stands in longsuffering silence before going into shock. The slant of the sun lends an opaque glow to the sky of dying summer. A few V's of geese have gone over with farewell cries. It is October tomorrow; and the countdown for winter will have begun. Are the winds more chilling? Perhaps, but the briskness is refreshing. The grasses are no longer green, but isn't the hay-color a bit like straw-spun-to-gold? The flowers of spring are resting; but up and bright-eyed are the amber-lashed pom-poms of fall. September, a time of subtle change, combines harvest at its height with nostalgia for a summer-gone. And so it is with our lives.

Maybe the past is crowned with a glory it did not wear. But for mature people to recall with delight fishing the stream when the bass were hitting, or dreaming when the stars stood still that special night—that's delightful. It is only when we look back on our lives as seasons wasted and refuse to believe that the same God is with us who was with us in our youth; when we fail to acknowledge that life begins anew with every season and at every age, that "looking back" becomes destructive. Let us look forward to October, aware that it, too, will soon become the November of our lives. Let us respect each day we have had, remembering it as a gift of God.

TO THINK AND PRAY ABOUT: Look for a brighter tomorrow and forever after by believing God is with you each moment, enjoying His presence each day, and praying for added strength to grow throughout each season.

October's Anniversary Prayer

LORD, I stand in a little village of golden aspen—not moving lest I disturb Your plan. A shuffle of my footsteps would disturb the bright-eyed mouse in search of one last acorn, the solitary robin that rescheduled its flight, a lad fishing in the nearby pond who perhaps thought he could learn more of You and Your ways here than within four walls. Let me be still, Lord; I have not come to crowd the wild things, to rush Your season or even to say goodby. The time of leisure is not yet, Lord. It is a time for me to be silent and think longer thoughts than summer allowed. It is a time for me to let the great rhythm of Your handiwork seep into my heart, reminding me of the glory that Your hand has brought. It is time for me to reach beyond myself, to seek wider horizons, more visible day by day as the leaves drift down one by one, and to know that their work is done. How good it is, Lord, that Your great clock should bring me this respite—a time for the sweet whisperings, a time to let go of summer tensions, a time to leave the valleys of my own making and ascend to view the autumn constellations of Your eternal love in an autumn sky. . . .

Lord, let me be still and savor the moment, remembering that spring is a prelude to harvest; insulating my soul with Your goodness against the winter cold. They, too, are a part of Your plan: for each leaf must leave its parent tree; each little mouse burrow into the sleeping earth and each robin take to its wing; so it is with our lives. Let me—let all of us—know that, Lord; but for now, let me enjoy the foundation You have laid for me: my life, my family, my friends, Your world.

Let me look upon the harvest of my dreams that the years have brought; but let me not touch it; for the time is not yet. Let me remember the first-time smile; the future shared in loving plans with faith in You that pays off in life's autumn; and make me even more thankful than I have been on other days—for each day brings us closer to You through earthly splendor. Yesterday is all around me, Lord. Give me tomorrow. Spring's youth gave way to summer's maturity. Lord, bless me, especially today.

Falling Leaves

OCTOBER HAS a way of putting us into a reflective mood. Old memories drift in like leaf-smoke; remembered sounds like gypsy calls echo against the canyon walls. Reflections and memories can and do mingle with dreams—with the young at heart. It's a beautiful time of year—the favorite season of "starving artists" who try to imitate the Master's hand; poets who try to paint it with words. Only hearts can see it as it is.

October comes in, blue and gold, urging one to do nothing but reflect. Reflecting is as beautiful as the gypsy-caravans of leaves that float down so leisurely. Yes, leaves are falling now that October's here. But it's not so poetic-feeling when the caravans camp in my front yard. The crimson sweetgum, the copper maple, the curling avocado fall all over. The yard is filled. The walks can hardly be walked upon. The porch is littered in peeling patchwork. As the days shorten, the slanting beams of autumn's sun tell the leaves it is time to rest. How freely, how gladly they float, their spirit set free after their labor. Once they were a source of light, shade and life itself. They have served their purpose well.

Have you ever thought of the similarity of leaves to the ideas which feed the mind, body, heart and soul? Ideas, like the leaves, bud and flourish in their maturity to give light; they speak of life and leave wisdom in their parting. When they have served God's purpose, He sweeps them away. If they cling too long, their beauty fades, withers, dies—blocking the way for the budding of new ideas to come. Life is a constant season of exchange.

TO THINK AND PRAY ABOUT: As you sweep away the leaves today, think of them as instruments of nature—tired, in need of rest, because their energy has been used up. Then sweep out the old ideas and let God come in with new growth!

Lord, Have I Failed Today?

October 3
Galatians 6:1-5

I need you, Lord, to start my day—
These gifts You have called hands—
For they have many tasks to do
To meet the day's demands.
Throughout the hours I need Your help,
And, yes, I need Your trust
In me to do the mundane things
We both know are a must.
I need You, Lord, at close of day
To tell You that I'm blessed;
I'm glad You hear my day-long prayer . . .
My hands must do their best. J.M.B.

HAVE I DONE the best I am able today, or have I failed? Was I impatient when my friend called? If so, it was probably because I did not know what to say.

My friend's daughter often flings this question in her mother's face: "Why did you bring me into this world? I didn't ask to be born!" Whatever caused such an attitude in a fourteen-year-old should have been corrected long ago, it seems to me—as long ago as crib-days. But I must not be judgmental. My friend needs understanding now. How should she cope?

She didn't ask to be born. Did you? It's childish thinking, of course. Most people feel abused at times. God doesn't ask anybody whether he or she wishes to enter this world—or leave it. There is no choice; there is only choice in how we accept and use up our days.

TO THINK AND PRAY ABOUT:

Each night my heart kneels down to pray; Thank You, Lord, for this day;
For all the blessings it has brought; lovely things—real and thought—
But teach me, Lord, that thought-things end unless I leave them with a friend.
So help me, please, to store away a part of You with them each day,
So they will one day come to feel You hold the key to thoughts made real. J.M.B.

The Value Of Things

"A WORD TO the wise is sufficient," said one of our great Americans. Benjamin Franklin's proverbs are afire with wit, wisdom and common sense. Do you recall Mr. Franklin's little story about the whistle? It brings home the laws of God and calls on just good ol' common sense.

When Ben was only seven, he was charmed by the whistle of a friend and impetuously offered to give him all the pennies he had for the worthless gadget. His purchase made him the target of his family, who pointed out to him the folly of bargaining before reflecting on the worth of one's purchase. "God helps those who help themselves," is another of his sayings; and while we may not be able to cure all the world's ills, we can begin by assessing some of the "world's whistles" to determine their worth.

Just what is a bargain? Will it bring more chagrin than pleasure? How much should a "pocket full of coppers" buy? How can we recognize a "boy with a whistle" who is out to grab four times what his wares are worth? How can we avoid "toy shop" folly? How can God help our dilemmas?

The Greens were childless. They had been unsuccessful in getting a child through the adoption agencies. A doctor heard of their plight, informed them of a case in which he could get a child for them providing they would pay the mother's hospital bill, pay him a fat fee and pay his attorney an equal amount. *Are they paying too much for the whistle?*

Mary is bored. Her husband's work keeps him on the road a lot. A "very nice" man began taking her out now and then. It breaks the monotony, so they see each other regularly now. Her children are upset; people are "talking"; her husband doesn't know. *Is she paying too much for the whistle?*

Don wants a family. Jean wants her "freedom." She had an abortion without telling her husband. *Is she paying too much for the whistle?*

Tom is ambitious and popular. He has no time for family, friends or church. Rita says he no longer prays. *Is he paying too much for the whistle?*

TO THINK AND PRAY ABOUT: Do you discuss "costs" at home? How do you keep values alive?

Happy Birthday—"Stranger!"

October 5
Ezra 9:2, 5-6
Isaiah 56:3, 5

OUR SON WROTE while on his tour of duty with the Intelligence Division of the USAF that he had met "the only girl I will ever love." I was the first to say with stars in my eyes, "How romantic!" He went on to state that "I wish to marry the young lady." The stars in my eyes turned to questions: "What are her credentials to qualify her as the 'right wife' for our son?" I asked my husband. George was working in the garage as I was reading him the letter. He seemed to be listening with half an ear; but when the third message came, his passivity vanished. Our son's fiance was Korean! My husband became an Ezra. While Ezra mourned "affinity with strangers," spreading his hands in despair, my son's father spoke in loud tones about "foreigners" and "irresponsible children" and he pounded his workbenches with hammer-clenched fists in Ezra-like lamentations. "Oh, well, it will spend itself," we consoled each other.

But it didn't spend, fortunately! We asked God to bring our son to his senses; instead He brought us a beautiful Korean daughter! We asked our friends for sympathy; instead they cited case after case in which "mixed marriages" worked. (I'd supposed our situation was unique!) We asked our son to reconsider; he asked us to do the same thing. . . . Those of you who have gone through the rigors that such decisions bring can understand fully. If you haven't gone through it, may I share with you the wisdom of our son? Perhaps it will meet a need.

Bryce returned from his station in Japan and re-entered college. A year passed—the waiting period we had agreed upon. Then, "Mother and Dad," he said one morning, "I want you to meet Sun; I'm sending for her. You'll love her, I think. I know you'll not let prejudice stand in the way—for that would be against all you've taught me!" How does a parent answer *that?*

Today is the birthday of the lovely wife God chose for our son! We love her.

TO THINK AND PRAY ABOUT: Examine your heart. Pray about prejudices. God handles with care.

October 6
Galatians 5:9

"SHANE AND JANE are raising Cain!" Mitty exclaimed. The young mother had been ecstatic five years ago when Betty, her firstborn, made her debut in October. She had been only slightly less ecstatic when the obstetrician confirmed her suspicions three years later—surprised when she found the addition to the family was to arrive in October, also; and overwhelmed when the doctor announced the addition was to be twins. No superlatives could describe the emotions of either mother or father when the identical bundles of humanity entered into the family with lusty shouts on Betty's birthday.

"They've been screaming ever since," she's said a thousand times. "They can out-scream the electric mixer, the vacuum cleaner and the too-loud T.V.!" Her voice can mimic theirs exactly: "Shane cut my Barbie doll's hair. He hates women!" "Jane took my purple chalk. She's gonna paint Betty's room!" And the oldest one yells, "I detest them both!" I can identify with her sometimes. Sibling love is a figment of some neurotic child psychologist's imagination. . . . Doesn't anybody know about sibling rivalry? And *three October sixth birthdays is tough!*

But this year was different. Betty had started to school. She had learned "new ways" and she was eager to teach the twins. The first-grader, who usually could live without her young rivals, took over completely with the birthday plans, and the twins—all eyes—looked on with awe. They formed a secretive triangle—the surprise (surprisingly!) being for their parents, whom they suddenly seemed eager to please. The house was a mess of Christmas decorations, which Betty decided it would be easier to leave up than clean up, with the holiday only two months away . . . but they sang happily, "Happy birthday to you . . . to me . . . to everybody . . . and I love you, me, God and the whole wide world!" They had discovered how much they loved one another.

TO THINK AND PRAY ABOUT: What do you think brought the change? Do you love God, others, self?

IT SEEMS ONLY yesterday that our son was clinching pink fists around my thumb as he kicked in his crib, clinging to my hand for security as we crossed busy intersections, tugging at my hand as he pulled me towards the toy department—and squeezing my hand briefly (if somewhat shyly) in a little secret code we had when we shared a joke as he became "one of the guys." Now he holds hands with another, which is as it should be. The "other woman" is his wife. At least I let God manage *that!*

Today as I thaw the top layer of their wedding cake, stale from too many freezings but still necessary for a "sentimental nibble" on their wedding anniversary, I find myself looking back on their rather unusual wedding. I am able to think now as I plan a menu for the evening meal; for our two cultures have blended rice (her staple) and steak (his indulgence)—because of love, understanding, prayer and constant vigilance on all our parts. The differences which once could have divided our house have strengthened it instead.

No ceremony is out of order these days, I guess. I continue to cling to tradition; and, yet, when I think back on the blindfold I must have been wearing in planning the wedding, I find myself in the position of "the kettle's calling the pot black." Writing one's own vows might be preferable to the act of unkindness I was guilty of—and worse, I was so sure I was right.

My only excuse is that it was a time of turbulence for us all. We'd hardly met Sun; she had no relatives or friends here; and, since we are long established, shouldn't our friends share in the celebration? Our minister proved indispensable; our friends stood by; and I patted myself on the back for being "mother of the bride" and "mother of the groom" in one blow! I attended to every minute detail—including helping my "new daughter" choose her wedding gown; and all went well—*American style.* The bride wore white and everybody cried—including the bride. How could I have known she'd brought a beautiful Korean gown from her own country, but preferred to bow to my wishes?

TO THINK AND PRAY ABOUT: It's easy to "take over!" Ask for forgiveness. I did! I consult my children and God more often now, too.

THE STORY CAME to me by reliable source. I wasn't around to hear the dialogue, but the quotes are fairly accurate, my source told me.

The boy was small for his age and wore a crown of chestnut curls—both of which he despised. He had a winning smile and a great ambition. He was not "the average," his teachers decided; and gradually, as the years walked on, the growing lad wondered if "not average" meant the same as "not normal." Was it peculiar for a man to put love first, as most women did?

People approached the child to compliment, always on the wrong things, according to the story. No "he-boy" wants adults "oh-ing" and "ah-ing" over frailty, curls and dimples. Those are "girl things." But it was his ambition that troubled him most of all. But openness was his manner, and he refused to compromise.

"What do you want to be when you grow up, little boy?"

"A husband."

"But—uh—I mean, your life work—"

"Being a husband will take all my time."

"But you'll want to prepare yourself. There are other things—"

"Yes," the boy replied patiently each time. "I'll be a good father, too."

The too-small boy suddenly loomed tall. The curls settled into acceptable waves. Dimples became laugh-lines; but the ambition never wavered.

The American male is expected to be the breadwinner, he knew, but he shied away from campus activities in preference to selecting a course of study that would "provide" but not dominate. His career was to be his family. When opportunity knocked, he asked, "How long will I be away from home? Will my evenings and weekends be free? Will I be my own man?" as opposed to "How fast can I climb? How far and fast can I advance? What will you pay?" He decided to sell his services (on his terms) to the highest bidder; he reserved his heart for family; his soul for God—so my husband's mother said!

TO THINK AND PRAY ABOUT: Women have changed their image; what do we expect of men?

Let Us Not Lose What They Found!

October 9
Psalm 54:4; 55:15

THE GINKGO'S fan-shaped leaves are turning buttery yellow. It's an old, old tree; does it remember its history? The Chinese Pistache is flaunting shades of bronze, burnt orange and flaming red—like dragon-tongues. It came from an old, old country . . . and the Spanish elm, what does it recall? One thinks of olden things on Columbus Day. This is a time to look back in gratitude and to look ahead and believe: believe in God, in country, in mankind, in each other—in life, here and hereafter. On our national holidays, shouldn't we focus our prayers on this great land and what it stands for—lest we lose what our nation's great men founded. God led them!

Thank You, Lord, for America—the land where dreams come as close to coming true as it is possible for earthly dreams to materialize.

Thank You, Lord, for giving hope to the weary and the downtrodden; thank You for the leaders You inspire daily to look out for them. We are a land of opportunity, but let us not forget the oppressed of the world.

Thank You, Lord, for the natural resources our forefathers found here. They walked close to You. They knew You had blessed this land. Remind us, Lord, for we forget.

Thank You, Lord, for the rights we possess—the right to work not being the least of these; but remind us often that we must work for You, too. We confess that all too often we look for added income, fringe benefits and early retirement programs—forgetting that You look after us day by day. Let us then pay off our mortgages and enjoy our earthly homes—ever mindful that You provided them—but let us remember the Home You are preparing. So, thank You, Lord, for the freedom of worship. Let us use it!

Lord, stir us up; move us from indifference! Give us a resurgence of faith: first and last in You; then add to it an abiding faith in this wonderful nation and its great men. Bless us with more like them!

TO THINK AND PRAY ABOUT: Let us try to perpetuate ancient spiritual values!

Why Hurry And Miss These?

We miss so much when we rush through
A meditation-walk:
The seas of grass in golden wheat,
The silver willow's talk,
A child at play in scented hay,
A birdsong in the trees
Are whispers straight from God, I think.
"Why hurry and miss these?"
From rosy dawn till day is gone
Beyond some lofty crest,
Sight, scent, and sound are gifts of God
We miss unless we rest. J.M.B.

TIMES CHANGE, but our basic needs remain stable. We need rest. You should see my neighbor. While I rush through one job with my mind on the next in line, she just drops down on the grass, idly chewing a pepperwood stem. "I'm unable to finish all that needs doing today, so what's the rush?" "I accomplish more if I sit a spell—not working—just thinking and appreciating." Let life settle around you; "Autumn's for a bit of resting."

Somewhere there's a recipe for people like me who try to do a year's work in one day—and rob themselves of "thinking time." My friend reads "so I can know the hopes and dreams in a world before my time," she says. My friend listens to music "so I can enlarge the heart and mind." My friend prays "so I can enlarge the soul." Her philosophy is contagious.

We can't change our patterns with one sitting, but one is a beginning! Today I tried it just once. When the pressure became unbearable, I just stopped, looked, listened and sniffed—like the watchful and appreciative family boxer who dropped in the grass alongside me, his bobbed-off tail fanning in a flurry of sheer joy. "Lord, it is good to be here," I whispered, remembering that God and His mysterious seasons remain the same.

TO THINK AND PRAY ABOUT: Take a quarter-hour; look at the lovely things you miss by rushing. Return to the mechanics of living refreshed, God's way.

You And The Lord's Prayer

"YOU AND THE Lord's Prayer," marked *Author Unknown*, came to me in yesterday's mail. I wish I were able to express appreciation to the writer for the blessing it brought me. Like a smile, it should be passed on:

"I cannot say OUR if my religion has no room for others and their needs.

I cannot say FATHER if I do not demonstrate this relationship in my daily living.

I cannot say WHO ART IN HEAVEN if all my interests and pursuits are earthly things.

I cannot say HALLOWED BE THY NAME if I, called by His name, am not holy.

I cannot say THY KINGDOM COME if I am unwilling to give up my own sovereignty and accept the righteous reign of God.

I cannot say THY WILL BE DONE if I am unwilling or resentful of having it in my life.

I cannot say ON EARTH AS IT IS IN HEAVEN unless I am truly ready to give myself to His service here and now.

I cannot say GIVE US THIS DAY OUR DAILY BREAD without expending honest effort for it or by ignoring the genuine needs of my fellowmen.

I cannot say FORGIVE US OUR TRESPASSES AS WE FORGIVE THOSE WHO TRESPASS AGAINST US if I continue to harbor a grudge against anyone.

I cannot say DELIVER US FROM EVIL if I am not prepared to fight in the spiritual realm with the weapon of prayer.

I cannot say THINE IS THE KINGDOM if I do not give the King the disciplined obedience of a loyal subject.

I cannot say THINE IS THE POWER if I fear what my neighbors and friends may say or do.

I cannot say THINE IS THE GLORY if I am seeking my own glory first.

I cannot say FOREVER if I am too anxious about each day's affairs.

TO THINK AND PRAY ABOUT: I cannot even say AMEN unless I honestly say, 'Come what may, this is my prayer.' "

Changing Roles

"ROLE PLAYING" always gets me uptight. Now changing roles is something else and is being done more so lately—or so one of my friends thinks. "You know, all the old tales told about men who thought their wives had it soft. Remember the messes they used to get themselves into when they tried to stoke the fire, keep the pot boiling, churn, keep the cow on the roof and mind the baby?" I remembered. "Well, today it's different—men and women are changing roles, sharing a balance of power."

My friend was suddenly inspired. "This should help us appreciate each other's roles more, and probably become more tolerant of each other." My friend giggled and went on, "Equal opportunity includes *sharing*—sharing our jobs, our joys, our frustrations, our needs—*whatever* with each other. The King of the Glass Mountains needs to know my struggles to keep the path from being slippery. I will probably sound something like this: 'I'm losing my mind, Darling. Did you notice? And the children, too, need to understand our roles: I'm willing to let you pitch in and help, children. Aren't you glad'?"

But *equal* means *empathy*—we need to feel for the other guy, too. "What was your day like, Darling? I'm sorry you have a headache." And children need the same considerations. Children are little people with good and bad days, busy schedules, and they need to be understood, just like we do. "So you got a "C" on your report, Joey. That's O.K. because I know you did your best. Don't cry, Susie, we all make mistakes."

God understands us better than we understand ourselves or each other, but He wants us to make the attempt.

TO THINK AND PRAY ABOUT: Mothers and Dads need to understand their children and each other. How you achieve it is up to you and God.

"Golden Rules" For Autumn

WHEN SKIES ARE painted your favorite shade of blue, it's autumn. When outside umbrellas are shedding scarlet leaves instead of raindrops, it's autumn. When rays of pumpkin-painting sun glisten across your lawn, it's autumn. It's a golden world, made so by the sheer artistry of the unseen Painter, who loves the world very much. The good Painter knows how to blend the colors before applying.

To keep autumn colors fresh and vivid in our lives, we need to know God's "Golden Rule" and follow it in everyday application. We know the rule. Why do we forget to make use of it? Perhaps it's from carelessness—surely not overconfidence! Take this day and make it golden for everyone you meet. Make it exciting—a challenge for yourself; a game for your children; an inspiration for others.

If you would have others write to you, write to them today; tomorrow may be busier for you; and someday there will be "No Forwarding Address."

If you wish friends to telephone you, phone them—to cheer them and share a bit of brightness.

If you wish to have others trust you, begin by trusting them; then become the kind of person in whom you yourself would wish to confide.

If you wish to have your husband admire you, admire him! And don't be afraid to say so. Have you ever known a man who complained about praise?

If you wish to have your children respect you, respect them. How? By listening in a way that shows you value their opinions, by being open with them when there is tension in the family; and perhaps most important of all by allowing time for feedback. You will be pleasantly surprised!

If you wish to have God love you, love Him! He is the one—the only One—who will love you no matter what the circumstances, but don't you agree it would be pleasing in His sight for us to obey the First Commandment?

TO THINK AND PRAY ABOUT: Now, what about all the little things? Borrow; return! Break; replace! Spill; mop up! Shout; apologize! Tear; mend! Secret; guard it—unless it's "I know something nice about you!" Thank God for His Rule!

Why Cry Over Spilt Milk?

WHAT KIND OF day have you had? Were you "all thumbs"? Did you break a cup from your best china, spill gravy on your new blouse, spill the breakfast cream? How much is worth repairing? Which should you replace?

"Crying over spilt milk" supposedly originated with this story. A small boy, many years ago, purchased a crock of milk at the grocer's. His mother had cautioned him to hurry, as the minister was coming for the evening meal. In his rush the little boy dropped the container, which lay broken in tiny fragments as the milk oozed down the street. He burst into childish tears; and that is how the minister on his way to the family home found the lad. "Now, now," he soothed, "maybe we can repair it." Together the two tried in vain to make some sense from the remains. It was no use, of course, and the child cried harder and harder. At last the kind gentleman took the little boy by the hand and said, "Son, now and then there are things in this life we can't put back together." So saying, he led the child into a pottery shop and purchased for him a sturdier container. Retracing their steps to the grocer's, they had the new container filled, and set out for home. The child hugged the new purchase, his face shining, "It's prettier than before, Sir. Anyway, why cry over spilt milk?"

So, repeating: *How was your day?* Can you repair the broken cup? There are some excellent cement products on the market; on the other hand, if it's beyond repairing, check your pattern and replace it. Maybe the new one will be lovelier than the old. As for the cream, why *cry now?* Just don't despair!

The same is true with our lives. Sometimes we "chip" ourselves—but a bit of prayer, a long talk with a friend or a talk with our minister, and we're repaired. But, like the kindly minister in the story said, there are some things we just can't fix. Sometimes no matter how hard we pray, God lets us try putting our lives back together before he takes over to "reshape" us. Believe!

TO THINK AND PRAY ABOUT: God saw a broken world try to redeem itself, and then He sent His son to give new life in Him. He will never let us down.

The Parting

October 15
Deuteronomy 22:6-7

NOW AND THEN one catches a glimpse of an out-of-season butterfly still sipping sweet nectar. The little strays must not tarry long, for their gossamer wings are little protection against the coming winter. The swallows know it is time to go. They hear and respond to some unseen voice within themselves even while the sun remains white-hot and humidity lays us low.

The little "Capistrano swallows," which have nested in the ruins of California's Mission San Juan Capistrano since St. Joseph's Day, March 19, left today. They have chosen mates and raised families here since Spanish colonial times; and with uncanny instinct, they leave us each St. John's Day, October 15. How they know remains a mystery even to learned scholars. Scientists continue to probe for clues. Skeptics shrug off the unexplained. And, while Christians would hesitate to attribute the constancy of their migrations to faith, we find a symbolism in the faithful flights of the little passerine birds. Instinct? Probably, but isn't instinct placed there by the handiwork of God?

Tourists and local residents enjoy taking pictures of the little feathered creatures as they lift off like countless aircraft above the Pacific Ocean. Our fancy lifts off with them—marveling at their courage and their strength and wishing our faith matched their instinct. Many times I observe the unshed tear of those who stand wordless with emotion. The little birds have done their work; they are going home. Some will make the journey safely; others will not; each will try. There is sadness in parting, whether it be with seasons and symbols or, eventually, with loved ones. And, yet, they leave a gift with us—a bit of God revealed in their spring arrival and in their departure.

TO THINK AND PRAY ABOUT: Consider the symbolism. Examine *your* faith. Pray.

My heart will follow the swallow
    When March blows in from the sea
Back to San Juan Capistrano,
    Searching for Things-Yet-To-Be . . .
My heart will follow the swallow
    When autumn takes them to the sea,
Filled to the brim with contentment;
    For they left cathedrals with me. J.M.B.

Button, Button, Who's Got The Button?

October 16
Matthew 25:1-13

I T'S A LITTLE embarrassing, my husband's carrying around an extra button in his coat pocket—not to mention a threaded needle (which broke me from the cozy habit of sticking my cold hands into his warm pocket when I forgot my gloves on fall and winter walks). Of course, a pricked finger isn't the worst thing that can happen to a wife; but surely George's telling *why* he carries the button is most embarrassing. All men have buttons that fall off, right? Right, but do all men take emergency measures—and let the world know their wives just never remember to replace the missing button? That's what creates the emergency, of course—my *not* remembering. His being prepared is sound.

Recently I read an article about a man who always took along an extra pair of shoelaces. His explanation of a broken lace sounded exactly like my mate's missing button. It all began, he said, when he was late for work and in his mad rush to catch the 7:05 commuter train, he yanked the shoe string, which responded with a snap. He called loudly (yelled!) for his wife to bring him a replacement. "Now," said his wife (reasonably), "I just don't happen to *have* an extra pair of men's shoelaces on hand." Angrily, he tried a slip knot (which lived up to its name) and unknotted quickly. The husband's anger increased as the knot untied twice, then continuously stabbed him after he secured it with a stapler.

By the time he reached home, the man was limping badly and ready to engage in battle with her who dared. The wife was a jump ahead of him, fortunately. If that string would break, so might others. Why not be prepared? "Here, dear," she said at the door and handed him a pair of brown ones, a pair of black ones and a set of rawhide strings for his snow boots. "May I suggest that you test your shoestrings each evening. Replace them if need be—and carry along an extra pair just in case." His great pain eased somewhat . . . and they lived happily ever after. I plan to buy buttons now.

TO THINK AND PRAY ABOUT: Life is unpredictable, but we can avoid many a crisis by being appropriately prepared. The people who live most successful know the value of Bible reading. Prayer—and, yes, shoelaces . . . and buttons!

Putting Others First

THE CONVERSATION began with guest towels and went multidirectional. One of our acquaintances asked the hostess, "Why do you put 'His' towels on the left side?" The answer was, "We read from left to right—so it comes out 'His' and 'Hers'. Anything wrong with that?" "Nothing wrong. I just wondered why it couldn't be 'Hers' and 'His'." "Hey! How about that!" said another guest. "Why *do* we wives always play second fiddle?" Have you given any thought to our language pattern? It's interesting.

For a while the group stuck to the husband-wife things, coming up with all sorts of revolutionary changes: "Mrs. and Mr., for worse or for better, marriage and love. . . ." Somebody said that would spoil the song "Love and Marriage." Somebody else said we'd change the second line to "They go together like a carriage and a horse," which still didn't rhyme. We went to other ideas.

Somehow the conversation shifted to grammar. " 'Me and Dick' has disappeared from my fourth-grader's speech," one commented. "But he still fails to understand why not 'I and Dick'. I told him it is a courtesy to put others first."

She was right. It is courteous to put others first; but doesn't the act go deeper than just a polite gesture? Are our behavioral patterns motivated by Christian love? We love our families, our friends, those who have done us favors and often those of short acquaintance with whom we find a lot in common. But what about the stranger at our gate . . . some unsavory character . . . an enemy? Jesus makes it clear we are to bless those who curse us. That would make hate "void and null!"

TO THINK AND PRAY ABOUT: "Love flows downward. . . . The love of parents for their children more powerful than that of children for their parents . . . and who among sons of men ever loved God with the love God manifested to us?"—Hare

I Have A Dream

"**I** HAVE A dream. . . ." The immortal words of the late Dr. Martin Luther King are familiar to us all. A dream come true is a wonderful thing; and through the inspired leadership of Dr. King and the acknowledged strength "furnished to me by God, the Father Almighty," his dream came true. But nightmares come true, too—even when we think we live in a safer world today than the one in which the great leader waged his war against injustice. Do you read the daily newspaper, shake your head in despair at what is happening somewhere else and say, "I'm thankful it's not happening here?" It can happen wherever you and I are—until the whole world says together with the remembered voice of Dr. King, "Love must be our regulating ideal." We must pray for people of all races to love each other all over the world.

TO THINK AND PRAY ABOUT: Dear Lord Jesus, there are racial problems all over the world and also in our country. Sometimes it's easy to criticize people in foreign countries for their lack of understanding of each other, but when it's right in our own country against a family living next door to us, it's a different story. We can often find fault with people who have a different colored skin than ours; we criticize them for not being neat and clean, for bringing down the value of property, for having different customs than ours or for not appreciating the things we appreciate. Lord, help us to realize that all people have been created by You, that You died for all people and rose again that all might have life everlasting. Lord Jesus, when You were here on earth the Jews despised the Samaritans, but You showed Your love for them by walking through the country of the Samaritans, stopping to visit with them and telling them that You were the promised Messiah. You even told a story about a Samaritan showing love to someone who had fallen among the thieves. You have also told us that on the Last Day You will say to us: "Whatsoever you have done to one of the least of these my brethren, you have done it unto me." Then help me to love all my fellowmen and to show it by my actions. In Jesus' name. Amen. (From The Lutheran Prayer Book.)

I know a word that has no end:
Some call it *love*; I call it *friend*. J.M.B.

October 19
Luke 15:8-11

A house is for adding on
A room as family grows;
A garden is for planting
A cutting from a rose.
A driveway is to welcome
A friend in as a guest;
A tree is for the shading
A stranger needing rest.
Then, finished with a shingle,
Or near-cathedral dome,
Your heart-door's standing open
And your house is a home! J.M.B.

A LADY WHO found dusting disdainful said she was guilty of inventing every possible excuse to avoid the dreaded chore. "I always dusted *around* things," she said, "never beneath them!" For a long time she'd avoided a dust-covered tile-plaque, wondering more where it came from than what it was. One day quite by accident she knocked it from the shelf. Only when she looked at the broken rubble did it occur to her to be curious. Carefully, piece by piece, she put the plaque together, patched it with household cement, and found inspiration in the inscription she could have been enjoying:

The Crown of the house is Godliness.
The Beauty of the house is Order.
The Glory of the house is Hospitality.
The Blessing of the house is Contentment.

My friend concluded: "There is dignity in a crown; and every homemaker wears one! I owe it to my family to share beauty as an all-pervading presence, and an orderly house is where it all begins; I shall dust diligently henceforth. If I want my home to be glorious, I must make it hospitable—and who wants to invite guests into an untidy household? My house needs the blessing of contentment, and contentment will come when I share my lot with others."

TO THINK AND PRAY ABOUT: What lies undusted in our Christian lives?

Secrets Of The Darkroom

MANY OF THE secrets of my husband's darkroom will remain secrets forever to me. Of all the modern-day developments, film must be the greatest! I stand amazed in the presence of a miracle when an ordinary-looking piece of paper, lying in a basin of water-clear chemicals, begins slowly to reveal an outline—indistinguishable at first, then fleshing into a life-like reproduction. Only moments before, George was explaining the process. "It is the function of photography to reproduce the differences in brightness of the subject so the result will bring to the mind of the observer the same impression one would get from looking at the original subject." Now I can understand *that*, but the process and emergence of the image is a mysterious miracle. Have you ever watched? If not, *do!*

Yesterday as he demonstrated to a group of students, I closed off the jargon of "liberated electrons," "bromide crystals" and "calfskin emulsions." My eyes focused instead on the black-and-white negative which soon would reverse itself into a positive print in all the charm of the little three-year-old. Light and shadow would exchange places. Darkness in the background would change to sunlight; the dark face would clear; and the unidentified object in the small hands would become a full-blown rose (responsible for the irresistible smile she wore).

I watch the capable hands at work—glad that my husband understood the work that I could only appreciate. He captures the fleeting things of nature (which I have studied in detail, meditated upon) recalling the glory of a moment which would be lost without his camera. The composition of his work comes from God. God furnishes the subjects through the process of nature. All of us can observe His creations walking the face of the earth He hung in the solar system. We can see the seasons come and go; we can see His purposes and His judgments work themselves out in the balance of nature, in our own lives, and in the lives of our nation and our world. Lovely as it all is, however, we are unable to see God until the image of Christ comes through.

TO THINK AND PRAY ABOUT: Read the prophet's pictures; then see Jesus, God in the flesh.

The Wisdom Of Poor Richard

IT IS STILL one of the marvels of modern literature. It has been translated into every tongue having any pretensions to literature. It is said to have more readers than any other publication with the single exception of the Bible. The annual was looked forward to by a larger portion of the colonial population and with more impatience than now awaits a President's annual message to Congress? *What is it?*

POOR RICHARD'S ALMANAC is as timely today as when its author, Benjamin Franklin, worked at instilling frugality and economy in the minds of colonists when frugality and economy were indispensable to the conservation of their resources and their independence. We could use a bit of the American statesman's philosophies now. Our needs are the same.

A good example is the best sermon. Who pleasure gives, shall joy receive.

A long life may not be good enough, but a good life is long enough.

Great beauty, great strength, and great riches are really and truly of no great use; a right heart exceeds all.

Content makes poor men rich; discontent makes rich men poor. Who is rich? He that rejoices in his portion.

Lost time is never found again. Never leave that to tomorrow which you can do today.

Search others for their virtues, thyself for thy vices. Wink at small faults—remember thou hast great ones.

Better slip with foot than tongue. Neglect mending a small fault, and 'twill soon be a great one.

The doors of wisdom are never shut. Fools need advice most, but wise men only are the better for it.

TO THINK AND PRAY ABOUT: "I believe in one God, the Creator of the universe. . . . He governs it by His providence . . . . He ought to be worshipped . . . . The most acceptable service we render Him is doing good to His other children . . . . Jesus of Nazareth left the best System the world ever saw or is likely to see . . . . I have no doubt of life's continuance, without the smallest conceit of meriting it."

Mothers In Autumn

WILLIAM JENNINGS BRYAN wrote: "There is one picture so beautiful that no painter has ever been able perfectly to reproduce it, and that is the picture of the mother holding in her arms her babe." Many artists have tried and failed; others have succeeded to the point of having their paintings called "great," but the lovelight in mothers-on-canvas somehow is missing—or maybe it's the stillness of the hands that robs the portraits of emotion. Mother-hands are always in motion. Motherhood, one of the most beautiful of all human relationships, cannot be captured in a painting.

We find mothers everywhere. There seems to be one of exactly the right size, shape and color to fit each baby. They are the indispensable bakers of cupcakes, stuffers of babies (whose insides seem to be fashioned around rubber balls) into snowsuits; and they are born knowing that kisses will cure what Band-Aids and iodine won't help. But the mother-instinct isn't limited to us women. Have you ever watched a mother cat lick her fluffy kittens? The pride in her eyes is unmistakable.

Maybe because of the symbolism of Mother Nature, we tend to think of birth in the springtime; but some other animals, like us mothers, pay no attention to the calendar. My neighbor called excitedly last night, "Heidi had puppies, thirteen of them!" I remember the last time her Heidi gave birth to a litter of mouse-size babies. She'd had a difficult time, and when it was all over and both she and her mistress were exhausted and happy, there was a look of perfect understanding that passed between them. New life at any season is an exciting thing; but it is generally born of pain.

Isn't it wonderful to remember that our Heavenly Father who planned it all is a Father of all seasons? He hears our cries and shares our triumphs twelve months out of each year. He is never "out of town." He never "moves to a new location." He never sends our prayers back stamped "left no forwarding address."

TO THINK AND PRAY ABOUT: It's harvest time again and the blossoms of spring offer crisp, juicy fruit from the parent tree. Thank God for His ever-ready plan.

Pastor Quits Sports!

THE HEADLINE in the Sunday bulletin was PASTOR QUITS SPORTS. His reasons followed:
Football in the fall, basketball in the winter, baseball in the spring and summer. Your pastor has been an avid sports fan all his life. *But I've had it!* I quit this sports business once and for all. You can't get me near one of those places again. And you can quote me on that.

1. Every time I went, they asked me for money.
2. The people with whom I had to sit didn't seem friendly.
3. The seats were too hard and not at all comfortable.
4. I went to see many games, but the coach never came to call on me.
5. The referee made a decision with which I could not agree.
6. I suspected that I was sitting with some hypocrites—they came to see their friends and what others were wearing rather than to see the game.
7. Some games went into overtime, and I was late getting home.
8. The band played some numbers that I had never heard before.
9. The games are scheduled when I want to do other things.
10. I was taken to too many games by my parents when I was growing up.
11. There was bickering and backbiting in my home team; there was criticism of each other between opposing teams.
12. I recently read a book on sports, and now I feel that I know more than the coaches do anyhow; so I won't be missing anything.

TO THINK AND PRAY ABOUT: Compare this analogy to your own feelings or those you hear expressed around you concerning the church. Most of us would profit by pondering whether we spend more time finding fault or helping spread the Good News of God, His Son and the Holy Spirit. DON'T QUIT!

It's A Good Day . . .

October 24
Job 5:17
Proverbs 3:13; 14:21

REMEMBER WHEN the world went around humming and sometimes singing, "It's a good day for shining your shoes; it's a good day for losing the blues; it's a good day from morning till night?" Maybe people have too many good-for-nothing days to sing about the good ones. Maybe it's easier to say "Have a nice day!" than to have one. Somebody struck it rich by replacing the American smile with a "Happy face" button.

The "pursuit of happiness" has shaped the American character, and I suppose it will continue to do so as long as each generation concentrates on building a happier (not better) world than the preceding generation. As a matter of fact, happiness has become big business from the happy-face buttons to—yes, believe it!—National Smile Week. You probably know about it; it's been around for a while—since 1949. Do we really need a button or a greeting card (a greeting card company promoted NSW) to remind us to be happy? Actually, would smiling prove we were happy inside? Maybe we should think less about the "pursuit of happiness" and concentrate on the "happiness of pursuit." This world is packed to the brim with causes that need pursuing: people who need understanding, love, a gentle hand, a kind word, a dinner invitation, a prayer, a listening ear, an introduction to God. And, yes, "Love has its own reward." Happiness, unsought, uninvited, un-campaigned-for, will perch upon your heart.

Two friends were talking about the happiness kick recently. One commented, "You know, this happiness campaign's not spread by happy people; it comes from the seekers who can't find." The other replied, "Agreed! And look at the money people spend trying to buy it." Don't they know it's free?

What does the Bible have to say? Certainly nothing about buttons and cards—or pursuits. Happy people are those "whom God corrects . . . find wisdom . . . have mercy on the poor . . . and trust in the Lord."

TO THINK AND PRAY ABOUT: Pray a lot; smile from the inside out; and make every day happy in the Lord.

The Hibernating Christian

SCIENTISTS ARE "waking up" from their former concepts of hibernation. Once upon a time they took it for granted that those animals which hibernated, instead of looking for a place in the sun or taking the risk of doing battle for food with their non-hibernating friends, simply curled up for a long winter's nap. Now they have discovered it is something quite different. Actually the animal which goes into hibernation lapses into a state of unconsciousness. Should you unearth such a creature, you might think it was dead. There's little respiration; body temperature is well below normal; heartbeat is barely perceptible; and muscles are stiffened to near rigor mortis. It's unlikely you could awaken the animal. These, of course, are the animals which have stored up layers of fat which their bodies absorb while they curl up in their deathlike slumber. (Sound familiar?)

Other animals store their foods away in a different manner. They use the pantries of their burrows. Chipmunks and squirrels nibble drowsily from nuts and acorns. If their supply runs out, they may shop around on top of the winter snow—only to return to their winter ways.

The discoveries scientists are making are interesting; but even they admit that a lot of the mystery of hibernation goes unsolved. Why, for example, do you suppose one hears the frozen cry of the timber wolf, undisputedly an intelligent creature, telling the world that he is dying of starvation; while the hibernating bear snores away, layered in fat and often glistening with ice? Wouldn't you suppose nature would provide for them all? Why are their instincts different? We don't know. We only know that the very thought of their hardships reminds us to store up a supply of goods, make sure the woodpile is weatherproofed, and gather our loved ones close for a long season of uninterrupted comfort. "Let's shut out the world!"

Is there anything wrong with that? Maybe. It all depends on the extent to which we close others and their needs out of our lives. As Christians, we are called upon to be on 24-hour call, whatever the need—yes, even ready to help those who neglected to store up a supply for themselves.

TO THINK AND PRAY ABOUT: How can you help others prepare for crisis? Stay alert!

Have You Forgotten Anything?

IT'S ALWAYS disconcerting to grab two shopping bags, a shoulder-strap purse, the sweater you needed this morning but no longer need and the hands of two small children to see the question posted: *Have you forgotten anything?* Even though you know it's for your protection, it's almost irritating. Unless, of course, there's something you're *trying* to lose—like my faded umbrella that's an embarrassment in its frayed condition, but loyal in its service. Now, if I could just lose it, I would feel no guilt in purchasing the new one I've had an eye on for years. No way! Some well-meaning lady always spies my "forgotten" umbrella and earns her Brownie Button by having me paged in a department store and confronted (before an audience) with the abandoned item. My guilt doubles.

Sometimes I wonder if we don't return people's trouble to them in much the same manner. We all mean well, to be sure, just like the good ladies who think I failed to read the sign in the ladies' room; but maybe we're handing them back something they've tried to lose. Recently a friend told me of her first trip to a local shopping center since her last surgery. She had gone to a sale, hoping to find a good buy that would keep her morale high. "I'd had a tough time snapping out of the doldrums," she confided. "And lo and behold! This is what I heard: 'Are you well enough to be out?' 'You still look peaked.' 'You know my sister had something like this, got up too soon, and she's never been the same'." My friend came home with a fever. Small wonder! Small acts can undo God's work.

Two other incidents (Praise the Lord!) cancel out such helpful "trouble finders." One elderly gentleman became so engrossed visiting boys and girls in a children's rest home, he lost his cane! I was proud of the attendant who did not rush up to confront him, but followed to hand it to him at the car. A crippled lady (sometimes having to rely on a wheelchair for legs) so enjoyed pouring at a church tea that she left the wheelchair in the building. It's there yet.

TO THINK AND PRAY ABOUT: "Healings" take place in many ways. Forgetting is one.

Spread The Good News!

THERE WAS A harsh and brassy wind this morning. Dry leaves swatted at each other as they met head-on—like the children next door. Their voices, like the leaves, came in uninvited. "He's using my panda for a cushion!" "She threw it at me!" Somewhere a siren screamed—but we could hear the childish screams above it. "Hush, both of you!" (That's Mother.) *Screeeeech!* (That's Father's tires as he leaves the scene.)

Across the street the Jones dog was chasing the Smith cat. Fifteen minutes earlier the Smith cat had been after the Adams canary. "Your dog's after my cat. . . . Your cat's after my bird and my bird never harmed anything!"

A straw hat cartwheeled across the intersection. Two cars nearly collided to miss the hat. There was a heated exchange of words between drivers; the owner of the hat tried to interrupt to see which smashed his hat. Both drivers turned on him. The hat caused the accident. The wind howled.

"Turn off the radio," my husband said. "I've heard enough bad news this morning without it." We laughed with the wind! What a way to start a day! I touched George's hand in unspoken appreciation.

The news media depend on disaster and near-disaster for their headlines. We say we want no censorship. "Tell it like it is!" we insist; then we shudder, complain and criticize radio, newspapers and TV for giving us what we asked to hear. "Wouldn't it be refreshing," we say to ourselves and each other, "if just now and then we heard some *good* news?"

Yes, it would! So why don't we begin at home? Seven days a week in the setting of our homes a private drama unfolds in which the family members (and their neighbors) star. How we start our day probably sets the stage for the scenes to follow. Each incident, like a pebble in a pond, spreads circles into our relationships—ever-widening, extending even into our church life. I have no way of knowing if they interfere with our prayer life. I only know that God says to make peace with others, *then* bring gifts.

TO THINK AND PRAY ABOUT: Say "Good morning, Lord! How can I spread Your Good News?"

The Golden Thread

Friendship is the golden thread
That circles, ties, and binds—
Heaven-sent togetherness
Of hearts, and hands, and minds. J.M.B.

WE'RE A GREGARIOUS lot—we human beings. God had every opportunity to let Adam live in the Garden alone; but He foresaw a need for companionship and love. Why, enjoying each other as we do, do you suppose we abuse friendship as we do? Some hearts must be black and blue all over. However, as Christians, we have the inside track. We know what God expects of us, so some of the pettiness is inexcusable. How can we go about improving relationships? First, one needs rules; and, second, we need to remember the sage advice of our grandparents: "Sauce for the goose is sauce for the gander." We must set examples.

In formulating rules of "Do's" and "Don'ts," let's take a pretest and a post-test. Try a few of these questions *today*. "Study to make yourself approved," and take the follow-up test until you can pass it!

1. Are you interested in others, or do you try to be interesting to them? *It takes hearts, hands and minds to secure knots of friendship.*
2. Do you wait to be pleased, or do you work at pleasing others?
3. Do you mope around waiting to be entertained, or do you furnish a spark that furnishes light entertainment for friends and family?
4. Do you say "You don't love me," or "I love you?"
5. Do you spend more time asking for help than in helping others?

TO THINK AND PRAY ABOUT: Add something to the list daily, and count your blessings!

Cutting Out The Deadwood

THE NEIGHBORS are pruning their Pyracanthas. I know it's good for the plants, but it pains me to see the beautiful branches go into neat bundles for the trash collector. Our house is so filled with the berry-strewn boughs, my husband insists I am confusing the birds! They try to fly right in through the sliding glass doors to the blazing hedge which provides their fall and winter salad.

These Firethorn shrubs are most practical and cooperative—just about the most emotionally stable hedge imaginable. They never sulk, refuse to bloom or fruit; and they never litter the grounds with cast-off leaves. In early spring the glossy leaves move apart to let sweet-smelling white-flower clusters form nosegays all over the bushes. Hardly have the petals floated away when fiery fruits appear—growing more rosy-checked by the day until time comes for the extravaganza of fall. As if being spectacular were not enough, they make wonderful fences. Their thorns teach persistent neighborhood dogs some valuable lessons!

And the plants themselves train as quickly as the dogs. You can coax them into any shape; but, of course, that's the big issue. I lack the courage to own a versatile Firethorn bush, either in a formal hedge or a well-disciplined miniature. You see, it takes cutting back in the fall. While Pyracanthas thrive in full sun and drink little water, neither of these "low maintenance" points would keep the bushes from becoming trees—absolute trees, say twenty feet tall—without a gardener bold enough to take shears in hand and cut the oldest wood down to the ground after the shrubs have set the last of their winter berries, but before the new spring growth appears. Bear in mind that "dwarfing" differs from "thwarting." It sets the plant in a planned course, determining its size and shape; it removes the ragged deadwood so the new growth will get benefit of the full sun; and it allows the plant to be all the more beautiful because someone cared enough to prune it.

TO THINK AND PRAY ABOUT: Are you able to lop off the superfluous in your life? Do you think God "shapes" us for His use?

Coming To A Close

OCTOBER IS coming to a close. Winds are rustling the leaves with taffeta whispers. Caterpillars, in homespun halloween suits of black and orange, hurry into hiding. Elk heads droop beneath the burden of antlers grown heavy for fall. Alaskan seal families bob playfully up and down in the Pacific waters as if teaching their new pups to swim. The burnished world is scented with mellow fruit. The nightlong symphony of the crickets limits itself to an occasional concert. Have they heard the rumor of frost? Evenings shorten; daylight saving is gone.

The doors have swung open on another school year. The air is filled with the smell of new leather and the atmosphere is charged with anticipation. For teachers, as well as the "seedlings" who rushed in, harvesttime comes in the spring. The children within the walls of the nation's schools stand on the threshold of a world about to be planted with new meanings. It is a world as new as Creation—great, wide, beautiful, wonderful—inhabited but uninhibited, and gloriously painted with imagination. Momentarily, they pause to marvel at the magnificence of the magenta of the October sunset or the copenhagen of the evening sky. Then they move on, for much of what these children are to become has yet to be determined. What contributions they will make to the world and what contributions the world will make to them will be measured by the questions they will ask and the answers they will find. Each must become a "see-er" of self. They look to Teacher and to us; we must look to God.

Who am I? What am I worth? What is going to happen to me? What should I do with my life? Is there hope for me in this indifferent, fallout-dusted world? Aren't these the questions we ponder with God? The creative thinker, the child, comes into existence with absorption in self—but ready to share unselfishly. A listening ear will hear the intricate blending of confessions, lamentations, hopes and fears—characteristic of mankind since the beginning of time. God listens to all ages!

TO THINK AND PRAY ABOUT: Someone cares! Hear the Voice: "The old has gone; the new has come."

A Birthday On "Death Day"

October 31
Matthew 8:22, 26

THE ONCE-BRIGHT leaves are now crisp-brown and give off sounds like morning bacon as the little feet of ghosts and goblins try in vain to slip from door-to-door in silence. The prominent symbol of Halloween grins from almost every window—his eerie candle-lighted smile lighting the corners of the dark. "Trick or treat!" sweet, young voices sing out. It is a fun-time of year for all ages. It's such fun to play along—remembering our childhood, that of our children, perhaps, or just continuing to have fun. This is the season of "spirits," so why not keep the spirit of fun alive? Why let it die? At a recent Couples' Club party a doctor-friend, during "get acquainted time," said of his wife, "This is the trick I treated!" Not to be outdone, my husband tilted his head in my direction and said, "And that's the treat who tricked *me!*" But Halloween has its sober side.

Observing Halloween is a relic of pagan times, encouraged by popular imagination of supernatural influences. There are some who associate the celebration with the occult; but research fails to bear out the claims. While there are secular influences and superstitions, does it surprise you to know that there is a Christian influence that ties in with the holiday? Because of the persecution of the early Christians, the day became one of memorial for the "dead in Christ" (meaning those who become martyrs for His cause). There was certainly nothing festive in the suffering they endured; neither was the commemoration one of costuming and partying. Rather it was a period of deep mourning. So while we harmlessly bob for apples and carve out jack-o'-lanterns, let us bear in mind that there was in ancient times—and ever will be—with us a very real Holy Spirit.

TO THINK AND PRAY ABOUT: Halloween is an excellent family time—a time of doing things together, enjoying the make-believe and the real. It's special in our family: my mother's birthday, furnishing material for joking. "Are you a witch, Mama?" "Grandma, are you a black cat?" My mother plays along, aware that once it was believed that those born on Halloween conversed with spirits! The Spirit she converses with is God.

A Prayer Of Thanksgiving

OPEN THE windows of heaven a little wider, Lord; hear the many prayers that come to You this month. This is the time when the whole world rejoices as it brings in the sheaves of Your fall blessings. How bountiful is Your harvest; how rich You have made us—in season's yield; in material things; in beauty of today, memories of yesterday and hopes of tomorrow. We all have our private sets of gratitudes, Lord, and yet they are much the same. In common voice we thank You for the great things and the small that make our lives worthwhile. Hear our prayer, Lord.

We want to thank You for bringing the early settlers to this land of plenty, for we believe that Your divine providence watched after them. You set them on course. Keep us on course, Lord, when our boats are too small and waves too high.

Thank You for the farsightedness of Governor Bradford, who recognized the need of gathering together our first Americans, the Indians and the small band of Pilgrims (strangers in a foreign land) to feast and to pray. Let us follow their example. Thank You, Lord, for peace. Let us guard it as kings guard treasures. Let neither the sacrifice of Your Son nor the olives of patriots be in vain.

And, Lord, we thank You for the more personal things—like loving husbands who take it in stride when we ignite over little things. Thank You, that no matter what statistics show, there are lovable children and trustworthy teenagers. Let us remember to praise them. Thank You for friends, Lord—the kind that know when we need to learn, but who know when it's time for us to stand.

Second Spring

The hawthorn bloomed in April,
A mountain-high bouquet—
The pinks and whites of springtime—
Then petals blew away.
And now it is November,
When breath is steamed with cold,
And hawthorn in the hollow
Blooms out in magic gold. J.M.B.

WHICH SEASON is the most beautiful? Which age is the most wonderful? Can we really say? So much is a matter of attitude.

A neighbor used to have a lone peach tree that bloomed early and yielded late—just why I was never able to understand. The peaches were enormous and his wife said they were rather tasteless. Consequently, she chose the late-blooming-early-yielding varieties for canning and left the enormous fall peaches on the tree. It was a wonderful arrangement for all the neighborhood children, for they were allowed to eat the fall peaches, whereas the early peaches were forbidden fruit.

I can see them yet—so crimson on one side, so golden on the other, as if they kept youth's blush on one cheek and absorbed the sun on the exposed one. One day the farmer came into the orchard, and, turning one of the beauties round and round in his hands, said, "Funny thing about this peach—'November's Choice' I call it. It's got no taste, my good wife says. And I guess maybe I'd agree if this tree saw fit to ripen in the summer; but come fall we forget how good those summer peaches were. So this one's mighty good—mighty good."

TO THINK AND PRAY ABOUT: Spend today as if it were your "November's Choice," God's bonus!

Have Thine Own Way, Lord

November 3
Ezra 7:11-20
Psalm 18:30

IT IS GOOD now and then to go back into the history contained in the Old Testament. Somehow God's people seemed closer to Him then. Although they questioned His ways, they feared the Lord, trusted and obeyed. While the Gospels assure us that there is no fear in love through the redemptive power of Christ, nowhere do I find that it is no longer necessary to obey; and can anyone think of love without trust?

"Authority" seems to be a bad word now. Whether those straining in the harness like it or not, there can be no freedom without authority. "Discipline me to show your love," the willful child is crying out to us—even when the behavior would indicate the exact opposite in thinking. We need protection. We need love. We need authority—which is to say: *We need God.*

Recently I watched a parent save the life of his child by use of heavy-handed authority when a gentle approach failed. The child was afraid of a dog and darted into the street. "Here, Son" the father called gently in an effort not to alarm the four-year-old. Instead of running to take the hand of his father, the child willfully rushed into the line of traffic. There was a screech of brakes, a scream and a father's firm voice, "Hold my hand! Don't you dare let go for one minute!" I hope the child learned.

We, too, could learn much by taking God's protective hand, walking with Him and saying, "Have Thine own way, Lord."

TO THINK AND PRAY ABOUT: "Have Thine own way, Lord, have Thine own way! Hold o'er my being absolute sway. Fill with Thy Spirit till all shall see Christ only, always living in me."

To Dream The Impossible

A S A CHILD after my evening prayer, recited with eyes shut tight and hands divided between my parents on either side of my bed, I said a little private prayer which was strictly between God and me. "And after You've finished blessing Mama and Daddy and all the people in the whole world, please let me dream good dreams tonight." The memories remain with me.

There was an art to how we went to bed when I was small. Nobody hurried. Nobody treated it as routine with an order to "Hit the sack!" We leisurely donned flannel nighties, brushed our hair and toasted our toes by the fireplace. Then came stories, prayers—and impossible dreams. Sometimes I carried a lantern that drove all the world's darkness away, or a painted clown that made every crying child start laughing. The best part was being a little "Helper Angel" who delivered all Heaven's blessings. Those dreams were the inspiration for the next day's games.

There's still an art to retiring—a time when we forget the cares of the day and the gloom of the late news. In the mellow glow of soft-light bulbs, the spots on the carpet don't show. In a warm, violet-scented bath, it is easier to place today's cares where they belong—behind—and prepare for beautiful dreams, part of which I can make come true, impossible though they be, if I place them in God's hands.

TO THINK AND PRAY ABOUT: "Daily retirement" can enrich your family relationships. Allow yourselves a little time together, no matter how you plan to spend it. Do you really want "dreamless sleep" or would you like visions impossible? Pray for faith and courage to face what the day may bring.

Greeting The Day

November 5
Psalm 30:1-5
Matthew 10:40-42

"GOOD MORNING, Lord. And hello, World, how can I help today?"

Did the conversation of the early birds make you want to soar up with them, or did they disturb your rest? Did the sound of the early garbage pickup give you a sense of security, knowing that the world went right on taking care of your needs, or did you resolve to telephone City Management about the noise? Does the grind of the juicer and the babble of the coffee pot whet your appetite or make you a little sick? Is it a matter of body metabolism, or is it a matter of attitude? How we greet the day may be more important than we think. Let's think about it.

One person I know has two alarm clocks set five minutes apart. She uses the time between the two bells for her devotionals. She thanks God for keeping her and her family safe through the night and prays for those on her prayer list. Another uses the same two-alarm system, only this is her physical fitness period, doing sit-ups for four minutes and letting herself go rag-doll limp for one precious minute afterwards. A third combines the two, breathing deeply with a silent "Thank You," and exhaling the same way. Then, there is the elderly lady who shared this with me: "I stretch and think beautiful thoughts. I see a little 'mother' in braids rocking her dolly, a kitten unrolling my knitting yarn, my grandson with his fishing pole, my friend feeding fat pigeons in the park . . . and behind it all, stained-glassed windows with a Madonna and her Child."

TO THINK AND PRAY ABOUT: Start today off for God, no matter how you do it. Prerequisite: a dream, a happy heart, and a helping hand. God gave you a gift of caring. Unleash it and see dreams come true!

A Moment On My Knees

The little church was crowded—
So many crowded there
They took no notice of me—
Just kept on with their prayer.
I knelt a while in silence;
Nobody seemed to know;
All arms reached toward heaven—
So no one watched me go.
I ever will remember
That moment on my knees
In nature's tabernacle—
The little grove of trees. J.M.B.

"**M**OTHER SCHAEFER" has a yardful of leaf-shedding trees, and she picks up every leaf unaided in spite of her son's repeated protests. "Jack offered to take the trees out. Ronald has one of those power tools that sucks the leaves up and pulverizes them. Bill says the boys can come over and rake and burn for me. They just don't understand. My basket and I want to do the job.

"You see, this life's just too busy nowadays. Everybody's busy rushing someplace so they can get back in time to rush someplace else. They want me to join this and that; they want me to go here and go there. It's all very nice, but they don't give me any time to *think*. I need to sort things out, to think them over and then talk about them—with God." Even as she explained, the fragile little lady knelt and kept on with the work she loved so well. She lifted each leaf gently, tracing a thin finger around its edges as if to memorize its shape. She lifted each to the sun as if in search of some bit of hidden color she might have missed. She rubbed each leaf against her pale cheek as if to feel each tiny vein. "Only a Master Painter who loved the earth very much could have painted it with such as these," she said. Then for a moment she closed her eyes, and I knew it was in prayer.

TO THINK AND PRAY ABOUT: Could it be that we push our activities upon others because we feel guilty about their loneliness? We all need solitude.

We, The People

THE DATES may vary, but the established patterns remain the same. Take any Tuesday following the first Monday of November, and you will see registered voters marching to the polling places to vote for candidates of their choice. Hopefully they march in throngs, because it is through the voters that our country maintains its strength. The key to a working democracy is its majority rule—found in togetherness, or "we-ness" among us all.

"We" is such a wonderful word, isn't it? It is the word that holds our Constitution together, letting it bend but never snap. The great document, with the countless people who have made it work, is an item we must remember to add to our "Blessings List." It has represented our freedoms since the time that a little band of early Americans huddled together to prepare our thrilling preamble: "We the people of the United States, in order to form a more perfect union, establish justice, insure domestic tranquility, provide the common defense, promote general welfare, and secure the blessings of liberty to ourselves and our posterity, do ordain and establish this Constitution of the United States of America."

How has that thin sheath of papers bound us together? How can we safeguard it and see that it works for the next generation? Today is a good day for some searching questions that probe beyond the person or issue:

Do we believe in the Constitution and its goals? Do we live by it? Would we die for it?

Do we read its terms and study platforms of candidates—and vote responsibly, ever aware that voting is a privilege denied citizens in some places?

Do we examine, question, challenge and pray over social issues?

Today let us thank God for the wisdom of the founding fathers, who prepared enduring guidelines. Let us remember that *we* must keep them alive.

TO THINK AND PRAY ABOUT: Apply the same questions to our Christian "Constitution," the New Testament. God, our Founding Father, should be praised.

With Experience Comes Faith

MY MOTHER WOULD take grand prize if ever there were a national contest to determine the homemaker with the greatest number of recipes. Sad to say, my father was allergic to "new recipes." The very mention gave him hives. Now and then she could get by with eggplant by making it into patties and calling them "mock oysters," but she served the dish infrequently enough to keep him from asking leading questions and she learned to be evasive when he asked the relationship between "mock" and "real." There was only one exception. Carrots made him "itch," but carrot cake did not—and we had the same rich, spicy dessert each holiday. Daddy never knew what was in the mixture, of course, and experience taught him that Mama's cakes were above suspicion. But what happened to his sense of adventure?

I was remembering the carrot cake recently as I watched a young mother feeding her puny, picky four-year-old—more in need of a good shaking, I think, than of spoon-feeding. "Ready? Watch Mommie now. Here comes the choo-choo train." The pouting child watched the silver "choo-choo" chug toward her as Mother nervously pushed applesauce towards her clenched teeth. "Open, darling. Open wide, so the choo-choo train can get inside the station." Finally the ordeal was over. The mother was exhausted and the child was satisfied—more because of the attention than the small intake of food. How long would she spoon-feed before the child ate alone?

How many wives and mothers coddle their families? Even as I wondered, I felt a twinge of conscience. Why should my father eat foods he didn't enjoy when the world was filled with equally nutritious food? And, if the young mother's anemic darling would eat no other way, maybe no harm would come of it. And who am I—a pot calling a kettle black when I never prepare my favorite desserts unless George likes them, and when we never elevated our son above the lowly hot dog?

TO THINK AND PRAY ABOUT: Compare devotional patterns to eating habits. Vary and grow!

And One To Grow On . . .

REMEMBER THE fun of trying to outrun teasing friends whose "birthday gift" was the traditional spanking? A swat per year was the prescribed dose—plus "one to grow on." Just how a stinging rap applied to the place nature prepared is supposed to promote growth is beyond me . . . but have you observed how many times disciplines and deprivations add growth to plant and animal life? Prune away dead wood, and new growth will heal the wound and add lush fullness to an ailing shrub. Irritate an oyster with a grain of sand, and the result may be a pearl. Tie a metal band around the trunk of some trees of the forest, and they, "thinking" they are dying (by way of nature's secret code), will yield as never before in order to keep alive their species. This is known as "artificial stimulation."

Has it ever occurred to you that some of the irritants that so inflamed, provoked, exasperated, nettled and peeved us in the past may have been blessings in disguise? The message came home to me yesterday.

The leader of our study group said, "When I call the roll today, please respond with some small thing—maybe overlooked at the time, but which you now know influenced your life—something that made you grow because it hurt!" A good many character-building ideas emerged—things our hearts, minds, and bodies grow on.

"I'm glad Mother made me eat my carrots. They never made my hair curly, but they improved my vision!"

"I'm thankful Mom refused to let me eat between meals. She made me mad enough to gorge on her fried chicken dinners!"

"I'm glad now that I had to dry silverware in the cafeteria to help pay my college tuition. That's where I met my husband."

"I'm thankful for the volleyball coach who always prayed before a game. She seemed real square, but that's where I learned to pray."

TO THINK AND PRAY ABOUT: Are most of your prayers about pleasure? Pain? Try both.

Bless Us, Lord, With Courage

"IT TOOK ME a while, but I figured out why Mike never entered the Junior Olympics at school," the boy's mother said. "He's afraid of failing."

His teacher was thoughtful. "It is a risk, but look at it this way: Nothing ventured; nothing gained. He's failing by not trying, too!" *Lord, give us the courage to try.*

"I need to have this lump in my breast examined, but I'm afraid of what the doctor may find," a woman said to a friend.

"I know," her friend consoled. "I felt the same way, but because I went to the doctor early, the problem was minor. Knowing could save your life!" *Lord, give us the courage to face truth.*

"You know, I would love to have one of those easy-care hairstyles," a patron told her hairdresser. "But it means a radical change . . . I might not like it . . . my family might not either . . . I just don't know . . . new things bother me."

"If I may say so, ma'am, your upsweep's outdated," said the stylist who had been doing her hair for years. "It's sticky with spray. Why are you more scared of something revolutionary than something out of style?" *Lord, give us the courage to face progress—in little steps and big ones.*

"I know my daughter is going along with the crowd. All this sexual revolution has me terrified, but I want to maintain communication." The mother's eyes dropped in humiliation, shame—and embarrassment because of her own weakness. *Lord, give us the courage to stand up for our convictions.*

"I'd like to go back to school," said the man to his psychiatrist (so an old story goes), "but you understand, Doc, I'd be forty-five years old when I earned my degree!"

"And how old would you be if you didn't?" was the reply. *Lord, give us the courage to follow our dreams.*

TO THINK AND PRAY ABOUT: It takes courage to try, to face truth, to face progress, to stand up for our convictions and to follow our dreams; but, remember, a courageous life is a full life. Ask God for courage. He has a bountiful supply.

The Unknown Soldier

November 11
Revelation 20:12-13
Matthew 26:36-37

HERE RESTS IN HONORED GLORY AN AMERICAN SOLDIER KNOWN BUT TO GOD. The inscription on the Tomb of the Unknown Soldier in Arlington National Cemetery, Washington, D.C., is a constant reminder of our great debt to those brave men who gave their lives to keep our country free. Today our President will lay a wreath before the front panel where the three symbolic figures commemorate the spirit of the Allied World: "Victory through Valor attaining Peace." The ceremony, like the tomb, is simple—but touching.

The first of the three Unknown Soldiers gave his life during World War I. To him went the Congressional Medal of Honor and Distinguished Service Cross. The Unknown Soldier was joined by two unidentified servicemen later: one a World War II casualty; the other, a young man who gave his life in the Korean conflict. If the magnificent old mansion of General Robert E. Lee could speak as it overlooks the murky waters of the Potomac River, it would say: "Be still, Americans! Lift up your voices in prayer. Here lie three heroes who kept you free!" With a click of his military heels and a snap of the rifle, the lone sentry would turn to resume his measured pace, that of guarding the symbolic tomb.

No President and no other national hero ever went to his final resting place with higher honors than did the Unknown Soldier on Armistice Day, November 11, 1921—and nobody knows his name or the names of those who joined him. Proudly, with fixed bayonets, the changing guards stand watch—ever watchful lest some person or some thing come between them and the symbol that they guard. The uniformed men would give their lives to protect the noble idea for which the Unknown Soldier died.

Far away, on the road leading from the Mount of Olives, eight olive trees stand like sentries guarding Gethsemane—traditionally supposed to have been the place where our Lord was crucified. He gave His life for an entire world and was an "Unknown Soldier" to almost all. On this day when we honor our dead, let us remember the New Life in Christ for us all.

TO THINK AND PRAY ABOUT: Pray that others will know Christ.

Who's To Blame?

November 12
Matthew 18:21-25

WE BLAME OTHERS for our failures. Do we credit them for our successes?

A teacher-friend came last night to borrow our post-hole digger. "I thought you'd be working on progress reports. Don't parent-teacher conferences start tomorrow?" I asked.

"That's *exactly* what I'm doing," he explained. "No way do I want a repeat performance of last year's meetings. The teachers blamed the parents; the parents blamed the teachers; they both blamed the administration. You know?"

Yes, I know—very well. What should be a confidential meeting between two people who want only the best for each child could be a free-for-all if all the "accused" were brought in for a hearing. Nobody is responsible (yet every witness points the finger of blame—always at somebody else). This sixth-grade teacher, for example, is certain that the fifth-grade teacher taught everything but basics; last year the fifth-grade teacher thought the same about the fourth-grade teacher, who said, "This is the kid's first year in solid subject matter. What on earth do they do down in those primary grades?" The third-grade teacher is caught between trying to teach what Miss Second Grade saw no need for and what Mr. Fourth Grade will expect.

The post-hole digger? Our friend made a list of every unpleasant little incident he could think of, including all the accusations he had made himself and all the transgressions of the children themselves. Now, he was literally going to bury them as things of the past, he said.

We all had a friendly laugh. Then he said, "All year I've been emphasizing how we are to live with each other. Now I'm going to set the example. There's to be absolutely no blame anywhere."

TO THINK AND PRAY ABOUT: Do you bury the past every day? Your implement is prayer. God has forgiven you; you are to forgive each other infinitely.

Rejection

November 13
Matthew 11:5, 28-29

A NEW FAMILY is moving down the street. Most of the houses in the neighborhood are sprawling and new or are old enough to have taken on character. This particular house is in sad repair. The fence has grown tired and has fallen down in a couple of places; the gate hangs on one hinge; and what few shrubs have survived look starved for food and water. We never get to know the people who live in the house because they don't stay long enough. The rent is low by today's standards, for as the long-time residents next door said, "Who'd rent a place like that?" Actually, I think, they were saying also, "And what kind of people would live there?"

As I stand by the window and watch the scene, I count: one, two, three . . . *five* children. And a dog, enormous, hungry-looking and somewhat mangy. Mothers at other houses are hustling their children inside their well-kept yards, telling them—undoubtedly—that "it isn't nice to stare." Really meaning, "You are to have nothing to do with these people." I hear a shrill whistle and know that neighbors are calling their well-groomed dogs home . . . not that I blame them for not wanting their dogs' contracting the mange . . . Still, I ponder, as yet another carload of people of assorted shapes and sizes arrives and files into the bulging house . . .

How accepting are we when a new family that's different moves into our community? Do we arch our backs and shake our heads in despair, wondering just how much their arrival will decrease our real estate in value? Do we whistle at our children and animals to remain aloof?

I remember many years ago having a college professor say, "So you think you're not prejudiced? Just wait till your kids grow up and pick out their friends. And, wow! Watch out for their marriage partners!" It meant very little until my son began associating with two little boys whose parents were "unacceptable" in every way. I explained to Bryce he was not to play with the children. His answer has remained with me: "They can't help it, Mother."

TO THINK AND PRAY ABOUT: Dear Lord, forgive me for my preconceived notions. They make me unworthy in Your sight.

Accepting One Another

"UGLY IS IN!" Now, that headline (no pun intended) may turn some people's heads, but I have my doubts. Personally, I think the Head Line Shoppe's ad in the Sunday paper blew it. The only thing they did well was to illustrate their slogan graphically: the drawings lived up to the words. "Would any woman in her right mind want to look like *that?*" I choked on my toast. George, thumbing through the want ads, answered absently, "If somebody told her she looked beautiful that way." And I guess he's right. We'd go to almost any extreme to be considered beautiful. We'd probably even go "ugly" if someone we loved said, "Lovely."

When God created a mate for Adam, He must have made her beautiful, for Genesis 1:1 tells us that in the beginning God saw that it was good. The verse refers to all the Creator placed in the Garden. But do you suppose Eve saw herself differently after they had sampled the tree of knowledge? Sometimes I think we have continued to sample too freely, and in so doing have wandered farther and farther from the image in which God once created us. Our behavior has changed; our attitudes have changed; and we are driving ourselves from His Garden and out into a world where relationships are no longer loving, warm, friendly and accepting. We hold ourselves in such low esteem that we fall for the "Ugly is in" thing. This is a little frightening, isn't it? Why do we see others but not ourselves as beautiful creations of God?

Removing some unwanted pounds that shapeless styles have concealed takes time. Restoring life to overbleached hair takes patience. Removing the old and putting on the new in our spiritual life takes both. Let's fight the "ugly" campaign; let's change it to "Beautiful is in!" "In" means inside. Getting back to God and His ways takes prayer. It takes seeing ourselves "beautiful in His sight." Then we can see the beauty of others, accepting and loving them as God accepted and loved the outcasts of Israel. Change a life today with, "You're beautiful . . . God made you so."

TO THINK AND PRAY ABOUT: Ask God for new inner beauty. See it in everyone you meet.

A Perfect Balance

GOD CREATED a world of perfect balance. There was no "open season" on animals and no slaughter on the battlefields of humankind. Now and then a sharp profile emerges, a person doing an incredibly fine job of attempting to put living things back into an environment which stimulates what their Creator must have had in mind.

Such a man retired recently from the San Diego Wild Animal Park. His title was Animal Care Manager, but he was more than that. He loved the animals. But to love a thing one must care for it, watch it grow—and then let it go. His love for animals extended to his never keeping a big, wild one and to his discouraging exotic pets whenever he could. What happened to "Shingoza" is an example.

The mother giraffe, "Ginger," had experienced a long labor when Bill stepped in to help her. This first birth was especially precious as the little animal's arrival was back in the days when endangered, and exotic animals were proving the thesis that, given enough space to roam in the right kind of human-free environment, they would reproduce in captivity. Wild animals were afraid; for man had not always been their friend.

Bill tranquilized "Ginger," hand-delivered "Shingoza" and raised her in the animal care center until she outgrew it. She was a beautiful and loving "child"—affectionately caressing him with warm-tongued licks and hugging him with her long, silken neck. He fed her warm milk through an enormous nursing bottle, watching the delicate eyelashes droop with sensuous content of sleep. He befriended her as one might befriend a person.

But animals grow up and find their own instincts back. They are no longer malleable, and their human owners must relinquish their hold. This animal-loving man knew that the way to love a wild animal is to respect it for what it is and to earn its respect. To treat it as an off-beat domestic would be a cruel thing: God's balance would never be restored.

TO THINK AND PRAY ABOUT: Do you see wild and domestic animals as serving different purposes in God's plan? Can you see a parallel in freeing those we befriend?

Where Does The Golden Rule Apply?

THE GOLDEN RULE should apply everywhere—in all circumstances. It is not always put to good use. Often we misuse this shining tool.

While the Golden Rule as we know it (Matthew 7:12) comes to us through the Gospels of the New Testament; it exists in the Old Testament also in similar meaning. Psalm 15 is a good example, when David writes of the qualities of the citizen of Zion. He concentrates on the spiritual requirements of truth, honor, righteousness and the sharing of one's possessions. He makes no mention of the race or the skin pigmentation of the good citizen; rather, he hits hard at the backbiters, the fault-finders and those who are reproachful of others in a sort of pre-Christian Golden rule.

Sometimes there are misunderstandings by the simple rule. While we let the words slide glibly off our tongues, "Do unto others as you would have them do unto you," there is something of the old "eye for an eye" that sticks with us. Could it be that we deliberately misunderstand? It's easier that way.

Recently I overheard a conversation between two small children which made me wonder why the parents made no attempt to clear up the misconception. The youngsters had mastered the Golden Rule as their memory verse for Sunday school. They were sing-songing it back and forth to each other as they played a game of hopscotch. "I like this rule," one of the seven-year-olds said. "It means I can take turns first and you aren't supposed to stop me!" "No siree!" the other yelled, "It means if you go out of turn, then I can go out of turn any time I want to!"

Perhaps we could smile if the cloudy concepts were only in the minds of children, but cleared up in adulthood. But misuses of the great passage can go beyond children at play; it can go on to school and follow them throughout life. And self-love is placed above love for others.

TO THINK AND PRAY ABOUT: The Golden Rule applies to all people in all circumstances. Pray about it.

Carrying On The Work Other's Started

November 17
John 5:20; 14:12-13

SARAH JOSEPH HALE believed in action. Back in the mid-eighteen hundreds, every fashion-conscious woman leaned on her advice in GODEY'S LADY'S BOOK, of which she was editor. But she had more to say in the publication than what the well-dressed woman should wear. The dedicated lady had a positive flair for taking up "unfinished business" and seeing it through. She filled her book with her ideas—most of which were carried out because of her tireless campaigns: the Bunker Hill Monument; the restoration of President George Washington's home, Mt. Vernon; and countless other projects. But we should remember to add her name to our list of persons whose contributions we are grateful for this Thanksgiving. The setting of the date was another of Sarah's victories.

After the first Thanksgiving, kept by the Pilgrim Fathers at Plymouth in 1621, there was confusion as to how and when it should be celebrated during the ensuing years. There was general agreement that a date should be set, but reasons for the setting became political to some degree. Congress recommended days of thanksgiving annually during the Revolution and in 1784 for the "return of peace"—as did President Madison in 1815. President Washington appointed such a day in 1789 after the adoption of the Constitution and in 1795 for the "general benefit and welfare of the nation." But the spirit of true thankfulness to God wavered.

It takes a hand like Sarah Hale's to put God back into a holiday! She began her campaign through her LADY'S BOOK in 1846, writing: "It is imperative that we pay nationwide homage to God by setting apart a specific day." It takes a faith like Sarah Hale's to grab a scattered, disorganized, casual tradition and demand that it have its meaning restored.

One has only to read a single page of today's newspaper to see the vast number of community, state and federal projects which have fallen to ruin because of public apathy. One has only to look at a single face to see some need—great or small—some little thing that perhaps somebody once nurtured and cared for and now needs a hand to carry on, Sarah-like!

TO THINK AND PRAY ABOUT: Meditate on today's reading. Jesus left us to carry on.

God Sees Us Through Our Loneliness

November 18
Isaiah 43:2:5-7

YESTERDAY'S buttered leaves are today's cinnamon toast as smooth gold turns quickly to sifted brown. Winds are unpredictable. Any day now they will collect the few remaining leaves. Are winds always hungry, or are they lonely, like they sound?

Jamie stood on one foot and then the other, dividing his attention between the autumn leaves and the overdue school bus. Are the leaves sad when they leave home?" he asked his mother.

"Oh, I think not. They meet their friends as you are going to meet yours today." (*Someday you'll know that loneliness comes to us all*, she thinks.)

"Will the tree be lonely for them?" Jamie seems deeply concerned.

"Maybe—for a little while. But, after the mother tree has rested, she'll get busy. There's so much to do getting ready for spring! And there's the big yellow bus. Run, little leaf!"

Jamie smiled happily. Mother has erased the little fears that sometimes grip a child. "The wind's a big gold chariot . . . coming to take me . . ." He waved and was gone to be with his friends. (*Another separation . . .*)

Children fear loneliness. They need constant reassurance from their parents in little ways such as Jamie and his mother shared: in sudden hugs, loving words, and in prayers that help them know God is always near.

"I wish," Jamie's mother said later to a friend, "that I could ease the loneliness in my own life the way I can in his. I play games for his sense of well-being, then spend the day feeling lonely—till he gets home."

Her friend replied, "How on earth could you be lonely? If I just had a child . . . you see, there's no bus for me to wait for!"

Down the street a recent divorcee has no one in whom she can confide. The divorce was inevitable; so is her loneliness. Her mother is no help. Recently widowed, she says, "I wish I could die."

TO THINK AND PRAY ABOUT: Psychologists tell us that loneliness and the fear of it are the greatest causes of emotional illness; and this is not reserved for the autumn season of life. How do you rely on God to see you through loneliness?

Now I Know Who I Am!

BEING OPTIMISTIC is important, but sometimes it's not appreciated. A happy-go-lucky attitude on life may seem like a handicap. You see, I am near sighted in a way that reading glasses won't help. Without them everything looks *small* and beautiful; with them, everything looks *big* and beautiful. The problem is that some people do consider what I have to be an affliction.

There were a few stray figs on the tree so I made Mrs. A a batch of preserves. She used to relish them before she contracted "near-diabetes" (her diagnosis; the doctor's is pending). "You know I can't eat these," she said accusingly. "Why do you tempt me?" Yes, I knew, and knowing had led me to use a sugar substitute. "You know that causes cancer!" She slammed the door, opened it again, and took the perserves.

I dropped by Mrs. B's house to give her the other jar, but she said that Mrs. A had telephoned her to come over for toast and preserves. "Wonderful!" I said (knowing misery loves company); "This lovely fall sunshine will do you good." She snorted. "It's ragweed time, but I'll try it."

Would Mrs. C enjoy the preserved fruit? I knocked and she called, "Come on in; the door's open. I can't move a muscle with this arthritis." I showed her the preserves. "The pulp gets under my dentures," she said, "and besides, chewing hurts." I explained that I'd taken care of the problem by straining this batch. The dear lady who couldn't move a muscle rose from her couch and said, "Why do you try to make everything sound so cheerful? When I sprained my ankle you said I'd have time to catch up on my reading. You know my eyes are poor and you go bringing in that big-print Bible—embarrassing me—" She must have known I was close to tears, for suddenly she said, "You know I lent that Bible to Mattie next door, and she never brought it back. Wish you'd go get it for me—and maybe you'll find her a copy? Guess this old world needs a few Christian Pollyannas—but not many, mind you!"

TO THINK AND PRAY ABOUT: Maybe only a few aren't enough, but even a few help, don't they? God needs you and your Pollyanna's "irrepressible optimism."

Do You Have A Problem Today?

November 20
Psalm 102:1-12

HOW ARE THINGS going today? Are you having problems as you prepare for the gathering of the clan, shop for a turkey that will fit into your oven, and think of creative things to keep the children busy during the holiday? Of course you've having problems. We all have; but do we have problems that God can't handle for us? The good news is that they don't come that big!

Do you take all your little frustrations to God, or do you suffer along, taking them out on others while reserving the big ones for Him? Do you engage God in conversation when you're wondering how you're going to seat twelve at a table for eight, when you're timing the minutes the cake mix is to beat and Junior gets a nosebleed; when Sally spills Elmer's glue in her sister's braids, and when the dog throws up on the shirt you just ironed and haven't had time to put away? Will prayer make them go away? Probably not; but it will make them more bearable—maybe even funny!

I can't handle things alone. I never could. So I developed the habit a long time ago of praying about all the little things: "Just get me through this minute . . . let me find the address . . . don't let this cake split on my husband's birthday"—that kind of thing. Actually, I think I pray more about incidentals—call it trivia—than the big things. God cares that it's important for me to survive this moment, to find an address if I'm to get a note of cheer to a sick friend, and to turn out a respectable-looking cake to keep the heart of the man I won with my cooking years ago! "I'd feel silly," some say. *Why?* "Because it's my first time." *Everything has a beginning:* landing on the moon, splitting the atom, harnessing the sun's radiation. Think of all that unleashed power waiting for you to get you over the little humps and big bumps—and you don't have to harness it at all. You don't even have to press a button. Just let go. It is difficult because human concepts get in the way. Consider this little girl's prayer:

"Lord, I know You're everywhere, but which day will you be *here?*"

TO THINK AND PRAY ABOUT: God wants to be in your life in the little things. Why not let Him help?

Feasting And Forgiveness

HOLIDAY TIME is friendship time. Thanksgiving has a big heart, but it has no room for holding a grudge. If there is to be warmth, we must add on a backlog of love and dust out all the ashes of hate. Thanksgiving is God's day—a time to honor Him with praise, but only after we have corrected the little hurts. Sometimes this means we must forgive. Sometimes it means we must seek forgiveness. Both call for us to stand tall—admitting to God that we stand in need of His help.

One reason that forgiveness is difficult is our misunderstanding as to its definitions and requirements. Recently I witnessed a sudden heated exchange of angry words between a husband and wife. "I can forgive you, but I shall never forget—never!" the wife said. Her husband replied, "To each his own. As for me, I'm going to forget. But I'm not going to forgive you." Yesterday I heard that they had parted. A sad thing any time.

Forgiveness works two ways. It hurts both persons to bear a burden of guilt. Persons who know the young couple say they are pig-headed, so maybe there's little hope of reconciliation—unless they forgive, forget and ask God to come to their table. But there are other examples of how grudges grow away at the insides until it leaves two human beings hollow shells. Here's an example. A woman borrowed a cup of sugar from her neighbor and was negligent about returning the sugar. The lender wasted many an hour complaining about what a poor risk the borrower was. Then, one day the lender, having heard the story and wishing to prove the talebearer wrong, rapped on the door and said, "Here is the sugar you so kindly shared."

Guilt-ridden herself, the lender said, "Oh! But you must keep it; returning it would prove me wrong about you."

Such seemingly small things slice marriages, friendships and relationships with God to the very core. Apologize quickly; erase guilt from your heart and restore faith in yourself and to others. Then you're prepared to feast.

TO THINK AND PRAY ABOUT: "To err is human; to forgive, divine." Pope.

Holiday List

IT'S FUNNY but serious the way a couple we know is making up their guest list. The hostess confided to me, "It's like the old holiday riddle about the goose, corn and fox." Once upon a time a man was carrying home a fat goose, a bag of corn and a young fox. All went well until he came to the lake where his boat was moored. Looking at his food for the Thanksgiving feast and the animal for the foxhunt to follow, he pondered, "Alas! If I leave the fox and goose together, the fox will gobble the goose. If I leave the goose and corn together, the goose will gobble the corn." The enterprising young man found a solution, of course. Since the light craft would support himself and only one of his prizes, he rowed across with the goose and rowed back for the fox. He then crossed the lake again, taking with him the fox and bringing the goose back. Leaving the goose alone, he took the corn across and left it with the fox. Finally, he took the last load: the prize goose.

My friend's problem is somewhat the same. She prizes all the friends she wants to include on her Thanksgiving list. "They'll gobble each other whole!" she said, and not without cause. She and her husband are friends with all the people she wishes to include, but none of them get along with each other. It's a sad predicament, for none of them have families and no one with whom to enjoy the lovely day. There are Mr. and Mrs. Newlywed; Mr. and Mrs. Businesspeople; and Mr. and Mrs. Golden-Age. The young couple is struggling to make ends meet and is both awed and embarrassed by successful older people. The ambitious, hard-driving business couple knows all the angles the youngsters should be using and envies their youth—while at the same time envying the leisure of the older couple. The retired couple is on a fixed income, and thinks both other couples extravagant, "heading for disaster."

TO THINK AND PRAY ABOUT: Do we work hard at understanding one another? Consider the wealth the guests could bring to each other: the energy of the younger generation; the reasoning of the middle years; the experience of age. It takes the love of Christ.

Every Good Gift

Thanksgiving, wearing somber hues,
Walks down November's lane;
She brings a secret (so she thinks):
"It's blessing time again!"
She enters into every heart
And finds a welcome there,
For she's a guest that God has sent:
This day of feast and prayer. J.M.B.

THANKSGIVING restores the soul like Grandmother's "molasses in the fall" restores the body. It is good for us to have blessings of the senses around us: colored smoke from burning leaves, cider-apple smells, brown bustlings in the cornfields—autumn things. One feels a sense of gratitude that is gratifying, affording a sense of pleasure like coolness after the heat. Let us be thankful for Thanksgiving.

No matter where we are our hearts turn home on this holiday. "Where to?" ticket agents ask at air terminals and stations. "Home!" we say. *Home*, that hallowed place still intact with the more fortunate; in memory with the rest. We elbow the crowds if there is a destination. We watch the mail, listen for the telephone and watch at the windows if we are the keepers of the flame. Or, again, the memory must suffice if there is no one to come home to us. The homing instinct refuses to die. We are like salmon swimming against the river's current to spawn in home waters. We are like migratory birds which turn from the southern climes homeward-bound, even when they feel ice upon their wings. Maybe we possess some of the homing instinct of the wild things.

A little girl said it so well. "I'm thankful for strangers—so I can ask them in" she wrote on her list of "What I'm Thankful For."

TO THINK AND PRAY ABOUT: Take a God's-eye view of Thanksgiving. Pull up an extra chair for someone whose destination isn't "Home." Erase loneliness with God's love.

Somewhere A Rose

TODAY IS the birthday of Izetta Jewel Brown Miller. A woman of gentility and enthusiasm, aspiration and conviction, constancy, warmth and cordiality. She is credited with more "firsts" perhaps than any other woman in America. Izetta won't admit to being "a day over ninety-five!" But early theatergoers will remember the flaxen-haired beauty who literally shot her way to fame in "Girl of the Golden West" in the early 1900's. West Virginians will remember her as Izetta Jewel Brown, first woman to second a Presidential nomination at a national political convention, and the first woman south of the Mason-Dixon Line to run for the Senate. Hers was the first face to appear on an experimental television screen. She was the first Portland Rose Festival Queen, and the list goes on.

But, most importantly, Izetta was always the first to appear when she was needed, in great things or small ways. In 1906, twelve days after the earthquake and fire, she was playing "Salome" in San Francisco to keep up morale. During the dark days of the Depression she was flying thousands of miles and speaking tirelessly in an effort to help President Franklin Delano Roosevelt drive fear away. But perhaps her greatest role came when she "retired"; after age sixty-five, this inspired woman did more than most of us packed into a lifetime.

Izetta was the daughter of a suffragette and a circuit-riding New England minister, which molded her into what she termed a "sort of missionary-actress." Even her Puritanical parents, though shocked by their daughter's decision to go on stage, must have sensed her inherent feel for "rightness" as they watched her performances become a ministry. One wonders how many lives she touched through inspiration, prayer and "grit." It was a man's world then, and she took losing with the same grace as winning: "Experience molds us for a brighter future," she said of this world and the next.

TO THINK AND PRAY ABOUT: "Every moment of this strange and lovely life from dawn to dusk is a miracle. Somewhere a rose is opening its petals. Somewhere a man is doing an incredibly fine thing for his fellowman," said Izetta recently.

November 25
I John 3:14

HAVE YOU HAD the experience of spending more time than you could afford looking for the just-right sympathy card, and, never finding it, sending some hackneyed verse instead? Greeting card companies do a commendable job offering thousands of cards from which to select: some touchingly beautiful and personal; others dignified and impersonal. But condolences differ from seasonal, holiday, anniversary and congratulatory messages. One feels that nothing is quite right. Grief is hard to deal with. The writer would almost need to have known the person a friend has loved and lost. And that's the point, exactly. You love the person to whom the message will go. You long to reach out and touch this friend in time of sorrow. Why not say so?

If you have experienced the loss of a loved one in your family, think back on what comforted you the most, and use that as your guide for helping others at such a time. If you have not lost a member of your immediate family or close friend, give some thought as to how you can let the other person know of your love and God's care. Wouldn't a warm, personal note be a greater blessing to you than some quotation by someone none of you knew? "I don't know what to say," is the usual comment. Why does death embarrass us? Would we have been so hesitant in selecting words in time of joy, victory or just in ordinary conversation? Be yourself. Say what comes naturally. Think of the other person. "Not knowing" is a turned-inward attitude.

Yesterday a friend whose husband was killed in the disastrous crash of a light plane and a PSA 727 over San Diego said, "You know, one of my greatest helps was a letter from a former teacher of my children who spoke of us as a family." Then I remembered a letter I received when I lost my father. "I always think of God as having a sense of humor, so heaven must be a happier place tonight." I reread it each September 25th, Daddy's birthday.

TO THINK AND PRAY ABOUT: God tells us to comfort one another. How do you give words of hope?

Gleaning The Fields

November 26
Ezra 7:1-10
Ephesians 4:14

THE VEGETABLE garden has succumbed—except for the faithful tomatoes. When we debated over plant names, "Wonder Yield" appealed to my fancy. It takes eighty days to bear fruit, but each tomato weighs nearly a pound, and the scarlet, overweight beauties just bear on and on. "Eighty days!" My husband (and live-in gardener) was aghast. "Why, we could go around the world in that time." True, but the tomatoes would be ripe when we returned. Actually, I liked the giants because they reminded me of the fruits of my childhood. My grandmother selected the plants and tended them with great care. When my grandfather complained at her insistence on perfection, she invariably resorted to her favorite punch line: "What this world needs is more Ezras!" I was unfamiliar with the passage then, but it silenced Grandpa. "We put up only the best," she used to say, "and strictly according to the letter of the law."

Once the tomatoes were gathered, she sorted each one with the same care she'd shown in selecting the plants. Then came the scalding of the jars and the long waterbath-type processing. Only the finest rated her pantry shelves. Results? Excellent! Botulism was unheard-of.

Were Ezra and Grandpa friends? No, more likely the friendship lay between Grandma's literal translations of her recipe and the biblical Ezra who never questioned an assignment or a commandment. His scholarship and dedication were the characteristics for which he was selected to journey to Jerusalem to introduce the reforms. He familiarized himself with every letter of the old laws and he "prepared his heart" with prayer.

Ezra offered a good model of strength and determination to deliver and carry out a decree. He never said, "Now, I have here a new way," or "Let's put this in the hands of a committee." He followed directions in a way that would have qualified him for Grandma's field!

TO THINK AND PRAY ABOUT: While we, as adults, need to maintain a flexible attitude, we are not to be "tossed by every wind of doctrine." Preserving the fruits of the Old Testament and our elders is important. Prepare hearts in prayer.

Needed: Time For Prayer And Memories

November 27
Psalm 105:1-8

TIME COMES as either an enemy or a friend. The memory of a certain time or a certain place can bring either joyous recollection or a regretful shudder. But one thing is for certain, we should allow ourselves time to appreciate the present.

Where I came from (many years ago), Christmas trees came right out of the woods. There the streets were swamped and the winds towered with flushed, crackling leaves, long before there was a hint of Thanksgiving; and winter spoke with authority into aching ears and racing hearts. For the adults who had to shovel the snow and chain the tires, the portent of winter may have seemed a curse. But for us children it was a blessing: the first clean sting of cold air in the nostrils was a welcome signal. The air was filled with expectancy. Silent and momentous, the wilderness of floating, marbelized flakes was almost a sign of grace to our formative theology. We saw the face of the Christ Child in each flake . . . Only nature rushed the seasons then.

What's the big rush? Candy-cane replicas and plastic greenery are on the streetlights downtown before the Thanksgiving holiday dinner is over. Do you ever wish merchants would stop rushing things—just let things come the way children do? Both holidays are so wonder-filled, it seems a shame to push them closer and closer together. We need time to go back and relive the days at Plymouth Rock.

We need time to savor their "positive dissatisfactions"—the kind that wasted no time in mumbling and grumbling but brought action in search of freedom. We need time to linger longer in their prayerful mood of a first Thanksgiving—adding to it our memories shared with our children of our own youth. For these hardy pioneers left signposts which our parents passed to us and which we need to pass to our children. There are no bypasses; there are no shortcuts. There is a long road—paved and smooth—but still straight and narrow. We need time to point it out. It leads Home!

TO THINK AND PRAY ABOUT: Take time to emphasize prayer, values, memories—and praise.

Climbing

November 28
Psalm 61:1-4;
116:9; 37:7

I wish that I might climb that hill
Which peaks up in the sky;
I might not ever reach the top,
But I should like to try.
To gain life's summit is to climb—
Or so to me 'twould seem—
For reaching up is natural
And climbing helps me dream. J.M.B.

THERE IS a story about two small roads that ran side by side. They chatted as they wound in and out of country places, laughing with the brook, sighing with the wind, and resting now and then along the level knolls. There they watched the trees put on their green gloves in springtime, raise their leafy umbrellas for summer shade, wind tawny shawls around their shoulders in autumn, and lace their limbs with snowflakes when winter came.

They were very happy little roads because they did their jobs well. Schoolchildren walked upon them, and wagons rolled smoothly upon them. Shy little creatures played games along their ruts when nobody was near. On and on they went until at last they came to a little incline. One road panted, but the other encouraged it to come along. The hill they must climb grew steeper, and the tired road said, "I can't make it. I'm going back." The other road worked very hard and grew very weary, but at last it came to the summit and danced over into the world beyond.

It is hard to tell the two roads apart until they reach the hill. There a traveler is destined for disappointment if he travels the weary road, for it leads back to the starting point. The person traveling the victorious road is greatly exhilarated at the top, for the little road slopes gently downward. It was the road that dared to dream!

TO THINK AND PRAY ABOUT: Praise God for the way of the Cross. It leads Home!

Remember This Life; Anticipate Another

November 29
Psalm 91:10-12;
95:1-4

THERE WAS a little hill in the country I grew up in, but it seemed like a mountain to me. To the south of the hill was a civilized world, a little village where I attended school. To the north lay the deep, dark woods filled with trolls and storybook characters—loved and lost by childhood's passing.

In foot-deep powder of early snow, the woods looked even more mysterious. My father, who must have savored the memory of his childhood sledding, saw to it that I had a proper sled. A sled is a child-sized raft with waxed metal runners instead of sails, built for voyages over the crests of snow. There was no stern—at least not according to my father's blueprint. There was a rope—like reins to which I clung for dear life with hands mittened against the biting cold. "Help me hang on," I always prayed.

How much fun we had with our tummies flattened against the rough boards as we swerved in and out of the snowbanks! At the bottom of the hill, we would pump with all the vigor of youth, just to gain another inch. Then, shrugging off the cold, each of us grasped our sled rope between numbed fingers and trudged back to the summit. Weekdays meant keeping to school schedules, but on Saturdays coasting time lasted from dawn to dusk and on Sundays from after morning church to evening church. We would play as hard as we could until we heard our names—unmistakably clear. We knew it would not be wise to claim, "We didn't hear you call," so we'd run like crazy. Once home, we paused, as taught, at the fogged glass panes to peel off boots ouch-by-ouch. Candles of welcome beamed through the frosty windows where welcoming arms were waiting . . . .

TO THINK AND PRAY ABOUT: It is good to remember the wonder-world of childhood. Holidays offer an excellent time to build a set for your children or those around you. It is good, too, to emphasize that God gave these gifts: life, beauty, family love and devotion, vigor and age. Someday He too will call.

Yielding

November 30
Philippians 3:20
James 1:19-20
Galatians 5:5

NOVEMBER'S cool blue flame has yielded to December's sober gray. Nature's garments are less brilliant now, for it's late autumn. A flip of the calendar tomorrow will take us into a winter world—brightened by the coming of Christmas. It will be a time for looking into shop windows, listening to carols and hoping for all sorts of happy surprises. It's a wonderful time of the year, coming now as it came 2,000 years ago, bringing light into our lives.

On the eve of the busy month ahead, let's pause and look at some other meanings of "looking, listening and hoping." The obvious is not necessarily the ultimate. The Ultimate is God.

The season is filled with blessings, some of which are less obvious. It is one thing to see a flock of robins in season; it is another to see a solitary bird as if it elected to stay behind to bring a message of joy. A single golden leaf may linger on the willow by the yet-unfrozen pond—what a beautiful sight! And don't the bayberries look more scarlet in their thicket of thorns now that the leaves are gone? Watch for the first idle snowflake—adding to the brightness of the holiday spirit ahead. See God in all of these. He is there, always, with the good and lovely.

Listening is another skill that needs practice during the season. Shopping crowds will be noisy; traffic will be heavy; and, with nerves frayed, we may find ourselves weary of taped carols over brassy speakers. But listen to their message. Can you hear the words of peace?

Open that little "Pandora's Box" inside you and take another look at its contents. Reread the story if you are a lover of mythology, and share its messages of hope with children around you. They need hope, for children are aware that they live in a troubled age with bomb threats, racial differences and unresolved problems. They need the Hope God offers through Jesus, friends, the future and the world—however troubled.

TO THINK AND PRAY ABOUT: Look, listen, hope: prepare for the coming of the King.

Each In Her Own Prayer

DEAR LORD, I covet a personal talk with You—as should each woman in her own way—as we enter the holiday season. It is with a full heart that I bring my writing to a close and listen to the carols that welcome Christmas and later for the bells which will tell me that the year has ended. The world is a year older, Lord, and hopefully a year wiser. I need this moment of solitude to audit the books before giving spiritual meaning to the countless greetings I will say and send.

First, I ask your forgiveness, Lord, for all those things I did which I should not have done. Next, I ask your understanding for those things I should have done—and didn't . And I confess I often have been impatient with my family: showing irritation instead of love, withholding my smile for the sometime-friend. You know that there are times when I said "Yes" to outside things that mattered little, when I said "No" too harshly to my loved ones because of it. Forgive me for my intolerance of their ideas when they conflicted with mine, for all the little deceits and subtle forms of dishonesty I unwittingly indulged in—to have my own way.

Right now, Lord, I desire to put on Your "full armor" to help You make this world a better place. It is not easy, Lord, for I am weary of wars and rumors of wars, of generaton gaps, distrust between ethnic groups . . . taxes, crowded freeways, merchandise that falls apart, smog, smutty comic books, pornography on prime-time television, talk of cancer-link with my family's food, and the cost of maintaining my body as your temple. Forgive me for saying I am weary—for I am weary, yes, of *caring!*

I need Your help. *We* need Your help. Bless our nation. Guide our President. Endow our lawmakers with knowledge; inspire our judges with wisdom. Lead them to combine justice with mercy, to be fair with the accused, to be truthful to and protective of society. Make them care.

Lead all groups to understand, to cooperate, to love one another: parent-child, clergy-layman, lawyer-client. Bring us into a new awareness of Your love and Your Gift at this Holy Season. And bear with me another year, Lord, and I will go on caring—*for I am a woman.*

The Advent Wreath

December 2
Isaiah 9:2, 6, 7;
11:1-6, 10
Ephesians 2:8-9

IT'S TIME TO gather the makings of the Advent wreath: A Styrofoam circle, evergreens and five candles—three lavendar, one pink and one white. An advent wreath and the accompanying ceremonies will add beauty and spiritual meaning to the holiday season.

If the idea is new to you (or even if it isn't), it helps to review the place of Advent in the history of Christianity. Most Western churches observe a four-week period before the Nativity. Even with the merriment and the buying of pandas and power saws, there is a touch of solemnity that touches the emotions of Christians, for the shadow of the cross hangs over the cradle of the King. In olden days marriages and public amusements were forbidden. It was a time of fasting and penance—dating back to the 6th century. Even though it is no longer considered a sober time, the Advent season is still a time of preparation. Lighting the candles, reading the Scriptures, singing the carols—sets a mood of preparation for the coming of the Messiah.

The entire family can help arrange the evergreens, discussing their significance as they work. The circle itself is important, representing the care of God with a love so great that it has no beginning and no end. The evergreens symbolize the hope Christ brought to the world—hope unchanging throughout Eternity. The colors of the candles have special meaning, too, the lavender ones representing the prophecies. On the first night, generally, the father reads the Scripture. But all share in the light of the first lit candle.

TO THINK AND PRAY ABOUT: Tonight as you light the candle of Prophecy, remember that Christ is the light of the world, and that the world no longer dwells in darkness. Pray for greater light during the season ahead than the universe has ever seen!

Life is filled with many things
No matter where we are
That take the darkness in their hands
And shape into a star. J.M.B.

THE BIBLICAL account of Creation thrilled me as a child—especially the division of day and night. I envisioned God hanging the millions of stars up there in infinity and felt a tingling up my spine. I still do.

As a child I could scarcely wait for the touch on our Christmas tree. After the cranberries, popcorn and paper chains came the star. The tree (always too tall) brushed the ceiling and there, in the topmost bough, went the "Guiding Star" the timeline of the Christmas story.

There were no Christmas trees when Christ was born, but there was a bright, unusual star in the heavens—visible for the first time to the human eye. It is good that the shepherds watched the skies and saw the sign. The prophecies would have remained unfulfilled had they followed another star. It makes us wonder at this time of year if we look up enough for guidance, doesn't it? Or, could each of us be hidden stars on which God needs to shed His Light?

On some days, when we are on the dark side of life, it helps to think about stars—knowing they are there and what special significance they have. Maybe darkness is a necessary ingredient before we take time to look up and see their brilliance. Do they seem to shine more brightly at Christmastime, or is it my imagination? Their light can make us feel so humble and yet so cared for. The world can be against us (or more often we are against ourselves), but there is a brightness in the stars that symbolizes truth: a guide to wayward feet. I am a child, again hanging a soon-to-tarnish star on a freshly cut pine . . . and I remind myself I am His child.

TO THANK AND PRAY ABOUT: Look for "new stars"—deeds that shine in the dark.

One Solitary Life

THE FIRST Christmas card of the season arrived today—early, and I am glad, for it reminds me of what the holidays ahead really mean. The message, "One Solitary Life" (author unknown) is a traditional greeting, but its words, like those of the Savior's birth, ring the bells of love.

"Here is a man who was born in an obscure village, the child of a peasant woman . . . He worked in a carpenter shop . . . and then He was an itinerant preacher. He never wrote a book . . . held an office . . . owned a home . . . had a family . . . went to college . . . put His foot inside a big city . . . traveled two hundred miles from the place where He was born . . . He had nothing to do with this world except for the power of His divine manhood. While still a young man, the tide of popular opinion turned against Him . . . friends ran away . . . one denied Him. He was turned over to His enemies . . . went through the mockery of a trial . . . was nailed upon a cross between two thieves . . . .

"Nineteen wide centuries have come and gone and today He is the centerpiece of the human race and the leader of progress . . . and all the navies that ever were built . . . parliaments that ever sat . . . kings that ever reigned, put together, have not affected the life of man upon this earth as powerfully as this One solitary life."

Jesus must have had "solitary" feelings, for surely He must have often been lonely. He was rebuked, doubted and denied. We know with Christian certainty that He is no longer lonely, having gone to join His Father; but we know also that there are others around us who feel rejected: in need of the peace and love Jesus offered to the world. I shall try to carry with me the message of joy and feelings of hope that were born again within me today—with the arrival of a first Christmas card.

TO THINK AND PRAY ABOUT: While we know that our lives can never reach the greatness of Our Master, let us read and reread what one solitary Life can do. You are but one, but you are one of many; and Christ has need of what you alone can offer. One Life changed a world. One deed may change a life this Christmas. "Here am I, send me!" Say it joyfully, and let the world know you volunteered; you didn't wait to be drafted.

Start "Giving" Early This Year!

December 5
Romans 1:8-12

IT STARTED before Halloween. There, amid the horror-masks—designed to fill the heart with fear—were the trappings of Christmas. Even crass commercialists would hesitate to say "Only nine more weeks till Christmas." But it's acceptable to begin the big *discount* sales and offer advice—the only free item—to shop early, before prices soar.

There's a lot to be said for shopping early; it helps keep one calm during the tempest. Maybe we should thank those enterprising merchants. Why don't we start early, too, cleaning out our hearts and preparing for the Celebration of the Birth before the rush sets in?

Let's get the jump on others. Instead of offering our merchandise at discount prices, we'll *give* it way. It's a wonderful phenomenon that at Christmas people seem to act more loving, to go out of their way a little more to be kind, to give of themselves, and to get in touch with loved ones by call, card or letter. Why not give your gifts away *early*? Mend a little fence. Do a special favor. Spread a little joy. Why wait for the countdown? How can you do it? Let us count the ways . . . .

How long has it been since you visited that aging fellow who lives in the tacky apartment where no children or pets are allowed? Wouldn't it be nice to take a basket of pre-holiday cookies to decorate a tree? How long has it been since you wrote to the dear friend who moved away? You used to talk so often on the phone then. You owe her a letter? Write and tell her how much you miss and love her. Don't wait until the holiday mail is cluttered with meaningless messages sent by many who are celebrating the birth of Someone they refuse to believe in!

How long has it been since you sat down with your family and talked things over: your innermost thoughts, your latest achievements and—yes—your disappointments? If we do these things, maybe October tinsel makes sense.

TO THINK AND PRAY ABOUT: Pray an early Christmas prayer and shop from a "soul list."

Faith, Hope And Love

December 6
I Corinthians 13:1-8, 13

FAITH, HOPE, LOVE: That's what Christmas is. These are the gifts without price, the ornaments which human hands cannot duplicate. They cannot be purchased at any price; and once you possess them, you must give them away. Christ brought the world an unlimited supply; yet they are hard to come by. They lie buried within the *self*; and the *self* is too busy to unpack the greatest gifts of all.

One always remembers childhood Christmases, but I remember another which brought back to me the real meaning of Christmas. It was during the dark days of World War II, when young wives were following uniformed husbands around. Only a few leaves were issued, and three of us couples spent our first holiday season away from home. We bought a tiny tree and put it up in one of the rented rooms. We purchased three spun-glass ornaments and carefully lettered one FAITH, another one HOPE, and the third one LOVE. We girls did a lot of talking as we arranged that special tree. "I'm glad we have faith that lets us know the war will end," Chris said in a way that was more a prayer than a statement. "And the hope of forever-after that Christmas brings," said Anne. "And Love," I added.

We drew names, as cash was scarce, and our fellows bought us gifts we knew they'd had to charge. Then the six of us opened our packages from home. How much we appreciated our "somethings from home." And how good it was to share with each other. Anne opened her cheese from Wisconsin; Chris, her Washington apples; and I, my Oregon prunes. Then, while singing, "Joy to the World", in came Mary and Hugh, who, even with a leave, had been unable to get tickets for home because of the conditions. With them they brought the paper-shell pecans from Down South. We all joined hands and sang the carols; we prayed for our loved ones at home and on the battlefields; and, as the Nebraska snow drifted up to the windows, we feasted.

TO THINK AND PRAY ABOUT: It is in the little things that we grasp the significance of that first Christmas. Wherever you are, you carry its gifts; share them.

Christmas Needs Some "Wise Women"

December 7
Psalm 38:18
James 5:16

The world is filled with Christmas;
My heart knows not a care,
But burns with tiny candles
That I have lighted there.
I've trimmed the tree with color
And made the silver shine;
And I am hearing carols
Within this heart of mine.
I've dusted out each corner
Of every waiting room;
The house is filled with pine cones
And poinsettia bloom.
Please help me keep it tidy;
Track in no thought that's soiled—
For it is Someone's Birthday;
I do not want it spoiled. J.M.B.

IT'S SO EXCITING, isn't it, making our homes lovely for those we love? And we want to make ourselves lovely too. The least expensive and most therapeutic beauty treatment is the most pleasant. Would you believe *talking?*

First, let's face up to unprofitable talk. That little unkind word stung. The sharp order was unnecesary. The "I have other plans" was untrue. Admit it to yourself, then apologize. It will make you feel tidier; it will bring back the smile you erased. And chances are ten to one that the person you hurt will admit having done or said similar things. Perhaps that person will follow your example and there will be forgivenesss all the way around.

Second, talk it over with God. He listened long before the modern-day psychiatrists. Talk as long as you wish or simply say, "I'm sorry, Lord, I need Your help to keep me following the right Star. Guide me."

TO THINK AND PRAY ABOUT: Be honest and talk to God and others. Then you have the Peace of Christmas.

December 8
Psalm 67:4

There's a tingling happy feel
In the air today;
All the little sadnesses
Seem very far away.
People shop for Christmas trees
With the utmost care
And tuck the memories in their hearts—
For it is Christmas there. J.M.B.

DECEMBER brings in the birth of the Savior; it culminates in the New established by the Old. For, lo, the prophecies have come to pass . . . .

"Blessed is the season which engages the whole world in a conspiracy of love," wrote Hamilton Wright Mabie. "Christmas is a quest," said Esther Baldwin York. "May each of us follow a star of faith and find the heart's own Bethlehem." Truly "Gladness of heart is the life of man" (Ecclesiastes 30:22). *Lord, bless us with a Christmas heart.*

The Christmas heart hears the angel songs repeated in the youthful voices of wandering carolers, church choirs and grade-school choral readings. It hears the happy greetings as shoppers hurry about with bundles much too heavy. It hears the age-old message of "Peace on Earth" in the holiday chimes, the church organ and the music shops. And it rejoices.

The Christmas heart smells evergreens before they appear . . . gingerbread before it is baked . . . woodsmoke before the Yule log is lighted. It smells the roast goose, unpurchased, the cranberries yet unpacked. And it sings.

The Christmas heart feels the warmth of voice, smiles and messages. It greets tirelessly . . . smiles unconsciously . . . and knows no writer's cramp. It feels a sense of oneness with the world: a Oneness with God. It kneels and prays.

The Christmas heart sees One Star that outshines the others: visions of everlasting love reflected in twinkling lights and bright ribbon. It loves.

TO THINK AND PRAY ABOUT: The Christmas heart *believes, gives and knows peace through Christ. Lord, bless us with a Christmas heart.*

The Second Candle Of Advent

December 9
I Samuel 16:1-3
Matthew 2:16
Luke 1:39-53, 57, 80

DAVID WAS excited this morning. He and "Charcoal" cut across the trail in the iceplant made by tennis shoes and dog paws. Both boy and dog were panting. "Don't forget we're going to light the second lavender candle tonight!" His face was glowing in anticipation as he hurried off to school. Christians can make God's love real to children through traditional rituals: giving, greeting, storytelling, candle-lighting . . . All these recreate the greatest Story ever told and pass it on to our young as their spiritual heritage.

We are one week closer to the Holy Birth. A second candle will be lit this evening, and your table will shine twice as bright. All week as you read the Scriptures and relit the first candle, you must have felt a glow within. What a bright light *two* nine-inch candles will make!

It's unlikely that the first candle of Prophecy will burn too low before the season of Advent ends. But even if the candle wore down, the symbolism wouldn't: the truth of the Prophecy remained firm until Jesus' birth. Should it spend all its energy, simply replace it with another. And remember the Eternal Flame is glowing in the center of the Advent wreath.

A friend, experimenting with the Advent wreath for the first time, asked, "Which candle do we light first?" It doesn't matter, of course, because whether the candle is in twelve-, six-, three-or nine-o'clock position depends upon where one is sitting. Our practice is that Daddy, who occupies the "Captain's chair," lights the one closest to him; and we continue counterclockwise. God's light shines all directions!

TO THINK AND PRAY ABOUT: Tonight we light the Bethlehem candle, remembering the time and place of Christ-in-the-flesh. Let's sing a carol for the Son of God.

They Do Not Believe Except They See

December 10
I Peter 1:6-9
John 3:12

OVER A DECADE ago an Associated Press item announced the hospitalization of Virginia O'Hanlon Douglas. I saved the article about the (over-ninety-year-old) teacher who had no idea her childish letter in 1908 would gain worldwide attention. The little girl wrote to the NEW YORK SUN: "Some of my little friends say there is no Santa Claus. Papa says, 'If you see it in the SUN, it is so.' Please tell me the truth, *is there a Santa Claus?*" The wise editor-in-chief wrote a tender letter, reassuring the child that the spirit of Christmas will live as long as we keep it in our hearts and retain that youthful faith in things we cannot see. Do you remember some of his words?

"Virginia, your little friends are wrong . . . They do not believe except they see. They think that nothing can be which is not comprehensible by their little minds . . . *Yes, Virginia, there is a Santa Claus.* He exists as certainly as love and generosity and devotion exist . . . Alas, how dreary would be the world if there were no Santa Claus! It would be as dreary as if there were no Virginias . . . Nobody can conceive or imagine all the wonders that are unseen and unseeable in the world. . . ."

Imagination is a gift of childhood. How sad it is when it is snuffed out too quickly, for—unlike a Christmas candle—it may never glow again. One year a group of third-graders decided to put down their thoughts and make an anthology for their parents. After binding the verses in folders, they designed them in crayon-colored stained-glass mosaics and labeled them "Christmas Windows." Some were rich with imagination.

One little boy wrote: "I think I saw Him in the baby's smile."

"How could you *see* Jesus?" A little girl challenged. "*You* couldn't!"

He replied "You colored your windows too dark!"

TO THINK AND PRAY ABOUT: Lord, let our faith glow—keeping alive Your Spirit.

The Unexpected

ONE ALWAYS expects the unexpected in O. Henry's stories, a little "reverse twist." His life may have been the influencing factor for his writing style, for it took many a strange turn. Indicted for embezzlement, he fled, returning when he heard of his wife's terminal illness. After her death, he was convicted and imprisoned. It was within prison walls that his writing became a reflection of the American way of life at the turn of the century. One of his best-loved tales is the GIFT OF THE MAGI.

Young Della had one dollar and eighty-seven cents to buy her husband "something fine and rare and sterling—worthy of the honor of being owned by Jim." Her only other collateral was her flaxen, knee-length hair—one of her husband's two prized possessions. The other was his gold watch.

"Please, God, make him think I am still pretty," she prayed as she sacrificed her hair for twenty dollars. A snip of the shears by the hairdresser and her lovely tresses were gone, but she had the price of a platinum fob chain in her hand. Oh, Jim's watch would look so beautiful . . . .

But Jim too, had been shopping—shopping for the expensive set of tortoise shell combs for Della's hair—her crowning glory. The money? "I sold the watch to buy your combs," he said.

Were they foolish? The author said they were, for they had "unwisely sacrificed for each other the greatest treasures of their house." Then, in an about-face, O. Henry explains that those who give and receive such gifts are in the long run the wisest, for they give as did the magi, those wise men who took gifts to a Baby born in a manger.

TO THINK AND PRAY ABOUT: This Christmas, place at least one person on your gift list who is unable to give in return. Give that person something you prize: something you or a member of your family wanted very much. Let's remind ourselves of God the Father's sacrifice. Anything we give is small by comparison; yet, given in loving sacrifice, it becomes "The Gift of the Magi."

Evergreen Cathedrals

The evergreen cathedrals
Reach high their ancient spires
To catch the muted wind-notes—
Or is it angel choirs?
The starlight is reflected
Upon the tulle-wrapped boughs—
Like virgins formed from snowflakes
Renewing ancient vows.
The air is filled with incense
Brought in from holy lands,
Speaking in an unknown tongue
Man briefly understands.
It happens every Christmas,
And then the moment's gone—
When trees repeat the story
And pass the glory on. J.M.B.

*B*ORN MORE *than two thousand years before the time of Christ, it is among the oldest living things on earth. Having survived the ravages of time and nature, it stands today in Kings Canyon National Park. What is it?*

It is the giant sequoia, discovered in 1862. As word of the monarch of the forest spread, people came from all points to see the ancient survivor. The idea of its becoming a "Christmas tree" came in the 1920's, when a small child, lifting her eyes to the highest needle, 267 feet in the air, said, "Won't it take a lot of lights to make it a Christmas tree?" Today some 2,500 people from all walks of life make the annual pilgrimage to the Nation's Christmas Tree to celebrate the birth of Christ.

Millions make ready for Christmas pilgrimages. Many would like to return to the setting of the holy birth. Although the message of the birth of Christ is "Peace on Earth," the threats of war remain, with explosions rattling windows in Bethlehem. Countless others flock to airports, railroad stations and bus terminals to reach home.

TO THINK AND PRAY ABOUT: The real pilgrimage is in the heart. Pass its glory on.

Christmas Around The World

AT FIRST my friend said, "No! Absolutely not." Then, seeing that her daughter's heart was broken, she said, "I'll speak to your father about it." Instead, she spoke to me. I could understand her concern.

Kristen had been chosen as "Lucia Bride" in the high school "Christmas Around the World" pageant. She was very excited. That was the part all the other girls wanted, she said, but she had the longest, blondest hair. Her long, lovely hair was the cause her for mother's refusal. "She is supposed to wear a crown of burning candles! I'm surprised they didn't have her wear a paper dress to make the fire hazard a little more complete!"

"Mother, *please*." Kristen turned stricken eyes to me. Her mother followed her gaze.

"You wouldn't understand. You couldn't. You've never had a daughter." *No, but I was once young!* Remembering gave me an insight into Kristen's desires. At the moment, the girl knew little of Swedish Yuletides—although they are of Swedish ancestry—but if she played the part, its memory would remain with her forever. Sometimes we must measure risk and benefits.

Kristen, the medieval saint, according to tradition became the embodiment of the Christmas spirit the night of December 13th. In her white dress with a crimson sash, and with her fair head adorned with flaming candles, she awakened members of her household on stage and served them steaming mugs of coffee. Accompanying her were baker lads carrying *Lussikattor* (cat-shaped saffron buns with raisin eyes), but all eyes were upon Kristen. She was the undisputed star. Her parents relaxed, held hands and were caught in the spell.

Their daughter's part as "Lucia Bride" led the couple to seek out both sets of Swedish grandparents and find out about the customs of their homeland: Saint Lucia's Day is the harbinger of the holy season, a time when weaving and threshing must be finished and everything put in order for "His coming."

Many of the Christmas customs we take for granted are very old and come to us from generations past. Studying the origin of one's ancestry can bring families closer, lifting the veil of centuries to gaze in wonder at the world's King.

TO THINK AND PRAY ABOUT: Let us bow in reverence to the universal gift—Christ for all.

Deck The Halls

AS YOU DECK the holly in your halls—together with fir boughs and sprigs of mistletoe—have you wondered about the ancient customs? Half-legend, half-truth, half-myth, somehow they all lead back to Christianity.

History tells us that Joel Poinsett, a goodwill ambassador to the Latin American countries, brought the first yule blossoms to California. Legend has it that a little Mexican waif had no gift to take to the cathedral on Christmas Eve. She picked a weed alongside the road, climbed the steep path to the great church and laid it upon the altar. As she rose to leave she saw that her humble offering had been transformed into *Flor de la Noche-buena* (Flower of the Nativity)—known as the poinsettia.

Mistletoe? All species have one common property: they are parasites and sometimes kill their host trees. While it might destroy a forest, it could provide "curative powers" in homes where it was hung, according to ancient myth. Once it was called the "wood of the cross." One group called its shining white berries "the symbol of purity and peace" because, so they believed, it was the first bouquet presented to the Christ Child on the first Christmas. The Norwegians thought it to be too sacred to touch the earth and be defiled, which accounts for hanging the mistletoe high at Christmas time.

The holly legends date back to the Druids, who believed that its evergreen leaves were proof that the sun never deserted it. Therefore, it was sacred. Legend also says that Christ's Crown of Thorns was composed of holly and that before the Crucifixion the berries were white. Afterwards, they turned to crimson—like drops of blood.

And no legend accounts would be complete without a dash of romance! The young lady who receives no kiss beneath the mistletoe will not marry that year. But there is jolly news for us homemakers. Should we be first to bring holly into the house during the holiday season we will rule the home for the ensuing year!

TO THINK AND PRAY ABOUT: Sharing the stories with children can help make Christmas more meaningful and can point to the manger.

'Twas The Night Of The Program

December 15
Mark 10:15
Hebrews 13:8

'TWAS THE NIGHT of the program and all through the house—was bedlam! If you are a parent or a Sunday school teacher or have ever been a child-participant, you know how it is. The heavenly choir is croupy . . . their leader is sneezing. One shepherd's scratching from his father's wooly robe (which touches him all over); another is hooking the angel in front of him with his shepherd's crook. An angel with a broken wing is noisily trying to shush them. The holder of the Christmas Star has lost one sneaker and will have to hop over the hills of Judea on one foot instead of rising slowly on the incline behind the stable. One Wise Man can't remember his lines. Joseph has disappeared . . . Mary is crying. Everybody is rattling scripts . . . somebody scatters the hay . . . somebody else breaks the pull-cord and the curtain won't budge. It opens with a jerk as the Littlest Angel announces he can't *wait* until taxes are paid!

"I will not go through this again—*ever!*" that's the Christmas program chairperson. You? Me? Oh, yes, we will. We will because out there sit proud and loving parents who see their private miracles, their children, acting out the greatest scene the world has ever known. Out there sit grandparents who remember the days of their youth and relive them through their grandchildren. Christmas programs have changed little. Out there sit younger brothers and sisters who watch with great round eyes the magnificence of the Nativity. Out there sits an audience waiting to be reminded that the old, old story is as new today as it was 2,00 years ago. The childish things make it better, as well as the glory in the faces of the children and the unquestioning faith as they sing, "Christ ·the Savior is born, Christ the Savior is born." Out there is a world trembling in fear, then kneeling to pray as peace creeps into their hearts—for they have "become as little children."

TO THINK AND PRAY ABOUT: Prepare your hearts for the rebirth that the Christmas story brings. Anticipate chaotic conditions. Remember, such was the condition of the world into which Jesus came. A sure peace will follow.

The Third Candle Of Advent

December 16
Luke 2:8-17;
Galatians 5:22-25

JENNY STOPPED BY after school to show me the clay turtle she was making for her father's Christmas gift. "Won't he be surprised!" Probably! But isn't it good when busy teachers take time to gently instill the importance of giving in the minds of children? School-age children, now past the self-absorption of toddlerhood, are naturally susceptible to generous feelings and enjoy assuming the grown-up role of the "giver." Most families, even those who make no profession of faith, appreciate this. Some parents let their children attend a pageant of a religious service that dramatizes the holiday's spiritual meaning. Sometimes this opens the door first for the children . . . and who can say when a little child will lead them?

Today, for instance, the little girl spotted the Advent wreath. She turned her attention from the turtle to the candles and demanded that I tell her all about it—up to and including the third candle, which we will light tonight. "Why are these three lavender?" I explained the foretelling of the Messiah in the Old Testament, and that lavender also stood for repentance of sins. "Is it too late for us?" Jenny asked.

"No, it isn't too late, Jenny. That's the nice part of an Advent wreath. You can be a latecomer, lighting three candles tonight—three times as bright as if you had begun with one. So make an Advent wreath, Jenny, and draw Mother and Daddy into the endless circle of God's Love. It's never too late."

TO THINK AND PRAY ABOUT: Have you kept up on your daily Bible reading? Did you remember to light the Candle of Prophecy each evening for the first week of Advent? Did you light the Candle of Bethlehem on the second Wednesday as well—making it twice as bright? Light them both again tonight and add to them the last lavender candle of repentance, the Shepherd's Candle. Tonight we light the third candle with great joy—remembering the joy the shepherds felt as they journeyed to see the Promised King. Let us share with others the peace and the joy He brought to the world. And let us share with others the joy of His Living Presence in our lives today!

To Observe Or To Keep?

COULD YOU perhaps see the glory of Christmas, sample its wholesomeness, and find it so spiritually satisfying that you keep it and serve it the year round? There is a way, but the recipe is exacting!

Arrange in advance (well out of reach of worry's hands) the celebration day. Select a house of any size (with a large heart) with evergreen boughs at the door; a fireplace flanked by a sleeping child, friendly dog and purring cat; and an open Bible.

Add from two to four proud grandparents; aunts and uncles in assorted sizes and ages and double the number of nieces and nephews; contented parents; a set of newlyweds; a dozen giggling teenagers; and a sprinkling of adolescents with braces. Have each generation bring at least one friend.

Mingle in the fruits of kindness and the spice of laughter. Blend with music. Add the sweetness of warm words, handshakes and embraces.

Gently remove all grudges, suspicion and mistrust; strain out malice, envy, complacency and irritation; replace with forgiveness, acceptance, trust, encouragement, loyalty and patience. Set aside until after church.

Fold in a prayer and sprinkle the top with "Amen" from all present; light the burner with candles from the Star; set the oven on "Moderate in All Things"; and let the hand of friendship open the door; bake until mellow, testing often for tenderness and the sweet aroma of love.

If baked on December 25th, this recipe will last throughout the year, providing it is served properly. When you serve children, stoop down and listen to their needs. When you serve those growing older, stoop down and listen to their pain. When you serve your family, say "I love you" instead of "Do you love me?" When you serve friends, remember what they have done for you instead of what you have done for them.

TO THINK AND PRAY ABOUT: Remind yourself that love is our strongest bond. It began in Bethlehem and leads into Eternity—keep Christmas all year.

Back To Our "Roots"

LAST YEAR you said you would have a sensible Christmas—no muss, no fuss—just a nice, quiet day. "After all, Dad's getting a little too old to keep up with freeway traffic," said Grandmother. "Well, we are not going *there!*" said Daughter. "It's too much taking the packages, cribs, training seats—." Then there's decorating, baking, shopping . . . The entire family agreed that this year would be different.

But something happens. Both sets of grandparents change their minds. One pair wants you *there*; the other is coming by plane! The children get to work pasting colored chains, stringing popcorn and making pomander oranges for their grandmothers. They cut out a star with three too many points and cover it with heavy-duty foil . . . And they rehearse a little Nativity Scene to perform for the family on Christmas Eve.

Something inside you sings a carol and you thank God that the children gave you an excuse to go on with Christmas—the biggest ever—and you work without protest on what you knew you'd be unable to resist all along. There is a need for "roots" at Christmas—a need to seek out those we love on earth, and a need to engage in something tangible to represent the heart-expanding Love within us that God placed there that first Christmas.

So here you are baking fruitcake. Your hands are pricked by holly. Somebody has ground mistletoe berries into the new carpet with a careless heel. The windows are sticky with peppermint fingerprints. It will take weeks to clean up the holiday mess. Utility bills soar for everybody. And it's time for Master Charge statements . . . .

But here you are together: laughing, loving, pushing, shoving—making plans for the snack after Christmas Eve communion. You have made the pilgrimage safely; you have reached the "roots " of joy; for, above the happy commotion, you hear an angel choir. You're home for Christmas once again.

TO THINK AND PRAY ABOUT: Ponder the ultimate homecoming that God has planned for us.

Lighting A Match

DECEMBER was "read aloud" time at our house. Just how I was supposed to work that into a baking, cleaning, shopping and wrapping-mailing schedule was always a mystery. But mysteries can be solved.

One year I was absolutely certain I would have to eliminate something. Story reading? First, George had a bout with flu and on the first day he was up, I went down. By the time I was up, Bryce was down. Our house would have qualified for a Disaster Area. I was suffering from iron-poor blood, and Christmas was only a week away. In the midst of all this my son said, "You'll just have to read to me." *Read!* But he continued, "I want 'The Little Match girl'."

I had no time to read *anything*—let alone that story. "Why do you always want to hear that? It only makes you cry," I said irritably.

"When I cry I feel better. I want to make bright lights for people."

Make bright lights for people . . . Isn't that what Christmas is all about? I pulled the dog-eared book from the shelf. I still read the old tale and see the same lovely visions, more aware each year of how we can brighten the darkness with such small lights described by Hans Christian Andersen.

The ragged little orphan-girl was trying to sell matches for a penny a box on a bitterly cold Christmas Eve. From where she huddled in a corner, pulling her ragged garments around her bare feet, she could see and smell the beautiful things of Christmas. *Just one little match*, she thought; and in its brief light she saw a cozy room. *A second match* . . . and there was a banquet table. With the third match the dying child saw candles, dazzling stars and the face of her grandmother. At last all the matches were gone . . . "But it didn't matter, Mother," Bryce said through his tears. "The lights of heaven had been turned on."

TO THINK AND PRAY ABOUT: There are so many ways we can share the real meaning of the holidays. Little deeds do count. A single match may turn "the lights of heaven on" for someone.

How To Eat An Elephant

December 20
Psalm 31:3; 71:3;
92:12-15

THERE IS ONLY one way to eat an elephant: a bite at a time. Maybe you knew that already. I didn't—until Beverly Johnson told the world after she, the first woman to do so alone, reached the top of 3,600-feet high *El Capitan* in Yosemite National Park, California.

"That's what I kept saying, 'A bite at a time, a bite at a time . . .'," the smiling Beverly said of her ten-day struggle up the gigantic granite mass that rises unbroken from the Yosemite Valley.

She was weary and afraid up there all alone, strapped with a hundred pounds of gear . . . climbing . . . climbing. Day after day she rose higher and higher, clutching to rocks and ropes self-hammered into the rock—praying that it would hold. What sleep she had was in slings on the sheer granite wall. "I often thought if I could magically leave, I would—" but there was no way—but up.

She kept climbing, saying to herself, "I'll climb here today." You can't do it, she told reporters, if you count the days. "Just a step at a time . . . a day at a time," she laughed victoriously, *"and a bite at a time!"*

We can all "eat elephants" by Beverly's formula, can't we? It makes little difference whether it's all the things we have to accomplish, a test we have to take, a physical condition we have to live with, a broken heart that needs healing—her reasoning works.

Haven't you often wished, as she did, that you could magically leave your problems? Most of us feel that way, but the world doesn't stop for us to get off. We dig in with whatever equipment we have; we work our way up slowly; and, remember this: We have the solid Rock to lean upon! God is always there.

I shuddered in listening to the brave woman's account. The universe whirls around me and my heart beats like a tom-tom when I look down. Beverly has the same sensations: "If I stood on one of those ledges and looked down—no! I looked up!" Why, then, should we waste time looking at bottomless pits when victory waits for us at the summit? Why look back when eternity lies ahead?

TO THINK AND PRAY ABOUT: Look ahead to a wonderful year. Resolve: A bite at a time!

You Hold The Key

TODAY OR tomorrow (it varies) the sun appears highest in the northern sky anywhere south of the Tropic of Capricorn. And, ready or not, here's winter!

"Old Man Winter" is the usual name of the visitor who packs enough snow to last three months and comes prepared to stay from mid-December until mid-March. Recently, however, I read an article in which the writer compared the season to "a capricious woman whose moods are uncertain and constantly changing." To that, our rebuttal can be that it carries with it an indefinable, intangible warmth that is the envy of the summer months. Winter is a lady: it is fierce and fickle, but how it allures!

The trees exchange their patchwork smocks of autumn for shawls of frost and capes of ermine. Icicles bediamond their bare arms. A deceptively innocent snowflake becomes a flurry and then a storm with all the "fury of a woman scorned." Spent, it moves on across the prairies, leaving drifts huddled in the fence rows like frightened children; and, beneath an unbelievably bright sky, a farmer walks out into the fields to thank God that his savagely thirsty grounds have been watered.

Winter paints a landscape, a winter wonderland! It fills the air with greeting-card bluejays; with rabbit-tracks that romp across the snow. It brings boots out of the closet, candles from the cupboard and blankets from the cedar chest. It brings runny noses; but we get to know our doctors better. It brings longer hours of darkness, but we have time to reacquaint ourselves with our families and our friends (maybe as we sit around the fire). There's time for new recipes, books and family prayer.

Winter is an aging process. Is the world's body less beautiful when it is wrinkled with ice and capped with snow? Winter is a good time to redefine beauty—both as to seasonal and physical changes. Let's update our thinking!

TO THINK AND PRAY ABOUT: "A person with a creative imagination can take the shambles of a dream and weave a new beginning, turn failure to success." Neil Strait.

The Gift Of Peace

EFFIE DROPPED by for coffee today unannounced. I was feeling a little hassled, especially because I just heard that frightening countdown, "Only three more shopping days left till Christmas!" I had the oven on "preheat" and was frantically greasing and flouring pans for fruitcakes that should have been mellow with age by now.

"Only three—" she began, but my look must have silenced her. I wasn't in the mood: cards, company, confusion. I motioned my friend and her four-year-old Eddie inside. "—days left to tell everybody what you want for Christmas!" Effie shifted emphasis.

"What do I *really* want? Would you believe just peace and quiet?"

She nodded understandingly, but it was Eddie who answered, "That's what the angels brung," he said happily.

"Not to grown-ups, apparently," his mother told him. I felt a little ashamed for us both and handed the child a candied cherry. "I'm sorry," I explained. "We get busy, honey. Every year it's the same old story."

He danced up and down. "Tell it to me. I like the same old story!"

Effie and I exchanged glances over his yellow curls. For a second I caught an illusion of a halo. "Plug in the coffeepot, Ef," I said. "I'll have these cakes in the oven in a jif and we'll chat. Eddie, you come and help me."

While I measured, Eddie, looking like a boy-angel, broke nutmeats into tiny pieces as I told him the Christmas story. By the time the cakes were ready to pop into the oven I had come to the "Peace on earth" part. Eddie interrupted me. "That's what the angels brung," he repeated convincingly.

I felt the sting of tears. *What did I want for Christmas?* I had my gift. A little child inspired that angel chorus 2,000 years ago, and it took a little child to remind me. How thoughtless we grownups can get!

TO THINK AND PRAY ABOUT: Let us thank God for His gift of peace and let us put it to **good use** during these busy days.

O, What A Difference A Word Makes!

THE CHURCH is empty and the hour is late. Somewhere in the pastor's study a clock tick-tocks loudly, the seconds tumbling over themselves as if eager to greet tomorrow. The city sleeps, except for the faithful workers of the night who keep our world in order—quietly, so as not to disturb our dreams—like the stars that keep watch in the sky. Here and there a light glows. Perhaps someone is frantically trying to wrap gifts or trying to soothe a child back to sleep. Christmas is not yet, but anticipation builds with the ticking of the clock; and tomorrow is Christmas Eve. Decorating's done. Soon I must go . . . but I need a moment here alone.

The sanctuary is spiced by the smell of freshly-gathered evergreens; and even in the harsh glow of the incandescent bulbs the improvised altar of potted poinsettias looks untouched by human hands. They will wilt slightly, warmed by the lights of tomorrow night's communion service; but by then their mission will have been fulfilled. Have I fulfilled my mission for today? It was so filled with phone calls, meal-planning and hurrying here and there that I found no stopping place. And even if I could have rested, the clock would not. It would have gone right on tick-tocking away the moments that I might have spent more wisely.

A church sanctuary, all alone at this hour, is a good place for such soul-searching. One comes face-to-face with truth. The pews are empty, but tomorrow night they will be filled. If some of my moments were empty ones today, tomorrow they can be filled with greater things. God will see to that. "The harvest is past and we are not saved" means that today has gone, but if I am more aware, I can enter into a great joy tomorrow. I can enter into a new life; I can offer new hope to others; I can become a better witness; I can use the new power of God's Spirit . . . for none of the things I did today were in vain. They were stepping stones—and stairs!

I look ahead with peace and joy to tomorrow evening's service. I know what the password is! We are saved by a single word: GRACE. I whisper a prayer and walk out with a light heart.

TO THINK AND PRAY ABOUT: Long on sin, short on grace? Place more faith in God's love.

The Fourth Candle Of Advent

December 24
Luke 1:13-14, 68-80;
2:10-14

THERE IS added color in the Advent wreath tonight—shining and alien, like the New Star that is destined to appear in the heavens; pink with promise, like the first hint of day in the predawn dark. It is the "voice in the wilderness" of John the Baptist . . . it is the hovering of wings as angels come close to earth . . . it is the pink candle of peace on earth.

And, indeed, there is a deep sense of peace that descends upon the circled-greenery of the centerpiece and mingles with the pink-and-lavender light. The candles have burned low enough to bring out the pungence in the green needles, creating a sort of incense. Tonight, all the pieces of the great prophetic puzzle of the ancients fit together to announce a King. We rediscover the splendor of the Star. We hear again the exultant song of heralding angels. We are drawn together by the immeasurable love, understanding and obedience of Mary and Joseph. Our hearts seek and find a Child in the manger, returning home with deeper understanding of brotherly love. In the rosy glow of the fourth candle we relive the miracle of Bethlehem. There is beauty in a quiet night that reaches out and holds our hearts. There is tenderness of a mother's smile, adoration of humble shepherds, and a million angels singing in the brilliance of the heavens. Christ the Savior is born!

TO THINK AND PRAY ABOUT: The four weeks of Advent draw to a close with the lighting of the Angels' Candle on Christmas Eve. The Prince of Peace has come; the Star and angel-song are leading the shepherds and the Wise Men to the place of His birth. Tomorrow the entire world will light up with His Love—symbolized by the remaining candle in the wreath. Tonight as we light the Angel Candle, let us remember the messengers who foretold the Holy Birth and those who sang of the glory of His Coming. Let us pray that the year ahead will be lighted by the love we feel tonight.

The Fifth Candle Of Advent

December 25
Luke 2:7
John 1: 1-20

The holly bush is burdened
With drifts of gentle snow,
And Something stirs the senses
That happened long ago.
Outside a crowd has gathered
To view the Child within;
The church is hushed and waiting
For "Peace, Good Will to Men." J.M.B.

TODAY IS THE DAY! God has kept His promise. Unto us a Savior is born. He has but one promise remaining: Jesus will come again. Until then it is up to us to let His light shine. There remains one candle to be lit in the Advent wreath—the biggest, the brightest, the most beautiful of all—the enormous white candle in the center representing Christ, the Light of the World. The lavender candles of Prophecy and Repentance and the pink candle of Peace become a part of the whole of Jesus Christ. How symbolic that the Christ Candle would be white for purity; for white, which appears to possess no color, holds every color of the spectrum.

Processions move in reverence
As squares of stained-glass light
Reflect upon their faces
The wonder of the night.
The candles' lighted fingers,
Like warm and fragile prayer,
Reach upward in the darkness—
And find the Savior there. J.M.B.

TO THINK AND PRAY ABOUT: It is my prayer that you have made use of the Advent wreath as a part of your devotionals this year. It can be the little "conversation piece" that removes a certain self-consciousness from more formal worship; or it can enrich whatever other family devotions you use.

Glory To God In The Highest!

THE TURKEY'S warm-brown scent mingles with evergreens. The kettle sings . . . George kisses me beneath the mistletoe . . . the doorbell rings again . . . and love permeates throughout the house.

Who can explain this feeling that seeps into the inner sanctum of the heart and lights a candle there? Can others see the glow in my face and hear the mellowness in my voice? I hope the warmth I feel radiates to show a world redeemed—new and beautiful. One word says it all: LOVE.

Rosy, young children are playing with the toys they were hoping they would receive. Their prayers have been answered; their dreams have come true; and it's a wonderful world. Aunt Jane is nodding comfortably in her chair, as if reaffirming last night's statement when we tucked the children in, "Yes, the little ones need Christmas."

The little ones. I think Jesus meant all of us when he said, "Let the little ones come unto me." And how the world needs to believe that! We all need Christmas: the dedicated Christian and the sophisticated agnostic who whistles in the dark instead of seeking a light. Christmas is for the believers and the nonbelievers; the charitable and the money-mad (who followed the sparkle of gold instead of the star). Christmas is for the innocent-eyed young who know they are loved; but it is for the old and infirm as well, who think the world has forgotten—for often it has. Christmas is for those behind the prison bars because of their weakness; it is for those inside prisons of their own making: bricks of hatred cemented together with false pride. Christmas is for the tormented, who have seen their castles crumble, their dreams fade and die, their old traditions walked upon by seemingly careless people.

TO THINK AND PRAY ABOUT: Christmas is for all people—maybe more especially for adults who have forgotten what children know. To them we must open our hearts, letting the Spirit out as well as in.

What New Year Brings

December 27
Ecclesiastes 3:1-13

Another chance to dream again;
Another trail to take;
Another chance to start once more—
New resolutions make.
Another chance to follow stars
That Christmas brought our way,
To keep our aspirations bright—
Renewing them each day.
Another chance for greeting friends;
There's no need for "Goodbye,"
For old years end to bring, I think,
Another chance to try:
For God has plans for each of us
Such as we never knew—
Until we reach the Higher Things
His Love can lead us to. J.M.B.

TRADITIONALLY, the tree, once pungent and parcel-laden, stands like a guest whose visit is over but is wondering how to take leave. It looks embarrassed with nothing left to offer and everyone ignoring its presence—unless you try moving it out before New Year's Day! Somewhere buried within us is a need to keep our universe in order, to mark its seasons with traditions, timepieces and calendars; to feel the ebb and flow of the tide and the shift of the stars which gauge it. Maybe it's continuity that reminds us of the excellency of God's works, one season overlapping the other as do minutes, months and lifetimes.

The year, like the holiday tree, has delivered its gifts. It furnished us with yesterdays which are the seeds of the new year's bright tomorrows. It brought us neither an end nor a beginning—simply a "going on" of God's plan. We stand on the threshhold of opportunity.

TO THINK AND PRAY ABOUT: By the grace of God we have another day; enjoy it! Try to go about your work calmly, lovingly and fearlessly. Face the year ahead rejoicing in your strengths, turning weaknesses over to God.

Expectations

December 28
James 1:2-4, 21-27

THE YOUNG man was brisk and professional as he interviewed the elderly gentleman he had met in the Kentucky hill country. "Tell me," he said, "do you expect the New Year to be happy?"

The eyes of the guest stared unblinkingly through his heavy growth of white eyebrows. "Years ain't never happy, Son, lest we help 'em. Best be askin' yourself what you plan to do to help it along. Then you get the glory!"

The old gent's right, I thought to myself. *Everywhere we are making ourselves hoarse with calls of "Happy New Year!"* The guests on the television talk show had the glory! There is no simple formula to happiness—even on New Year's Day. No number of greetings, no turning of a calendar—not even a long list of resolutions—can usher in a happy new year. There *is* a formula, of course, but it lies within ourselves. So we'd "best be askin' " what we can bring into the lives of others. Therein lies the secret: give and get that inner glow! But, first, let's examine our feelings.

Do you believe you must pursue happiness? Use caution: there is no way to run it down; it's always over the hill; it sifts through the fingers like sand. It's caged inside you—waiting for release!

Are you afraid to be happy? It is surprising how many people feel guilty in possessing what others have been denied. Nobody is denied happiness. One can deny that it exists. One can have failed to experience it because (maybe) you and I failed to share. Or one can refuse to accept what God wants for each of us. If happiness frightens you a little, or if you know someone who sees life as a funeral march to the grave, remember: Jesus explained His coming "that My joy might remain with you."

Do you want to be happy? You'd be surprised at how many *need* to sulk, complain, and yes, suffer in "this world of sin and death." How can we help them (and ourselves) find a happiness-packed year?

TO THINK AND PRAY ABOUT: Let's bring our happiness to the surface by being open and honest with God, ourselves and others; forgiving at all times; dismissing unworthy thoughts; returning good for evil; and praying for New Year's Joy!

The Heart Is Young At New Year

December 29
Luke 1:46-55

HOW GOOD that the carols aren't hushed at the stroke of twelve on New Year's Eve. The continuation of the carols and the bells gives one the feeling that the spirit goes on and on. I guess it's the carols I like most of all.

The carols of Christmas are more than folk songs: they are hymns; they are the glorious tidings that "came upon the midnight clear" from out of a star-struck sky; they are the overture to the cry that has rung down through the ages, "Fear not: for, behold, I bring you good tidings of great joy." They proclaimed the advent of a child born in a manger with the status of a King. Can you imagine a more humble setting, a more glorious title?

It seems symbolic somehow that the carols, too, have remained simple for the simple ears of us all. Think of the words to "Silent Night," one of our most universally loved and certainly one of the most simple—so simple that little children can sing with understanding about a little child they can adore. Yes, it is good that the songs go on and on. Hearing the children sing them after the season is past reminds us of the everlastingness of the real meaning of Christmas; that instead of New Year's Day ending the holiday season, it opens the gateway to the next one—beckoning invitingly like an oasis in the long, barren landscape of the commonplace. May every New Year remind us of that first carol.

TO THINK AND PRAY ABOUT:
> The angels sang sweet carols first
> While shepherds watched their sheep;
> They sang in voices soft and low
> To let the Baby sleep.
> Glad shepherds heard them in the fields
> And saw the Star on high;
> And then perhaps they joined the song—
> The world's first lullaby. J.M.B.

The End Of The Way

THERE WERE DAYS during the last twelve months when you felt like an amoeba . . . a blob of protoplasm . . . the lowest form of life . . . a single-celled animal . . . perpetually changing shapes . . . and spreading all directions at once. "I'm falling apart!" you cried (but you didn't). "I can't go on!" you said (but you did). Look around you. See all the growth? And chances are that you've forgotten the growing pains already. God goes with us all the way, right into the delivery room. He hears our agonized cries, and then in the joy of new birth we say, "It was a good year." God took the pain away!

And so it is with our spiritual lives. We agonize. We doubt. We fear. We often stumble and sometimes fall. But we go on, for the time of our delivery is not yet. It will all be worth it when we see Christ face-to-face; for we, as Christians, know the roots of joy!

TO THINK AND PRAY ABOUT: God keeps His promises! Do you remember this old hymn?

The sands have been washed in the footprints of the Stranger on Galilee's shore,

And the voice that subdued the rough billows will be heard in Judea no more.

But the path of the lone Galilean with joy I will follow today

And the toils of the road will seem nothing when I get to the end of the way.

He loves me too well to forsake me or give me one trial too much;

All His people have been dearly purchased, and Satan can never claim such.

By and by I shall see Him and praise Him, in the city of unending day;

And the toils of the road will seem nothing when I get to the end of the way.

Unfinished Book

December 31
Acts 1:25
III John 13-14
Hebrews 13:20-21

LIFE IS THE BOOK I've not finished because its pages
won't hold
The treasured chapters I'm writing . . . Would that it all could
be told!
I want to tell of my garden and flowers that it has grown—
In enormous plots of friendship—for I have loved all I've known!
I want to tell of my doormat, in rainbow colors so bright
That shades of sadness add contrast to the glad fabrics of light.
I want to tell of the beauty I found in detours unplanned—
When floods had destroyed all the bridges and brooks built
castles in sand.
Why does my garden keep growing? Each year I add a new row
And brilliant blossoms surprise me—rewards for kindness I
show?
The rug needs cleaning and mending; the edges need a new
braid;
But feet keep crossing my threshold—ignoring the spots they
have made.
Then the circumstantial by-way that found me a chatty brook
Set foot and heart meandering . . . I'll never finish my book!
Yes, life's the book I've not finished—just love-sheaths of memories:
Yellowed, old, but sketched out in gold with priceless treasures like
these. J.M.B.

And, as the old year fades away, reflect momentarily with
Margaret Sangster: "There was so much of splendor and glory,
there was so much of wonder and delight, that there can be no
ending of our story, though the book is closed and it is night."

TO THINK AND PRAY ABOUT: Go in peace. Love
one another as Christ has loved us, and "May the grace of our
Lord Jesus Christ, the love of God, and the fellowship of the
Holy Spirit be with you now and forevermore." Amen.

Other Good
Harvest House Reading

GOD'S BEST FOR MY LIFE
by *Lloyd John Ogilvie*

Not since Oswald Chambers' *My Utmost for His Highest* has there been such an inspirational yet easy-to-read devotional. Dr. Ogilvie provides guidelines for maximizing your prayer and meditation time.

THE NARRATED BIBLE—In Chronological Order
by *F. LaGard Smith*

Dr. Smith's narrative combines with the New International Version in chronological order to guide you easily through the incredible unfolding drama from Creation to Revelation. Reading sections for each day of the year.

LORD OF THE DANCE
by *Deidre Bobgan*

Thoughtful Christian women who long for a richer and more intimate walk with God will deeply appreciate this refreshing new look at the disciplined Christian life as seen through the eyes of a professional ballet dancer.

IN TOUCH WITH GOD—How God Speaks to a Prayerful Heart
by *Marie Shropshire*

Knowing how to have life-giving fellowship with God in the midst of life's challenges is the key to fulfillment in the Christian walk. From this personal journal we learn that there is no difficulty or wound that is out of reach of His healing touch.

SURVIVAL FOR BUSY WOMEN—Establishing Efficient Home Management
by *Emilie Barnes*

A hands-on manual for establishing a more efficient home-management program. Over 25 charts and forms can be personalized to help you organize your home.

THE GRACIOUS WOMAN—Developing a Servant's Heart Through Hospitality
by *June Curtis*

June shares the secret of being a gracious woman and shows how to become the gracious woman God intended.

Dear Reader:

We would appreciate hearing from you regarding this Harvest House nonfiction book. It will enable us to continue to give you the best in Christian publishing.

1. What most influenced you to purchase *Quiet Moments for Women?*
   - ☐ Author
   - ☐ Subject matter
   - ☐ Backcover copy
   - ☐ Recommendations
   - ☐ Cover/Title
   - ☐ _____

2. Where did you purchase this book?
   - ☐ Christian bookstore
   - ☐ General bookstore
   - ☐ Department store
   - ☐ Grocery store
   - ☐ Other

3. Your overall rating of this book:
   - ☐ Excellent   ☐ Very good   ☐ Good   ☐ Fair   ☐ Poor

4. How likely would you be to purchase other books by this author?
   - ☐ Very likely
   - ☐ Somewhat likely
   - ☐ Not very likely
   - ☐ Not at all

5. What types of books most interest you?
   (check all that apply)
   - ☐ Women's Books
   - ☐ Marriage Books
   - ☐ Current Issues
   - ☐ Self Help/Psychology
   - ☐ Bible Studies
   - ☐ Fiction
   - ☐ Biographies
   - ☐ Children's Books
   - ☐ Youth Books
   - ☐ Other _____

6. Please check the box next to your age group.
   - ☐ Under 18
   - ☐ 18-24
   - ☐ 25-34
   - ☐ 35-44
   - ☐ 45-54
   - ☐ 55 and over

Mail to: Editorial Director
Harvest House Publishers
1075 Arrowsmith
Eugene, OR 97402

Name _____

Address _____

City _____   State _____   Zip _____

Thank you for helping us to help you in future publications!